HERACLITUS

ALSO AVAILABLE FROM BLOOMSBURY

Nature, History, State, Martin Heidegger
Towards the Definition of Philosophy, Martin Heidegger
Basic Problems of Phenomenology, Martin Heidegger
Mindfulness, Martin Heidegger

HERACLITUS

The Inception of Occidental Thinking
Logic: Heraclitus's Doctrine of the *Logos*

Martin Heidegger

Translated by Julia Goesser Assaiante
and S. Montgomery Ewegen

BLOOMSBURY ACADEMIC
LONDON • NEW YORK • OXFORD • NEW DELHI • SYDNEY

BLOOMSBURY ACADEMIC
Bloomsbury Publishing Plc
50 Bedford Square, London, WC1B 3DP, UK
1385 Broadway, New York, NY 10018, USA
29 Earlsfort Terrace, Dublin 2, Ireland

BLOOMSBURY, BLOOMSBURY ACADEMIC and the Diana logo are trademarks of
Bloomsbury Publishing Plc

First published in *Martin Heidegger Gesamtausgabe vol 55: Heraklit. 1. Der Anfang des abendländischen Denkens 2. Logik. Heraklits Lehre vom Logos*, edited by Manfred Frings, © Vittorio Klostermann GmbH, Frankfurt am Main 1979. 3rd edition 1994

English translation © Julia Goesser Assaiante and S. Montgomery Ewegen, 2018

This edition published by Bloomsbury Academic 2018
Reprinted by Bloomsbury Academic 2019 (twice), 2020, 2022

Julia Goesser Assaiante and S. Montgomery Ewegen have asserted their right under the Copyright, Designs and Patents Act, 1988, to be identified as Translators of this work.

Cover image: *Diana of Versailles* © Bridgeman Images
Cover design: Irene Martinez-Costa

All rights reserved. No part of this publication may be reproduced or transmitted in any form or by any means, electronic or mechanical, including photocopying, recording, or any information storage or retrieval system, without prior permission in writing from the publishers.

Bloomsbury Publishing Plc does not have any control over, or responsibility for, any third-party websites referred to or in this book. All internet addresses given in this book were correct at the time of going to press. The author and publisher regret any inconvenience caused if addresses have changed or sites have ceased to exist, but can accept no responsibility for any such changes.

A catalogue record for this book is available from the British Library.

A catalog record for this book is available from the Library of Congress.

ISBN: HB: 978-0-8264-6240-4
PB: 978-0-8264-6241-1
ePDF: 978-1-4742-4919-5
eBook: 978-1-4742-4920-1

Typeset by RefineCatch Limited, Bungay, Suffolk
Printed and bound in Great Britain

To find out more about our authors and books visit www.bloomsbury.com and sign up for our newsletters.

CONTENTS

Translator's Foreword ... xv

THE INCEPTION OF OCCIDENTAL THINKING: HERACLITUS ... 1
Summer Semester 1943

    Preliminary concerns: Philosophy as the authentic thinking of the to-be-thought. On the inception of "Occidental" thinking ... 3

INTRODUCTION: PRELIMINARY CONSIDERATION OF THE INCEPTUAL AND THE WORD ... 5

§ 1 Two stories concerning Heraclitus as introduction to his word ... 7

    a) Heraclitus's thinking in the region of fire and strife and in the nearness to play ... 8
    b) Heraclitus's word under the protection of Artemis ... 12
    c) The obscurity of the thinker Heraclitus ... 16

    Review ... 18
    1) The reference to 'fire' and 'play' in the two stories concerning Heraclitus ... 18
    2) The to-be-thought in the signs of Artemis: lyre, bow, and torch. The obscurity of the thinker ... 20

§ 2   The word in the inception of thinking   23
    a) The 'obscurity' of essential thinking: the essential self-
       concealing of the to-be-thought (i.e., being)   23
    b) The essentially oppositional, and dialectical thinking. The
       unfitting language of dialectic   26
    c) The form in which the word of Heraclitus's is passed down,
       and the elucidation of the fragments in terms of the experience
       of the to-be-thought   28

    Review   31
       Regarding the problem of the sameness of what is thought in
       inceptual and contemporary thinking. The inherited word of
       inceptual thinking (Heraclitus) and dialectics   31

MAIN PART: THE TRUTH OF BEING   35

§ 3   The inception of the inceptual to-be-thought.
     Fragment 16   37
    a) Parenthetical remark on the task of translating   37
    b) The question pertaining to the 'never submerging thing' and its
       essential relation to 'concealing'   38
    c) The characteristics of the foundational word τὸ δῦνον and its
       exposition in the guiding question of metaphysical thinking
       (Aristotle)   42
    d) Mindful consideration of the words 'being' and 'is'   47

    Review   49
    1) On translation and interpretation: the compulsion into an
       originary understanding from out of the experienced
       restiveness of 'the same'   49
    2) 'Submerging'—thought in a Greek way—and the question
       concerning the essence of the word   50
    3) Elucidation of τὸ δῦνον in terms of the structure of the words of
       the main question of metaphysical thinking (Aristotle, Plato).
       Concerning the problem of retroactive interpretation: the
       inceptual thinkers and the later beginning of metaphysics   56
    4) The characteristics of the word ὄν. The primacy of the verbal
       meaning over the nominal meaning (in participles)   61

§ 4 The foundational words of inceptual thinking (φύσις, ζωή), and their relation to metaphysical thinking and to the thinking of being   65

    a) The peculiar poverty of inceptually thoughtful utterance in the structure of the words τὸ μὴ δῦνόν ποτε and their transformation into 'perpetual emerging' (φύειν). On the word φύσις in inceptual thinking, and on the concept of 'nature.' Note on fragment 123   65

    b) The foundational words φύσις and ζωή as obtained through the translation. The fundamental meaning of ζῆν and ζωή in inceptual thinking over and against the concept of 'life' in the metaphysical tradition. Note on fragment 30   68

    c) The 'violence' of the translation and the explicit consideration of negation   72

    Review   73

    1) The μὴ δῦνόν ποτε of Heraclitus's, thought inceptually, and the ὄν of metaphysics   73

    2) The inceptually unblemished meaning of φύσις as the 'pure emerging' and its essential nearness to ζωή. The essential nearness of 'life' and 'being' in ἀείζωον (fragment 30). Rejection of the metaphysical interpretations of the concept of life   76

§ 5 Exposition of the essential connectedness of emerging and submerging. Fragment 123   83

    a) The 'contradiction' of emerging and submerging. The failure of logic and dialectic in the face of this 'contradiction'   84

    b) The standing-still of conventional thinking in the face of the 'irreconcilable,' and the leap into essential thinking. Philological translations as flight in the face of the claim of the saying   88

    Review   92

    On the essential relationship of emerging and submerging. Rejection of logical (dialectical) interpretations   92

§ 6 Emerging and submerging. Favor (φιλία) as the reciprocal bestowing of its essence. Notes on fragments 35 and 32   97

    a) Emerging (φύσις), favor (φιλία), and self-concealing (κρύπτεσθαι)   97

    b) φιλία (favor, bestowal) as the reciprocal essential relation of emerging and submerging (self-concealing). φύσις as the simple essence of the favor (φιλία) of the concealing emergence   100

§ 7   φύσις as the essential jointure (ἁρμονία) of emerging and submerging (self-concealing) in the reciprocal bestowal of its essence. Indication of the same in emerging and submerging. Fragments 54, 8, and 51   107

    a) The inconspicuousness of the jointure of φύσις as the unique feature of its revealability. The originarily precious essence of pure emerging   108

    b) The contra-tension and counter-tension as the essential moment of the jointure. Concerning the difficulty in thinking the counter-striving at one with the jointure: the difference between conventional and essential thinking. The jointure of φύσις and the signs of Artemis (bow and lyre). Note on fragment 9   110

    c) The inadequacy of logic (dialectic) in the face of the jointure thought in φύσις. The two-fold meaning of φύσις and the questionable 'priority' of emerging   116

§ 8   The essence of φύσις and the truth of being. φύσις in view of fire and cosmos. ἀλήθεια thought in the μὴ δῦνόν ποτε (φύσις) as the dis-closing into the unconcealment of being. Fragments 64, 66, 30, and 124   121

    a) Fire and lightning as the enkindling of the lightening. The cosmos as the fitting, inconspicuous jointure and the originary adornment. The same in fire and cosmos: igniting and lightening of the decisive measure-dispensing expanses   121

    b) ἀλήθεια as essential inception, and as the essential ground of φύσις. The essential relation between unconcealment and self-concealment in φύσις, thought inceptually. ἀλήθεια as the unconcealment of the self-concealing   129

c) On the hearing and saying of being in inceptual thinking: λόγος and signs. The signs of Apollo as the self-showing of φύσις. Fragment 93. On the truth and the word of beyng in Occidental history   133

LOGIC: HERACLITUS'S DOCTRINE OF THE *LOGOS*   137
Summer Semester 1944

Preliminary remark   139

FIRST SECTION
LOGIC: ITS NAME AND ITS MATTER   141

§ 1   The term 'logic'   143
     a) The logic of thinking and the logic of things   143
     b) ἐπιστήμη and τέχνη in relation to modern science and technology   146

     Review   149
     1) The intimate connection between thinking and things. Logic, pure thinking, and reflection   149
     2) Return to the Greek context at work in the naming of the words ἐπιστήμη λογική: ἐπιστήμη and τέχνη   152

§ 2   Logic, ἐπιστήμη, τέχνη. The related meanings of ἐπιστήμη and τέχνη. An analysis regarding the questionable relationship between thinking and logic   153
     a) τέχνη, φύσις, and ἐπιστήμη. τέχνη (to bring forth, to place-forth) and φύσις (to emerge from out of itself) in their relation to unconcealment. A rejection of the interpretation of τέχνη and ἐπιστήμη in terms of the differentiation between theory and practice   153
     b) Logic as ἐπιστήμη λογική in connection with ἐπιστήμη φυσική and ἐπιστήμη ἠθική. On the dominance of reflection   156

Review 157
　　　1) Logic as the reflection about reflection without an attachment to things. On the power of the self-reflection of subjectivity and pure thinking (Rilke, Hölderlin) 157
　　　2) ἐπιστήμη λογική, ἐπιστήμη φυσική, ἐπιστήμη ἠθική 161
　　c) λόγος and ἦθος. The universal role of λόγος as *ratio* and reason in the determinations of the human essence and its consequential consummation in the "will to power" (Nietzsche) 163

　　　Review 165
　　　3) On the dominance of reflection and subjectivity. The question concerning the depth of pure thinking and the re-turn (Rilke, Hölderlin) 165
　　　4) Logic as the doctrine of the assertion (concept, judgment, inference). λόγος, *ratio*, reason: on the universal meaning of logic in the determination of the human essence. The equating of thinking and logic as the origin of Occidental fate 168

§ 3　Logic and λόγος. The discipline and the matter. Logic and Occidental metaphysics 171

　　a) The origin of the three-fold division of logic, physics, and ethics as the scientific disciplines comprising philosophy, and the fate of Occidental metaphysics 171
　　b) Logic and the inhibiting of the unfolding of the essence of the Λόγος 174

　　Review 176
　　The dominance of the discipline over the matter, and logic as the grounding essence of Occidental philosophy as metaphysics 176

SECOND SECTION
THE RECLUSIVENESS OF THE ORIGINARY Λόγος AND THE PATHS TO APPROACHING IT 181

§ 4　Preparation for the listening to the Λόγος 183

　　a) On the meaning of λόγος as speech, saying, and assertion. The necessity of a renewed questioning concerning the inceptual meaning of the Λόγος 183

    b) Access to the hearing of the Λόγος. The hearkening listening to the Λόγος as an entryway into authentic knowledge. Fragment 50. The question concerning the originary concordance (ὁμολογία). References to fragments 32 and 112   186

    Review   192
    1) λόγος as assertion about beings by way of the idea (εἶδος), and the category in meta-physical thinking (Plato, Aristotle, Kant)   192
    2) The return to the pre-metaphysical Λόγος through λόγος as assertion. Fragment 50   197

§ 5   Three paths toward answering the question: what is the Λόγος?   199

    a) The first path: the Λόγος as One and all. Access to the Λόγος (as being) through the ἓν πάντα εἶναι in fragment 50   199
    b) The second path: access to the Λόγος through the original meaning of λέγειν. The Λόγος as harvest and gathering   203

    Review   205
    1) Expanded reconsideration of λόγος within the horizon of the meta-physical doctrine of ideas, and of the to-be-thought pre-metaphysical essence of the Λόγος as the naming of being   205
    c) The third path: access through the λόγος of the ψυχή. Fragment 45. The question concerning ὁμολογεῖν   211

    Review   215
    2) A reconsideration of fragments 50 and 45. The Λόγος as the self-disclosing all-uniting One and the original meaning of λόγος and λέγειν. The Λόγος as the for-gathering that dispenses the origin and thereby retains it   215

§ 6   The absent presence of the Λόγος for the human and the indication of the objectless region of the originary Λόγος   223

    a) The harmony of fragments 50 and 45. The homological relation of the λόγος of the soul to *the* Λόγος. ὁμολογεῖν as the self-gathering toward the originary forgathering of the Λόγος of being   223

Review ... 231

1) The λόγος of the ψυχή as the gathering toward the originary, all-preserving gathering. The erroneousness of psychological views. Fragments 45 and 50. References to fragments 101 and 116 ... 231

2) A reconsideration of the harmony of fragments 50 and 45. The drawing-in drawing-out of the λόγος of the ψυχή as the relation to beings as such and as a whole. The absent presence of the Λόγος for the human ... 236

b) The two-fold relation of the human to beings and to being: the forgotten, concealed presence of being in the everyday use of λόγος. Fragment 72. References to fragments 16, 45, 50, 101, 43, 118, 30, 64 ... 238

c) The apparent contradiction between the Λόγος understood as gathering and understood as what has been 'separated.' Fragment 108. πάντων κεχωρισμένον as the distinct, to-be-thought determination of the Λόγος as ἓν πάντα, and as the object-less region of the Λόγος ... 246

d) The Λόγος as the regioning presencing in which and from out of which everything presences and absences, and the originary difference between beings and being ... 251

Review ... 253

3) The ambivalent two-fold of turning-toward and turning-away as the relation of the human to being and beings. The rupture in the two-foldedness of the two-fold and the relational rule of λόγοι. Fragment 72. References to fragments 50 and 108 ... 253

THIRD SECTION
RETREAT INTO THE ORIGINARY
REGION OF LOGIC ... 259

§ 7 On the illumination of being, experienced through inceptual thinking. Fragments 108, 41, 64, 78, 119, 16, 115, 50, 112 ... 261

a) The 'steering vision' and the jointure (ἁρμονία) of the originary forgathering. γνώμη and the Λόγος as the unifying One in the advising, counseling presence of the originary sheltering forgathering ... 261

  b) Reconsideration of the ὁμολογεῖν of the ψυχή and the interpretation of the self-enriching of the human λόγος as the self-forgathering residing in the presence of the originary Λόγος   264
  c) Knowledge, the true (i.e., the unconcealed), and the Λόγος. The revealing gathering of the concealed toward unconcealment in true λόγος as the essence of knowledge (σοφία). The demand and imposition of the Λόγος   268

§ 8 The human, the Λόγος, and the essence and truth of being. Final part of the interpretation of saying 112   279

  a) The Λόγος as ἓν πάντα: the originary forgathering presence. On the sameness of the Λόγος and being. The human as safe-keeper of being and the relation of being toward the human: the divining of the event   279
  b) Summary of the guidelines and perspectives according to which the Λόγος, which has yet to unfold inceptually, is to be thought. The truth of being and the fate of metaphysical thinking   281

Supplement   289
Editor's afterword   299
German to English Glossary   303
English to German Glossary   307

TRANSLATORS' FOREWORD

"In the realm of transportive translation, all translations are poor, only more or less so."
—Martin Heidegger, GA 55, 45

The following is the first complete English translation of Volume 55 of Martin Heidegger's *Gesamtausgabe*, published by Vittorio Klostermann in 1979 (three years after Heidegger's death) and revised in 1987. Edited by Manfred Frings, GA 55 contains two lecture-courses offered by Heidegger at the University of Freiburg: the first, *The Inception of Occidental Thinking* (given in the Summer semester of 1943); the second, *Heraclitus's Doctrine of the Logos* (given in the Summer semester of 1944). Taken together, these two lecture-courses offer Heidegger's most sustained and focused engagement with the early-Greek thinker Heraclitus, whom Heidegger considered to be one of only three thinkers (the others being Anaximander and Parmenides) who thought within the region of the inception of Occidental thinking, and who thought something of that inception itself.

Heidegger's playfulness with the German language is at its best in GA 55—a play that is a joy to read, but is often difficult (and occasionally impossible) to translate adequately into English. As anybody who has read Heidegger in German knows, the path and trajectory of his thinking is much more visible in the German language than it is in English, as the connections between words (and therefore concepts) are more conspicuous in the former. While many of our word choices in the translation that follows were governed by a desire to maintain and display Heidegger's wordplay, the chasm between the English and German languages often made this impossible (or, at the very least, insufferably awkward). In light of this, we have done our best to preserve the spirit (and spiritedness) of Heidegger's text, while simultaneously rendering an enjoyable and mellifluous translation. To aid the reader in getting underway, a few words should be said regarding some of the more prominent terms that appear within the lecture courses. (For a more extensive list of German words and our translations of them, please see the Glossary provided at the end of this volume.)

Two of the most fundamental German words at play within the volume—and certainly of the first lecture course—are *Aufgehen* and *Untergehen*. For reasons that we hope will become quickly obvious, we elected to translate these terms as 'emerging' and 'submerging' respectively, a rendering that allowed us to capture the directionality of these German terms (*auf-* and *unter-*), while still employing a common root (as is the case with the German). This latter consideration is important given the manner in which Heidegger thinks these terms (and the processes they name) as inseparable, and as being grounded in a more fundamental process of *Gehen*. Still, even while 'emerging' and 'submerging' are, in our view, the best-suited English terms available to make manifest the process that Heidegger is describing, they are nonetheless inadequate to capture every nuance of *Aufgehen* and *Untergehen* of which Heidegger makes use within this volume, as would be any other rigid pair of English terms. The ability to catch all of these nuances demands a patience and flexibility of thinking that we encourage all readers of this volume to practice.

Throughout the volume, and especially in the first lecture course, Heidegger makes great use of a cluster of related terms all sharing a common etymological (and, for Heidegger, conceptual) history: *fügen*, *Fuge*, *Fügung*, *verfügen*, etc. Following precedent, and in order to capture the linguistic play forever at work in Heidegger's thinking, we have translated these terms as 'join,' 'joint,' 'joinedness,' 'jointure,' etc. The related term *Gefüge*, which is of special importance within the text, we most often render as 'conjoined,' in order to denote the sense of *gathering* that Heidegger often intends with his use of the *ge-* prefix. However, on occasion, *Gefüge* is used to refer specifically to the *structure* of something, or the *combination* of multiple things, or the *articulation* of a thing. In these instances, we have rendered it accordingly.

The German word *Edel* plays an important part in the culminating sections of each lecture course, though its meaning differs somewhat between the two. Within the context of the first lecture course, we have favored the word 'precious,' whereas we have used 'noble' to capture the various nuances at play in the second lecture course. (With the latter term, one should think, for example, of the 'noble' gases.) In both cases, one should think of what, in being unique and rare, is distinguished from all others, and therefore preeminent among them.

In the second lecture course, Heidegger favors the German word *Versammlung* to refer to the originary operation of gathering (*Sammeln*) or harvesting (*Lesen*) whereby the Λόγος sets beings forth into unconcealment. In order to distinguish *Versammlung* from (mere) gathering (*Sammeln*), we have translated it as 'forgathering.' When encountering this term, the reader should be aware that the prefix 'for-' denotes more of an operation of placing-forth or setting-forth than it does any kind of anteriority (though, on several occasions, Heidegger emphasizes the manner in which the forgathering of Λόγος precedes and makes possible any subsequent gathering). If anything, the 'for-' should be read as adding emphasis, though perhaps such emphasis in-and-of-itself already implies a certain priority (or even apriority) at play in the term.

During the latter-half of the second lecture course, Heidegger delineates the operation of the λόγος belonging to the human soul (ψυχή) as consisting of reciprocal and interrelated movements of *Ausholen* and *Einholen*, which we have translated as 'drawing-out' and 'drawing-in'. The German words are meant to be able to explain 1) the reaching-out-toward and bringing-back-in of the Λόγος that characterizes the very essence of the human, 2) the reaching-out and gathering-in that takes place in harvesting (such as, for example, the harvesting of grapes), and 3) the fundamental operation of breathing, properly understood. It is our hope that the dyad 'drawing-in' and 'drawing-out' is sufficient to capture these many nuances.

In the final section of the second lecture course, Heidegger employs a play on various words related to *schweigen* (i.e., 'to keep silent'). In setting out the nature of the relationship between the human being (and its λόγος) to the originary Λόγος (i.e., being), Heidegger speaks of the silent word of Λόγος that, in its stilling of beings for the human being, makes language possible. To capture this rich and important play of words, we have used the related words 'quiet (*schweigen*),' 'acquieting (*Erschweigen*),' 'quiescence (*Schweigen*),' 'requiesence (*Verschweigung*),' and 'acquiescence (*Beschewigen*).' In all cases, what is pointed to is the manner in which the Λόγος (i.e., being) silently gathers beings together in such a way as to make them graspable by the human being and articulable through her λόγος.

Throughout both lecture courses, Heidegger often employs the archaic verb *wesen* and the much more common corresponding nominal form *Wesen*. We have translated the verb as 'to unfold,' and the noun as 'essence,' 'essencing' (when a more verbal sense is clearly intended), or 'unfolding.' On one or two occasions we have translated the noun *Wesen* as 'being,' owing to context.

Translators of Heidegger must be punctilious in their attention to the many different variants of *sein* and its cognates, as must readers of an English translation be fastidious in their attentiveness to the many different formulations of *being*, *beings*, *the being*, etc. In what follows we have translated *Seiende* as 'beings,' though on one occasion (for purposes of euphony) we rendered it as 'that which is.' *Sein*, of course, we have rendered as 'being'; however, despite the convenience of doing so, we have avoided the custom of capitalizing the word, as such a practice risks losing the verbal sense of *Sein* that Heidegger goes to such great lengths to retrieve. The more archaic word *Seyn* has been rendered as '*beyng*.'

To make this volume as readable as possible, we have included only a few bracketed German words, and have done so only when it is absolutely instrumental to deciphering the meaning of the passage. All footnotes are Heidegger's own, unless otherwise indicated as belonging to the translators or to the German editor. We have provided the German pagination in brackets embedded within the body of the text.

With the exception of omitting quotation marks that either Heidegger or Frings introduced into the Greek quotations, we have reproduced the Greek script exactly as it appears in the German volume, including the avoidance of capitalizing the first letter of a Greek word that appears at the beginning of a sentence. The reason we have done so is that Heidegger occasionally capitalizes the first letter of a Greek term in order to give it special emphasis. This practice is extremely important in the second lecture-course in particular, where Heidegger uses capital letters to differentiate between λόγος in a general sense, and *the* Λόγος in a much more specific and ontologically rich sense (i.e., as being itself). Standard English rules governing capitalization would have been fatal to preserving this difference and would have resulted in intolerable confusion. We have also allowed our English renderings of Heidegger's German translations of Heraclitus's Greek to follow Heidegger's sometimes peculiar grammatical constructions, all for the sake of fidelity to Heidegger's engagement with Heraclitus 'The Obscure.'

Although we have done our best to leave as many interpretive decisions as possible up to the reader, we have surely allowed our own understanding of Heidegger's text to guide our interpretation of certain terms, and ineluctably. As Heidegger himself writes in this very volume: "every translation is in itself already an interpretation [...] Interpretation and translation are, in the core of their essence, the same" (GA 55, 63). Though we hope readers will find this translation eloquent and smooth, as well as faithful to the original, we have no doubt that some of our decisions will be questioned, challenged, and perhaps even outright refused. We welcome such criticisms and look forward to the conversation. Above all we look forward to a new generation of scholarly work on the *Heraclitus* lectures: work which, we hope, we will have been aided by, or at the very least instigated by, our translation.

Out of deference to Heidegger, but also in a manner that is shamefully self-serving, we give him the final word of this foreword: "... one can easily criticize any translation, but can only rarely replace it with a 'better' one" (GA 55, 63).

Julia Goesser Assaiante and S. Montgomery Ewegen
Connecticut, Spring 2018

[1] THE INCEPTION OF OCCIDENTAL THINKING
Heraclitus

Summer Semester, 1943

[3] PRELIMINARY CONCERNS
Philosophy as the authentic thinking of the to-be-thought. On the inception of "Occidental" thinking

This lecture concerns the origin of Occidental thinking. The word 'thinking' means here the thinking of the thinkers. Since antiquity, this thinking has been called 'philosophy.' Philosophical thinking is authentic thinking because it thinks that which in its essence is the "to-be-thought," and thereby takes thinking as a claim for itself. Thoughtful thinking is essential thinking. The old name 'philosophy' hails from the region of the inception of Occidental thinking. Thought in a Greek way, it means φιλία τοῦ σοφοῦ: friendship for the to-be-thought.

However, if the friendship between humans can neither be planned nor contrived, then the friendship for the to-be-thought is entirely, and before all else, not something forged by the thinkers, but is rather the gift from what is in, and for, essential thinking the to-be-thought.

The title of this lecture speaks of Occidental thinking. The expression "Occidental Philosophy" is here being avoided, because this expression is, strictly speaking, redundant. There is no philosophy other than Occidental philosophy. 'Philosophy,' in its essence, is so primordially Occidental that it bears the ground of the history of the Occident. From out of this ground alone, technology has arisen. There is only an Occidental technology. It is the consequence of 'Philosophy' and nothing else.

Instead of the thoughtfully adopted title "The Inception of Occidental Thinking" one would even like [4] to say: "The Beginning (or the Origin) of Philosophy in the Occident." Why we have chosen to remain with the other title must come to light through the course of this lecture.

Kant, in the introduction (Part IV) of his *Lectures on Logic*, says the following: "*When* and *where* the philosophical spirit of the Greeks first erupted, one cannot properly determine."[1] Our consideration of the inception of Occidental thinking does not set out to determine when and where philosophy erupted. We content ourselves with the attempt to experience, from a distance, something of the region of the ground of the 'inception' of 'philosophy' (i.e., metaphysics). We call those thinkers who think in the region of the inception 'the inceptual thinkers.' There are only three such thinkers: Anaximander, Parmenides, and Heraclitus. In this lecture course, we concern ourselves with only the last mentioned. We would like to experience something of the 'inception' in the word of Heraclitus's.

---

[1] Immanuel Kant, *Logik*, in *Werke* (Cass.), VIII, 346.

[5] INTRODUCTION

Preliminary consideration of the inceptual and the word

§ 1. Two stories concerning Heraclitus as introduction to his word

Regarding the life of Heraclitus, which fell in the decades between 540 and 480 BCE, we know as little as we do of the lives of Anaximander and Parmenides. It would be a mistake, however, to lament this lack of biographical information: for who Parmenides and Heraclitus *are* is alone determined from out of *what* they thought, and we experience nothing of this through 'biographies.' Thus, the biography of a thinker can be largely correct, while the presentation of his thinking remains quite untrue. This is what happened with Nietzsche, who composed quite a lively description of the 'character' of Heraclitus; however, this lively description did not obviate the fact that Nietzsche's legacy on this score was to bring into circulation the most awful misinterpretation of Heraclitus's thinking.

The question of who Heraclitus is, provided that it is asked within the limits within which it is here able to be asked at all, finds its answer in the word that the thinker, as thinker, has said. A faint glimmer of this word conceals itself in the 'stories' concerning the thinker that are occasionally preserved and passed on. Such 'stories,' even if they are invented (indeed, precisely then), contain a truth that is more originary than the correct information determined through historiographical research. Historiographical/biographical findings always (and only) move within the medium of indifference, and serve only the satisfaction of curiosity regarding the biographical.

[6] We attend here first to two 'stories' concerning Heraclitus. It cannot be proven that what is therein recounted actually occurred. But the fact that these 'stories' are preserved shows us something of the word that this thinker spoke. Of course, we understand these 'stories' only from out of what Heraclitus himself thought and said. Nonetheless, they can in turn serve to make us heedful of Heraclitus's word, albeit at some remove. These 'stories' should not replace the

missing 'biography' in order ultimately to introduce the representation of the so-called 'work' 'biographically'; rather, the 'stories' should lead us to recognize the 'biographic' and the 'historiographical' as inessential. The stories let us be attentive to the realm from out of which Heraclitus's word is spoken.

a) Heraclitus's thinking in the region of fire and strife and in the nearness to play

The first 'story' is as follows:

Ἡράκλειτος λέγεται πρὸς τοὺς ξένους εἰπεῖν τοὺς βουλομένους ἐντυχεῖν αὐτῶι, οἳ ἐπειδὴ προσιόντες εἶδον αὐτὸν θερόμενον πρὸς τῶι ἰπνῶι ἔστησαν, ἐκέλευε γὰρ αὐτοὺς εἰσιέναι θαρροῦντας · εἶναι γὰρ καὶ ἐνταῦθα θεούς ...[1]

Regarding Heraclitus the following (story) is recounted: namely, that he spoke to the visitors who wanted to approach him. Coming closer they saw him as he warmed himself at an oven. They remained standing there (very surprised by this), on account of the fact that he bid them (including those who were still hesitating) to have courage and come in, calling with the words: "Here, too, the gods are present."

The crowd, in its curious intrusiveness upon the thinker and his abode, is disappointed and baffled. They believe that they should be allowed to find the thinker in conditions [7] that carry the characteristics of the exceptional, the rare, and the exciting, and thus unlike the usual day-to-day life of people everywhere. In visiting the thinker, the crowd hopes to find things that (for a while, at least) will serve as fodder for entertaining chatter. Those wanting to visit the thinker hope to catch him precisely at that moment in which he 'thinks' in raptured profundity; not, however, in order to be affected by his thinking, but rather only so they can say that they have seen and heard someone who has the reputation of being a thinker.

However, instead of such a situation, these curious spectators find the thinker at an oven. This is an everyday and modest place where (for example) bread is baked. But Heraclitus is not even at the oven engaged in baking; rather, he abides there only in order to warm himself. He thereby reveals in this everyday place the whole indigence of his life. The sight of a freezing thinker offers little of 'interest.' The curious spectators, owing to this disappointing sight, lose their desire to come closer. Why should they bother? This commonplace and charmless indigence of

---

[1] Aristotle, *Parts of Animals*, A.5, 645a17 ff.

freezing and standing at the oven can be found at anyone's house at any time. Why, then, should they seek out a thinker? Heraclitus reads the disappointed curiosity in their faces. He recognizes that, for the crowd, the mere absence of an expected sensational event suffices to turn them toward leaving. Therefore, he tells them to have courage and prompts them to enter with these words: εἶναι γὰρ καὶ ἐνταῦθα θεούς: "Here, too, the gods are present."

These words cast the abode of the thinker and his occupation in another light. Whether the visitors understand these words instantly or at all, thereby seeing everything in this other light, the story does not say. But the fact this story has been told and passed down to us [8] moderns is based upon the fact that it hails from out of the atmosphere of the thinking of this thinker and thus designates it. καὶ ἐνταῦθα—even here at the oven, in this everyday and ordinary place where each thing and every circumstance, each action and every thought, is familiar through and through, common and ordinary; 'even here,' in this region of the familiar, εἶναι θεούς, the 'gods presence.' θεοί are the θεάοντες καὶ δαίμονες. The essence of the gods who appeared to the Greeks is precisely this appearing, in the sense of a peering into the ordinary in such a way that what peers both into, and out of, the ordinary is the extraordinary that presences in the region of the ordinary. Even here, says Heraclitus, at the oven, where I warm myself, the presencing of the extraordinary in the ordinary prevails. καὶ ἐνταῦθα—'even here'—says the thinker, thereby speaking to the expectations of the visitors, and therefore, in a certain sense, in accordance with the desire and disposition of the crowd. Supposing, however, that the words of a thinker say what they say in a way that is different from everyday language, so that in each common surface meaning of his speech a subtext necessarily conceals itself, then these words of Heraclitus's, when we heed them as the thoughtful word, have a strange meaning.

When the thinker says καὶ ἐνταῦθα ("even here"), ἐν τῶι ἰπνῶι ("at the oven"), the extraordinary presences, then he wants to say in truth: the presencing of the gods unfolds *only* here. Where, namely? In the inconspicuousness of the everyday. You need not avoid the customary and ordinary and chase after the eccentric, exciting, and tantalizing in the misguided hope of thereby encountering the extraordinary. You should keep only to your daily and familiar, as I do here, abiding with the oven and warming myself. Is what I do here, and how I abide, not full enough of signs? The oven gives bread. But how can humans live properly without the gift of bread? This gift of the oven is the sign for what the θεοί (the gods) are. [9] They are the δαίοντες, those who give themselves in the ordinary as the extraordinary. I warm myself at the oven and thereby remain in the nearness of the fire: the Greek πῦρ, which at the same time means 'light' and 'glow.' You find me here near the fire, in which alone the ray of light of those peering in is possible and is one with the ray of warmth, and which lets 'emerge' into appearance that which, in the cold, would otherwise fall victim to the numbness of nothingness.

In what follows, we must watch for whether, and in what way, the thinking of Heraclitus remains always in the nearness to, and within the region of, the thinking of fire, in order to gauge what 'truth' the story of the thinker at the oven conceals. But, if this story should contain something significant regarding the thinking of Heraclitus's specifically, and not only what in a certain sense applies to every thinker, then something must be said in the word of Heraclitus's that the story hands down, something that we have indicated but not yet properly seized.

καὶ ἐνταῦθα θεούς: "even here," and precisely there, in the inconspicuousness of the ordinary, unfolds the extraordinariness of those who shine-in. This means: here, where I (the thinker) abide, is the inconspicuous together with the highest of that which appears and shines. Here, where I have my abode, what seems mutually exclusive has come together into one. Here, in the realm of the thinker, what stands in opposition and appears to be mutually exclusive—namely, what turns against but also toward the other—is everywhere. Perhaps this turning-toward *must* even exist in order that one may turn itself against the other. Where such turning-toward prevails, strife (ἔρις) unfolds. The thinker resides in the nearness of strife.

In what follows we must watch for whether, and in what way, the thinking of Heraclitus remains always in the region of [10] what the word ἔρις names, in order to recognize that this 'story' in particular allows a light to emerge upon Heraclitus's thinking.

The other story concerning Heraclitus reads:

ἀναχωρήσας δ'εἰς τὸ ἱερὸν τῆς Ἀρτέμιδος μετὰ τῶν παίδων ἠστραγάλιζε · περιστάντων δ'αὐτὸν τῶν Ἐφεσίων, τί, ὦ κάκιστοι, θαυμάζετε; εἶπεν · ἢ οὐ χρεῖττον τοῦτο ποιεῖν ἢ μεθ' ὑμῶν πολιτεύεσθαι;[2]

But he had himself withdrawn into the temple of Artemis in order to play knucklebones with the children; here, the Ephesians stood around him, and he said to them: "What are you gaping at, you scoundrels? Or is it not better to do this than to work with you on behalf of the πόλις?"

This second story gives a similar picture, insofar as the crowd, gaping curiously at the thinker, has once again come close to him and is hovering around him. The Ephesians—i.e., the countrymen of Heraclitus's—are named. In this story, however, he does not abide in an everyday and modest place. Rather, he has gone into the holy precinct of the temple of Artemis. Thus, in this story too, the nearness to the gods is reported, but in a way that does not touch upon the astonishing fact that the gods presence in the oven. The holy precinct of the temple speaks for itself clearly enough. Certainly, here, now more than ever, there is the opportunity for

---

[2] Diogenes Laertius, IX, 3.

astonishment. Yet, the thinker does not particularly concern himself with the goddess; rather, he plays a dice-game (ἀστράγαλος: the vertebrae; knuckles; die) with the children. A thinker, from whom even the average person expects seriousness and profundity, plays a child's game. However, if, according to his own words from the first story, the nearness to the gods is so important to him that he found them even in the oven, how can he then, in the precinct of the house of the goddess, [11] do ἀλλότρια (i.e., inappropriate things)? Once again the thinker reads perplexed wonder in the expressions of the by-standers, and once again he speaks to them. But now his words have a different tone. The words of the first story are encouraging, inviting. Now he asks: τί, ὦ κάκιστοι, θαυμάζετε;—"What are you gaping at, you scoundrels?" These words are severe, scornful, and dismissive. The former words invited the bystanders to experience the presence of the gods with him. Now the thinker cuts himself off decisively from that with which the bystanders are engaged. The thinker, or so it appears, wants nothing to do with the πολιτεύεσθαι, the care of the πόλις.

One might be tempted to interpret this 'situation' in a modern way and remark that the thinker admits here to being an 'unpolitical' person, one who self-centeredly spins around only within the circle of his 'private existence.' But such modernizations and the almost inevitable 'allusions' by historiographers to the respective present are always unfitting, because from the start they refuse to allow the past its historically proper-essence, and thereby fail to think historically in an authentic way. It is one thing to produce a historiographic image of the past for the respective present; it is another to think historically, that is, to experience what has-been as what is unfolding as what is to come. All merely historiographical revivals of the past are always the poor facades of historical errors.

In the case of Heraclitus, it is not at all decided whether the renunciation of πολιτεύεσθαι includes a refusal of the πόλις. Indeed, how could this be so, if—when thought in a Greek way—the concern with the presence of the gods is the highest concern of the city? This is in fact the case: for the πόλις, still thought in a Greek way, is[3] the pole and the site around which all appearing of essential beings, and with it also the dreadful non-essence of [12] all beings, turns. Understood in this way, and thus always thought in a Greek way, the thinker with his care for the essential nearness of the gods is the authentically 'political' human. Thus, πολιτεύεσθαι and πολιτεύεσθαι, even among the Greeks, are not immediately and in every case the same. Therefore, with his words to the Ephesians, Heraclitus refuses only their expectation that he, as thinker, drops out of the care allotted to him in order to degenerate into a common endeavor with them toward the πόλις (cf. fragment 121). This refusal refers indirectly to the necessity of the plight of thoughtful care: namely, to be thoughtfully concerned with the extraordinary that presences in all things ordinary.

---

[3] Cf. *Parmenides* (GA 54).

But, when Heraclitus plays 'dice' with the children in the temple-precinct of the goddess, does this exhibit his care about the extraordinary and about the particular goddess of his particular πόλις? We shall ask this question, as do the Ephesians within the fragment. Heraclitus, however, in no way refuses the bystanders this question. Rather, he addresses it directly in order to properly ask about why they marvel about his present action.

τί ... θαυμάζετε; — "What are you gaping at?" Are you surprised that a thinker, set off from commerce and its successes, spends his time only in useless games and not even pursuing his thoughts, which is the least of what may be demanded of a thinker? If they wonder solely about these things, they understand altogether nothing about his conduct. Were it a mere pastime, the game with the children would in fact be no better than the gaping of the Ephesians. Then why should this activity be granted the privilege of being better for the thinker? What truly astonishing thing conceals itself in the harmless actions of the thinker? Does the nearness to an extraordinary game lie hidden in this perfectly familiar and ordinary playing with the children? If so, then the harsh words of the thinker to the Ephesians would be unwelcoming only in appearance, just as the words at the oven had the appearance of a mere, glib invitation, as though [13] the gods let themselves be encountered by just anyone in any disposition.

In what follows we must be attentive to whether, and in what way, the thinking of Heraclitus's is always determined from out of the nearness to a game, and whether even the to-be-thought of thoughtful thinking is revealed to him to be something like a game.

b) Heraclitus's word under the protection of Artemis

Both stories regarding Heraclitus show, albeit in varying ways and with varying distinctness, that in the thinking of the thinker a nearness to the gods prevails. If one attended sufficiently to this, one could easily explain it in accordance with the later imaginings of metaphysics through the suggestion that, precisely in thoughtful thinking, where the entirety of the world will be presented, the universal world-ground—i.e., the godly in a broad and undetermined sense—would also necessarily be represented. One can also easily prove how, in all metaphysics from Plato to Nietzsche, a theological moment predominates, because of the fact that 'the godly' is thought therein as the universal world-cause. Herein also lies the ground for a far-reaching process within the history of the Occident: namely, the reciprocal relation between metaphysics and Christianity.

By contrast, we would do well, already at the beginning of this lecture course, to keep all theological interpretations—and thereby also the opinion that philosophy, already at its beginning, was determined through theology—away from inceptual thinking. For the gods and the godly of the ancient Greek world are not suitable for a theology, even when we take this designation very broadly and understand it not only as the rational explanation and ordering of doctrines belonging to a given 'religion.' There is, after all, no Greek 'religion.' The word *religio* and its concerns are essentially Roman. Because there [14] is no Greek 'religion,' there is also no Greek 'theology.'

However, the fact that the essential nearness of the gods to the thinker Heraclitus has its own essence is expressed in the second story. Specifically, the goddess Artemis is named here. One would perhaps like to contend that the mentioning of Artemis is in no way characteristic of Heraclitus the thinker, but rather is characteristic of Heraclitus the Ἐφέσιος: for since ancient times, there was a sanctuary of Artemis in Ephesus. It still stood in the late-Greek period when Paul, while on his mission, preached there to the Ephesians. During an Ephesian uprising against Paul's Christian preaching, the chant μεγάλη ἡ Ἄρτεμις τῶν Ἐφεσίων rang for two long hours.[4]

But the question remains whether, taken by itself, the historiographical explanation that the Artemision was a popular cause of the Ephesians can at all grasp and express the truth. It remains to be asked whether the goddess Artemis was only mentioned in the report about Heraclitus because Heraclitus was an Ephesian, or whether the thinking of this thinker in relation to this goddess is in tune with what this thinker had to think as an inceptual thinker of the Greeks.

We state the following, and for the moment only in the form of a supposition: Artemis is the goddess of the thinker Heraclitus, and not merely the goddess of the Ephesians. But she is the goddess of the thinker because she is the goddess of what the thinker has to think.

Who is Artemis? It would be presumptuous if we thought that we could respond to this question by means of some observations about 'mythology.' Here, the only possible and, indeed, necessary response takes the form of a responsibility that entails the historical decision regarding whether or not we choose to safeguard the 'essence' of this goddess and the Greek realm of gods as something having-been. Whether the forms of the gods still amuse us in a 'literary-poetic' [15] sense, or whether we explain them in mythological/historiographical terms, amounts to the same. In both cases, they are only the objects of our 'lived-experience,' which turns out in one case as moving and sentimental, and in the other as stiff and boring. It is an entirely different question, however, whether the concealed essence of the history to which we belong is compelled, from out of an essential need, into a dialogue with what was, to the Greeks, their θεοί. The proper answer to the questions 'Who is Artemis?' and 'Who is Zeus?' conceals itself still in our history to come, insofar as it alone responds to the having-been.

---

[4] Cf. *The Acts of the Apostles*, XIX, 34.

The observations concerning the 'gods' of the Greeks offered here and periodically in what follows remain, above all, cautious hints and makeshift clues that do not carry much weight. Familiarity with these observations should never lead to the opinion that, by mastering mythological evidence and the poetic description of the same, knowledge of the gods is obtained in such a way that this knowledge enacts the relation to the gods in and through which they bestow themselves to humans. Moreover, the relation of the Greeks to the gods is a *knowledge*, and not a 'faith' in the sense of a willful taking-to-be-true on the basis of an authoritative proclamation. We still do not fathom the inceptual way in which the Greeks were the knowing ones. It is not the case that they were the knowing ones because they possessed a philosophy; rather, it was because they were the knowing ones that they thereby founded the inception of authentic thinking.

Who, then, is the goddess of Heraclitus? Who is Artemis? Artemis is the sister of Apollo, and both were born on the island of Delos. The last strophe of the poem "Song of the Germans,"[5] in which Hölderlin poeticized the essence of the Germans, begins with the question that the poet poses to the Muse (i.e., to the 'angel' of the German fatherland). The question asks, in the end, about the island Delos, [16] the birthplace of Apollo and Artemis. The final strophe of the poem reads:

Where is your Delos, where your Olympia,
    That we all find ourselves at the highest festival?
        Yet, how does the son divine what you,
            For yours, Immortal, have long prepared?

Artemis, the sister, who along with her brother hails from Delos, bears the same signs as her brother Apollo: lyre and bow, which in a mysterious way, and hence also in their 'outer form,' are the same. The lyre is the symbol of 'string music' and its ἁρμονία. Here, the 'essence' of play strikes us again. The Greeks know Artemis as the huntress and as the 'goddess of the hunt.' Naturally, we believe we know approximately what the concept 'hunt' means, and apply this notion in an unreflective way to the goddess of the hunt. Hunting and animals belong in 'nature'—i.e., φύσις. Artemis is the goddess of φύσις. Her playmates, the Nymphs, play the game of φύσις. This word names the self-opening coming-forth and emerging 'up' and upwards into an unconcealed standing-there and rising (πέλειν). The goddess of φύσις is the rising one. Hence she appears in an elevated form. Her beauty is one of lofty and stately appearance. Those maidens to whom Artemis is well-disposed are given great stature.[6]

---

[5] Hölderlin, *Werke* (Hellingrath), IV, 129–131.
[6] Cf. Homer, *Odyssey* XX, 71: ... μῆχος δ'ἔπορ Ἄρτεμις ἁγνή—"but Artemis the holy gives high stature."

If φύσις should prove to be what remains for the inceptual thinker the sole to-be-thought, we must then linger in amazement, at the appropriate time, at the fact that Artemis appears in the nearness of Heraclitus. Such nearness would be precisely the sign that Heraclitus is an inceptual thinker. Artemis appears with torches in both hands. She is called φωσφόρος—the Light Bringer. The essence of light (φάος, φῶς) is the illumination that first lets something appear [17] and thus lets the unconcealed come forth from out of concealment. But the essence of φύσις is at the same time the emerging and self-expanding into the open and lightened. φῶς and φάος (light) and φύσις (emerging), as well as φαίνω (to shine and appear), are all rooted in one and the same essence that neither the inceptual thinker of the Greeks, nor any later thinking, has thought in the unity of its essential richness.

(We call it by the single, but still unconsidered word: clearing. The clearing in the sense of the illuminating and opening sheltering is the inceptual hidden essence of ἀλήθεια. That is the Greek name for what is otherwise known as truth, which, for the Greeks, is unconcealment and disclosure. φύσις (nature) and φάος (light) have the ground of the concealed unity of their essence in the veiled essence of ἀλήθεια. The fact that recently modern linguistics, without any notion of the stated essential intimacy between φύσις and φάος, has come to the discovery that the words φύσις and φάος indicate the same thing, may here only be mentioned in passing. This linguistic discovery proves nothing, because it is only an addendum to, and consequence of, insights into essential intimacies that it exploits mindlessly and thoughtlessly.)

Artemis is the goddess of emergence, of light, and of play. Her sign is the lyre, which appears in the form of the bow: thus, thought in a Greek way, it is the same as the bow. The lyre, understood as the bow, sends the arrow that brings death. But the deaths that her arrow sends are 'sudden,' 'gentle,' and 'loving.' The goddess of emergence, play, and light is also the goddess of death, just as if light, play, and emerging were the same as death. Rather, emerging, self-illuminating, and play mark the essence of ζωή, 'life,' and of ζῷον, 'the living.' Our word 'life' is already so burdened by Christian and modern-day thinking that it cannot [18] designate what the Greeks understood by ζωή and ζῷον. Even if our word 'life' remains only an imprecise and confused translation of the Greek word ζωή, it nevertheless allows us to think that 'life' is the opposite of death. How, then, can the goddess of the self-illuminating, of emerging, and of play be, at the same time, the goddess of death, i.e., of the dark, of submergence, and of the rigid? Life and death turn against one another. Certainly. However, what turns against one another turns, at the moment of its most extreme opposition, intimately toward one another. Where such turning prevails, there is strife, ἔρις. For Heraclitus, who thinks strife as the essence of being, Artemis, the goddess with bow and lyre, is the nearest. But her nearness is pure nearness—i.e., farness. We must of course think nearness and farness in a Greek way, and not in the 'modern' sense as the numerically greater or lesser distance between two spatial points.

But if, as we claim, Artemis is the goddess of Heraclitus, then must not also the brother be of the same nature as the sister? To be sure, the name of Apollo is not mentioned explicitly in the words of Heraclitus's that have been handed down to us. Although this god is not spoken of in a saying of the thinker, he is nonetheless named unequivocally, and indeed in connection with something that clarifies for us the essence of this thinking in a decisive way.[7] The thinking of Heraclitus's, in which the to-be-thought is characterized by the nearness of Artemis (brother to Apollo), is, on account of this nearness, 'Apollonian.' We use this designation in a sense yet to be clarified, one that differs no less from Nietzsche's concept of the Apollonian than from those concepts customarily employed within 'humanism' and all of 'classicism.' The 'Dionysian' interpretation of Heraclitus's thinking—already employed by Hegel [19] and then coarsened by Nietzsche and pushed further into the quagmire—is eliminated in advance through the observation that Artemis is the goddess of this thinker.

In light of this, an old fragment only now obtains its proper complexion and gravity. The story reads:

ἀνέθηκε δ᾽ αὐτὸ (τὸ φερόμενον αὐτοῦ βιβλίον) εἰς τὸ τῆς Ἀρτέμιδος ἱερόν . . .[8]

He [namely, Heraclitus] brought it (that is, his still-intact writing) into the sanctuary of Artemis, in order to shelter it there.

Thus, the word of Heraclitus's stands under the protection of Artemis. The *word*, surely, though not the writings—for the latter were apparently abandoned unsheltered and broken up into pieces. For us today, only fragments of these writings are preserved. Because of this, every attempt to think-after the thinking of Heraclitus's by bringing it into the light of understanding is difficult. We are faced with the incoherence of the isolated pieces and sentence fragments and do not know the unity in which they belong. By contrast, if we possessed the entirety of the unbroken writings, then we could easily let the thought of this thinker present itself clearly and brightly from out of its own proper cohesiveness. But this idea is admittedly misguided, and for various reasons.

c) The obscurity of the thinker Heraclitus

Even at the time when the writings of Heraclitus's were still preserved intact and well-known, this thinker, on the basis of his still directly accessible writings, had a reputation that has remained for centuries: ἐπεκλήθη ὁ Σκοτεινός—"He

---

[7] See fragment 93.
[8] Diogenes Laertius, IX, 6.

(Heraclitus) was called by the epithet 'The Obscure.'" However, we can find nothing special in the fact that the thinker Heraclitus was called 'The Obscure,' [20] since each thinker who truly is a thinker easily (and often) attains a reputation for 'lack of clarity' and 'obscurity.' The crowd happily agrees with this reputation, since they feel insulted in the face of whatever they do not immediately understand, and retaliate by describing the thinker as 'unclear.' Often this reputation for 'lack of clarity' (where, incidentally, thinkers are safest) also carries with it the suspicion that the thinkers themselves seek to portray their thoughts as 'difficult' and as 'obscure' as possible, in order that they may appear 'mysterious' and 'important.'

(Schopenhauer, whose work was Nietzsche's downfall, demonstrated that he is not a thinker through his self-indulgent rant concerning Schelling and Hegel and their lack of clarity. Nevertheless, we should give Schopenhauer his proper due as an accomplished novelist who, in the middle of the last century, imparted to the Germans only a pale notion of what 'philosophy' is.)

This widespread opinion concerning the thinking of the thinker—namely, that it deliberately sheaths itself in obscurity—has an old and famous example in the view that the Roman author Cicero voiced regarding Heraclitus 'The Obscure.' Since, to be sure, the Romans have notoriously grasped nothing beyond this from the thinking of the Greeks, the opinion of Cicero's concerning Heraclius is hardly surprising. Cicero believes[9] that Heraclitus has purposefully written so opaquely. The German thinker Hegel, who after all must have known something about the essential nature of a thinker, has already given the definitive reply to this opinion of Cicero's in his *Lectures on the History of Philosophy*.[10] Hegel there says that such intentionality (as Cicero has imputed to Heraclitus) would be very vapid indeed, were it true, but that it is in fact nothing but Cicero's own vapidity that he forces upon Heraclitus. But then Hegel himself, immediately following the aforementioned remark, gives the following judgment concerning Heraclitus's obscurity: [21] namely, that it is probably a consequence of the careless combining of words and unrefined language.

We are tempted to reject this explanation of Hegel's as being no less 'vapid.' However, we must keep in mind that Hegel in his time (i.e., the time of Goethe and Humboldt and classicism), but also in accordance with the Occidental tradition of the time, held the thinking and saying of Plato as *the* paradigm of classical Greek philosophy. However, at the same time, Hegel still placed Aristotle over Plato with regard to speculative power and profundity. Regarding Aristotle, Hegel says the following in the same lectures:[11] "There is certainly a lack in Aristotle of Plato's beautiful form, of his sweetness of language (the chatting) [one could almost say:

---

[9] *De Natura Deorum*, I, 74.
[10] Hegel, *Sämtliche Werke* (Glockner), XVII, 347.
[11] Ibid., XVIII, 314.

the chatter], his conversational tone that is as lively as it is cultured and humane." Given such an assessment of Plato's language and, more importantly, given the opinion that the thinkers before Plato must only be construed in terms of this and only by means of it, and thus taken only as 'pre-Platonic' and preliminary thinkers, is it then any wonder that Hegel finds in Heraclitus "unrefined language" and "the careless combining of words"? We think about the thinking and the language of the inceptual thinkers differently now, in the same way that one now judges the 'archaic style' of Greek art differently than classical art history did, whereby it may remain undecided whether or not the now customary interpretation of the 'archaic' is in agreement with the Greek world. 'Archaic' comes from the word ἀρχή, which means 'inception.' Without knowledge of the inception, the interpretation of 'archaic art' no doubt fumbles in the dark. Furthermore, we should not measure the inceptual language of the Greek thinker by means of the yardstick of subsequent Hellenistic grammar.

[22] REVIEW

1) The reference to 'fire' and 'play' in the two stories concerning Heraclitus

Three thinkers approach us from out of the realm of Occidental thinking: Anaximander, Parmenides, and Heraclitus. In the present lectures, we are attempting to become attentive to the word of Heraclitus's. At the outset of this attempt, it may be prudent to experience straightaway the atmosphere in which the word of Heraclitus's was said. Because Heraclitus is a thinker, the air that envelopes him is the crisp and cool air of thoughtful thinking, which is itself a daring deed. Two 'stories' concerning Heraclitus should help bring it about that perhaps, from time to time, we feel the draft of this air, if only from out of the farthest distance.

The first of these two stories reads, in translation:

> Regarding Heraclitus the following (story) is recounted: namely, that he spoke to the visitors who wanted to approach him. Coming closer, they saw him as he warmed himself at an oven. They remained standing there. He bid the surprised ones to have courage and come in, with the words: "Here, too, the gods are present."

The other story reads:

But he (namely, Heraclitus) had withdrawn into the temple of Artemis in order to play knucklebones there with the children; there, the Ephesians (his countrymen) stood around him, and he said to them: "What are you gaping at, you scoundrels? Or is it not better to do this [what I am now doing] than to work with you on behalf of the πόλις?"

One story shows the thinker near the oven, the other shows him playing a game with children. Where, in either of these stories, is there a trace of the crisp and cool air from which hails the daring deed that is called 'thinking'?

[23] One story shows an everyday place, the oven, where nonetheless, according to the thinker's own words, gods are present. The other story shows, by contrast, the place of a god (i.e., the temple of the goddess Artemis); but here the thinker does not attend to the presence of the goddess, whose presence means everything to him during his stay at the oven. The sojourn of the thinker shows in each case precisely the opposite of what one expects. At the oven one is disappointed; in the temple one is surprised. Regarding the manner and the essence of the thinker, and regarding his thinking, nothing shows itself, at least not immediately, and certainly not for the mere gaping eye of the crowd: for this eye sees only what falls immediately in front of it, and only what is obvious and pleasing to it. This eye of the crowd is not inclined to notice what the appearance points to beyond itself. This eye of the crowd is not at all practiced at following what such a pointing points to in each case. The eye of the crowd is blind to signs. Whatever exceeds appearance is considered to be fantasy and fabrication by the many (i.e., the πολλοί, as the Greeks say). Against this, the crowd believes in so-called 'reality' and simple givenness. Moreover, the eye of the crowd does not have the sight for the inconspicuous, in which alone genuine signs are concealed. The oven points to bread and to fire and, in the 'fire,' to glowing and brightness. The 'reasonable person' just sees an oven. And whoever still today reads this harmless story of the thinker at the oven as a 'reasonable person' must rightly conclude that one goes 'too far' in finding here a sign of the fire and a hint of the glow and the light.

The children's game of which the second 'story' speaks points to the relaxed and easy-going, to the dynamism and freedom of play which, as play, nonetheless has its rule and its law and thus remains [24] in the unified and circumscribed (what we call a *world*) in which the players are immersed without, however, drowning in it.

When we thoroughly ponder the two stories regarding the sojourns of the thinker, suddenly we no longer think of the thinker, but rather of that with which he lingers. We follow the signs that point to fire and play. We can now set aside the 'personality' of the thinker. We hold now only to that with which he sojourns, because it is this that determines the character of his sojourn and, from out of this, his posture and his ownmost comportment (i.e., his thinking). When we say 'Heraclitus,' we think not of this man as a 'creator' of a philosophy; rather, we think of the 'fire' and of the 'play.' We think of this because it points to what remains, for his thinking, the to-be-thought, the very one with which he stands in a friendship that is the φιλία τοῦ σοφοῦ in which the thinking that is later called 'philosophy' is grounded.

We must thus be attentive hereafter to whether, and to what extent, the word of this thinker speaks essentially about 'fire' and 'play,' and whether, and how, with 'fire' and 'play' something essential is named that at the same time points to the presence of the gods. We will then only later—perhaps suddenly, one day soon, or perhaps only after years—notice at once what a note-*worthy* explanation these two harmless 'stories' about the thinker Heraclitus give.

2) The to-be-thought in the signs of Artemis: lyre, bow, and torch. The obscurity of the thinker

Both stories point out in different ways that a presencing of the gods belongs to the sojourn of the thinker. Both stories, however, also give us the hint that this nearness of the gods is of a unique sort. Hence, we would do well not to speak too much, too loudly, or too often about the gods. With all due caution in this regard, [25] we cannot presently ignore the peculiarity that in the second story, and also in still another narrative, the goddess Artemis is specifically named. One could, in reference to this, offer the plausible explanation that Heraclitus was, after all, an Ἐφέσιος, and that, thus, the goddess Artemis is distinctive not of Heraclitus the thinker, but rather of Heraclitus the man from Ephesus. For in ancient times there was a sanctuary of Artemis in Ephesus, the 'Artemision.' Artemis is also called Διώνη or 'Diana.' The goddess Artemis is the sister of the god Apollo. The essence of both, who according to legend were born on the island of Delos, has emerged into that world whose domain is the light and the illuminating. Artemis appears with the torches in her hands, because she is the φωσφόρος, the Light-Bringer. Artemis streaks through the mountains and wilderness and is encountered there as the Huntress. She seeks out the animals in which the 'lively' appears in an exceptional way, so that today still with the words 'zoological' and 'animalistic' we mean not only the animal, but rather above all the living. The Occidental definition of the essence of the human should be recalled: ζῷον λόγον ἔχον, *animal rationale*, the rational living being; instead of 'living being' Nietzsche says, for example, simply 'animal.'

Animals and the way of tracing their tracks, thereby engaging with the consummation of their 'life,' belong in φύσις, which one renders inadequately as 'nature.' The word φύσις means: emerging from out of itself into the open, into the free emerged standing-there of appearance, and giving itself within appearance to the free, and thereby still following a rule. Accordingly, 'to unfold' is the essence of play. Play belongs to φύσις. The nymphs, who play the game of 'nature,' are the playmates of Artemis. The sign of 'playing strings,' and perhaps of play generally, is the lyre. It appears in the shape of a bow. For the Greeks, who experienced 'appearance' as being, the lyre 'is' therefore the bow. The bow sends forth the death-bringing arrows. The Huntress, who [26] tracks the living so that it may find death, bears the signs of play and death—lyre and bow. Her other sign, 'the torch,' is, as the fallen and extinguished torch, the sign of death. The Light-Bringer is the Death-Bringer. Life and death, like light and night, correspond to one another, in that they at the same time 'contradict' one another. Artemis the elevated one, through her appearing, lets this 'contra-diction' peer into beings as a whole. She is the appearance of the oppositional, and nowhere and never is she disposed to balance the oppositional, or give up the oppositional entirely in favor of one side. The Light-Bringer *is*, as the Death-Bringer, the appearance of the oppositional. She is this because she originally lets the unfamiliarity of strife peer into the familiar. Artemis is a bringer of the essential strife, ἔρις. This strife is not only unresolved; rather, it belongs to the essence of strife to strive-against each resolution and every attempt at such.

Here, with our use of the word 'strife,' we clearly must stay away from the common notion of the word, which points in the direction of conflict and discord. Neither 'battle' nor 'war' attain to the richness of the essence of what is here called 'strife,' ἔρις. Each battle and every war is a type and variety of what is here called ἔρις, 'strife,' but nowhere is this in its essence and by necessity the same as 'battle' or 'war.' The attempt to consider what is for the inceptual thinker Heraclitus the to-be-thought will encounter light and fire, play and life, and will discover strife in all of them. What the goddess Artemis lets appear through her own appearing points to what is, for the thinker, the to-be-thought.

Artemis is the goddess of Heraclitus insofar as she, as goddess, is θεά, i.e., the one who peers into and is near to that which opens itself to the inceptual thinking of this thinker.

[27] The word of this thinker, as the saying of the to-be-said, stands under the protection of this goddess. However, because the word is not grounded in the reading of words, and because the word-sound only rings out as what it is from out of the inceptually soundless word, the words and the word-configurations found in writings and in books can break apart and fragment, while the word itself remains intact.

We possess only fragments of the writings of Heraclitus. How much more convenient our attempt would be to think-after the thinking of this thinker were we able to possess the writings intact! Yet, we take some steps in that direction when we hear that Heraclitus, even at the time when his writings were still accessible in their entirety, bore the epithet ὁ Σκοτεινός, 'The Obscure.' Thus, the thoughtful appropriation of his writings, even if they remained for us intact, would still be a difficult task. Unless perhaps the epithet ὁ Σκοτεινός is merely a label that is attached to him that obscures, through some misunderstanding, his otherwise clear thinking. If this were so, the epithet 'The Obscure' would originate only from the lack of understanding of others while hitting upon nothing about the essence of the thinker himself. Heraclitus has only the 'reputation' for obscurity, a reputation that a thinker can all too easily obtain. Cicero explained the obscurity of the thinker as resulting from a deliberate obfuscation of his own thinking. Hegel reproved this explanation of Cicero's and set down another in its place, one that seeks to locate the reason for the obscurity in the defective combining of words in Heraclitus's use of language. Surpassing this view, we gradually attain to the insight that the 'primitiveness' of the early thinkers is not characterized by lack of skill and maladroitness, but rather by the primacy of the inceptual, and the simplicity proper and exclusive to it. The language of the inceptual thinkers has the nobility of the inceptual. The word is in the inception of the saying.

[28] § 2. The word in the inception of thinking

a) The 'obscurity' of essential thinking: the essential self-concealing of the to-be-thought (i.e., being)

When we measure the nobility of the word in terms of what remains to be said in it, what could be more joined to what is to be said than a saying of Heraclitus's? Where, after all, does a higher concern for the word speak? To be sure, the reason for the inceptual nobility of this thoughtful speaking lies not in a special linguistic ability belonging to the thinker, but rather in the essence of what is thought in this thinking and what remains the to-be-thought, and which, *as* the to-be-thought, calls forth the word in such a way that the thinker is merely summoned to echo this call. In the inception of the saying, the word has not yet degraded into a mere 'linguistic expression' and 'turn of phrase,' such that any arbitrary phrase can replace any other. The word here still preserves its inceptual essence—i.e., *the word*—without the inceptual poet and thinker possessing or even needing knowledge of this concealed essence.

The to-be-thought of inceptual thinking, as the ground of the nobility of the word, is of course at the same time also the reason for the obscurity of this thinking. Hegel would certainly not be the thinker he is if he had stopped at the superficial declaration concerning the obscurity of Heraclitus mentioned in the previous lecture, and had not also said the following about the latter's philosophy:[1] "The obscurity of this philosophy lies mainly in the fact that a profound, speculative thought is expressed in it": for the concept, i.e., the idea, is contrary to the understanding and cannot be grasped by it, whereas (for example) mathematics is very easy for the understanding to grasp. In order to understand this declaration

---

[1] Ibid., XVII, 348.

of Hegel's adequately, we would need to clarify for ourselves [29] what Hegel means by 'concept' and 'idea' and by the designation 'speculative.' To accomplish this, a discussion concerning the essence of modern metaphysics would be necessary, as well as a demonstration of the essence of truth in which the modern experience of beings as a whole stands. However, for the immediate purposes of the present investigation, we can see, even without such an extensive discussion, wherein Hegel 'primarily' located the ground and essence of the 'obscurity' of Heraclitus's thinking. The obscurity lies not in Heraclitus's unclear style, but rather in 'philosophy' itself, owing to the fact that philosophy thinks in a way that is not familiar to common understanding and which is therefore always very difficult for that understanding to grasp. Philosophical thinking thereby remains, in its very essence, obscure, at least when viewed within the horizon of conventional thinking. Philosophy is thus always and necessarily obscure so long as it is regarded from within the horizon of mere understanding (i.e., of everyday imaginings and opinions). Heraclitus is thus ὁ Σκοτεινός, 'The Obscure,' not because he intentionally or unintentionally expresses himself in a manner that is incomprehensible, but rather because every merely reasonable thinking excludes itself from the thinking of the thinker (i.e., from essential thinking). For this reason alone, however, philosophy as such is not obscure. Its essence consists, following Hegel, precisely in bringing that which is first veiled and inaccessible into the light of the knowledge of unconditional certainty. The to-be-known places itself into the clarity of unconditional knowledge in which each and every trace of obscurity (i.e., what is still not unconditionally known) is obliterated. In regard to the essence of the truth of philosophy as the absolute 'science,' Hegel, on October 28, 1816, concludes his inaugural lecture at the University of Heidelberg with the following words:

> The essence of the universe, at first concealed and closed-off, does not have the power to offer resistance to the courage of cognition; it (the essence of the universe) must open [30] itself up before him (the philosophical thinker) and lay its abundance and depth before his eyes and for his pleasure.[2]

Hegel proceeds to consider the thinking of Heraclitus in terms of modern (and of his own) speculative metaphysics, which consummates its presentation in the work that Hegel has deliberately entitled *Science of Logic*. Regarding how he himself understood the relationship of his *Logic* to Heraclitus's thinking, and thus how he understood this thinking itself, Hegel offers the following: "There is no proposition of Heraclitus's that I have not taken up into my *Logic*."[3] Nietzsche states something similar in a passage in which he enumerates his

---

[2] Ibid., XVII, 22.
[3] Ibid., XVII, 344.

'forerunners' as first Heraclitus, then Empedocles, then Spinoza, and finally Goethe.[4]

For Hegel, however, Heraclitus does not first make an appearance within the *Logic*, and thus within the historical context of the consummation of Hegel's metaphysics. Indeed, Heraclitus is already there for the young Hegel, the student of philosophy, as well as for his friends Hölderlin and Schelling. The three of them lived together in a dorm room (called 'the Augustine Room') in Tübingen. At that time, and still later, it was customary to enter commemorative words about friends into the ledger book associated with the dwelling. Hölderlin wrote the following entry for his friend Hegel:[5]

>   Goethe
>   Lust and love
>   Are the wings to great deeds.
>
>   Written in commemoration,
>   Your friend,
>   M. Hölderlin

Tüb.
12. Feb.
1791.
S(ymbolum). Εν και παν[6]

[31] Owing especially to his *Hyperion*, we know of Hölderlin's nearness to Heraclitus. While in conversation during the passage to Athens—a journey on which they perhaps traveled past the island of Delos—the question arises regarding "why in particular the Athenians also had to be a philosophical people?" In approval of the words of Diotima's, Hyperion says: "The grand word, the εν διαφερον εαυτω[7] (the One differing in itself) of Heraclitus, only a Greek could find, because it is the essence of the beautiful; and before that was found, there was no philosophy. Now one could determine: the whole was there. The flower had ripened; one could now dissect."[8] Ὑπερίων is the name for the one who goes further than all others, going precisely to what 'goes too far' for the 'reasonable human.'

If we recall, however, that between Hegel's metaphysics and the word of Heraclitus's lie two and a half millennia of Occidental history; if we also recall that, already since Plato, Occidental thinking had transitioned away from its inception

---

[4] Nietzsche, *Werke* (Großoktav), XIV, 263.
[5] Hölderlin, *Werke* (Hellingrath), VI, 232.
[6] Translators' note: The Greek appears in the German volume with no diacritical marks.
[7] Translators' note: As is the case immediately above, the Greek appears in the German volume with no diacritical marks.
[8] Ibid., II, 188 ff.

into a self-rigidifying essence—namely, into metaphysics—then certainly Hegel's explanation for the obscurity of Heraclitus's thinking cannot be sufficient for us.

For precisely the above-mentioned presupposition and fundamental experience of Hegelian metaphysics—namely, that the universe cannot withstand the courage of cognition and *must* open itself to the will for unconditioned certain knowledge (i.e., the will for absolute certainty)—is entirely and utterly non-Greek. The universe—ὁ κόσμος, as the Greeks said—is rather, in the essence of its very being, the self-concealing and therefore the *essentially* 'obscure.' The relation of inceptual thinking to the to-be-thought is inceptually determined by this fact. But if thinking is to think the self-concealing, it must allow the self-concealing to unfold as what it is, in which case the knowledge of [32] this essential thinking can in no way be a 'will' that compels the universe to divulge its closed-ness. Because the to-be-thought is in its essence the self-concealing, and thus the 'obscure' in this sense, in this way and only in this way is essential thinking, which remains in agreement with what is experienced as 'obscure,' itself necessarily obscure. Thought in this way, 'obscurity' now means: an essentially necessary way of self-concealing. The thinker Heraclitus is The Obscure because his thinking of the to-be-thought preserves the essence that belongs to it. Heraclitus is not ὁ Σκοτεινός, 'The Obscure,' because he intentionally expresses himself opaquely; he is also not 'The Obscure' because every 'philosophy' looks 'obscure' (i.e., incomprehensible) within the horizon of habitual understanding. Rather, Heraclitus is 'The Obscure' because *he* thinks being as the self-concealing and must speak the word according to this thinking. The word of inceptual thinking attends to 'the obscure.' It is one thing to attend to the obscure; it is something else entirely merely to push against it as though against a wall. The obscurity attended to in the way of thinking is essentially divorced from every 'mysticism' and mere sinking into the darkness of obscurity for its own sake. Because inceptual thinking thinks the essence of that to which self-concealing belongs, obscurity remains here necessarily, and always, a theme of thinking. As a result of its theme, Heraclitus's philosophy, as it shows itself to conventional thinking, is also 'obscure' in an emphatic sense. This outstanding and therefore exemplary obscurity in Heraclitus's thinking that derives itself from its 'theme,' when taken alone as an 'impression,' prompted some to demarcate this thinker by the epithet ὁ Σκοτεινός, and thus to understand the aforementioned obscurity exclusively in a conventional sense.

[33] b) The essentially oppositional, and dialectical thinking. The unfitting language of dialectic

'Artemis,' who bears the epithet 'bringer of light,' is now seen to be the goddess of the thinking of the thinker who is called 'The Obscure,' and who also *is* 'the obscure.' The thinking of the thinker who thinks the obscure, and himself is called The Obscure, is thus 'Apollonian,' i.e., essentially related to the light. How are the two to be reconciled? For φωσφόρος, 'bringer of light,' and σκοτεινός, 'the obscurely minded,' are as different as night and day.

However, through these few introductory remarks we have already recognized that every time we bump up against the apparently irreconcilable and oppositional, the essential is stirred. The obscure (i.e., the dark) and the light belong together, and not only in the sense that, where darkness is, generally light must also be, and vice versa. Rather, the dark 'is' in its essence the light, and the light 'is' in its essence the dark. In the first place, we recognize this for the following reason: where the brightness in question is *pure* brightness, and is thus a brightness that shines on its own terms beyond the measure of what is adequate to us, one can see nothing precisely on account of this pure brightness. Such a situation is not due to us, but rather has its ground in the fact that the bright and the light are, in their very essence, somehow also a concealing.

When we say "the dark 'is' the light, the light 'is' the dark," or "what is alive is dead and what is dead is alive," then we appear to be speaking in a Heraclitean manner. In truth, however, such speaking is mostly idle chatter, and we should not fool ourselves into thinking otherwise. For precisely there, where the possibility exists within essential thinking to think what is decisive and singular and at the very limit of thought, there is also the constant danger of a superficial leveling-down into mere mechanical chatter. [34] Where this danger is not conquered ever anew, there arises the clamorous clatter of the empty opposition of contradictory words: light and dark, life and death, wakefulness and sleep, movement and rest, freedom and necessity, infinity and finitude. Already since Plato's time, and especially since the metaphysics of German Idealism, one has called the thinking of opposites together in a higher unity 'dialectical' thinking. Some have already contrived, through such easily learned 'dialectical' noise, to feign profundity and to ape the gestures of the thinker. With the help of the dialectical back-and-forth of the words of Heraclitus's, a clever person can easily make it seem as though he himself were a thinker like Heraclitus, if not still 'greater' than him, since such a person supposedly understands Heraclitus and thus believes he has surpassed him. All of this is of little help in regard to a genuine understanding of Heraclitus. But we must note that, after Hegel, and especially after Nietzsche, an atmosphere formed around the figure, the thinking, and the word of Heraclitus's that is difficult to escape both for the inexperienced and for the all-too-clever in equal measure. This atmosphere surrounding Heraclitus springs from a hasty application of dialectical thinking, which harbors within itself a peculiar danger that even the experienced thinker cannot entirely escape. Indeed, sometimes even Hegel's thinking, and also that of Schelling's, are caught in the gears of dialectic. Why, then, would those who trail behind such thinkers, and who no longer think from out of the experience of the 'substance' of the matter, be any less vulnerable?

Why should they renounce the expedient vehicle of dialectic, when such oppositional sayings almost leap in front of their eyes from out of the words of thinkers such as Heraclitus? We are all still, without even knowing it, exposed to the danger of an inappropriate application of dialectic. Therefore, a warning is necessary.

When we attempt to enter into the thinking of Heraclitus, we in truth set out on dangerous ground. By means of a certain and entirely incorrect image—but one which, precisely owing to its incorrectness, appeals to the modern imagination— [35] we could say that the region of the words of this thinker is like a minefield where the slightest misstep annihilates everything into dust and smoke. We should be careful not to turn essential obscurity into mere murkiness. We consider the fact that, although Heraclitus's thinking was under the protection of the goddess Artemis, we ourselves (still) must go on the path of this thinking without the aid of such gods. For this reason, care is required at every step, and it is necessary to have a view of what is and is not possible. Therefore, with this merely preparatory consideration, we must now ponder the form in which the word of Heraclitus's approaches us.

c) The form in which the word of Heraclitus's is passed down, and the elucidation of the fragments in terms of the experience of the to-be-thought

The more inceptual the thinking, the more what it thinks is intimately one with the word. The more unblemished the originary thought remains secured in the word, all the more carefully must we safeguard the intact word and consider its appearance. In order to do this, it is necessary that we know even more precisely the form in which the word of Heraclitus's is passed down. If there is no chance or accident within the region of the essential history wherein the history of thinking belongs, then there must be a specific reason for the way in which the inceptual word of Heraclitus's still speaks to us.

Tradition is familiar with so-called Ἡρακλείτου σύγγραμμα, the 'writings' or, as one also says, the 'work' of Heraclitus's. Of this work we have only 'remains'; we must make do with 'fragments' of the writings. The later thinkers Plato, Aristotle, and Theophrastus—and still later scholars of philosophy such as Sextus Empiricus and Diogenes Laertius, the author Plutarch, but also Christian church fathers Hippolytus, Origen, and Clement of Alexandria—all quote in their writings 'passages' [36] from the writings of Heraclitus. These quoted statements comprise the fragments we possess. These fragments sometimes consist of multiple phrases, sometimes only one single phrase, and occasionally only sentence fragments and individual words. Because the particular choice of passages quoted by the aforementioned authors is determined from out of their own unique paths of thinking or writing—paths that occur later than Heraclitus—we can only make out, through meticulous consideration of the position of these later writings, the context in which the quotation is embedded, but not the context from out of which it was torn. The quotations do not directly pass on to us what is essential in the writing of Heraclitus's (i.e., the authoritative and organized unity of its inner structure). Only in persistent view of the unity of such a structure could it be demonstrated where each of the individual fragments belongs, and only through such arrangement could the pieces, homeless and scattered among themselves, be restored into their proper and sustaining coherence.

In recent times, people have begun to gather the fragments together. Today, we know of approximately one hundred and thirty fragments. Should they be laid out only in a muddled heap, or can they be ordered? Given this number—and, above all, given the importance of the content of many of the fragments—the hope arises to assemble the whole again from out of the remaining ruins, as with the broken shards of a Greek bowl or vase. But things are not so simple with the fragments of Heraclitus's writings. The broken shards of a bowl we find gathered together in one place; moreover, and most importantly, we have other complete and well-preserved bowls with which to compare it. By contrast, Heraclitus's writings occurred only once. Here, there are no possible objects of comparison. Thus, each attempt to reconstruct the whole from out of the present fragments must operate on its own. Therefore, we can abandon this hopeless enterprise of reconstructing past 'philological research.' We ask only about the [37] 'content' of the fragments and seek to think-after the thinking enunciated therein.

This is easy enough to say, but the following question immediately announces itself: in which of the one hundred and thirty fragments can the inner core of what this thinker thinks be seen? If, as is fitting, we attempt right at the outset of this elucidation to cultivate an attentive view of this core, which fragment should we consider first? Further, from where do we grasp the guiding directive for the determination of the sequence of the fragments? Does not everything here remain arbitrary? Or is there rather an obligation to be followed here? These questions are important, but only so long as we are regarding the ordering of the fragments from the outside, thereby perpetually evading the primary and sole necessity to experience what is essential from out of the word of the fragments themselves. Nevertheless, the fragments must now be laid out in a purely external but somehow measured arrangement, and thereby made recognizable and accessible.

Presently, there exists a collection in which the fragments are numbered and brought into an ordered sequence. This collection comes from the philologist Hermann Diels (1901), who has gathered all of the fragments of the early Greek thinkers into a large collection that appeared for the first time in 1903 under the title *The Fragments of the Pre-Socratics*. (His ordering of the fragments of

Parmenides already appeared in 1897.) Today, the fragments are everywhere cited and numbered in accordance with this edition. Other collections of Heraclitus's fragments are not currently available. Since the fragments are generally short in length, each of them will be written and translated on the board as they are dealt with within the lecture. Though we shall retain the numbering of the fragments provided by Diels, we do not follow the sequence determined by this numbering. The fragment ordered by Diels [38] as number 1 is, for us, by no means essentially first.

If we now translate and elucidate the fragments in another order, this in no way means that the ordering attempted by us can reconstruct the structure of Heraclitus's writings better or more correctly. We must perhaps forever do without such a reconstruction. But, suppose that the impossible one day becomes possible; suppose that the writings of Heraclitus's were suddenly given to us intact. What then? Then philology would be relieved of the arduous task of textual reconstruction. However, even in such a situation, nothing more would be achieved—for the task of appropriation begins first. For a long time we have had the dialogues of Plato's and the treatises of Aristotle's, both of which lay chronologically nearer to us than Heraclitus does. We possess the writings and the letters of Leibniz; we are acquainted with the original and complete texts of the major works of Kant. All of these possessions, taken on their own terms merely as present-to-hand works, give not the least guarantee that we 'know' what they contain. Even such knowledge can remain a mere knowledge of the bygone without the word of this thinker being awakened into its historical future. The merely 'erudite' knowledge of its contents is as without insight into the historical as the bowdlerizing of its content for popular consumption. The library's possession of the writings of the thinker in no way guarantees that we are able or disposed to think-after what is thought therein. More essential than the complete preservation and possession of the intact writings of the thinker could ever be is this: that we ourselves, if only from a distance, attain to a relationship with the to-be-thought within the thinking of this thinker. We do not strive after a philological/historiographical reconstruction of the writings of Heraclitus's; rather, we seek to prepare ourselves for the as-yet delivered word to meet us from out of its essential core. If this elucidation is to be thoughtful, [39] and thus in accordance with its matter, it must think only of experiencing this to-be-thought. Whether and to what extent this succeeds can neither be proved beforehand nor calculated afterwards from a 'result.' It can neither be established 'objectively,' nor remain the effort merely of a 'subjective' undertaking. The to-be-thought is not 'objective'; the thinking of it is not 'subjective.' The difference between object and subject has no place here, as it is a difference that is alien to the world of the Greeks and especially to the sphere of inceptual thinking. Consequently, the barely touched upon questions regarding the possibility and impossibility of the adequate reconstruction of the writings of Heraclitus's lose their importance. Lastly, we recognize that it is probably a blessing if the word of the inceptual thinkers is given over to us only in fragments: for such a situation requires from us a sufficient attentiveness at all times. If instead we had the supposed good fortune of having the inceptual words preserved intact, the obstinacy of a supposed better knowledge would likely implant itself in us still more easily and rigidly. Given that this is not the case, it should be clear why no extensive assurance is needed here that we do not presume to reconstruct the 'one true Heraclitus' for all time. It is already enough if the intimation of one way of moving toward the word of Heraclitus's has a shimmering of the true, i.e., a shimmering of that which brightens.

REVIEW

Regarding the problem of the sameness of what is thought in inceptual and contemporary thinking. The inherited word of inceptual thinking (Heraclitus) and dialectics

Heraclitus is called 'The Obscure' because he is the obscure. He is the 'obscure' thinker because he, more inceptually than others, thinks [40] what in the to-be-thought can be called 'the obscure' insofar as it has the essential feature of concealing itself. The name ὁ Σκοτεινός, 'The Obscure,' was therefore attached to Heraclitus because one dimly suspected straightaway that his thinking was on the trail of what prevails as the obscure within the to-be-thought itself. The attribution of this sobriquet, however, does not derive from a keen insight into this obscurity.

In the meantime, the sobriquet has been explained in manifold ways. Next to the facile prattle of Cicero stands the 'speculative' ground of Hegel. But the one is just as untrue as the other. Hegel's explanation for the obscurity of Heraclitus is untrue because it is un-Greek, and also because it veils the essence of inceptual thinking. Hegel presupposes, along with the entire metaphysics of modernity, that what philosophy thinks not only cannot resist the will of thoughtful disclosure, but in its very essence does not want to resist it. Rather, he supposes that the entirety of beings is determined through the will to show itself, i.e., the will to step out into appearance. The highest manner of this appearing is accomplished within, and also for, the thinking of metaphysics, provided that it speaks through the appearing essence of the absolute as it shows itself. In Greek, such speaking-through is called διαλέγεσθαι. The language of dialectic is the word (λόγος), in which the appearing (φαίνεσθαι) actuates itself. The appearing of the absolute, whose absoluteness consists in wanting to appear, is, in the idiom of dialectic, captured by the single name 'phenomenology' in the sense that Hegel thinks this term. Phenomenology, the bringing-to-appearance-of-itself within the word of dialectic, is the essence of the absolute (i.e., of 'Spirit' in Hegel's idiom). Spirit itself exists in no other event than phenomenology. Phenomenology is the ownmost matter 'of' Spirit. It cannot be shown here to what extent also Schelling, [41] who at first appeared to be in sharp contrast to Hegel's metaphysics, nevertheless generally thinks from out of the same fundamental experience of modern metaphysics and, just as Hegel, thinks the absolute as that which *wills* to manifest itself, understanding this will to be nothing other than the being of the absolute. Unfathomably different from all of this is what emerges to the inceptual thinkers as the to-be-thought. It is neither a will *to appearance*, nor, indeed, a 'will' at all. However, if Hegel and Nietzsche (though the latter in a modified way) see Heraclitus as their great precursor and ancestor, then a historical blindness occurs [*ereignet*] here within the nineteenth century (a century of historiography), the outermost ripples of which have still not dissipated and whose still prevalent ground is to be found all the way back at the inception of Occidental thinking. Hegel's and Nietzsche's misunderstandings of Heraclitus's thinking are therefore based in no way upon any errors in their own thinking that could have been circumvented by the two thinkers, and which could perhaps be rectified through the understanding of a well-trained and avid scholar of philosophy were he to reckon together all of the errors that have occurred to thinkers since Anaximander in order to then 'improve' upon them.

However, we would paint for ourselves a fairly absurd picture of the thinkers were we to claim here that their thinking is totally without error. Indeed, they are essential thinkers precisely because of the fact that they, despite the many errors that 'befall' precisely them, think the true. Because of this, the confrontation between thinkers has a character and sense that is different from the criticisms and polemics that are customary and necessary for the sciences. The confrontation between the thinkers does not deal critically with whether what is said is correct or incorrect. Their confrontation is the reciprocal enunciation concerning in what way what is thought is thought inceptually and nears the inception, or whether it distances itself from the inception in such a way that, even in that distance, what is thought remains essential and thereby [42] remains the one and the same thing that each thinker thinks. The 'originality' of a thinker consists solely in the fact that it is given to that thinker to think, in the highest purity, the same and only the same as what the early thinkers have 'also already' thought.

One could reply to this that, in that case, the thinkers, precisely through their 'originality,' make themselves superfluous, if all they ever do is say the same thing. Most people, owing to their desire to reach a swift 'conclusion,' have concluded precisely this, all the while lacking the courage 'to truly look.' The same remains the same for us only so long as we behold the same as itself, holding it in view and not forgetting it. But because human beings now concern themselves, for various reasons, with the continually new and up-to-date, whatever exhausts itself in always and only being the same is completely boring to them. It is precisely in order to ensure that this absolute (i.e., the boring same) will not be forgotten through the course of the history of a people that a thinker occasionally arrives. Admittedly, this is perhaps not the sole reason, and certainly not the true reason, that the thinker arrives. Why do we now say such things about the thinkers? So that we, when the moment calls for it, remember all the more that the thinkers and their thoughts belong in a peculiar atmosphere to which we attain neither through vain admiration nor through empty criticism. We must therefore heed the uniqueness of this atmosphere: for it happens all too easily to us through the course of a lecture that a word said against a thinker appears as a flippant criticism, while perhaps it is only the attempt to enter into a discussion with that thinker. So understood, the comments given here in the last hour on the danger of dialectic, and the compulsion toward a dialectical interpretation of Heraclitus's thinking, are anything but a dismissal of the essence of dialectic. In and through dialectic, whose beginning goes hand-in-hand with the beginning of metaphysics (with Plato), an as yet illuminated relationship to λέγειν (i.e., to saying, to the word) conceals itself. The word of inceptual [43] thinking is essentially other than the language of dialectic. The full consideration of this will certainly only happen after we have first heard the word of Heraclitus's. If within the region of essential history it is no coincidence that the history of thinking belongs first and foremost with that of poetry, then such a situation must have its peculiar explanation in the way and the form in which the inceptual word of Heraclitus speaks to us.

This word is passed down to us only in fragments, found ripped out and collected as quotations from later thinkers, scholars, and authors. Today there are approximately one hundred and thirty fragments gathered together and ordered into a numbered sequence. The ordering established by the classical philologist Hermann Diels is authoritative everywhere, and the fragments are quoted in accordance with it. Without wanting to offend or evaluate the scholarly merits of philologists, it nonetheless must be said that the ordering of the fragments that has become customary (owing to H. Diels), when viewed in terms of the sequence of its content, is rather nonsensical. That does not preclude the possibility that, from time to time in the sequence of the fragments, those which belong together also occur together, since already a crude understanding of the wording of the fragments compels one to associate them. However, when we in this lecture course follow a different sequence of Heraclitus's fragments, the intention is not to reconstitute in a superior way the eternally lost writings of Heraclitus's. Rather, our sole concern is whether we enter into an experiential relation with what prevails in inceptual thinking as the to-be-thought. But let us suppose that the inception prevails over all of its consequences in advance and beyond them: in that case, the inception is not what lies behind us, but rather one and the same with what comes before us and, in a mysterious turn, still approaches us.

[44] MAIN PART

The truth of being

§ 3. The inception of the inceptual to-be-thought. Fragment 16

a) Parenthetical remark on the task of translating

With that fragment of Heraclitus's that we now take as the first in the preliminary succession we are presenting here, thinking would like to arrive at the constitutive core of what is, for thinkers of the inception and therefore for Heraclitus, the inceptual to-be-thought. We place fragment 16 at the 'inception.' It says:

τὸ μὴ δῦνόν ποτε πῶς ἄν τις λάθοι;

From the not ever submerging (thing), how may anyone be concealed (from it)?

This and all other translations in what follows should, if possible, be true to the word. 'True to the word' means something other than 'literal.' In mere literal translations, single words are confronted by almost mechanically lexical counterparts. But mere words are not yet words in the fullest sense. Therefore, when translation seeks to be not only literal, but also true to the word, the words must receive their naming power and their structure from the already presiding fidelity to the unifying word (that is, to the totality of the saying). Nevertheless, every translation remains makeshift. When the stakes are low, a makeshift approach suffices—for example, in the case of translating business paperwork. Here, both sides understand what is at stake, perhaps even too well. In the case [45] of translating the sayings of Heraclitus's, the stakes are very high indeed. Here trans*lation* becomes a kind of trans*porting* to the other shore, one which is hardly known and lies on the opposite side of a wide river. Such a voyage is easily led astray, and most often ends in a shipwreck. In the realm of transportive translation, all translations are poor, only more or less so. The translations attempted here will not be exempted from this judgment. Translation undertaken in the realm of general understanding and through the course of business dealings can largely be accomplished without interpretation. Translations undertaken in the realm of the vaunted word of poetry and of thinking, however, are always in need of interpretation, for they themselves are an interpretation. Such translations can either inaugurate the interpretation or consummate it. But it is precisely the consummating translation of Heraclitus's sayings that must necessarily remain as obscure as the originary word.

b) The question pertaining to the 'never submerging thing' and its essential relation to 'concealing'

τὸ μὴ δῦνόν ποτε πῶς ἄν τις λάθοι;

This saying of Heraclitus's names several things. To begin with: τὸ μὴ δῦνόν ποτε—"the never ever submerging thing"—which we can easily reformulate (but thereby also weaken) as "the never submerging thing." What precisely it is that never submerges is not expressly said in the saying. At any rate, this appears to be so; for the saying only names it in the neuter case, "the never submerging thing." Then the saying states: πῶς ἄν τις, "how may anyone"; a τις, an "anyone," is therein named, not a τι, so not an object or a thing, but rather what we address in regard to itself (and its self) with the interrogative pronoun "who." We ourselves—human beings—are so addressed. In any case, human beings are meant by the τις— "anyone." Whether something else is also meant, [46] something else that can be addressed by the questions "who" or "who are you," remains undecided for the time being.[1] Furthermore, there is talk in the saying of λάθοι, λαθεῖν, λανθάνειν—that is, of a being concealed. More precisely, there is the question of whether anyone from the sphere of human beings can be concealed.

The saying ultimately has the form of a question. However, the question is of the sort that appears already to answer itself. Transcribed into the form of an answer, the questioning saying reads:

From the never submerging thing, no one can remain concealed.

---

[1] Cf. fragments 30 and 53.

From this modification of the saying—one suggested by the saying itself—we can, in any case, clearly conclude one thing: namely, that the saying names a relation existing between the never submerging thing and human beings. The relation is such that no human being can withdraw from the never submerging thing. We are immediately tempted to ask why this is so. We would like to know in what sense this relation exists and in what it is grounded. This leads us immediately to two questions: first, who is the human being such that, in relation to him, there can be talk of being concealed and not being concealed? And second: what precisely is that before which and in the region of which the human can never be something concealed? Heraclitus's saying quickly becomes pervaded by questions for us, questions that practically pose themselves all at once. But this, after all, cannot be a surprise for us: for the saying itself is a question, only one out of which we have prematurely made an answer and a predicative statement that almost sounds like a doctrine. But is not the saying simply a rhetorical question, i.e., a question that is not a question at all and that thereby prohibits questioning by allowing the questionable to disappear through an easily destroyed pretense to questionability? But is it so [47] readily evident that there is no way for the human being to be concealed before the never submerging thing?

Assuming that this is so, then certainly the saying states that we should know this. But how *can* we know this, if we do not consider all that is being said there? And how can we consider it without questioning? Perhaps it is precisely here that questioning comes upon the unquestionable. But how shall we ever arrive there, if we do not go forth along the path of questioning in order to learn the proper way of questioning? The proper way of questioning is based upon knowing where, and in the face of what, one may no longer question. Thoughtful questioning and being able to question in the manner of the thinkers is in itself already an originary form of knowledge. We should approach such knowledge, and only such knowledge, in the manner of questioning: i.e., by taking the saying as a purely rhetorical question, which would mean not grasping it in advance as the dictum of a thinker. Additionally, when dealing with a thinker who is himself obscure, we will only attain understanding with difficulty. Therefore, we ask: what is the saying asking? It is asking: πῶς—how, and in what way and by what means, could a human ever remain concealed before the never submerging thing? In saying 'before' the never submerging thing, we are inserting a word not present in the Greek text. This 'before' inserted by us also easily leads to the misunderstanding that the 'never submerging thing' is some sort of object or being that everywhere stands opposite to the human and watches over him, as it were. Therefore, we formulate it more carefully in the translation: "From the not ever submerging thing, how may anyone be concealed (from it)."

Admittedly, this also brings with it the misinterpretation that the never submerging thing is some kind of watchful being in whose custody the human finds himself such that, try as he might, he can never escape from this being to safety. Yet, what kind of relation the never submerging thing has to the human, and conversely, how things stand with the relationship between the human [48] and the never submerging thing, could surely be easily determined if we finally just directly stated what the 'never submerging thing' is: for it is the lack of clarity surrounding this name that alone accounts for the enigmatic nature of the saying, since surely the other part that is mentioned in the saying—namely, the human being—is sufficiently known to us owing to the fact that we ourselves are human. However, precisely the opinion that we already know what the human is, and that we therefore also know how the essence of the human was experienced in inceptual thinking, is the greatest barrier we can encounter on our path toward understanding the saying. For the saying is, after all, a question. And we shall retain it as the question it is. We shall retain it even in the face of the suggestion, brought forth by the dictates of grammar, that the question is merely a pseudo-question, a so-called rhetorical question, precisely because it already contains the answer. Such a suggestion would further maintain that it is only the form of the speaking, and not the content of what it says, that has a questioning nature. Certainly, in some sense, the saying contains the answer in what it asks and how it asks. But how can someone understand an answer—and thus think of it *as* an answer—if he does not first take seriously the question that the answer answers? 'Rhetorical' questions are, in truth, themselves ambiguous. They can serve to distract from precisely what is questionable. They assume the appearance of the question, thereby giving the appearance that the question has already been posed, thus bringing it about that no further questions arise. Or, in assuming the mere guise of the question, they give themselves the appearance of an unquestionable answer, which so dismays us that it leads us to the questionable in the first place. The 'answer'—namely, that no human could ever be concealed before the never submerging thing, as the saying of a thinker posed in the form a question—shifts into a thinking-after how, in what sense, and why that should be the case. [49] In this, however, the following question conceals itself: *what* is it that is named here as submerging (i.e., being-concealed)?

If no human can be concealed in relation to the never submerging thing, then it must be owing to the never submerging thing that every human—that is, every human *as* human (i.e., in accordance with his essence and indeed from out of the essential core of his human being)—stands in the unconcealed, so that in and through the never submerging thing the human is that which cannot conceal himself. What, however, is this τὸ μὴ δῦνόν ποτε?

At first, we will linger with the attempt to think what has been named here in its essence. We will therefore initially only contemplate the first 'part' of the whole saying, and not yet pursue the question posed in it. For we can already see that the μὴ δῦνόν ποτε obviously remains the determinant from which arises the concealment and unconcealment of the human. We shall return to the question of the saying itself only when the sufficient illumination of the μὴ δῦνόν ποτε leads us there of its own accord. This illumination naturally demands that we also think through other fragments, and in such a way that the first-named fragment encompasses those inserted in the meantime.

In the words τὸ μὴ δῦνόν ποτε, something is named whose essence determines itself in relation to δύνειν. δύνω is connected to δύω, which means *to envelop, to sink*. δύνω means: *to enter into something*; the sun enters into the ocean and dives down into it. πρὸς δύνοντος ἡλίου means: toward the submerging sun—'toward evening,' 'toward the West.' νέφεα δῦναι means: to merge beneath the clouds, to disappear behind them. 'Submerging' understood as δύνειν (and thus thought in a Greek way) is the disappearing from presence in the manner of departing and entering into that which envelops, i.e., that which conceals. 'Submerging,' thought in a Greek way, has its essence in *entering into a concealment*. However, in connection to the words 'submerging' and 'submergence' [50], we are prone to think of an indeterminate disappearance. 'To submerge' can mean to fall victim to decay or destruction. 'To submerge' is also to go over into non-existence. To be victorious or to submerge in defeat—to be or not to be. But 'submerging' understood in a Greek way, and thus in the sense of 'entering into a concealment,' is in no way merely a situation of no longer existing or of non-being. Submerging, in the sense of an entering into concealment, is precisely 'a' being—yes, perhaps even *being* itself, thought in a Greek way, and thus inceptually experienced. 'Submerging' is a becoming concealed and a concealment: in Greek, λανθάνω, λάθω, 'submerging' and 'submergence' in the sense of the submergence of the sun; the submerging of the sun is clearly not its 'destruction' and in no way brings about its non-existence. But certainly, since the time of Copernicus, we have known that the submergence of the sun is merely an optical illusion: for modern science holds the key to all understanding. Sunsets are now only for 'poets' and 'lovers.' The enchantment of the world has been displaced by another enchantment. The new enchantment is now 'physics' itself as an outstanding achievement of the human. The human now enchants himself through himself. The modern human is now what is enchanting. We have already heard it in the words of Hegel: the universe itself cannot offer any resistance to the human will to unlock it. This certainly presupposes that what the will subjugates through its unlocking is the universe, i.e., that which is oriented toward the one and singular: *versus unum*. The 'universe' is that which unlocks itself and offers itself up for pleasure. But Heraclitus speaks of the same. His saying speaks not of 'submerging,' but rather of its opposite, μὴ δῦνόν ποτε, the "never submerging thing." Certainly. Nevertheless, the question remains whether what Heraclitus names as the never submerging thing is the same as what Hegel conceives of as the essentially self-disclosing.

[51] Even supposing that both were the same, Heraclitus's saying would nevertheless be saying something different: namely, that the human cannot conceal himself before the never submerging thing. The reverse sentiment is true for Hegel's thought (and for that of the contemporary era): namely, that the

self-disclosing is that which cannot withdraw itself from the grasp of the human. However, perhaps the contemporary and the inceptual have yet another relationship with one another beyond that of a mere inversion. The inceptual word, in any case, demands that we think 'submerging' and 'submergence' in the sense of 'entering into concealment.'

We need only to regard the saying of Heraclitus's from the outside in order to recognize more clearly that an essential relationship exists between δῦνον and λάθοι. The only two substantive words of the saying think the same thing: namely, that which has the essential feature of concealment, that which perhaps is nothing other than concealment and self-concealment itself. In order to recognize this, we must listen to the saying even more carefully and remain mindful that it is the saying of a thinker whose thinking is different from conventional thinking. The saying of Heraclitus's directly compels us into testing the difference between conventional and essential thinking, and thereby to practice the latter. So long as we fail to endure the test of this difference, we remain incapable of thinking-after the saying of the thinker. Thus, we must first put ourselves to the test. We must first reflect upon whether we, with all of our hurried zeal to understand the saying, are really thinking with care.

[52] c) The characteristics of the foundational word τὸ δῦνον and its exposition in the guiding question of metaphysical thinking (Aristotle)

As soon as we hear the saying, we would also like to know what τὸ μὴ δῦνόν ποτε, "the never submerging thing," is. We are therefore asking about that which never falls prey to submerging. We thereby differentiate something that submerges, or alternatively does not submerge, from submerging itself. The latter we can name the process or the event by which something—namely, the submerging thing—is affected.

Through this question we do not so much want to find out something about the event of submerging; rather, the question wants to know what that is which, as the never submerging thing, remains withdrawn from the event of submerging: for in the saying there is talk of τὸ μὴ δῦνόν ποτε. By asking in this way, we penetrate into the substance of the saying. Or at least it appears so.

In truth, with this apparently forceful question about the submerging thing, we do not think properly about the saying of the thinker, on account of the fact that we are not thinking essentially but rather only 'conventionally.' How so? Where is there in reference to the talk about τὸ δῦνον—the submerging thing, or the never submerging thing—even the possibility of misunderstanding? τὸ δῦνον means, unequivocally, the submerging thing. That is what we say—we who are thinking conventionally—when we allow our conventional imagination to consider that which submerges. By this, we mean something that is subject to the process of submerging. However, τὸ δῦνον does not only mean the submerging thing in the sense thus explicated; the word τὸ δῦνον is by no means unambiguous. In fact, the very character of this word is ambiguous. Expressed grammatically, the word has the character of a participle. The word 'participle' is the Roman translation of something that the Grecian grammarians signified through ἡ μετοχή: 'participation.' The word δῦνον is characterized by [53] participation because it, as the word that it is, can participate both in the part of speech that is called a 'noun' or 'substantive,' and in the part of speech of which the participle itself is a derivation—namely, the verb, or 'time-word.' Thus, for example, 'the smelling' is on the one hand that which emits smell—say, the rose—but also the activity itself of emitting the smell, the activity by which the rose smells.

τὸ δῦνον can mean 'the submerging thing,' whereby we think of the substance that is subject to submergence. But τὸ δῦνον can also mean the submerging thing precisely in its submerging, and thus the activity of submerging itself understood as such. Hence, the word τὸ δῦνον, as a participle, gives two meanings according to which it may be thought.

If we keep only to the substantive meaning, as has happened thus far, then we leave out the 'verbal' meaning. But suppose that Heraclitus, precisely because he thinks the word τὸ δῦνον not in the conventional sense but rather as a thinker, intended only the verbal meaning. If this were the case, then by thinking the word τὸ δῦνον in the substantive sense, we would be missing the essential meaning of the word and would not at all be grasping what is here the to-be-thought. In this event, the question that we pose when we inquire about *what* does or does not submerge is misguided.

But by what right do we claim that the verbal meaning of the participle is the one thought by essential thinking, and thereby the one meant by the thinker Heraclitus? What is it that the thinkers think—most importantly, the thinkers at the inception of Occidental thinking and, generally, the thinkers of the Greeks? Perhaps the saying of Heraclitus's, considered before all others, may one day give us the proper answer to this question, insofar as inceptual thinking here directly has its say, and thereby is itself not required to think 'about' the task of essential thinking and to deliver information 'about' it in a pedantic way.

However, for the time being we do not yet understand this saying. That is why we turn to a thinker of the Greeks in whose [54] thought the tradition of Greek thinking consummates itself, even though this thinking is at a distance to inceptual thinking. Let us consider a saying from Aristotle, who lived a century and a half after Heraclitus (384–322 BCE). In one of his most important treatises, Aristotle states the following at the end of the first chapter:

καὶ δὴ καὶ τὸ πάλαι τε καὶ νῦν καὶ ἀεὶ ζητούμενον καὶ ἀεὶ ἀπορούμενον, τί τὸ ὄν,...²

And so the question that from antiquity has been, is now, and shall (before all else) remain the-sought-for—i.e., that which we (when we think it) continually cannot penetrate—is: what is the being?

τί τὸ ὄν—"What is the being?," asks the thinker. In the above-articulated definition of what the to-be-thought of the thinker is, we encounter the word τὸ ὄν—"the being"—and so once again a word possessing the character of the participle. And once again we have taken this participle according to the meaning closest to that of conventional understanding—namely, as the substantive. According to the consideration of the wording of Aristotle's quotation undertaken thus far, the to-be-thought of the thinker is τὸ ὄν. From this we can surely neither deduce if this participial word τὸ ὄν should be understood 'substantively' or 'verbally,' or indeed in some other way entirely. However, Aristotle himself helps us out with this dilemma. The first sentence of another among his treatises, which sketches an outline of the realm in which essential thinking should reside, begins with the following:

Ἔστιν ἐπιστήμη τις ἣ θεωρεῖ τὸ ὄν ᾗ ὄν καὶ τὰ τούτῳ ὑπάρχοντα καθ' αὑτό.³

[55] It is (by chance and by inner necessity) some kind of knowledge that takes into consideration the being, insofar as it is the being, (a knowledge, therefore, that) thus also (takes into consideration) that which belongs to it (i.e., to the being insofar as it is the being).

According to this sentence of Aristotle's, essential thinking is some sort of knowledge. This knowledge is characterized by its consideration of what is to be known by it. What is considered is τὸ ὄν, the being, but it is considered ᾗ ὄν—this means that the consideration is in view of the fact that the being is a being. In regard to beings, it is not what lies nearest that should be gaped at—namely, that the being is a house or a tree, a donkey or a man, or something else entirely. Rather, the being should 'only' be considered in regard to what is seemingly distant, insofar as the being is determined as a being. But the being is only a being because it 'is': i.e., it is only a being by virtue of 'being.' τὸ ὄν, the being, is τὸ ζητούμενον, the sought-after; but what is sought-after in the thinking of the being is the being of beings, and whatever belongs to it.

---

² *Met.* Z 1, 1028b2 ff.
³ Ibid., Γ 1, 1003a21–23.

In Greek, being is called τὸ εἶναι. This word εἶναι is the infinitive of the verb whose participle is τὸ ὄν. From this it becomes clear that, when the thinker thinks τὸ ὄν, he does not take this word in its substantive sense, but rather in its verbal sense. The abridged and thereby ambiguous question—what is the being?—is indeed the guiding question of thinkers. But in pursuing this question they do not ask if the being is a rock or a bone or a donkey or a triangle. Rather, the question asked by the thinker—what is the being?—means only this: what is the being of the being? What is that in and through which something that 'is' is? What is it that characterizes the 'being' as such? [56]

Now, what characterizes 'the free' as such, and what designates 'the free' as 'the free,' language calls 'freedom.' Similarly, justice is what makes the just the just. Correspondingly, we may be allowed to say, even if the conventional understanding rebels against it, that what characterizes the being as such is 'beingness.'

This word, however, is only the literal translation of the Greek word οὐσία, the word that was translated by the Romans as *substantia* and was thereby distorted in its meaning. In Aristotle's sense, the thinker is seeking what the being *as being* is, i.e., he is seeking the being of beings—or, phrased otherwise, he is seeking *beingness*. That is why Aristotle elucidates the first of his quotations considered here—in which the eternally sought for, but also the forever newly question-worthy, is the question τί τὸ ὄν—with an addendum that immediately follows. It reads: τοῦτό ἐστι τίς ἡ οὐσία: "this—namely, what is actually sought-for in regard to beings—is, for us, beingness." οὐσία, being, is that whence each being as such comes: the origin of beings, γένος. In this way, Plato and Aristotle designate being in relation to beings. Because being is the origin to which each being as such owes itself, being, in its relation to every being, is τὸ κοινόν (to follow Plato and Aristotle here)—the commonality that concerns every being καθόλου (i.e., every being as a whole and generally).

If, therefore, the thinker thinks τὸ ὄν, he thinks τὸ εἶναι—the being (of beings). He thinks being as that from which all beings originate. Being 'is,' with respect to beings, always already the 'older.' When being is thought, the being is conceived as that which it already was—τί ἦν. That is why Aristotle determines what the thinker is to think—τὸ εἶναι—more precisely as τὸ τί ἦν εἶναι: being as that which, for beings, always already is, i.e., "what was."

The way of thinking the being of beings briefly outlined above was established by Plato and Aristotle. By thinking the being in a manner [57] that proceeds out of beingness and is oriented toward it, this thinking moves beyond the particular being under consideration. In Greek, movement from one over to the other is designated by the word μετά. Beings—the sea, the mountains, the forests, the animals, the heavens, but also the human and the gods—which of their own accord lie before, sometimes in one way and sometimes in another, without the assistance of the human, are what-occur-in-the-fore, are the coming-forth, and are thereby the lying-before—i.e., ὑποκείμενον (i.e., what approaches the human and encounters him). Here, what is present, which the human does not first need to produce, appears. What is present presences 'toward' the human and concerns him in such a way that it comes upon him and even assails him. Those things that appear from out of themselves as 'presencing toward' the human are, for the Greeks, authentic beings, because the Greeks, for reasons about which we cannot yet inquire, only experience being in the sense of a presencing-toward. That which emerges from out of itself and is therefore what appears and, in all of this is the presencing-toward, is called τὰ φύσει ὄντα, or τὰ φυσικά. This appears as what abides here-and-now and there-and-then—i.e., the particular thing that abides. But when τί τὸ ὄν is asked, the question is not aimed at that particular being, but rather beyond it (μετά), 'over' it toward the being of beings. The question τί τὸ ὄν does not think τὰ φυσικά, but rather μετὰ τὰ φυσικά. The thinking that thinks οὐσία—i.e., beingness—moves beyond the particular being and over toward being. It is a thinking μετὰ τὰ φυσικά—that is, "metaphysics." From Plato and Aristotle up to the current day, Occidental thinking is 'metaphysics.' By contrast, the thinking of the inceptual thinkers is not yet metaphysics. However, they too think being, yet they do so in another way; they too are aware of beings, but they experience them in a different way. When, therefore, the inceptual thinkers say the words τὸ ὄν/τὰ ὄντα/the being, then they are not for the most part thinking, as thinkers, the 'participial' word substantively, but rather verbally; τὸ ὄν, the being, [58] is thought in the sense of its being, that is, in the sense of being. τὸ ὄν—or, according to the older formulation, τὸ ἐόν—means, for Parmenides, the same as τὸ εἶναι.

We will remain with the question of how to think the participle τὸ δῦνον in the saying of Heraclitus's. We have said that it must be thought according to the way of the thinkers. The thinkers think the participle τὸ ὄν verbally. We must accordingly think τὸ μὴ δῦνόν ποτε—the not ever submerging thing (i.e., the never submerging thing)—in a manner analogous to how the thinker thinks the word 'the being': namely, in the sense of being. Therefore, we must think τὸ μὴ δῦνόν ποτε verbally as 'the never submerging.'

We will therefore change the translation of the saying we initially gave to now say: "from the not ever submerging, how may anyone be concealed (from it)?"

Now, one could surely object that what applies to the philosophical understanding of the participle τὸ ὄν need not also be applied to the participle τὸ δῦνον. However, this concern is too superficial to allow ourselves to tarry with it for long. Regardless of which way in particular 'submerging' and 'never submerging' relate to 'being,' it is clear that each are a manner of being. The participle τὸ ὄν—i.e., the being, i.e., being—is the participle of all participles, because the word 'being' is the word of all words. In every word—even in the word 'nothing,' into which we let all beings drift—being is thought and named, even if we never expressly think about it or speak it. Supposing, therefore, that in the saying of the thinker the word δῦνον is meant in the sense of essential thinking, then what is thought and named by it is being, understood 'verbally.' Instead of *verbum* (verbal), a term used by Latin grammarians, we will say 'time-word.' The word being, as the word of all words, is the inceptual 'time-word' as such. The time-word 'being,' as the word of all words, names 'the time of all times.' Being and time inceptually belong together. Thinking must think this [59] togetherness of 'being and time'; otherwise, it runs the risk of forgetting what remains, for the thinkers, the to-be-thought.

d) Mindful consideration of the words 'being' and 'is'

There is another concern, however, that is weightier than the apparently frivolous consideration of whether the verbal sense of Heraclitus's word τὸ δῦνον necessarily follows from the meaning of the foundational word τὸ ὄν, which itself must be thought verbally.

We are speaking in a circuitous way of the never submerging thing and of never submerging; we are speaking, before all else, of beings and of being. We are speaking empty words which bring nothing to mind, and we fail to find ourselves in an immediate relationship with what is meant by those words. We are being led around in an abysmal region of a strange manner of speaking and ushered through an elucidation of words and word meanings, and thus are passing by the things themselves. The suspicion arises, and it has been spoken of and repeated often enough, that an empty sorcery with words is being practiced here. 'Word mysticism' is the polite term used by those who suspect all of this to be mere word games. It would indeed be dangerous were we simply to shove aside the suspicion and the impression that only words are being negotiated with here: for this impression—namely, that it is only mere words that are being manipulated here, words through which we fail to represent anything actual to ourselves—does not arise from this lecture alone. Rather, the observations made here merely bring our attention to a state of affairs that we otherwise disregard hourly, daily, and often for a whole lifetime.

That state of affairs is this: in our explicit, but also our implicit speech, we constantly use the little word 'is.' We are now thinking, for example, without saying it [60], that this lecture 'is' boring; the theme being covered 'is' dry. You need not speak these sentences out loud; rather, you, as though half-asleep, simply think unreflectively "this lecture 'is' boring." Yet, even here—in this indeterminate, unreflective thinking—you nevertheless understand the unuttered, entirely unremarkable and inconspicuous word 'is.' Please—take a moment and test yourselves whether you can 'imagine something' in relation to the word 'is.' Even if not, the word 'is' is not just some empty sound. Everyone understands it, yet no one grasps what is thereby understood. Only rarely can someone be motivated even to pay any attention to this 'is.' How often in the course of days and nights, how often and in what manifold connections do we say, mean, and understand this 'is'? It never bothers us that we cannot imagine anything by it. But what else is the little word 'is' but a variant of the word 'being'? Presently, however, we are making a fuss about the fact that one cannot imagine anything in relation to the words 'being' and 'beingness.' And it is good that we are making a fuss about this, and even better if we become outright agitated about it; it is best if we never inhibit this agitation surrounding our continual use of the word of words and the demands we make of it to mean something, while at the same time failing to conceive anything by it when we are suddenly asked: what do you actually mean when you utter the little word 'is'? It is best if we become horrified that the human, whose essential characteristic consists in 'having the word' and being able 'to say something,' never thinks about the word of words and, by neglecting to think about it, forgets the very word in which all saying sways and rests.

The impression that discussions about beings and being are carried out through an empty sorcery of mere words [61] may very well remain. What's more, it does no harm if thinking continually makes the 'impression' on the thoughtless (which it must necessarily make) that it is a consciously contrived devilry to make contemporary thinking even more difficult than it already is. Someday perhaps those who are spirited enough will lay hold of the insight that the estranging impression left by thinking does not have its origin in the circuitous thinking of the thinkers, but rather in ourselves: namely, in the simple and thereby also frightening event [*Ereignis*] that we all, as historical humans, no longer think of being, but only chase after beings. This forgetfulness of being hangs like a cloud over historical humanity, and due precisely to this forgetfulness, this cloud is also the reason that considerations about the 'substantive' or 'verbal' meanings of the word ὄν seem empty and foreign to us.

If, however, it is the case that the word 'being' and its variants—especially the little and familiar word 'is'—constantly pervades all of our thoughts and behavior, and in such a way that without an understanding of this word we, even while amidst beings, could not relate to it and ourselves be beings; if everything and all, the highest and the lowest, only encounters us in the 'ether' of being, how close must being still remain to us, notwithstanding all of this forgetfulness? If we can first ponder this, then perhaps the moment will one day arrive at which the horror at this forgetfulness of being will turn into astonishment in the face of our nearness to that which first only appears as the esoteric sorcery of an errant thinking—i.e., our nearness to that which names the most vapid of all common words (i.e., the most inconspicuous 'is'): nearness, namely, to 'being.' Yet, this is also the sole thing that awards itself to the thinkers as the 'to-be-thought.'

[62] (Once we have considered all of this, we will perhaps wish to become more attentive to the apparently merely circuitous explanations of the words τὸ δῦνον and τὸ ὄν. If, since the inception of Occidental thinking, the forgetfulness of being has spread beyond all measure—spreading, indeed, into philosophy as well—then we should not be surprised if the attempt to think toward the inception of

Occidental thinking must itself be slow beyond measure. Haste is anathema to essential thinking. Certainly, it is imperative that we make haste, if by that we mean that we think toward the 'to-be-thought' without delay or neglect. But such a hastiness of diligent care is not the same thing as rapidity.

The hastiness of essential thinking is subject to the law of slowness. Slow haste determines the way toward the inceptual. The inceptual word demands of us the kind of diligent care in which every step allows the next to come forth from it.)

REVIEW

1) On translation and interpretation: the compulsion into an originary understanding from out of the experienced restiveness of 'the same'

The attention that this lecture is attempting to steer toward the word of Heraclitus's places fragment 16, in distinctive to the usual order of the fragments, at the inception. It says:

τὸ μὴ δῦνόν ποτε πῶς ἄν τις λάθοι;

From the not ever submerging thing, how may anyone be concealed (from it)?

A parenthetical remark on the task of translating should briefly allude to the fact that one can [63] easily criticize any translation, but can only rarely replace it with a 'better' one. This occurs only occasionally, and only owing to much experience. Such a case is exemplified by the recently published translation by Karl Reinhardt of Sophocles' *Antigone*. The sovereignty and beauty of this translation guarantees that some, at least, are on the right path. Every translation, taken just on its own without its corresponding interpretation, remains subject to all manner of misunderstandings: for every translation is in itself already an interpretation. Silently it carries within itself all the attempts, aspects, and layers of interpretation from out of which it originates. The interpretation itself, on the other hand, is only the carrying out of the translation which, still silent, has not yet been brought into the consummating word. Interpretation and translation are, in the core of their essence, the same. That is why, even in one's own language, translation is constant and necessary, given the fact that the words and texts of the mother tongue are often open to interpretation. All speaking, all call and response, are translation. Therefore, the essence of translating does not consist in two different languages entering into a dialogue. We Germans, for example, must each time translate Kant's *Critique of Pure Reason* in order to understand it. Such translation does not entail degrading the sophisticated language of the work down to the level of everyday speech: rather, it means *trans*porting the thinking of this work into a thinking and saying that engages and confronts it. By this process it occasionally appears, strangely, that the interpreter 'actually' understands the thinker 'better' than the thinker understood himself. For the empty vanity of the 'heady' pendants, this appearance is dangerous: for they conclude from this that, in this case, Kant himself did not quite know what he himself wanted, but that now the subsequent interpreters know it precisely. However, the fact that a thinker may be 'better' understood than he understood himself, is surely not a deficit that may be attributed to him retroactively; rather, it is a sign of his greatness. [64] For only originary thinking harbors that treasure within itself the pondering of which remains forever inexhaustible, and which can be 'better' understood each time it is pondered (i.e., can be understood as other than what the words only apparently mean). Mediocre thinking, by contrast, contains only the easily intelligible, and possesses nothing that continually compels toward a more originary understanding and interpretation. Moreover, mediocre thinking cannot call forth those epochs that are compelled once again to recognize and translate what is taken to be familiar.

(That is why thinkers, and only thinkers, have the experience that they one day come to understand themselves better in light of what they have already thought, in such a way that the entire edifice of their earlier thought suddenly collapses, even though they always think the same. But this 'same' is not the boring emptiness of the identical, which is only a semblance of the same. There are those, however, who do not know of the restiveness of the same, and who are proud of the fact that they, at seventy, still think the same as what they already thought and knew as high school students.)

Only what is truly thought has the good fortune of being continually 'better' understood than it first was. This superior understanding, however, is never due to the merit of the interpreter, but is rather a gift bestowed by what is interpreted.

2) 'Submerging'—thought in a Greek way—and the question concerning the essence of the word

We will now attempt, from the outside and with insufficient preparation, to dissect the saying of Heraclitus's in a crude way. In this saying there is talk of the "never submerging thing"; furthermore, the word τις is mentioned—"anyone," a word that in every case designates a human. (Whether it designates the human alone is a question that must remain open.) Moreover, there is talk of a "being concealed." The saying itself has the form of a question that already seems to bring its answer with it.

Our elucidation of the saying must first attempt to make clear, in a general way and from out of the thinking of Heraclitus itself, [65] what this talk of the "never submerging thing" means. How is "submerging" to be thought here? Certainly, it needs to be thought in a 'Greek' way. δύνειν signifies submerging in the sense of an entering into a concealing. We speak here of 'submergence' in the sense in which we still speak of the "submerging of the sun" that disappears behind the mountains or sinks into the ocean, in the manner poeticized, for example, by Stefan George in his poem "Song of the Sea":

When along the horizon in soft fall
Dives down the fiery red ball,
I halt on the dune and rest
To see if to me shows itself a dear guest.

Jean Paul once wrote:

I have thought to myself a hundred times that, were I an angel, were I to have wings, were I to have no specific weight, I would soar upward just enough so that I could see the evening sun glimmer at the edge of the earth; and while I flew along with the earth, though at the same time against its axial motion, I would maintain myself in such an attitude that I could gaze for an entire year into the mild, wide eye of the western sun.... But in the end I would sink down, drunk on the resplendence, like a stupefied bee in the grass overfull on honey![4]

However, for the contemporary imagination, insofar as it clings to *the* true (or what it values as 'the true'), the sight of the submerging sun is untrue and mere appearance. 'Since Copernicus'—and please note that I said 'since,' and not 'owing to,' Copernicus—the 'world' has appeared differently. Listeners who are quick to make up their minds—perhaps, after all, they are only eavesdroppers—may now think that 'Copernicus' was mentioned in the previous hour owing to the fact that the commemoration of Copernicus was last week. I regret to say, however, that this lecture cannot be so 'close-to-life.' There are certainly more substantial reasons to think of 'Copernicus' in connection with the elucidation of Heraclitus's [66] μὴ

---

[4] Jean Paul, *Werke* (E. Berend), §1, V, 265.

δυνόν ποτε, reasons to which the eyes of some may perhaps be opened over the course of this semester.

In those notes of Nietzsche's that serve as the draft for a planned magnum opus to which he occasionally lent the title *The Will to Power*, one finds statements regarding a plan for the presentation of 'European nihilism.' The note in question (written in 1885/86) begins: "Nihilism is standing before the door: whence does this most uncanny of all guests come to us?"[5] Nietzsche then sketches out, point for point, the 'consequences' of nihilism, which have already begun to appear. Under point number 5, Nietzsche says the following:

> The nihilistic consequences of contemporary natural science (in addition to its attempts to escape into the otherworldly). From out of its practice *follows* finally a self-subversion, a turn against *itself*, an anti-science. Since Copernicus, the human has been moving out of the center into the X.

The last sentence means to say that, since then, the place of the human has become an X, that is, it is still undetermined and therefore must be determined. Nietzsche's metaphysics of the will to power is meant to accomplish the new determination of the place of the human. The earth, and the human of this earth, shall regain their lost meaning anew. The 'meaning of the earth' is the 'over-human,' that is, the human who goes over and beyond the prior human, the one who experiences all that is real—and thereby also experiences itself—as a configuration of the will to power. With this most modern of all modern humans, the human not only moves back 'into' the center; rather, the human himself now [67] finally becomes the center itself. A saying of Nietzsche's from 1888 may illustrate this most concisely:

> All the beauty and grandeur that we have bestowed upon actual and imagined things, I shall reclaim as the property and creation of the human being as its most beautiful apology. The human as poet, as thinker, as god, as love, as power: oh, what kingly munificence with which he has endowed things, precisely in order to *impoverish* himself and make *himself* feel wretched! His most selfless act heretofore has been to admire and to idolize and to know how to conceal from himself the fact that *he* himself has created those things that he admired.[6]

The saying unequivocally states this: everything that *is*, only *is* insofar as it is "the product" and thereby the "property" of the human—namely, of the human as

---

[5] Nietzsche, *Werke*, XV, 141 ff.
[6] Ibid., XV, 241, *The Will to Power*, between aphorisms 134 and 135.

the highest configuration of the will to power. The human is precisely that concrete thing from whose gaze nothing may remain concealed and from whom no being can withdraw, for the human alone and in the first place stamps all beings with the mark of 'being.' In the above-quoted note of Nietzsche's regarding the nihilism of modern natural science, he criticizes it for still attempting to 'escape into the otherworldly,' that is, of still occasionally speaking of 'providence' and a 'divine plan.' By contrast, Nietzsche wants an absolute nihilism, one that does not teach that everything is merely 'nothing,' but rather that the human is everything. Nietzsche himself describes his metaphysics as an 'active' and 'classical' 'nihilism.' In it he sees the proper and positive consequence of the Copernican revolution, as well as the future of Europe. Here nothing remains before which the human could still be concealed or not concealed, for the human himself has become the judge of what appears and what, by virtue of its appearing, 'is,' as well of what does not appear and therefore 'is not.' [68] We say too little, therefore, if all we do is point out the abyss that gapes between the consummation of Occidental metaphysics in Nietzsche and the saying of Heraclitus's positioned at the inception. However, from this we can anticipate approximately which interpretation of Heraclitus must manifest itself, if Nietzsche sees his metaphysics already modeled in Heraclitus's thinking.

One more comment must be added here, however, before we put an end to all this unavoidable but, admittedly, annoying beating around the bush. The attempt being dared here to elucidate Heraclitus's saying in no way plans on 'renewing' this inceptual thinking, or even being able to erect it as an 'archetype.' In the historical context of the centuries of modernity, through which not only beings in their entirety but also being itself is jeopardized, not one free moment remains to reproduce something from an earlier era, if such a thing were even possible. Since there is no longer time for 'reproduction,' we must make do without those archetypes that themselves can only be continually recreated, refreshed, or replaced. This renunciation of historiographical archetypes of ages, styles, tendencies, situations, and ideals is the sign of an extreme and distressing need that we and future generations must first endure before it announces what it conceals. In order that we or those who come after us are even able to hear the saying, we must first slowly learn how to listen to the thinking word.

If we now think δύειν (submerging) in a Greek way as the entering into a concealment, then we recognize that, between δύνω and λάθω, there stands an essential relation.

(The necessity governing any translation is variously determined in accordance with the dominant 'need' at the time. These 'needs' span from the lowly depths demanded by hurried business communications, to the merely academic engagement with foreign literatures, upward to the peaks of those moments in which inceptions of history gesture toward one another in recognition [69], and where a dialogue from peak to peak awaits consummation. Here, in the valleys between these peaks of history, every historiography (i.e., the learned, comparative conveyance of ages and cultures in the indeterminate space of an ideal braced up in accordance with educational norms) fails. All historiography must necessarily cling to an archetype (indeed, any classical one) because the passing back-and-forth between styles, tendencies, and situations arising necessarily from out of its own historiographical activity of mediation is threatened by the merely mediate and comparative, i.e., the relative. Any implementation of a classical model and a classic age is in itself already Classicism, which is an offspring of historiography—that is, of the calculating and fundamentally technical relation to history.

However, because the philosophy of the ancient Greek world, along with all of antiquity, is often counted as belonging to the 'Classical,' it is important to consider that for us the inceptual thinkers cannot be archetypes for the single reason that we may no longer be permitted to contemplate mere reproductions. For to do so would mean closing off our thinking to the fact that the temples of the earth have either collapsed in upon themselves, have left the holy sites where they once were, or are now only inhabited by empty convention and have therefore lost their historical essence. Not only does it remain to be decided whether or not the German people will remain *the* historical people of the Occident, but it is also the case that the human, along with the earth to which he belongs, is jeopardized—and, indeed, by the human himself.)

In the saying of Heraclitus's, the two foundational words τὸ δῦνον and λάθοι appear. Since 'submerging,' thought in a Greek way, conveys an entering into concealment, and λάθω means "I am concealed," and since being concealed is being asked about in relation to that which never enters into concealment, the saying is, at the first attentive glance, pervaded by a singular thinking oriented toward concealing and not concealing. But given that a thinker [70] is speaking here, we must immediately strive from the very first to hear the word within the realm of essential thinking. The elucidation of the word τὸ δῦνον, which seems to be merely grammatical in nature, can help us get there.

Still today we must contend with the puzzling fate that in the Occident, for more than two millennia, the relation to the word has been determined by grammar; that grammar, for its part, is grounded in what is commonly called "logic"; that "logic" itself, however, is merely one (and not the only) interpretation of thinking and saying: namely, the interpretation of the essence of thinking that is proper to metaphysics. Any explanations about the word—be these psychological, physiological, aesthetic, or sociological—are, according to grammar and logic, merely added on to the word understood grammatically as a linguistic sign. Moreover, if we consider that in the modern world the word is generally only 'evaluated' as 'language,' and language itself is evaluated only as an instrument of communication, then it is not surprising that every consideration of the word immediately appears to be merely an empty reflection on a kind of thing that one calls "words," "with" which "scholars," as one says, "occupy" themselves. Words are a type of useful object that one should best leave to the arbitrariness of unrestricted usage.

Now, certainly there would emerge a distinct image of the modern relation to the word, were one to present this relation only as a neglect of language. Over against this—but also dependent upon it—are the efforts of some writers who practically form a cult out of the technics of language and reckon themselves to be members of The Guild of "Splitting-Hairs." Here, however, even with all due care, language has merely a technical character or, in the idiom of Ernst Jünger, a "work-character." The word is an instrument of the hunt and the strike [71] in the 'process' and the 'work' pertaining to the 'bulletproof' objectification of all things. The machinegun, the camera, the 'word,' and the billboard all have this same fundamental function of seizing and arresting the object. The technical precision of the word is the counterpart to the neglect of language that occurs when it is treated as a mere means of conveyance. Considered metaphysically, both relations stay on the level of that particular relation to reality which, since Nietzsche, appears as the "will to power," and both experience reality itself as the will to power.

Were we now to abandon ourselves to the common relation to the word (which is in fact an uncanny and skewed relationship), we would never be able to consider a saying of Heraclitus's. Therefore, we must first, through some kind of 'reflection,' approach the inceptual word. However, it is not as if the inceptual thinkers produced 'reflections' 'about' the word; it is only *we* who need to take such long detours to the word, on account of the fact that our much-acclaimed 'immediate experience'—not in its 'content,' but rather in its basic structure—is perhaps the most abstract and abstruse form that Occidental history has ever taken. However, since we have not yet found a way other than that of grammar in order to grasp, even just superficially, the word in its essence, this provisional path must suffice.

The word δῦνον is a participle. As such it takes part in both the substantive and verbal meanings. 'The submerging thing' can mean that which is either subject to submergence or not; but it can also mean the submerging thing in its submerging, that is, the submerging thing during its submerging and in the endurance of it. Which meaning the thinker intended, and thereby which meaning we must think, cannot yet be decided. Seen in terms of form, we can think the participle either nominally or verbally; but there also exists the possibility of understanding the participle as simultaneously both 'nominal' and 'verbal,' in which case the emphasis can be placed [72] either on the verbal or the nominal aspect. All of these possibilities of understanding reside in the so-called 'participle,' and indeed within a unity proper to it. In this unity, the richness of the word flourishes in a way that cannot be exhausted by grammatical dissection. The word whose meaning has come to be reduced to a single form has still another richness precisely because it comes from the originary unity of speaking and saying.

3) Elucidation of τὸ δῦνον in terms of the structure of the words of the main question of metaphysical thinking (Aristotle, Plato). Concerning the problem of retroactive interpretation: the inceptual thinkers and the later beginning of metaphysics

In order to see a path along which we could arrive at the way of thinking by which the Greek thinkers thought such participial words, we now address our question to that thinker in whose word the thinking of the Greek world consummated itself. However, in doing so we must be careful not to impose the later thoughts of Aristotle back onto the thinking of the inceptual thinkers. In *Metaphysics* Z 1, 1028b2 and following, Aristotle states:

καὶ δὴ καὶ τὸ πάλαι τε καὶ νῦν καὶ ἀεὶ ζητούμενον καὶ ἀεὶ ἀπορούμενον, τί τὸ ὄν, . . .

And so the question that from antiquity has been, is now, and shall (before all else) remain the-sought-for—i.e., that which we (when we think it) continually cannot penetrate—is: what is the being?

τί τὸ ὄν—this is the question that directs the thinking of the thinker. Once again the to-be-thought is named through a participial word: τὸ ὄν—the being.

With this word, we initially think of things, living beings, humans, the heavenly vault, and—in order to imagine these things as the Greeks did—also the gods. [73]

The question "what is the being" thereby initially means: what are things, what are plants, what are animals, what are humans, what are gods? In order to find the answer to each question regarding each particular thing asked about, we turn to what is named and seek to grasp what it is. In doing so, however, we shall never find that about which the question "what is the being" asks, even if we should spend an eternity searching.

The question "what is the being?" does not demand information about this or that particular being, but rather about being. What is asked about here, as Aristotle states at the beginning of the discourse *Metaphysics* Γ 1, is ὄν ᾗ ὄν: the being, but with regard to the fact that it *is*—in other words, with regard to the being of the being. That to which our gaze is drawn is τοῦτό ἐστιν: τίς ἡ οὐσία—it is the beingness of the being. The suffix -ness (as in 'just-ness,' 'free-ness,' 'rapid-ness') means that which, for example, is proper to all that is just as such, to all that is free as such, and to all that is rapid as such. For example, all that is proper to trees as trees is 'tree-ness.' One therefore likes to designate this quality as the universal, the 'general.' But tree-ness is not proper to individual trees because it is the 'universal' in distinction to the particular specimen. Rather, this universal only is the universal because it is the tree-ness of trees: it is their γένος, that from which every tree *as* tree, δένδρον ᾗ δένδρον, derives. The οὐσία, the beingness, is τὸ γένος, the origin, that from which every being as being originates. In short: τὸ εἶναι, being, and τὸ ὄν, the being, are not thought substantively, but rather verbally in view of the being of the being.

To name beingness and being, Aristotle uses a term he likely coined himself: τὸ τί ἦν εἶναι, i.e., being as that which every being, insofar as it is a being, already was. In the determination of that which for thinking is the to-be-thought, Plato's thinking advanced beyond the thinking of Aristotle's, who [74] listened to Plato over the course of two decades and thereby learned to think. Plato himself names the to-be-thought of beings by means of an idiom that the Greeks, as a thinking people, could be trusted to understand. What the thinkers think is τὸ ὄντως ὄν, "the being in terms of being" [*das seienderweise Seiende*], the being solely in view of being. This then is also considered 'what is of the utmost being' within beings [*das Seiendste am Seienden*].

Now, admittedly the designations ὄν ᾗ ὄν, οὐσία, τὸ τί ἦν εἶναι, and ὄντως ὄν communicate next to nothing to our stuffed and stubborn ears. These designations are like empty word husks. The reasons for this state of affairs cannot be found solely in the contemporary inability and disinclination to think. The reason Plato's thought in particular, and above all the philosophy of Aristotle as an expression of Greek thought in its originary directness, remains closed to us, is owed to the fact that the philosophy of Aristotle, by way of Jewish–Arab thought in the Middle Ages, was transformed by ecclesiastical theology into an entity that has only the words in common with the Greek Aristotle, and even these are translated into the language of Latin.

How immovably Aristotle's thought lies entombed by the Middle Ages is shown in the fact that even a thinker such as Leibniz was incapable of scaling the wall that medieval theology, through its own particular use of the Aristotelian doctrines, erected between the Greek thinker and the later ages of the Occident. Even the classical philology of recent decades, from which one could perhaps expect an inkling of the Greek essence, interprets the philosophy of Aristotle in terms of the theology of Thomas Aquinas. That is why even today most people think that when one says 'Aristotle,' it is Thomas Aquinas who is meant, or that when one says 'Thomas Aquinas,' [75] a justifiable claim has been made to knowledge of Aristotle and his thought.

As a result of this widespread thoughtlessness, a few years ago a rector of the local university informally suggested removing the figure of Aristotle from the main entrance of the university building, since today we are no longer concerned with the 'Middle Ages.'

But perhaps it is good that Aristotle, as the last thinker of the Greeks, continues to stand in proximity to the first poet of the Greeks and the Occident [i.e., Homer].

These two figures are right where they should be. However, I often think that all of this is lost on those of us who simply sit there on the steps allowing our slightly thoughtless brains to fry in the sun.

Fragment 16 of Heraclitus's, to which we have tried to attend thoughtfully as the first in the ranking of sayings, speaks in the form of a question:

τὸ μὴ δῦνόν ποτε πῶς ἄν τις λάθοι;

From the not ever submerging thing, how may anyone be concealed (from it)?

In order to get to the essential core of this question, we must first interpret the words that, through their 'content,' bear the sentence. What does the particular combination of words τὸ μὴ δῦνόν ποτε—"the never submerging thing"—mean? And how is the participle τὸ δῦνον to be thought? In order to get a Greek answer to this question we asked Aristotle, the last thinker of the Greeks, through whom the following was revealed: the principal question in accordance with which thinkers since Plato think is τί τὸ ὄν;—"what is the being?" Once again we encounter a participle referring to what is being examined by the thinkers: τὸ ὄν—"the being." However, the thinkers think the being ᾗ ὄν—i.e., they think the being in view of the fact that it is a being. The thinkers bring the being into the essential view [76] of being. Thus, Aristotle elucidates the above-quoted question as τί τὸ ὄν, and then further transcribes it into the question τίς ἡ οὐσία;—"Which and what is the beingness of beings?" Seen from the perspective of the being, what accounts for the commonality of beings such that every single being (ἕκαστον) is subject to this commonality (κοινόν)? Instead of the name οὐσία (beingness), the word εἶναι ("being") (the infinitive of that particular verb whose 'present' participle reads ὄν) also occasionally appears.

When the thinkers think the ὄν in view of the εἶναι, they thereby understand the participle 'verbally.' Thought philosophically, τὸ ὄν always means the being in its being. Why, then, do the thinkers not directly and exclusively use the infinitive εἶναι in order to state clearly what they are thinking? What purpose, then, does the ambiguity of the participle ὄν—i.e., the participle 'being,' which can be understood both nominally and verbally—have? It almost seems as though the common suspicion that philosophers purposefully express themselves 'stiltedly' and 'awkwardly' applies no less to the thinkers of the Greeks.

Now, it cannot be denied that the participle is included within the structure of the question of all questions. Aristotle asks τί τὸ ὄν, and not τί τὸ εἶναι. Therefore, we must postpone our peculiar desire for straightforward expressions. 'We,' with our perhaps very limited intellect, must conversely try for once to think about the fact that thinkers on the level of Plato and Aristotle perhaps did have their reasons for using the ambiguous participle τὸ ὄν. One who attempts to think in the manner of these thinkers must indeed think the participle nominally as well as verbally, so that the nominal and verbal meanings can be thought in their own determined relatedness.

With Plato and Aristotle, the guiding question for all thinkers was brought onto a pathway on which, even if one allows for all of the differences in the basic positions of later thinkers, it still remains today [77]. The questions is: "What is the being?" This question unfolds itself more clearly into the question: What is the being *of* the being? Here the question is directed from out of the being toward being, and from being back toward the being, all with the sole purpose of thereby determining the being itself specifically in its 'being.' Because the being is here thought with regard to being, the only proper naming of what the thinkers think remains, in truth, the participle τὸ ὄν, which expresses both the nominal *and* the verbal.

The nominal sense of τὸ ὄν, according to which the being—and, indeed, beings as a whole—is meant, can be transcribed more clearly through the plural τὰ ὄντα, and the verbal meaning can be more clearly transcribed as τὸ εἶναι. After being thus amplified, the guiding question τί τὸ ὄν means: τί τὸ εἶναι τῶν ὄντων;

Thus, strictly speaking, it is only conditionally true when we say that the participle ὄν, thought in the manner of the thinkers, must always be understood verbally. Philosophy—or, as we could now also say, metaphysics—does indeed constantly think being, but it exclusively thinks the being of the being: that is, it in fact thinks the being, and indeed with regard to being. The casual manner of speaking that often sneaks its way into the thinkers' speech speaks at one time of 'the being,' when the being of the being is meant, but at another time of being, when the being is presented with regard to being. One speaks even more casually and more vaguely of the 'question of being,' saying that this is the question concerning being, when in fact, already after a short reflection, it becomes clear that one is actually asking about the being, about what the being is. In the oft-mentioned 'question of being,' one asks so blindly and implicitly about the being that one cannot hear a different sort of question that suddenly, and for a change, asks about being and its truth. One hears only what one wants to hear.

[78] Aristotle, in fact, gives us an elucidation of how the participle ὄν is to be understood and how the guiding question of the thinker reads—τί τὸ ὄν;—but it nevertheless remains doubtful whether we can directly interpret the doctrines of Aristotle back into the thinking of the inceptual thinkers, even though he, like them, is Greek through and through. To be sure, such retroactive interpreting happens constantly. Indeed, Aristotle himself is in fact the originator of the attempt to locate the metaphysical manner of thinking that begins with him and Plato already in the thinking of the 'pre-Platonic' thinkers. Aristotle habitually begins each of his treatises with a critical review of the prior doctrines of earlier thinkers that he then contrasts with his own doctrine, but only after having already translated their doctrines in such a way that they are on the level of his own manner of questioning. The manner in which Aristotle, and also already Plato,

distinguish themselves from earlier thinkers, still today remains the paradigm according to which the sketch of the outlines of earlier thinking is carried out. According to this paradigm, one compares, and does so from the perspective of the later thinkers. Thus, it naturally results that the earlier thinkers appear as those who did 'not yet' know what afterwards was thought by Plato and Aristotle. That is, in fact, the case. However, the question remains whether the later thinkers are, precisely because they think what the earlier thinkers did 'not yet' know, the 'progressive ones.' Perhaps they are in truth the pro-gressive ones—but the question remains whether this pro-gress is not in fact an e-gress away from the inceptual. It is certainly the case that, from Heraclitus to Aristotle, thinking 'developed.' But the question remains whether 'development,' only because therein something 'develops,' is itself already the true and protects the true. It is the same question that we must also direct at modern science when 'researchers' are being applauded for (as the strange formulation has it) 'driving research forward.' Forward? To where, if you please? Perhaps to the shattered cities on the Rhine and the Ruhr? What is going [79] on with this mere driving forward for its own sake? Does it even have a meaning, especially when one has forgotten to ask along what path one is driving, and who, after all, is doing the driving? 'Driving research forward'—why *forward*, and by what right? What are fore and aft here? In any case, we must not take forward-driving and forward-driven 'modern research' as a schema in order to construct a so-called 'historiographical' development from Heraclitus to Aristotle. For us the question here and now is precisely this: whether the inceptual thinkers, because they did 'not yet' think as Plato and Aristotle did, remain 'behind' the thinking of later thinkers, or whether they, because they did 'not yet' think as Plato and Aristotle did, were already thinking ahead of all later thought, and indeed so essentially far ahead that all later thinkers up to the present day have yet to make up this leap ahead, and indeed cannot even perceive and experience it *as* a leap ahead. The question that is thus touched upon about the relationship between the inceptual thinkers and the later beginning of 'metaphysics' is for us not a historiographical question that only compares past positions of thinking: for if the inceptual thinkers thought ahead of all that came later, and thereby thought beyond even today's thinking, then what comes to light in their thinking is what already and only lies before us as the fatefully sent that has yet to approach us—that is, what lies before us as history.

This consideration also reveals that the common representation of time as a consecutive succession is in no way adequate to properly think history as it is. However, insofar as history is presented as historiographically and chronologically ordered, this chronological conception of time leads to the fact that only a superficial understanding of time has bearing upon our consideration of history. Through this view, we see [80] the inceptual as what came earlier and has passed: it lies behind us. So understood, we must only count backwards in order to find the inception. However, we will never find the inception of Occidental thinking as long as we count backwards in a historiographically comparative way. We will only find the inception when we think ahead in a manner that experiences history.

4) The characteristics of the word ὄν. The primacy of the verbal meaning over the nominal meaning (in participles)

If we consider this, then surely the information we have requested of Aristotle regarding the meaning of the participle carries less weight. Indeed, it becomes questionable if we may continue, without sufficient consideration, to take the δῦνον of Heraclitus's in the sense of Aristotle's ὄν. We could easily eliminate this concern by saying that δῦνον, in comparison with the ὄν, is something singular— i.e., that the submerging or, on the other hand, the never-submerging, is only a type of being: the δῦνον thus belongs, as does emerging and any process whatsoever, 'under' the general concept of the ὄν. Moreover, if the never-submerging 'is' something at all, and if the submerging 'happens,' a being and a being [*ein Seiendes und ein Sein*] are present here.

Therefore, what applies to the ὄν as the most universal also applies to the specific case of the δῦνον. The possibility, and perhaps even the necessity, of construing Heraclitus's δῦνον in the sense of the Aristotelian ὄν thus rightly persists.

Yet, there is a matter that still remains undecided, for, indeed, it has not even been asked yet: namely, whether the δῦνον, or more precisely the μὴ δῦνόν ποτε, is only a singular appearance and occurrence within the ὄν (i.e., within what *is*), or whether the relation of the μὴ δῦνόν ποτε to the ὄν must be thought altogether differently and in a way for which we find no model in common ways of thinking.

[81] Through the preceding lecture we have decided, almost in one fell swoop, to think the δῦνον 'verbally,' thereby hearing the saying in such a way that therein the word of the never-submerging has become audible. Initially, this emphasis on the verbal meaning only has the purpose of allowing the thoughtful gaze to align itself to the viewpoint within which the thinking of the thinkers moves when they name 'the being.' In this sense, the 'never-submerging' would be a process— something that *is*, after all—and that therefore still belongs to the category of being. In any case, this relationship between the never-submerging and being must be illuminated, if indeed the thinkers think the being of beings, and Heraclitus, as a thinker, thinks the never-submerging.

The question that remains can hence be captured in the following formulaic way: is the never-submerging only one manner of being among others, or does the concealed essence of 'being' perhaps altogether rest in the never-submerging? If the latter is the case, whereto are we being led—or thrown—by the saying of

Heraclitus's when it asks: "From the never-submerging, how could anyone be concealed from it?" Is not the appeal uttered within this saying, which has withstood the fleeting timespan of two and a half millennia, directed to *us*? Who, if not us, is being addressed therein—we who are sitting here, and who are perhaps still of the opinion that this lecture on Heraclitus is enacting a flight into 'intellectual history' and antiquity? Certainly, we could simply process this saying in a purely historiographical way and designate it as the erstwhile opinion of a past philosophy. We could indeed do this. The saying certainly does not suffer as a result: however, the question remains if perhaps *we* suffer as a result. The saying does not need us: but the question remains whether someday we will need this saying that speaks to us in a hidden way about being. Should this prove to be the case, then it is perhaps good if we ourselves gain some clarity about how we—those of us sitting and standing here, [82] listening and speaking—all relate to 'being.' It is perhaps good if we consider, for once, on what terms we are with the most common and fleeting word wherein being speaks itself: namely, with the unremarkable word 'is.'

We say 'is' constantly, even when we are not saying it expressly. We think it in the form of every time-word; we think it in every naming, every call and command, every appeal and every greeting. We think it constantly and understand it everywhere, and yet utterly fail to grasp it and reflect upon it. We think it in every silent reflection; we think it in thoughtless opining; we think it even when we believe ourselves merely to be 'feeling' or 'experiencing' something. The word of all words; the very ether of language; the word that names that in which all saying and all silence are suspended: for us, this word has remained up until now the most innocuous of all that is innocuous. It is surely strange how carelessly the human proceeds with the word that is always already named in advance of all his often hasty and loud pronouncements, even though it is not always spoken aloud.

According to the Occidental determination of its essence, the human is that being who has found its distinction in λόγον ἔχειν, in having "speech," in "having the word." The human has the word in the sense that for the human—and, as far as we know, only for the human—that to which he is relating addresses him, and he is able to respond to this address by speaking, so that everything that appears also and at the same time comes into the word, even if it is not spoken aloud each time. This event [*Ereignis*]—namely, that whatever comes to appearance already comes from out of the word—is the sole reason that the human is also occasionally affected by the un-sayable. The un-sayable would not appear if all appearing did not remain originally interwoven with the sphere of saying and the word. Every statue, every temple, every playing of the flute would be nothing, if it could not find a home in the realm of the word. [83] What is revealed, however, through a consideration requiring the courage to embrace the simple, rather than the profound or the scholarly, is this: namely, that the human, who in its essence 'has the word,' 'has' just lost the word of all words, insofar as he thoughtlessly says the word 'being' as though it were the most trifling of all trifles. At the same time, the human never fully throws this word away, since doing so would apparently bring about the loss of his own essence.

Let us imagine, if only for a few minutes, what would become of the human if it came about that every possibility of saying and understanding the words 'is' and 'being' were revoked. No catastrophe that could befall the planet can be compared with this seemingly most trivial of events [*Ereignisse*] in which the human's relation to 'is' is suddenly suspended. But this catastrophe has long since arrived, only no one has noticed it in its essence. The human, in its history, has reached the point where he has forgotten the 'is' and 'being,' insofar as he renounces any consideration of what is named by this word. Indifference to 'being' has besieged the planet. The human being allows himself to be washed over by the flood of this forgetfulness of being. But, in truth, this is not even a 'diving into' the flood anymore, for that would still require an awareness of the forgetfulness of being. Precisely this forgetfulness of being has itself already been forgotten, which is surely in accordance with the essence of forgetting, sucking up everything in its radius like an undertow.

But what do the thinkers of metaphysics say who, since Plato, have been appointed as the 'guardians' of the being of beings? What does the last thinker in the history of metaphysics say about the being of beings? Nietzsche says: 'being' is the last vapor of an evaporating reality. Is not the forgetfulness of being justified here by metaphysics itself? Certainly. So, it is not worth our while anymore to remember something [84] that is a mere vapor. It is enough if the human 'lives' and acts 'true to life' and 'true to reality.' Why does the human need being, if beings and reality are already enough for him to, as it is often said, 'fulfill' his life? With this, one concedes that otherwise there is obviously an emptiness. In fact, through Nietzsche's metaphysics, 'being' is rendered into a mere value: however, this devalued 'being' is 'worth' even less than 'becoming,' i.e., even less than the will to power. For in Nietzsche's metaphysics the being of beings, which has remained the to-be-thought for all metaphysics, evaporates in one last vapor, which is why Nietzsche's metaphysics is the end of all metaphysics: for in this final stage a decision is made about being, against which any patchwork solution on the part of a prior metaphysics or a flight into a rehashed Christianity is no longer viable.

But how stubbornly and tirelessly must metaphysics remain within its forgetfulness of being if, as it seems, even two world wars cannot wrest the historical human from out of his mere engagement with beings and awaken humanity's fear regarding the forgetfulness of being, placing the human before being itself.

Suppose that, however, we were to be placed before being in a less painful way. Suppose that, with one fell swoop, the modern human were to be deprived of such things as the movie theater, the radio, the newspaper, the theater, concerts, boxing matches, and 'travel.' Suppose it came about that the human were forced to subsist with only the simple things: he would rather 'die' than remember being!

But if we are all so unfamiliar with being and cannot find our way into a thinking of it, how can we be expected to be able to think, as if overnight, what is thought in advance within the inception of our hidden history? Here the only help [85]—if it is indeed any help—comes from the care with which we think-after the inceptual word. This care also entails that we are already attentive to the possibilities of the appropriate translation. By now it has come to light that the thinkers, when they think words that are essentially participial, primarily think the verbal meaning of those words. In accordance with that thinking, and perhaps even somewhat hyperbolically, we now translate Heraclitus's saying as: "the not submerging ever." We can contract the "not–ever" into "never," thus yielding: "the never submerging."

§ 4. The foundational words of inceptual thinking (φύσις, ζωή). Their relation to metaphysical thinking and to the thinking of being

a) The peculiar poverty of inceptually thoughtful utterance in the structure of the words τὸ μὴ δῦνόν ποτε and their transformation into 'perpetual emerging' (φύειν). On the word φύσις in inceptual thinking, and on the concept of 'nature.' Note on fragment 123

Up to this point we have determined the first substantive word of the saying of Heraclitus's τὸ μὴ δῦνόν ποτε only in terms of its character as a word. When there is talk of 'the submerging thing,' we no longer think only of what falls prey to submerging or remains withdrawn from it, but rather of 'submerging itself.' However, we think of this in the previously elucidated Greek sense, where submerging is understood as entering into a concealing. And yet, in Heraclitus's saying, there is no mention of submerging. To the contrary, the saying speaks with unique emphasis of τὸ μὴ δῦνόν ποτε—'the not ever submerging.' μή is a word of negation. Yet, it negates differently than οὐ, which straightforwardly states only a non-being. By contrast, μή negates in the sense that whoever experiences what is negated wants to know what is kept from him by it (namely, the negated). We therefore translate μή as 'not ever.' [86] What is named here is experienced as that which, not for anything, not even 'for all the world,' is a submerging or is dissolved within one. However, with this it is in no way already decided whether what is named here is not still determined in its essence through a submerging, or indeed whether "the not ever submerging" must nonetheless remain determined in relation to a submerging. For only if within what is named here a trace and a sign of submerging appears does the μή—the 'not ever' of repulsion—have a hold and sense. The μή says, then, that in what is named here, submerging indeed prevails and unfolds, but that this submerging does not dominate in this unfolding, not just now and from time to time, but rather essentially not and therefore consequently 'never.' The μή in the saying is hence still more narrowly qualified through the ποτέ—'ever,' 'at any time,' a word that indicates a temporality: μή–ποτε—"not ever, ever," i.e., "never." But here, as would be perfectly possible, the much more common combination of words τὸ μή ποτε δῦνον is not used, but rather we find τὸ μὴ δῦνόν ποτε—the negated word (δῦνον) is set between a combination of negating words. Precisely through this combination of words (i.e., the δῦνον between the μή and the ποτέ), the verbal, temporal sense of δῦνον is made conspicuous, and the eventful [*ereignishafte*] essence of the above-named is brought to appearance through this simple and straightforward way of naming. Already here, with the first saying of Heraclitus's, we learn, if we have eyes to see and ears to hear, something of the harmony of what is said and thought, heard and questioned, in this thinking. However, we also sense something of the austerity of care, that is, of the poverty proper to thoughtful saying.

Certainly, we could now (as we already did above in a makeshift way) simplify the combination of words within the translation (i.e., the expression "the not ever submerging") and instead say "the never submerging." Such a translation almost compels us on its own to further transform [87] the saying into the following: "the constantly (i.e., perpetually) emerging." For what never is a submerging must therefore constantly be an emerging. Through this shifting of words, the bothersome 'negation' in the saying of Heraclitus's is done away with. We hear now a 'positive' word which, as such, has priority over all 'negatives.' The word, now transformed into a positive, makes the expression easier for us to understand by opening our eyes for the first time to what is named here, supposing of course that we are mindful and able to learn to see in a Greek way. This is perhaps the minimal precondition under which every attempt to think the inception of Occidental thinking remains situated.

If we undertake to use the affirmative turn of phrase "the perpetually emerging" instead of the negating phrase "the not ever submerging, ever" or the phrase "the never submerging," then we say in our own language a word that Heraclitus also at one time very well could have said in his own language. "The perpetually emerging" names the Greek τὸ ἀεὶ φύον. In place of τὸ φύον could also stand ἡ φύσις[1] which,

---

[1] See fragment 123.

thought literally, means emerging in the sense of coming out of the closed and veiled and simple one-folded. (φύσις is the foundational word in the saying of the inceptual thinkers.) This 'emerging' becomes immediately clear to us through the emerging of the seeds sunken in the earth, the sprouting of shoots, the emerging of the blossom. Additionally, the spectacle of the emerging sun points to the essence of emerging. All of this, however, is different from the sort of emerging one sees when the human being, gathered into view, arises from out of himself; or how the emerging world unveils itself to the human through speech and thereby, at the same time, unveils the human himself; or how the mind, through gesture, displays itself; or how, in play, the essence of the human shows itself transparently; or how, in simple presence, the essence of the human reveals itself. To say nothing here of the greetings of the gods, [88] there is everywhere a reciprocal unfolding-toward-one-another of all 'essences' and, within that unfolding, appearance in the sense of the emanating self-showing. *That* is φύσις. Therefore, it is fundamentally erroneous to hold that what this foundational word φύσις names in the saying of the inceptual thinkers was first of all gleaned from the emerging seed, the emerging plant, or the emerging sun, and was only then accordingly extended to all so-called natural processes, and then finally conferred upon humans and gods, and in such a way that, from the point of view of φύσις, 'gods and humans' are also presented as being in a certain sense 'natural.' As if it were not in fact the case that what we call 'nature' first obtained its determination only through a lack of understanding of φύσις. φύσις, pure emerging, is neither merely abstracted from out of the narrow sphere of what we call 'nature,' nor is it subsequently assigned to humans and gods as an essential characteristic. Rather, φύσις names that prior emerging within which earth and sky, sea and mountain, tree and animal, human and god emerge and thereby show themselves as what emerge, so that they, in light of this emerging, are known as 'beings.' What we call 'natural processes' first became visible to the Greeks in the way of their 'emerging within the light of φύσις.'

By contrast, modern natural science experiences the emerging of seeds as a chemical process that is interpolated in terms of the grinding gears of the mechanistically viewed interaction between seeds, the condition of the soil, and thermal radiation. In this situation, the modern mind sees only mechanistic cause-and-effect relationships within chemical procedures that have particular effects following upon them. Modern natural science—chemistry no less than physics, biology no less than physics and chemistry—are and remain, so long as they exist, 'mechanistic.' Additionally, 'dynamics' is a mechanics of 'power.' How else could modern [89] natural science 'verify' itself in 'technology' (as one says)? The technical efficaciousness and applicability of modern natural science is not, however, the subsequent proof of the 'truth' of science: rather, the practical technology of modern natural science is itself only possible because modern natural science as a whole, in its metaphysical essence, is itself already merely an application of 'technology,' where 'technology' means here something other than only what engineers bring about. The oft-quoted saying of Goethe's—namely, that the fruitful alone is the true—is already nihilism. Indeed, when the time comes when we no longer merely fiddle around with artworks and literature in terms of their value for education or intellectual history, we should perhaps examine our so-called 'classics' more closely. Moreover, Goethe's view of nature is in its essence no different from Newton's; the former depends along with the latter on the ground of modern (and especially Leibnizian) metaphysics, which one finds present in every object and every process available to us living today. The fact that *we*, however, when considering a seed, still see how something closed emerges and, as emerging, comes forth, may seem insubstantial, outdated, and half-poetic compared to the perspective of the *objective* determination and explanation belonging to the modern understanding of the germination process. The agricultural chemist, but also the modern physicist, have, as the saying goes, 'nothing to do' with φύσις. Indeed, it would be a fool's errand even to try to persuade them that they could have 'something to do' with the Greek experience of φύσις. Now, the Greek essence of φύσις is in no way a generalization of what those today would consider the naïve experience of the emerging of seeds and flowers and the emergence of the sun. Rather, to the contrary, the original experience of emerging and of coming-forth from out of the concealed and veiled is the relation to the 'light' in whose luminance the [90] seed and the flower are first grasped in their emerging, and in which is seen the manner by which the seed 'is' in the sprouting, and the flower 'is' in the blooming.

b) The foundational words φύσις and ζωή as obtained through the translation. The fundamental meaning of ζῆν and ζωή in inceptual thinking over and against the concept of 'life' in the metaphysical tradition. Note on fragment 30

If, therefore, in the word τὸ μὴ δῦνόν ποτε the "never submerging" is named as the perpetually emerging, and if φύσις/φύειν/φύον is the word for "emerging," then the above-mentioned phrase very well could have been rephrased by Heraclitus as τὸ ἀεὶ φύον, or even contracted into the single word τὸ ἀείφυον. However, this word does not appear in the saying; indeed, we find it nowhere among the sayings of Heraclitus's. In place of it, Heraclitus used the word ἀείζωον,[2] perpetual life/the

---

[2] See fragment 30.

perpetually living. Thus, rather than φύον, ζῷον appears, the participle of the verb (or 'time-word') ζῆν. We blithely translate this as 'to live,' and believe we know what this means. 'To live': how could we not know what that is, since we ourselves 'live,' and since we, in accordance with the founding principle of modern metaphysics, create our notion of beings (and also of being) from out of the experience of our own 'I'?[3] Along these lines, Nietzsche (entirely in accordance with his epoch) considered 'life' as what is best known: namely, the absolutely self-evident. Because everything is understood from the perspective of 'life,' every objective thing is the 'experienced,' and experience is therefore the relation to the world. Everything comes from 'lived-experience.' *Poetry and Experience* is the name of a famous book by Dilthey. Because Nietzsche also thinks from out of experience, he does not hesitate to interpret the foundational word of all thinking—[91] namely, the word 'being'—in terms of 'life.' In a note from the year 1885/86 Nietzsche writes:[4] "'Being'—we have no other conception of this than '*to live*.' How, then, can something dead 'be'?" Already at Nietzsche's time, 'being' had been conceived by 'us' (which is to say, by 'anyone') for a long time as 'life.' The question nevertheless remains which conception 'we' have of 'life.' Nietzsche interprets 'life' as 'will to power.' In the second part of *Thus Spoke Zarathustra* (1883), in the section entitled "On Self-Overcoming," the connection between 'life' and 'will to power' is expressed for the first time:

> He certainly did not arrive at the truth, he who shot at it with the phrase 'will to existence': this will—it does not exist!
> For: what is not, cannot will; but how could what is in existence will existence! Only where life is, there is also will: not, however, will to life, but rather—so I teach you—will to power!
> There is much, to the living one, that is valued as higher than life itself; but from out of the process of valuing itself speaks forth—the will to power![5]

In the same passage, prior to the above-cited, one sees the following:

> Where I found living things, there also I found will to power; and even in the will of the servant I found the will to be master.[6]

In all of this, it is decided that whatever does not have the character of the will to power is not 'being,' and thus is, insofar as it is not thought as will to power, a

---

[3] See Leibniz, *Monadology*, § 30.
[4] Nietzsche, *Werke*, XVI, 77, *The Will to Power*, Aphorism 582.
[5] Ibid., VI, 168.
[6] Ibid., 167.

mere vapor. To be sure, this vapor is still necessary for 'living.' It is, according to Nietzsche, even that 'truth' that humans must perform for themselves in order 'to live'—that is, to be capable of existing as will to power. But, [92] we also see here that the appeal to what is alive and to 'life' always already contains within itself an interpretation of its essence. Nietzsche finds 'living things' only where he finds will to power. Said a bit more generally: one finds 'living things' only where what is encountered already corresponds to the superimposed conception of what 'life' is. Unfailingly, we believe we know in an immediate way the 'living' as such, even without an expressed essential determination of life. We distinguish, for example, the living from the dead. However, we do not group the dead together with the lifeless which, like a stone, has no life at all and therefore cannot die and can never be dead. We distinguish life and death and yet do not know what 'life' and death are. It probably belongs to the same oppressive forgetfulness of being that, with respect to 'life' and 'death', we have only very indeterminate, flickering, and adventitious notions, whereas life and death can be nothing incidental, since indeed the entire planet erupts in a clamorous uproar concerning the 'living' and 'dying' of its people. By means of 'modern science,' we will not be able to learn to experience what 'to live' means in the sense of the Greek word ζῆν, even after the previously adduced example of the word φύσις. Even if modern biology were built upon a clear and grounded experience of the essence of life (which, to be sure, is certainly not the case), then its underlying essential experience of the essence of life would still never be gained nor grounded 'biologically.' All 'biology,' as is the case with every science, is merely an addendum to the determination of what in its essence has been brought into knowledge only through essentially thoughtful experience. We never experience what art and poetry really are through the historiography of art and literature. For when these disciplines make claims about artworks and speak about poetry, they must already know beforehand what art and poetry are: and if they do not know this, then they do not know what they are doing. [93] Therefore, they 'busy' themselves. Because, however, we are all always entangled in the web of contemporary conceptions of 'life,' it is very difficult for us to put our own opinion aside and think the inceptual of inceptual thinking like beginners, like 'inceptors': that is, it is very difficult for us simply to think, and to think simply.

What does the word ζῆν mean to the Greeks? How must we understand our word 'to live,' if we intend to use it as a faithful translation of the Greek ζῆν? ζῆν, ζάω—therein lies the root ζα. From this word-form, which is 'composed' from out of the consonant ζ and the vowel α, we can certainly not extract the 'essence of life.' We do not understand such word-forms at all if the word whose meaning is rooted in such roots does not speak to us. However, instead of immediately considering those words that grow directly from out of this root, it may be more instructive to attend beforehand to those word-forms in which the root itself, in its purity, comes forth.

Toward that particular end of illuminating the words ζάω and ζῆν, let us consider words such as ζάθεος and ζαμενής, words that the poets Homer and Pindar[7] used. Linguistics 'explains' that ζα here is an 'intensifier'; accordingly, ζάθεος means 'very godly,' 'very holy'. In a similar way, ζαμενής means 'very powerful' or 'very forceful,' μένος on its own meaning *power* or *might*. This linguistic explanation of ζα as an 'intensifying' morpheme is perfectly correct—yet, it is also untrue. Such an explanation thinks 'mechanistically' and not in a manner that attends to what is said: that is, it does not arise out of what is named through the 'intensifying' word ζα, nor from out of the context in which the poetic saying is compelled to speak in such a way. The words ζάπυρος ('very fiery') and ζατρεφής ('well-fed, distended, inflated,' which one finds in Homer)—words which, owing to ζα, signify 'intensifying'—abide in a uniformly essential domain, [94] the present pursuit of which would lead us too far astray. Pindar refers, for example, to localities, regions, mountains, and borders (e.g., the banks of a river) as ζάθεος, in order to indicate that in these places the gods—i.e., the appearing ones—often and properly are present and, as we say, 'show their faces.' These places are 'especially holy' because here the appearing ones give forth their appearance, and the localities and mountains emerge entirely within such appearing and are enveloped therein. ζαμενής—'very forceful'—is that which emerges in its pure form in the breaking-forth and commencing, such as, for example, a storm breaking into μένος (τό). μένος is that to which μένειν, understood as anticipation, corresponds: namely, the coming-up and coming-forward, the gushing-in and breaking-in (which is one way of coming-forth and appearing). It is as all of this that the word μένος first acquires its meaning of force, might, strength, and power: words which, while different, mean the same with regard to the approximate, but nonetheless determinate, realm of the incoming surge. μένος is said of the sun and of the storm, but also appears in the following phrase from Homer: ψυχή τε μένος τε. 'Soul' and 'power,' however, have long since been thought in terms of 'action' and 'dynamism,' and thus in a Roman and modern way, leaving the Greek sense thereby buried. When the root ζα is thought in terms of the merely dynamically intensifying 'very,' we have the same misunderstanding before us that inconspicuously and stubbornly persists precisely because it is 'correct.' That the earth revolves around the sun is perhaps—but *only* perhaps—correct: but is this correctness therefore already the true?

Thought in a Greek way, ζα means the pure emerging within the various ways of emerging and appearing, for example, in breaking-forth. It is not accidental that the root ζα is here associated with words that themselves mean peering into, looking into, and breaking into (as do the words θεός and μένος); likewise, ζα is associated with 'fire' and 'gleam,' 'growth' and 'storm.' ζάω and ζῆν mean nothing

---

[7] For the latter, see *Olympian Odes*, III, 22, and X, 45; *Isthmian Odes*, I, 32; *Pythian Odes*, V, 70; *Nemean Odes*, VII, 92; Fragment 90 (60), 4; Fragment 105 (7).

other than emerging into ..., i.e., self-unlocking and self-opening into the open. This fundamental meaning of ζῆν and ζωή [95] is such that poetic saying is prompted to elucidate the essence of what we translate as 'life' through beholding the light of the sun. Homer says simply: ζῆν καὶ ὁρᾶν φάος ἠελίοιο—to live, i.e., to see the light of the sun. For the Greeks, the early foundational words ζῷον and ζωή have nothing to do with zoology, not even with the biological in a broad sense; just as little does the early foundational word φύσις have to do with what is later called physics or the physical. What the Greek word ζῷον names lies so far from all modern understandings of animal life that the Greeks could even call the gods ζῷα. In its original signification, this name—which names precisely what emerges and is present in emergence—accords absolutely with the essence of the Greek gods, who are the ones who peer in and are, thus, the appearing ones. (The Greeks call even the statues of the gods ζῷα, i.e., those who have emerged on their own and have come to stand in the open.) When we say that the originary word ζῷον/ζωή lies remotely from all animal life, this does not mean that the Greeks lacked knowledge of 'animals.' Indeed, they bring them into an appropriate relation to the essence of the gods. However, animality is not thought by them 'zoologically,' vaguely, or in a Christian way as the mere lowly in distinction to the 'higher' (i.e., the human). Animality, thought in a Greek way, determines itself from out of the ζῷον, from what emerges and then rests properly in itself by not expressing itself. For example, we need only to take a few steps away from the vague and indeterminate modern conception of the bird in order to experience and recognize the bird as the Greeks did: namely, as the animal through whose swaying and hovering the free dimension of the open unfolds, and through whose singing the tidings the call and the enchantment unfold, so that its bird-essence whiles away and disperses in the open. To all of this also necessarily belong closure and the protecting of what is closed, for example, as in mourning. The bird, flying, singing, connects to and points to the open: it [96] is entangled in this. In Greek, σειρά means tether. The Sirens are, 'in Greek,' the captivating ones in a manifold sense of the word.

The essential connection between φύσις, ζωή, and 'light' manifests itself in the fact that the Greek word for 'light'—namely φῶς—has the same stem as φύσις and φάος. Also, even still we speak of the 'light of life,' though we certainly think neither 'life' nor 'light' from out of its proper Greek essence of φύσις (and, that means, from out of ἀλήθεια).

c) The 'violence' of the translation and the explicit consideration of negation

Heraclitus's word ἀείζωον says the same as his word τὸ μὴ δῦνόν ποτε. Nonetheless, if we now translate τὸ μὴ δῦνόν ποτε as "the perpetually emerging," our thinking does not faithfully follow that of the thinker. Moreover, we commit violence to his word, because we unilaterally modify the negating word into an affirming one, and thus eliminate the negation that belongs to the word. However, the fidelity we owe to the inceptual word demands that we leave it in its negating form, especially since, presumably, the negation in the inceptual word is something other than a mere form of linguistic expression. For example, for all thought and knowledge and experience, which word could be more essential than the word for 'truth'? For the Greeks, this word bears a negation within itself: ἀ-λήθεια—un-concealment, not-concealment.

However, insofar as we first call explicit attention to the negating moment and ourselves become attentive to it through our apparently reasonable (but in truth unfaithful) effort to invert the negating word into an affirming one, it is perhaps advisable to persevere in this attentiveness. For, when we do so, we see that this combination of words in truth contains yet a second negation. How so? Not only does τὸ μὴ δῦνόν ποτε contain [97] the particular word for 'not' (μή), but, indeed, submerging itself (δῦνόν) is already a negation, if indeed submergence, thought in a Greek way, is a departing and a vanishing, and thus is the not-emerging and no-longer-emerging and thereby what turns against emerging. Thus, the combination of words τὸ μὴ δῦνόν ποτε contains a double-negation. However, the double-negation yields, as if by itself, an emphatic affirmation such that, when considered correctly, it seems once again appropriate if we forthwith translate and substitute it with a positive expression. If we think the matter in this way, we reckon well with words and put forth the 'equation' that a double-negation is the same as an emphatic affirmative; in this case, we are dealing here with coin-counting rather than with the foundational words of saying as such. Certainly, in this all-together cheap and calculative procedure, we renounce properly contemplating what is said and named here in an essential thinking.

REVIEW

1) The μὴ δῦνόν ποτε of Heraclitus's, thought inceptually, and the ὄν of metaphysics

Within the saying of Heraclitus's that we prioritize before all others, thus considering it to be the first saying, there stands in first position the combination of words τὸ μὴ δῦνόν ποτε, "the never submerging, ever." This first word of the first saying names what, above all and before all else, inceptual thinking thinks, supposing, of course, that there is good reason that this saying shines as first through all the others.

The elucidation of this prioritized first word demands special care. First of all, the characteristics of the foundational word τὸ δῦνον should be clarified. The word is a participle. [98] Thoughtlessly, we use the word τὸ δῦνον to mean "the submerging thing," thinking the word in accordance with its nominal meaning. Indeed, our previous consideration, which in its essential features contained the elucidation of the guiding question of metaphysical thinking, revealed this: namely, that the thinkers understand τὸ ὄν (beings) in accordance with the way in which they think the being of beings, in the sense that they question beings on the basis of being. Being itself is unquestioned and taken for granted, for it is only in the light of being that beings can be asked about, and the question concerning what beings are can be answered.

However, the light itself remains unnoticed, just as one takes the day for granted and in its 'light' concerns oneself with the matters of the day. 'Everydayness' is a peculiar case;[8] one lives, as one says, 'one day at a time.' Metaphysics from Plato through Nietzsche, which questions beings within the light of being, lives 'one day at a time.' One must, however, also know that in the 'question concerning being' so understood, for which being itself remains what is foremost unquestionable and before all else unquestioned, it is not only the case that being remains unquestioned, but also that metaphysics as metaphysics can never even ask the question concerning being itself. At the moment when the question 'What is metaphysics?' is asked, it is already asked from out of an entirely different sphere of inquiry. As a result, the question 'What is metaphysics?' is taken as a genuine question, and not only as the form by which the perpetually unquestioned metaphysics expresses its shape, structure, schemata, and disciplines. The chatter circulating today regarding the 'question concerning being' is the sign of a boundless bewilderment. This organized confusion of thinking was once even called 'the revival of metaphysics.'

However, the current and dominant confusion of all concepts and ways of posing questions does not arise from a mere [99] shallowness of thinking: rather, the reason for the confusion conceals itself in an estrangement from being. When Nietzsche says that being is the last vapor of an evaporating reality, then he only pronounces, in his language and with the boldness of a metaphysical thinker, the final consequence of the truth that all metaphysics as such holds: namely, that being is the emptiest and most abstract concept, 'the most general.' It is still more honest to pass off being, taken as this conjectural abstraction of all abstractions, as a mere vapor, than it is to pretend that one is even asking 'the question concerning being' from within the estrangement from being.

---

[8] See *Being and Time* (GA 2).

For the sake of the consideration necessary here, only the following is of importance: namely, to recognize that the thinkers understand this foundational word in its verbal sense, and in such a way that the being, understood verbally (i.e., as being), is that in view of which the particular being, understood nominally, is questioned. The consideration necessary here depends upon the simple and ubiquitously operative experience—which is nonetheless quite rare—that what the inconspicuous words 'is' and 'being' name is neither a mere vapor nor merely 'the most general,' but rather 'is' that in whose light any being appears as such.

The reference to the way in which the participle ὄν is thought in metaphysics should provide us with a guide by means of which we might arrive at an understanding of the participle τὸ δῦνον.

If we understand τὸ δῦνον in a manner that corresponds to the metaphysical understanding of ὄν, then the former means the submerging thing in light of submerging. The submerging thing is hereby treated as some existing thing; were it not some existing thing, it could not submerge, i.e., it could not be deprived of the customary conception of being. Submergence, as a process of the deprivation of being in view of the still existing thing that submerges, is a way of being. Thus, when thought [100] in the manner of metaphysics, the submerging thing in its submerging (i.e., the δῦνον) falls under the highest genus and the most general concept of the being of beings. What applies to being thus also applies to submerging. 'Never submerging,' which after all means a persistent presence (i.e., οὐσία) is all the more so attributed to 'being.' Therefore, we must grasp δῦνον and τὸ μὴ δῦνόν ποτε in a manner that corresponds to the metaphysical view of ὄν.

This conclusion is legitimate only under the assumption that the thinking of Heraclitus and the inceptual thinkers is already or solely a metaphysical thinking that asks about the beingness of beings. One takes this assumption as so self-evident that one further takes the inceptual thinkers not for metaphysicians, but rather assigns to them the 'honor' that their metaphysics is still something primitive and unformed, but is nevertheless the preliminary stage of metaphysics (i.e., the preliminary stage of the philosophy of Plato and Aristotle, who for many centuries in the Occident, and still today, count as 'the' philosophers *par excellence*). This, however, is the question: is inceptual thinking metaphysics or preliminary to it, or does something entirely different occur [*ereignet*] within inceptual thinking? This question is certainly not meant 'historiographically': rather, the question pursues whether and how being itself inceptually clears into the open within the history of the Occident, and whether and how being, even now, gleams in a faint light, which some suppose to be a mere vapor. Above all else, the question asks only how things stand with being and where we stand with regard to it.

The question of whether or not the μὴ δῦνόν ποτε of Heraclitus's may be thought in the sense of the ὄν of metaphysics should not be used to bring about an academic controversy regarding how pre-Platonic philosophy is to be grasped in the most historiographically accurate way: rather, the question is meant to provoke us into thinking about whether being lights itself in what Heraclitus calls τὸ μὴ δῦνόν ποτε in such a way that we also stand in this light, even though it, as only an [101] evaporating vapor, obscures and darkens the horizon of human existence.

2) The inceptually unblemished meaning of φύσις as the 'pure emerging' and its essential nearness to ζωή. The essential nearness of 'life' and 'being' in ἀείζωον (fragment 30). Rejection of the metaphysical interpretations of the concept of life

Through the course of our preceding elucidation, we have translated the combination of words τὸ μὴ δῦνόν ποτε in various ways: first as "the not ever submerging thing"; then, we resorted to the purely verbal sense, "the not submerging, ever"; then, we contracted the two words between which δῦνον is set—μὴ and ποτέ—into the familiar Greek expression μήποτε, and translated it as "the never submerging"; finally, we gave this negative expression a positive twist and replaced "the never submerging" with "the perpetually emerging."

Through this process of rendering the Greek into German, we recognized the original meaning of the Greek word φύσις, which is the foundational word of inceptual thinking.

In order to think-after its inceptual meaning to the greatest possible extent, we must forestall a common prejudice: namely, the customary equating of φύσις with 'nature.' In the course of this equating it is of little importance how this latter concept (nature) is defined, whether it is taken in the sense of nature as opposed to Spirit, or whether 'nature' is meant in the broader sense of 'essence,' such as when one speaks of 'the nature of a matter.' Even when we consider that the Greeks had an essentially different 'view of nature' that cannot be compared with the contemporary one; even when, according to this incompatibility of an equating of φύσις and 'nature,' we determine φύσις otherwise, we nonetheless still remain [102] constantly caught in the prejudice that φύσις means for us so-called 'nature' (earth and heaven, sea and mountain, plant and animal), although now thought in a Greek sense. Moreover, this means that the human and the gods have also been thought, in a Greek sense, from out of this φύσις-concept and in accordance with it: that is, they have been thought 'naturally.'

This prejudice is just as fatal as the first. In truth, φύσις means the pure emerging in whose prevalence any appearing thing appears and thus 'is,' without specifying any particular being such as mountain, sea, or animal. However, even with this clarification we could now still easily succumb to an additional prejudice by thinking that φύσις is the pure emerging in whose openness and brightness everything appears. Mountain and sea, plant and animal, house and human, god and heaven are thus all things that appear, and do so in the manner in which we nowadays conceive such beings. We may make efforts to take φύσις in the appropriately Greek sense of the pure emerging: however, even when we do so, we treat it like a gigantic, all-encompassing container into which we stuff those things that we currently conceive of as beings. When we do this, we thereby fail to grasp what is decisive: for φύσις, as the perpetually emerging, is not an inert receptacle, a so-called 'container' in the manner that a lampshade spreads over the lamp in such a way that the lamp remains what it is whether the shade 'contains' and 'covers' it or not. The pure emerging prevails throughout the mountain and the sea, the trees and the birds: their being itself is determined through and as φύσις and is only experienced in that way. Neither mountain nor sea nor any being needs the 'container,' for each being, insofar as it is, 'is' in the manner of emerging.

If we consider the above-mentioned and intrinsically convoluted result of the prejudices that stand over against the inceptual meaning of φύσις; if we further consider that these prejudices are hardly recognized, let alone sufficiently thought through; if we even further consider that [103] our insight into the hitherto dominant prejudices that stand over against the inceptual meaning of φύσις is only the preparatory step for entering into the correspondent experience of φύειν itself; if we consider all of this, then we surely cannot expect that, even in light of the superior instruction regarding the matter that has just taken place, we will all henceforth refrain from translating φύσις superficially as 'nature,' but will instead say 'the pure emerging.' This empty substitution of words is almost worse than the stubborn retention of the customary interpretation: for when one now no longer translates φύσις with 'nature,' like common people do, one thereby believes oneself to be a superior human being. The same situation exists when, as has been the case for some time now, one no longer translates the Greek word ἀλήθεια with "truth," but rather with "unconcealment" and even "openness," and yet betrays in the very next sentence that one is indebted to a conception of the essence of truth that can be obtained from any textbook of modern epistemology, while in fact this conception of truth is and will forever remain untouched by the essence of ἀλήθεια.

However, the inconspicuous modification of the translation of the words φύσις and ἀλήθεια, when truly executed, is nothing other than a sign of the change of our fundamental stance toward being itself. The abiding within this alteration is something that may only be historically prepared in thinking, and neither forced nor contrived. Without this experienced relation to being, the modification of the meaning of the above-mentioned word dissolves into an unimportant historiographical reckoning of derivative concepts.

However, this suggestion may seem to imply that we must think through what is said in each case with an eye toward the modification and, above all, toward the awakening of being's relation to us. Being, however, is not 'something' that lies hidden in some supersensory place and in the heights of some vast soaring speculation. As the little word 'is' makes clear to us each time it appears, being 'is' the nearest of the near. [104] Yet, because the human being troubles himself first and foremost only with what comes next, he constantly avoids the nearest, particularly since he appears to know very little about the near and its essence.

The series of steps in which we elucidated the translation of τὸ μὴ δῦνόν ποτε finally yielded the equating of the expression "the never submerging" with "the perpetually emerging," or, in Greek, τὸ ἀεὶ φύον. Instead of this phrase, which is not found within Heraclitus's writings, we could say τὸ ἀείζωον, "the perpetually living," a word used by Heraclitus in fragment 30. Again we stand before a foundational word: ζωή, ζῆν ('living'). This word of Heraclitus's indicates the essential nearness of 'living' and 'being' already at the inception of the history of Occidental thinking, and throughout the course of that history taken as a single moment.

In the final stage of this history, Nietzsche has articulated the equivalence of 'being' and 'living,' and indeed in the sense that 'living' is experienced and grasped as "will to power." With this, the word 'being' loses its role as the foundational word of philosophy. 'Being' continues to designate 'constancy.' This is thought, in the mind of modern metaphysics, as 'certainty' and 'security.' But constant, certain security, and thus 'being,' is not the will to power itself; it is not 'living' itself, but rather only a condition living itself sets for itself. The will to power can only want what it alone wills and must want: namely, 'more power,' i.e., an increase in power in which the approached degree of power is secured from which and beyond which the next step is carried out. What is in each case secured (i.e., the particular being) and the actual security (i.e., being) remain, seen from within the perspective of the will to power, the perpetually and merely temporary, i.e., that which only 'is' in order to be overcome, and therefore what must necessarily evaporate in the blaze of the will to power. Certainly, however, the highest thinking of this metaphysics must itself remember being: [105] for if the will to power appears as the actuality of the actual and should remain determined as this, then the 'living' (i.e., the always becoming) must enter into the fundamental character of being; and even this 'becoming,' this will to power, must itself be willed as being. In fact, Nietzsche's thinking in the vicinity of the metaphysics of the will to power is radical enough to admit this extreme concession to being. At the beginning of a long note, which he characterizes as a 'recapitulation,' Nietzsche says the following: "*Imprinting* the character of being onto becoming—that is the *highest will to power*."[9] The note appears in a draft consisting of 97 folios and double-folios that derives from two

---

[9] Nietzsche, *Werke*, XVI, 101, *The Will to Power*, Aphorism 617.

bound notebooks which contain notes that span from 1882 to 1888, and thus from the decisive years in which the majority of the material regarding the metaphysics of the will to power unfolded. Judging from the manuscript, the notes in question hail from the years 1885/86, and thus from the two years during which the preparation for the planned magnum opus began. The highest will to power is to will becoming, but to arrest this becoming as being.[10]

We could now easily retrace the metaphysical interpretation 'of living' as will to power in our historical 'past' and show the manner in which 'living' was construed in the metaphysics of German Idealism, or the manner in which Leibniz decisively defined the essence of 'living' for modern metaphysics, or the manner in which the Renaissance, the Middle Ages, Augustine, Christianity, late antiquity, Hellenism, Aristotle, and Plato [106] each determined the essence of 'living.' We could open a gallery of 'intellectual history' featuring the concept of living, and everyone could then pick out, as if in a warehouse, what appeals to him and his 'life experiences.' A person could, by virtue of this magnificent presentation of intellectual history, decide—unreflectively and with a wink—upon the 'concept of living' as defined by Christianity. However, on the same day this person (who is, for example, a renowned researcher from Berlin) must fly on an airplane to Oslo for a lecture. Such a person finds the 'experience' wonderful, all the while utterly failing to notice and consider that this experience is the purist affirmation of the will to power, upon whose essence the possibility of an airplane and a trip in it depends. This person, owing to the perspective of their Christian experiences, would surely find Nietzsche's doctrine of the will to power horrid, even while flying merrily in the plane over the Norwegian fjords. Having arrived, this person perhaps presents a lecture against 'nihilism,' one rich in intellectual history, while also flying around in an airplane, using a car and a razorblade, and finding the will to power too dreadful to bear. How is such splendid hypocrisy possible? Because this person does not think of being for even a moment, either with his Christian standpoint or during his trip on the airplane, and is driven by this forgetfulness of being into the purest oblivion.

Likewise, the historiographical stroll through the history of the 'concept of living' would only be an optical illusion and in truth a flight away from the consideration of what 'is' and of what prevails in the 'is.'

Yet, are we ourselves not in the very same situation when we elucidate the meanings of ζωή and ζῆν, only that we in this case go back several hundred years further, where the determination of concepts becomes even less certain?

However, if we heed what was said in the preceding sessions, we soon see that the situation is not the same. What is at stake here is not a historiographical

---

[10] Cf. Descartes, who thinks in his meditations on metaphysics that *mansurum quid et firmum stabilire*: to make something enduring and solid. [In *Med.* I, paragraph I, literally: . . . *si quid aliquando firmum et mansurum cupiam in scientiis stabilire.*—Ed.]

reckoning of varying conceptual views [107] in various time periods carried out in such a way that we, in confronting this assortment of concepts and testimonials as if we were spectators and shoppers, had the choice to opt for some Romanticism, or for a Goethean classicism, or a culturally joyful Christianity, or for some other historiographically concocted and ersatz fabrication, with the help of which we could squint our eyes and save ourselves for an alleged 'transcendence.' We are within the forgetfulness of being, and in such a way that we are willed by the will to power as the actuality of the actual, whether we know it or not, and whether we find it dreadful or not. We are, insofar as we are historical, what is willed in the will to power. The will to power is not some deranged idea conceived by the insane Nietzsche. It is not the fiction of an eternally dissatisfied and arrogant human being. The will to power is the being of beings, which unfolds historically: and it is precisely because of that fact that it had to have been discovered by a thinker and had to be endured by someone suffering immeasurably, and can only have been found as what is suffered through. The will to power is neither an invention of Nietzsche's nor of the Germans, but is rather the being of beings upon whose ground the European nations (together with America) have existed over the past centuries, and upon which beings have been actualized. In knowing and reflecting upon this, one has already lost all 'time' and opportunity to move around historiographically within intellectual history and to take up, from the catalogue of the enumerated concepts of 'living,' those of Nietzsche's, and with a sanctimonious remark against this 'anti-Christian philosophy' pretend as though one were among the saved—or, indeed, the savior himself. We are not here practicing historiography with an appended moral application and mixed-in allusions from the current state of things: rather, we *question*, and in a questioning way also *know* that this questioning can only be a very preliminary knowledge, [108] and that this inquisitive knowledge must exist if the Germans (and only they) are to save the Occident in its history.

Let us ask: what is happening to us here? Let us ask: what does it mean that being in the form of the will, and finally in the form of the will to power, determines beings as a whole? Let us ask about being. If being, as the 'luminance' of unconditioned self-certainty of the will to power, even if only in its most veiled form and in its decaying deformity belongs to the ground of the essence of φύσις and its ground (i.e., belongs to ἀλήθεια), then within the question concerning being we also already ask about the inception and in advance of it (and not after the fact). We are, in this question, referred to the word of the inceptual thinkers that we might hear and reflect upon their foundational words.

ζῆν, ζάω grow from the root ζα. We reach this root through word formations such as ζάθεος, ζαμενής, ζάπυρος, and ζατρεφής. Everywhere the ζα correlates to what manifests like a god peering in, like a storm irrupting, like a fire emerging into its luminance, to what emerges and disperses like the well-nourished and thus appears as the unfurling. The ζα signifies the essential ground upon which the ever-varying arising, dispersing, and going-forth emerges. ζῆν means the emerging itself, the self-opening into the open.

τὸ ζῷον is not "the animal" nor "the living being" in any casually conceived or indeterminate sense. Rather, ζωή means the essence that emerges from out of itself and into emerging. τὸ ἀείζωον means "the perpetually emerging." It means the same as τὸ ἀείφυον, which we here equate with τὸ μὴ δῦνόν ποτε.

[109] § 5. Exposition of the essential connectedness of emerging and submerging. Fragment 123

If we consider all that has been said up to this point, we stand before a two-fold necessity. First, we must simply acknowledge that, in the combination of words τὸ μὴ δῦνόν ποτε, there lies a double-negation, provided that we take the saying as it speaks. However, this is the least important issue to which we must attend: namely, that what most essentially belongs to the saying is not harmed through a reinterpretation. Second, the transformation of the negative saying into a positive one certainly all but compels us to retain this positive meaning. For, through this transformation it appears that the "never submerging" means the "perpetually emerging": φύσις/ζωή. But these are the foundational words of inceptual thinking. They name straightaway what is, for the inceptual thinkers, the to-be-thought. This is why the writings of the inceptual thinkers all bear the same title: περὶ φύσεως—'On Emerging.' Thus, not only *can* we transform τὸ μὴ δῦνόν ποτε into "perpetually emerging"; rather, we *must* do so, if indeed this saying of Heraclitus's is to be ranked as first, and if it is thus to name what is above and before all else the to-be-thought: namely, φύσις.

Moreover, we think entirely within the spirit of Heraclitus when, instead of τὸ μὴ δῦνόν ποτε, we simply say φύσις—for Heraclitus himself used the word φύσις. Indeed, he uses this word in a saying whose content directly points to that essential connectedness that is named with μὴ δῦνόν ποτε, "the never submerging": namely, the not-going-away into concealment and, thereby, concealing in general.

[110] a) The 'contradiction' of emerging and submerging. The failure of logic and dialectic in the face of this 'contradiction'

What does Heraclitus say about φύσις? Even before we have thought through the first saying in its entirety, we already hear yet another saying. However, with the quotation of the following saying, and as was the case with the first saying, we abandon the typical ordering of the fragments, taking instead fragment 16 as the first and, from now on, fragment 123 as the second. The latter fragment reads:

φύσις κρύπτεσθαι φιλεῖ.

Emerging to self-concealing gives favor.

We are astonished to hear such a thing regarding φύσις. φύσις as "the perpetually emerging," as the "never submerging," is obviously the same as the "never going into concealment." The perpetually emerging is indeed what is purely concerned with emerging and only with this. The perpetually emerging constantly rejects submerging from itself: it is averse to entering into concealing. If the perpetually emerging, φύσις, at all turns away from something and indeed turns itself against it; if, further, the perpetually emerging in its very essence does not know one particular thing and is not permitted to know this thing, then surely this thing would be concealing and going-into-concealment. Yet, now Heraclius says: "emerging gives favor to self-concealing." Accordingly, emerging belongs in its very essence to self-concealing. How does this square with the essence of φύσις? Here, it seems, Heraclitus contradicts himself. Conventional understanding always 'feels' a deep satisfaction when it discovers that a thinker has contradicted himself. For example, one has hardly even 'read' (if you could even call it 'reading') [111] the first pages of Kant's *Critique of Pure Reason* before making the discovery that Kant 'in fact' contradicts himself.

(With this discovery of contradiction, one obtains the longed-for superiority over the thinker: one finds him 'illogical.' One 'finds much' in that fact: and, indeed, one is *only* preoccupied with such finding. In addition to this particular way of occupying oneself, there is yet another, whereby one keeps oneself busy finding things to be 'so and so.' One listens to concerts and one finds the violinist to be good, bad, or otherwise. Everywhere 'one finds'. One listens to a lecture and finds it to be too technical. One further finds that the speaker has a poor voice, and one finds more still. In addition to this way of occupying oneself, one seeks after further opportunities where one can find things to be 'so and so'; indeed, one finds that such bustling about is just 'life,' and naturally one finds it annoying when one is made aware of this activity of 'occupying oneself' and 'finding.' Or, what is even more fatal, one finds such awareness interesting and entertaining.)

Before we content ourselves only with finding that Heraclitus's word concerning φύσις entangles him in a contradiction, we would first like to actually consider this saying.

If φύσις, in its proper essence, belongs to self-concealing, then is it the case that emerging would thereby be in its very essence a self-concealing? Emerging—a submerging? For serious thinking, this is clearly a pure contradiction that cannot be evaded through quibbling, sophisticated subtlety, or deceptive maneuvering. To say that emerging is submerging is like saying that day is night and vice versa, and sounds just like the statement 'light is dark.'

However, keep in mind that during a previous session concerning the elucidation of Heraclitus's nickname ὁ Σκοτεινός, we already pointed to the fact that in the sayings of Heraclitus's we come across strange sentences that assert something contradictory. We also heard that, in [112] contemporary metaphysics, 'dialectical' thinking does not only treat such contradictions as a nuisance and eradicate them, but actually holds the self-contradictory as the 'true.' We also heard that today one attempts to interpret Heraclitus's thinking 'dialectically' according to the model of Hegelian thinking. Seen in the light of dialectic, which thinks the unity of the self-contradictory and sublates the contradiction as contradiction, Heraclitus's saying φύσις κρύπτεσθαι φιλεῖ—which, however, Hegel did not yet understand—is no longer strange.

However, it was already pointed out that Hegel's doctrine of 'contradiction' and 'dialectic' is grounded upon foundations that belong specifically to contemporary thinking and are foreign to the inceptual thinking of the Greeks. Thus, the lazy wisdom that proclaims that one must 'obviously' understand the aforementioned saying of Heraclitus's (and everything similar) 'dialectically' is of no help to us. This escape into dialectic is easy and has the advantage of appearing profound: however, it remains, when viewed with respect to Heraclitus, merely an escape, a flight, and a cowardice of thinking—that is, it remains an evasion of the being that clears itself here.

When faced with fragment 123, we think much more seriously (than do the acrobats walking on the rope of self-strangling dialectic) when we initially 'find' a 'contradiction' within it. It is another question entirely whether we should be allowed simply to halt in the face of what we have initially found to be a 'contradiction.'

To say that emerging, and what essentially unfolds in emerging, 'loves' and 'is' submerging is, when taken straightforwardly, a 'blatant' contradiction that screams and shouts at us from out of the saying. We must certainly ask at once: who are *we* who are being shouted at by this contradiction? 'We'—here that means human beings who are not encumbered with an erudite understanding [113] of Hegelian philosophy and the 'ways' of dialectic. We are human beings who think 'normally,' who take white for white and black for black, who think emerging as emerging and submerging as submerging and not as all mish-mashed together, and who, unlike others, also lack any ambition to avert their gaze quickly from the bald-faced contradiction and merely to parrot that it is emerging *and* submerging, just because they have heard it is fashionable to think dialectically. To think 'normally' means: to think according to the norm of all thinking. This norm is, however, the axiom and the principle that holds for all thinking and, according to Kant, "for all cognition in general." This principle is the *principium contradictionis*, the principle of contradiction, which Kant formulates in the following way: "To no thing belongs a predicate that contradicts it."[1] To apply this to the 'present case': to emerging, the predicate 'submerging' cannot belong, owing to the fact that the latter directly contradicts the former. φύσις ('emerging') and κρύπτεσθαι ('self-concealing,' 'submerging') contradict one another. If they are at all able to be brought into a relationship, then it cannot be one of φιλεῖν, of love, but rather can only be one of 'hatred'. Whoever thinks against this principle violates the law that establishes the doctrine of thinking.

Ever since Plato—that is, ever since metaphysics—appeared, so too did that determination of the essence of thinking that one calls 'logic.' It was not just the name "logic" (ἐπιστήμη λογική), but also the matter designated by it, that arose in the 'school' of Plato, a matter that was then advanced in an essential way by that great student of Plato's, Aristotle. 'Logic' is an offspring of metaphysics—perhaps one could even say a misbirth. If it were the case that metaphysics itself were a mishap of essential thinking, then 'logic' would indeed [114] be the misbirth of a misbirth. In this lineage, the strange consequences and implications to which logic has led and has brought itself perhaps hide. But, with what right do we speak here so 'contemptuously' of 'logic'? Even if the preceding statements about 'misbirth' and 'mishap' judged and evaluated the misfortune in an essentially historical (and not merely historiographical) sense—one that has the appearance here of being derogatory—it cannot be overlooked that, despite this purported misfortune 'of logic,' we everywhere are bound to 'the logical.' Thus, the thinkers—Heraclitus no less than Plato, Aristotle no less than Leibniz, Kant no less than Hegel, Schelling no less than Nietzsche—cannot escape the bondage of 'the logical.' Moreover, one tends even today to invoke the following as the ultimate arbiter about a matter: namely, that it is 'entirely logical,' whereupon one eliminates every contradiction.

And yet, what does one mean when one says that 'something is logical,' an expression that one hears more and more frequently? 'Logical' can here mean: correctly inferred from premises. 'Logical' can also mean: 'reasonable,' and therefore thought in a manner that corresponds to, and follows upon, fundamental principles.

When we in this way make use of the oft-invoked 'logical,' we make use of a bindingness that consists merely of *consistency*. However, many and various things can be consistent. The merely consistent (i.e., 'the logical' strictly considered) entails no bindingness, and lacks in any case the distinctiveness and weight of the

---

[1] Kant, *Werke*, III, 149.

true. What is 'logical' need not be true. The manic errancy of history can be arranged 'logically'. The endlessly invoked 'logical' is never able to give or establish the true. A criminal also thinks logically—indeed, perhaps even more 'logically' than some honest men. We should guard against [115] taking the 'logical' that results in wrongdoing as the true only because it, as one thoughtlessly says, is 'logical'. The invocation of the 'logical' as the authority of the binding is always the sign of thoughtless thinking. It is the 'uneducated' human being in particular who exhibits a special fondness for the use of the expression 'logical'. The 'uneducated' human being is the one unable to get a grasp of the matter under discussion, and who is ignorant of how a relation to things looks and how this relation must always be won anew, and can only be won through the articulation of the matter from out of that matter itself. The popular expression 'that is logical' is, for the most part, characteristic of an ignorance of things. To think 'logically', to comply with 'the logical', does not yet entail a guaranteeing of the true. Additionally, the 'illogical' can also harbor the true. 'The logical' may be in accordance with the standard of thinking: however, this standard, which is thus also the common and the conventional, can never rise up to the authority of the true.

The statement 'the light is the dark,' when viewed with respect to the tin-god whose name is 'the logical,' means the same as 'A is the opposite of A,' which is clearly 'illogical'. The statement 'the emerging is the submerging' is similarly 'illogical'. Were 'the logical' also already the true, and 'the illogical' already 'the false,' then normal understanding would have to judge Heraclitus's saying regarding φύσις to be false.

However, the 'normal' thinking of the understanding that thinks 'logically' is able to decide nothing regarding Heraclitus's saying, owing to the fact that, precisely by and through its appeal to the authority of the logical, it precludes the possibility of a decision, for such thinking renounces in advance the bringing of what is said in the saying into essential view. The decision of conventional thinking concerning the saying of the thinker is in essence more reckless than a judgment made about color by one who is colorblind. Conventional [116] thinking, in its initial grasp of Heraclitus's saying, focuses only on the apparent fact that emerging is just emerging, and self-concealing is just self-concealing (i.e., 'submerging' thought in a Greek sense). The singular focus of conventional thinking finds that emerging itself by itself, insofar as it is emerging, does not tolerate submerging: the two are incompatible with one another. Against this obvious incompatibility, the saying of Heraclitus's says that emerging indeed tolerates self-concealing, and in such a way that it gives its favor to it. Accordingly, emerging, precisely insofar as it is an emerging, is a submerging. For conventional thinking, the understanding comes to a standstill in the face of this saying. We all—those of us here who come from conventional thinking—must first actually reach that place where our understanding stands still: only then, when this everywhere bustling and at the same time 'normal' understanding (which jostles about with the phrases 'logical' and 'illogical') comes to a standstill, can the other, essential thinking perhaps come to pass in such a way that the understanding that is standing still, with all of its vindictive and vainglorious presumptuousness, no longer interferes with it.

We would certainly be going directly against the way of thinking of this lecture, and more generally against every attempt toward an essential thinking, if only on the basis of what was heard in earlier sessions we now thought ourselves to be above conventional thinking, which continues to retain its undiminished law within its sphere. It was said previously that essential thinking thinks, for example, the light as the dark and the dark as the light. That is a thinking which, in the era of the absolute metaphysics of German Idealism, developed the form of a 'dialectic.' With a little effort and practice it is not all that hard to acquire the 'flair' of this dialectic; and with the implementation of this 'flair,' all windows can be opened. Yet, it nonetheless remains questionable [117] whether this mere cleverness is able also to look through the opened windows into the rooms that are wandered through by the dialectical speculative thinking of Schelling and Hegel. It also remains questionable whether the person who possesses solely this flair is actually able to see and to hear.

Phrased otherwise: it is far better for us if we do not know the flair of dialectics, and that we, in our initial attempt to ponder the saying of Heraclitus's, only make it so far that our understanding truly stands still.

b) The standing-still of conventional thinking in the face of the 'irreconcilable,' and the leap into essential thinking. Philological translations as flight in the face of the claim of the saying

When our thinking imagines and juxtaposes 'the emerging' and 'the submerging,' and then finds itself in a situation where it is supposed to understand these juxtaposed terms not (simply) as differing, but also as the same, it seizes up: for obviously emerging is not submerging. If this were not the case, then why do they have different names? The one is not the other; they do not tolerate each other. However, if we take Heraclitus's saying in its most obvious sense—"emerging loves submerging"—then conventional understanding can still find something understandable here with which it can calm itself: we do not need to let it go so far as our understanding having to come to a standstill, because something previously understandable has ceased to be so. Let us ponder, however, what the saying says: "emerging loves submerging"; emerging inclines itself toward submerging and thus merges into it. We observe the workings of such a merging constantly and for the most part annually in 'nature.' What in the spring sprouts and blooms ripens into fruit and then disappears. Thus, the fact that some emerging thing emerges but nevertheless [118] drifts toward its contrary submergence, indeed seeking it out, is not after all as strange as it may initially appear.

However, in the way that we are translating the saying, it says something different: emerging gives favor to submerging. This does not mean that some emerging thing subsequently falls prey to submergence or drifts over to it: rather, it means that emerging is in itself already submerging.

It is easy to imagine a situation wherein, subsequent to an emerging, a submerging follows, and in such a way that 'the emerging' meanwhile disappears. In such a scenario, there remains nothing to which submerging is contradictory and nothing with which it would be incompatible, once emerging has drifted into submergence. However, according to Heraclitus's saying, submerging should not just come to replace emerging: rather, emerging should in itself be a submerging, and should indeed actually 'bestow favor' to this. Thus, what is to be thought here commands our imagination to halt.

(Here our understanding must come to a standstill; it stands before something irreconcilable. However, when the understanding represents to itself in each case some represented thing 'as' this and that—for example, a house as the possibility of lodging—it binds, through such representation, the one with the other: it binds, in this example, the house and the possibility of lodging, and finds the two to be entirely reconcilable with each other. By contrast, emerging and submerging are irreconcilable, supposing both are simultaneous and not merely successively supplanting one other. In the face of this irreconcilability, understanding can no longer reconcile or combine: it must relinquish its characteristic procedure of reconciling by means of representation and instead stand still.

However, this standing still must only be the initial preparation for beginning to think the saying in the manner of the thinker. Of course, this demand is only legitimate if we let the saying come up to meet us as a saying of a thinker. [119] That the saying is such a saying is something that we, strictly speaking, arbitrarily presuppose. The merely historiographical fact that Heraclitus has been taken as a thinker since antiquity is in and of itself no proof that he is indeed one. That is something 'proven' to us only through the process of first learning to understand, and then actually understanding, his sayings as those of a thinker. However, as is now obvious, such an understanding is only possible if we, in our attempt at offering guidelines and elucidations, presuppose that Heraclitus is a thinker and that his sayings must be thought in the manner of essential thinking. Thus, we spin around in a circle: we presuppose the saying to be a saying of the thinker and demonstrate on this basis that the saying, thought essentially, says something other than what conventional thinking supposes. When we demonstrate by such methods that the presupposition is valid, we are only able to do so as a result of the fact that we make use of the presupposition for the demonstration itself. This procedure is entirely 'illogical.' Certainly; and conventional understanding indeed makes this determination. It seems as though we cannot escape its desire to brand as 'illogical' whatever is not agreeable to it. Indeed, we never and nowhere escape the covert obtrusiveness of conventional understanding in its many guises. However, if we nonetheless succeed someday to think essentially rather than merely conventionally, and thereby to reside within the vicinity of a thinker, then we shall do so only through a leap, and not by climbing higher up a ladder rung by rung, as it were, from the supposed lowlands of conventional understanding, and then suddenly by means of certain, higher rungs, ascending this ladder into the 'higher region' of philosophy.

The previously mentioned circle (*circulus*) in which our procedure of elucidating the saying necessarily moves is already a sign of the fact that the domain of essential thinking is essentially other than that of conventional thinking, [120] which is why there is not a continuous passage from one over to the other. The domains of conventional and essential thinking lie as two distinct worlds, separated by a chasm, either next to each other or one atop the other. Or so it seems. This perspective is adopted above all by philosophy itself, and especially by philosophy in the form in which it has presented itself for more than two thousand years (namely, metaphysics). At the present moment, we cannot offer extensive comments 'concerning' the relationship between conventional and essential thinking. We must, however, become attentive to one thing in particular: that in all cases, and necessarily, essential thinking enters ever anew into the strange illumination that conventional thinking unceasingly spreads around itself, and that this repeatedly and almost unexpectedly leads us to grasp the words of the thinker in a 'much simpler' and more plausible way, without the unnecessarily numerous considerations and provisos that we are now bringing forth through our elucidation of Heraclitus's saying. In terms of the present case, why in the world do we speak here of emerging and submerging, of reconcilability and irreconcilability, and of the relation of conventional and essential thinking? Why these remarks concerning 'the logical' and 'dialectic'? These long-winded expositions have not the slightest to do with the fragment in which Heraclitus speaks of φύσις. Why do we not just accept the standard view? Why do we not just grasp the saying in the way that philological research—which, after all, has mastered the Greek language—translates it? Philosophical speculation can go in whatever directions it wants with its interpretations, but it must first nevertheless stay true to the text and what it is saying.

If we translate entirely 'conventionally' and adhere to the 'sober' and 'exact' philological translations, then the saying immediately becomes clear. The grand edition of [121] the fragments put forth by Diels-Kranz translates fragment 123—φύσις κρύπτεσθαι φιλεῖ—in the following way: "Nature (essence) loves to conceal itself." In his special edition of Heraclitus's fragments, Snell translates as follows: "The essence of things likes to hide itself." Another, somewhat more grandiose translation from an author who clearly has heard through hearsay something about the 'question of being,' reads: "The essence of being loves to conceal itself."

Throughout these translations, φύσις is taken generally as 'nature,' and indeed in the sense that we speak of the 'nature' of a matter, and thereby mean its essence. Every being has its 'essence,' its 'nature.' Now, it is well known that the essence of things, their nature, is not always easy to discover. This difficulty may in part be owed to the inability and limitations of human cognition: however, it is owed in greater part to the fact that the essence of things, φύσις, 'likes to hide,' so that the human being must struggle to retrieve the essences of things from their hiding place. "The essence of things likes to hide itself." So Heraclius has already said. Should we attribute such a platitude to the thinker? If we do this, which is effectively what happens through the above-mentioned translations, then we subsequently 'have' a saying that conventional thinking could also say. Well, why should we not expect a thinker to at least once utter a statement that abides in the lowlands of conventional thinking? Must everything he says always be spoken from on high?

Did Heraclitus say, "The essence of things likes to hide itself"? Let us set aside the question of whether or not we should impose upon Heraclitus's saying such a platitudinous interpretation. Let us ask only this: in terms of the content, could Heraclitus have said anything of the sort? No. For the meaning of φύσις that is now supposed in the translation—namely, φύσις = nature = essence, [122] and this latter in the sense of *essentia* = οὐσία—is only operative in Greek thinking beginning with Plato.

φύσις κρύπτεσθαι φιλεῖ, translated absolutely literally, means: nature likes to hide itself. This, at least, everybody can understand. Why, then, always engage in these insulting methods, matters, and expressions that nobody understands? Indeed, why engage in such insulting things, ladies and gentlemen, when everything is just fine and dandy and has been for decades and even longer? How is everything fine? In that we simply demand that what is said must at all costs be such that 'we' understand it straightaway. In the face of all of this, I ask: where, really, is the insult? Does it consist in the fact that it is expected of us to take the essential seriously, or rather in the fact that we demand that everything should be familiar to us as we find ourselves off the beaten path before the saying of the thinker? 'We'—who are we, anyway? How does it come about that 'we' have taken control of history, and even the inception of the essential fate of our history? How does it come about that we make use of this history only as though it is ours? Is it because we are the latecomers who, precisely because of coming late, can look back historiographically at everything and claim that the history is *ours*, that we have it at our command, and place in it our claims regarding what is allowed to be intelligible and what 'we' hold as unintelligible? I ask again: where is the insult? Does one not see here the insult that lies at the core of the arrogance of the historiographical outlook? Does one not see here the destruction and 'nihilism' that lie in the ever-so-reasonable demand to speak about things 'as simply as possible' so that everyone understands them, as though what is essential for the human must simply 'be' 'present' for him, and not the other way around? We do not measure up, in a historical way, to the demand that history places upon on us simply by filling our calendar with numerous commemorations, [123] only to forget all 'commemorating' the following week because we then have to race out to see the latest film. The flight in the face of this demand is not an invention of the present: it begins rather with Christianity, and only changes its form with the emergence of the present. The planet is in flames. The essence of the human being is out of joint. A mindful consideration that is sufficiently world-historical can only come from the Germans, provided that they find and safeguard 'the Germanic.' This is not arrogance, but rather the knowledge of the necessity of bearing out an inceptual poverty. We must learn to let our thinking span from the most ephemeral flickering of the fleeting day—the pedestrian, the 'is'—all the way into this poverty so that it may experience a single fate in its entirety.

Previously, when we pointed out that in the saying it is said that emerging is in and of itself a submerging, conventional understanding was brought to a standstill. Now that we are presented with the saying draped in the clothes of conventional understandability, perhaps it is the understanding of those who have already attempted to think essentially and to persevere in the vicinity of the inceptual thinkers that must stand still.

Thus, for all of us, the understanding stands still. Let us allow it to stand still as we leave hasty thinking aside, instead opening our eyes and ears as we prepare ourselves simply to hear the word. We will no longer assail the saying with our haphazard thinking, and will instead allow the saying to speak the following word to us:

φύσις κρύπτεσθαι φιλεῖ.

Emerging to self-concealing gives favor.)

[124] REVIEW

On the essential relationship of emerging and submerging. Rejection of logical (dialectical) interpretations

If we repeat it according to its faithful translation, the word configuration τὸ μὴ δῦνόν ποτε says: "the not ever submerging." This combination of words contains a two-fold negation: 1) the explicitly articulated μή ('not ever'); 2) the negation that lies within δῦνον itself, insofar as 'submerging,' thought in a Greek way, means entering into concealing, departing into concealment, ab-sence, non-presence. When we take this combination of words, which is thoroughly permeated by negation, and not only translate it faithfully, but also try to think faithfully what is said in it, then something confronts us whose fundamental structure consists in a two-fold 'not,' and in such a way that its condition is of a thoroughly negating sort. At the same time, however, it becomes clear that the combination of words τὸ μὴ δῦνόν ποτε names the same 'in terms of content' as the foundational words of inceptual thinking: φύσις, ζωή—"the perpetually emerging." When we meditate upon this—and thus upon φύσις—we do not come upon a negating essence determined by the 'not.' Therefore, we stand in front of a double necessity: on the one hand, we must faithfully think-after the negating foundational word, and on the other, we must think precisely this foundational word without negation as 'the perpetually emerging,' i.e., as φύσις.

And yet—is it the case that what Heraclitus names φύσις is without negation? We have indeed maintained this so far, on the basis of a rough elucidation of what the word names. When we do this, however, we maintain something about φύσις without hearing what Heraclitus himself expressly says about it. So long as we do not consider this, we are not authorized to decide whether φύσις and ζωή stand as words without negation while τὸ μὴ δῦνόν ποτε stands [125] full of negation, nor whether each term vitiates the other, nor whether they all name the same and, if so, how this is possible, since within the concept of φύσις no negation is thought.

Before we consider fragment 16 (which we here place as the first fragment) in its entirety—that is, before we simply ask the question posed therein—we will listen to that fragment that is conventionally ordered as fragment 123, but which we here rank as second. It reads:

φύσις κρύπτεσθαι φιλεῖ.

Emerging to self-concealing gives favor.

Even on a cursory hearing it is immediately clear that φύσις (i.e., emerging) stands in an essential relation to 'self-concealing' (i.e., to 'submerging'), thought in a Greek sense as entering into concealing. Thus, Heraclitus thinks in φύσις something 'negative' after all, and he presumably thinks this because he *must* think it, and he must think φύσις thusly because it shows itself to him in such a way. To the superficial view, however, what immediately jumps out is the way in which the saying seems to assert something about φύσις, about emerging, that contradicts it: namely, submerging. If we want now to think what the saying of the thinker says, we must first deny two different positions that stand before us that are seemingly equally compelling. We should avoid hastily arming ourselves with 'logic,' 'the logical,' and the law of metaphysically construed thinking—namely, the principle of contradiction—in order to declare that the saying of Heraclitus's contains a contradiction, that it is illogical and thus 'untrue.' The logical is neither an authority nor a source of the true and the truth. If, in light of the saying of the thinker and on the basis of the preceding observation, we dismiss 'logic' and conventional thinking, but still nevertheless must consider what is said in the saying, a solution is immediately provided for us—namely, that we throw ourselves headfirst into 'dialectic,' which we know (at least from hearsay) [126] not only does not eliminate 'the contradiction' and 'the illogical,' but indeed recognizes in the contradiction the 'true.' In the absolute metaphysics of German Idealism, after Kant had already made the significance of contradiction visible in his 'Doctrine of the Antinomies,' contradiction is not taken as something to be avoided in thinking, but rather as what thinking preserves so that the contradiction may be overcome and dissolved within a higher unity. As Hegel writes: "The dissolved contradiction is thus the ground, the essence as unity of positive and negative";[2] "*Speculative thinking* exists solely in the fact that thinking retains the contradiction and thereby itself therein, but does not let itself, as is commonly thought, be governed by it nor allow its determinations to be steered toward yet other contradictions or dissolved into nothing."[3] Hegel also writes, in his *Lectures on Aesthetics*:

> Whosoever claims that nothing exists that bears within itself a contradiction as an identity of opposites must also maintain that nothing living exists. For the power of life and, even more so, the might of the Spirit consists in just this: in positing contradiction in itself, enduring it, and overcoming it. This positing and dissolving of contradiction between the ideal unity and the real separation of the elements constitutes the unceasing process of life, and life exists only as *process*.[4]

(It was from out of this metaphysics of contradiction that Kierkegaard formulated his doctrine of paradox, thereby demonstrating himself to be the most extreme of all Hegelians.)

Whether we overzealously and rashly drag the saying of Heraclitus's before the tribunal of the so-called logical, or whether we indiscriminately attack the saying of the inceptual thinkers with the method of a later metaphysics, in each case we miss what is the primary and simple necessity for us: namely, that we attempt to think the saying in what it says, [127] and truly carry out this attempt of thinking in such a way as to thereby exert our understanding.

---

[2] Hegel, *Werke*, IV, 540.
[3] Ibid., IV, 547/8.
[4] Ibid., XII, 171/2.

We attempt here to think emerging as what stands in an essential relation to submerging and *thus* is, in its essence (as emerging), somehow also a submerging. We attempt to think this—and our understanding stands still. We must first of all reach that place where our understanding—that is, conventional thinking—stands still and sets itself on a different course.

§ 6. Emerging and submerging. Favor (φιλία) as the reciprocal bestowing of its essence. Notes on fragments 35 and 32

a) Emerging (φύσις), favor (φιλία), and self-concealing (κρύπτεσθαι)

Of φύσις, Heraclitus says: φιλεῖ. Translated literally, this means: φύσις 'loves.' We could take this word φιλεῖν in a variety of ways: however, we must be careful not to let our initial inclinations lead our thinking here.

φύσις 'loves to,' it 'likes to.' So understood, one could translate the saying as "the essence of things likes to conceal itself," which reads nearly the same as the phrases 'children like to snack,' or, 'the grandmother likes to sit near the stove.' The essence of things—φύσις—"likes to hide itself." Even if it is philologically precise, we must leave aside this profusely quaint presentation of φύσις. Why, then, do we bother even mentioning it? Only because this way of translating shows merely the final offshoots of the very widely held view regarding the inception of Occidental thinking: namely, that one must understand it to be the unrefined preliminary stage of metaphysics. The inevitable consequences of this view reveal [128] themselves in the above translations. Therefore, we are not 'criticizing' the translators here, but are rather only considering our position, i.e., the position of the Occident with regard to its historical inception.

φύσις κρύπτεσθαι φιλεῖ. At first we are constrained to the interpretation that sees φιλεῖ being said of φύσις: φύσις ... φιλεῖ. The word φύσις names what is, for the thinkers, the to-be-thought. Such essential thinking had already obtained a designation among the Greeks, a designation in which the word φιλεῖν is also heard: "philosophy"—i.e., φιλία τοῦ σοφοῦ. We translated this in the first session as: friendship for the to-be-thought. In fragment 35 of Heraclitus's, there is talk of the φιλόσοφοι ἄνδρες, that is, of the men who subsist on the φιλία for τὸ σοφόν. σοφόν, σαφές, originally means the bright, the manifest, the light. τὸ σοφὸν μοῦνον—that which is in the strict sense solely and uniquely the light— is ἕν, i.e., the One. In fragment 32, Heraclitus says the following about the One: ἓν τὸ σοφὸν μοῦνον λέγεσθαι οὐκ ἐθέλει καὶ ἐθέλει Ζηνὸς ὄνομα—"The One, alone to be thought, does not let itself and lets itself be called by the name 'Zeus' (i.e., The Lightning)." When we translate τὸ σοφόν with "the to-be-thought," it is merely a very preliminary translation that only receives its content and ground when the to-be-thought is determined. We now translate the φιλεῖν in Heraclitus's saying as "to give favor." In doing so, we understand favor in the sense of the originary granting and bestowal, and therefore not in the secondary meaning of 'benefit' and 'patronage.' This originary granting is the bestowing of what is owed to the other because it belongs to the other's essence, insofar as it bears that essence. Accordingly, friendship, φιλία, is the favor that grants to the other the essence that the other already has, and in such a way that through this granting the granted essence blossoms into its proper freedom. In 'friendship,' the essence that is reciprocally granted is freed to itself. Neither excessive solicitude nor even 'jumping in' to help in emergencies and dangerous situations is the defining characteristic of [129] friendship: rather, it consists in being-there for another, which does not require any kind of event or proof, and which works by abstaining from exerting influence.

It would be a mistake to believe that such bestowal of essence comes about all by itself, as though 'being-there' were here nothing other than something present-to-hand. The bestowing of essence requires knowledge and patience, and granting is the ability to wait until the other finds itself in the unfolding of its essence and for its part does not make a big fuss about this discovery of essence. φιλία is the granting of that favor that gives what strictly speaking it does not possess, while also guaranteeing that the other essence can remain as its own.

Friendship so understood, which reaches its apogee in the form of friendship for the to-be-thought (and receives its essential determination from there), is, to mention this only in passing, the concealed essential ground of all "upbringing." Without 'philosophy' in the correctly understood sense, a historical people catches no glimpse of the essential, i.e., of the simplicity of all that is. Without this essential glimpse there can be no ability to stand in relation to the simple, i.e., to what prevails from out of itself. Without this relation there can never be the grounding relationship in which all upbringing rests, for upbringing merely awakens the attraction toward, and the state of being-drawn-toward, the essential. Without the concealed, prevailing essence of upbringing, all instruction and every schooling, all discipline and every training, go without this proper and nourishing foundation. What they bring forth instead is a training that caves in on its own vacuity just as it becomes serious. But the upbringing itself and its essential ground—namely, philosophy as the friendship for the to-be-thought—for their part establish themselves upon the fact that the to-be-thought, which from ancient times has been called 'being,' is in itself pervaded by a favor and a granting. So says, in any case, Heraclitus's saying: φύσις κρύπτεσθαι φιλεῖ.

[130] (There is nothing to dispute here. Also, we should not here suppose what might easily occur to someone: namely, that Heraclitus superimposes 'personal' and altogether human 'lived experiences' onto φύσις—as if it were clear what 'lived-experiences' are, and as if it were not in fact the case that these 'lived-experiences' themselves receive their origin from out of the essence of life, and thus from out of ζωή, and therefore from out of φύσις.)

However, whatever we understand φύσις to be, the saying φύσις κρύπτεσθαι φιλεῖ makes it sound as though, with φιλεῖ, a human attitude is being attributed to nature, and that thereby something that is in itself objective is 'felt' to be something subjective. With this very widely held argument we act as though it were the case that everything that has the manner of favor and bestowal were the special right and property of the 'subject,' and as if the determination of the human into a 'subject' were the most obvious thing in the world, when in fact such a determination is scarcely three hundred years old (though certainly during this time, as an incomprehensible frenzy of history, this determination has taken the essence of the human into its will). Only since that time when the human became a 'subject' has 'psychology' existed; and the prerequisite for the formation of the passion for psychology is Christianity. There is no 'psychology' in the ancient Greek world. Aristotle's treatise περὶ ψυχῆς has nothing to do with 'psychology.' In its consummation, metaphysics becomes the metaphysics of 'psychology': psychology and anthropology are the final word of metaphysics. Psychology and technology belong together like right and left.

That is why to us living today, even the possibility of the following thought is entirely strange, let alone the thought itself: namely, the thought that what we straightaway claim as 'our experiences' could in their essence perhaps not belong to us. Within our sphere of thinking, we have no place for the possibility that the so-called 'subjective' along with the corresponding 'objective' (and the relationship between them) [131] might not be principal and originary, but rather might be an especially question-worthy 'issue' and consequence of a more inceptual essential comportment.

The view that Heraclitus 'anthropomorphized' the world in a naïve-primitive way of thinking when he attributed φιλεῖν to φύσις—a view that is not even simple-minded, but just merely stupid—will certainly one day collapse under the weight of its own helplessness: for, within the assertion that the saying of Heraclitus's carries out an anthropomorphizing of 'nature,' there lies buried the arrogant pretense to possess an authoritative assessment regarding both the world itself and, above all, the human. Instead of insisting upon our subjectivity and the metaphysics of unconditional intellectual presumptuousness, it is necessary first to take the word spoken by Heraclitus seriously. It says:

φύσις κρύπτεσθαι φιλεῖ.

Emerging to self-concealing gives favor.

The favor of emerging belongs to self-concealing. κρύπτεσθαι—to conceal itself—is, in relation to emerging, the self-occluding. In this sense, we seek to think κρύπτεσθαι first, though not in a complete way. Emerging grants to self-occluding that it be, because self-concealing itself, from out of its 'essence,' allots to emerging what it is.

b) φιλία (favor, bestowal) as the reciprocal essential relation of emerging and submerging (self-concealing). φύσις as the simple essence of the favor (φιλία) of the concealing emergence

(One grants itself to the other and thus allots to the other the freedom of its own essence, which rests in nothing other than this granting that thoroughly prevails in concealing and revealing in which the essence and prevailing of unconcealment freely commences. This free commencement is the inception itself: the inception 'of' beyng as beyng.

[132] And yet, with these last sentences too much has already, but unavoidably, been said: 'too much' in the sense that the simpler the to-be-said is, the more the proper elucidation of it lags behind the to-be-thought. The above sentences had to anticipate what we could perhaps one day experience in our understanding of the saying of φύσις, so that we may, given such experience, direct our thinking toward the unforgettable.

Before this, however, we must first attempt to gain insight into the reciprocal essential relation that is here called by the name φιλία/φιλεῖν—favor. Emerging grants to self-concealing that the latter might unfold in the proper essence of emerging; self-concealing unfolds, however, by allotting to emerging that emerging may 'be' emerging. In φύσις, favor prevails: not any old favor and privileging, but rather favor in the sense of the granting that grants nothing other than the allotting, the bestowing, and keeping safe of that which unfolds as emerging.

If for the modern human, who is just barely three hundred years old, everything was not already bent toward the subjective and experiential and was not made conscious through the calculating consciousness (and at the same time shuffled off into the fatal region of the so-called 'unconscious'), then we could now, without the danger of misinterpretation, refer to a word of the thinker Parmenides who, along with Heraclitus, thinks the inception. The word of Parmenides (fragment 13) reads:

πρώτιστον μὲν ῎Ερωτα θεῶν μητίσατο πάντων.

As first, certainly, Eros, of all the gods, (she) was devised.

To de-vise means here to con-ceive in advance: to give, as the pro-vision, the poverty of all necessity. 'Eros,' thought essentially, is the poetic name for the contemplative word 'favor,' insofar as this word names the now dawning essence of φύσις. According to the word of Parmenides (as quoted from Plato's *Symposium*)[1], [133] who here brings about the de-vising cannot immediately be identified. The word of Parmenides is being adduced here to illustrate that, in the inception, it is relationality that unfolds, and not some thing or condition. However, the word of Parmenides could only be adequately considered if we were first to bring to mind a sufficient concept regarding what the Greeks meant by θεοί.)

Emerging as emerging in no way evades self-occluding, but rather claims self-occluding for itself as that which bestows emerging and that which alone and always grants the sole bestowal for the emerging. One grants itself to the other. In this granting, the intimacy of both is granted the simple 'essence.' φιλία and φιλεῖν do not first befall φύσις. The establishing of emerging back into a prior self-occluding; the overcoming of emerging by self-occluding; also, the pre-establishing of self-occluding in emerging: favor is the manner in which these unfold. Favor, again, is not something separate and apart from φύειν and κρύπτεσθαι: rather, granting has the essential character of emerging and self-occluding. Favor is the intimacy of the simple differentiation; granting lets the pure clearness arise in which emerging and self-concealing are held both apart from, and toward, one another, and thus struggle with one another for the simple bestowing of the simply granted essence. Favor is the essential feature of ἔρις (strife), provided that we think this inceptually and do not conceive of it only as discord and disputation based upon the contrariety of disfavor and resentment.

Emerging grants to self-occluding that the latter allot the essence to the former, thus vouchsafing itself in the favor of its own essence, which is granted to it through emerging. Whatsoever unfolds as the simplicity of the favor of the concealing emerging allows itself to be called by the single word φύσις. [134] We hear and read this isolated word according to the customary way in which a word corresponds to an object. We say 'house' and mean the corresponding object. We say 'mountain' and mean that particular, imagined thing. We say φύσις and at first believe, at least according to the preceding explanation, that our imagination must

---

[1] Plato, *Symp.* 178b.

be able to represent some corresponding object to itself. We demand such representability, because with its help we orient ourselves amongst things, affairs, and situations. But, even if we were to become attentive to the fact that what is named with φύσις does not let itself be represented immediately in such a way, we would nevertheless still demand that the many things that have been said about φύσις should be lucidly assembled together in such a way that they could be easily understood by everybody. Otherwise, we would find the matter to be convoluted. We use what we take to be 'the simple' as the measure by which we judge what, according to and for us, is 'complicated.' The 'natural' and healthy understanding finds such 'complication' to be offensive, and meets it with hostility. The exegesis offered here of the saying φύσις χρύπτεσθαι φιλεῖ is manifestly 'complicated.' There is, however, a simple way to grasp its content without thereby degrading the saying into a platitude. 'Emerging' and 'submerging' can easily demonstrate their relationship in an 'image' that perhaps even Heraclitus himself 'had in mind.'

Within the figure of the morning's twilight one finds an emerging: from out of the morning blessedly ensues the luminous day in which emerging consummates itself. Of course, the evening follows with a twilight of an opposite sort. With the morning one has, so to speak, a box that opens slowly. Then one has the day itself, which is the second box (for, 'the morning' and 'the day' are something different). [135] The second box stands open. Then comes, of course, the third box, which once more slowly closes: this is the evening. One privileges the second box, in comparison to which emerging and self-occluding are merely unavoidable additions. When one observes the third box, the one called evening, in its relation to the others, it reveals moreover that it 'properly' stands in relation only to the open box, the day: for through the evening the day comes once more to a close. Thus, according to wisdom, submerging (the evening) stands not in opposition to emerging, but rather simply to the day—just as, indeed, 'death' is not in opposition to being born, but rather stands in opposition to life. We say, 'to live and to die,' not 'to be born and to die.' Against these three boxes and the underlying box-like conception of beings on which they stand, one can say no more than this: that every mode of conceiving that 'thinks' according to boxes is itself clearly limited and boxed-in. One indeed talks about the opposites life and death, through which talk it is taken for granted that death is the opposite of 'life' and not of birth. Here, too, the box plays its role. One thinks (insofar as one thinks anything at all regarding such things) that through birth the human being is placed into a box called 'life,' and that through death he is taken out of this box, as if the human being did not already begin to die straightaway at birth; as if, indeed, death were not the constant possibility of so-called life; as if, as regards life, being born were not on the same plane with death. 'The box' is certainly a convenient thing, and whoever thinks in boxes can accommodate much therein. But, regrettably, being is not a box: rather, a box is at best some particular being and, indeed, something quite insignificant.

φύσις (i.e., emerging) stands in an essential relationship to self-occluding (i.e., to entering-into concealment), and thus to 'submerging' understood in a Greek way. The essential relation is named in fragment 123 (φύσις κρύπτεσθαι φιλεῖ) with the [136] word φιλεῖ. We understand φιλεῖν as favor and granting.

Emerging, insofar as it is emerging, grants to self-occluding that it unfold in the proper essence of emerging. Self-occluding, insofar as it is self-occluding, grants to emerging that it unfold from out of the proper essence of self-occluding. Favor is here the reciprocal granting of bestowal that one essence gives to the other, in whose granted bestowal the unity *of* that particular essence that is called φύσις is safeguarded. This we think when, and only when, we think it from out of the originally unifying unity of favor. Thinking this way, we hold ourselves outside of the domain of the common way of thinking that conceives of things only objectively and places everything into individualized conceptions and categorizes and files them, as if into boxes.

Now, this box-like thinking (though, to be sure, not the box itself) is something essential that dominates the relation of human beings to beings. It must therefore be taken seriously. This box-like conceiving is in no way merely the consequence of a superficial way of thinking, but is rather its ground. This box-like thinking is founded upon the fact that beings are compelled on their own accord to become and to remain the standard and horizon for the determination of being. (The essence of metaphysics is founded upon this compulsion belonging to beings.) In the case of Heraclitus's saying regarding φύσις, the box-like way of thinking, which as boxed-in remains closed-off from the free prevailing of the essential, thinks emerging as one process and self-concealing as another. Self-concealing can follow from emerging, and in such a manner be connected with it: the box of emerging can exist next to the box of submerging. 'Normal' thinking prevents itself from thinking that, contrary to this box-like view, emerging unfolds in itself as self-concealing. However, the saying of Heraclitus's says precisely this, [137] insofar as it names φιλεῖν as the relation between φύσις and κρύπτεσθαι. How should we understand this?

Let us assume the following: that ἀείζωον/φύσις (i.e., the never submerging/the perpetually emerging) is pure emerging in the sense that every self-concealing and self-occluding remains excluded from it in every respect. What, then, is the situation with this bare emerging that in every respect stands naked before the self-occluding? Then emerging would have nothing out of which it emerges and nothing to which it opens itself in emerging. Even if we were to take emerging as something that has already happened, and take it on its own terms, so to speak, emerging would still have to withdraw itself and float away from that which bestows a coming-forth (i.e., a self-occluding), resulting immediately in its dissolution into the nothing, even at the very moment of the separation. Emerging does not unfold as what it is if it does not beforehand and always remain retained and secured in a self-concealing. Therefore, it is owing precisely to its essence, and only to its essence, that emerging gives favor to self-concealing. What would happen if the spring, emerging into the light of day, were without the favor of the water flowing to it beneath the ground? It would not be the spring. The spring must belong to the concealed water, a belonging that means that the spring in its essence is secured by means of the concealed water and only from out of it remains the spring. To be sure, this reference to the spring is only an 'image,' by means of which we grasp more easily the imagelessness of the essence of the coming-forth emerging that rests in self-concealing. All 'essence' is in truth imageless. We falsely understand this to be a lack. We forget thereby that the imageless, and thus imperceptible, first gives to the image its ground and necessity. Indeed, what could a painter be able to paint, if he were not first and continually able to see above and beyond what colors and lines represent? Everything perceptible is, without the imperceptible that it purports to reveal, merely an eyesore. The increasingly [138] shrill cry for 'perceptibility' passes from the comic directly into becoming a sign of the tragic—that is, the sign of a will which, while it wills itself, in fact only wills against itself and counteracts itself and thereby even perceives itself as 'logical.'

The implementation of cinema in 'school' (and above all in research) is an important and beneficial development: however, this process immediately leads to disaster if through it the opinion and attitude become solidified that only what 'shows up on film' properly exists, an attitude not owed to cinema in and of itself, but rather to the context of contemporary reality (i.e., of the will to the will) in which it takes place. But the 'cinematically' un-presentable and 'cinematically' imperceptible is not thereby the invisible: for, indeed, it provides the view for the imperceptible, the view that our entire essence bears in its ground, inasmuch as we understand the 'is' and 'being', and thus have being itself 'in sight.' But the danger persists also that we will equate cinematic perceptibility with 'reality.' If we do not recognize this metaphysical danger belonging to our historical existence, then we do not yet know where we are and in what world-moment we stand. Even if it never becomes perceptible to the 'cinematic' view, the following still holds true: φύσις κρύπτεσθαι φιλεῖ.

Concealing guarantees to emerging the latter's essence. And because this self-concealing thus guarantees, it must also therefore unfold in such a way that it conceals. Self-concealing guarantees [*verbürgt*] by concealing [*verbirgt*]. The two are the same and therefore sayable with the same word. This is not an empty play *on* words, but rather the concealed play *of* the word that we ourselves should not disrupt. Our crude way of dealing with language treats the communicative employment of language as its normal and therefore authoritative function. What remains—what otherwise strikes us occasionally as the prevailing of the word—is taken as the exception: attention to the [139] self-arising and self-playing wordplay that is neither contrived nor forced seems to be mere self-indulgent frivolity. In fact, it is often difficult to recognize the boundary between the wordplay that comes from the word itself and the frivolous playing with words contrived by us, and thus easy to overlook completely when the wordplay degenerates into a method and a technique that becomes blindly imitated. Then it comes about that, to speak colloquially, the credit of the already deflated words becomes overdrawn.

However, the play of the word is played from out of the play of essence itself that comes to its word. φύσις is the play of emerging in self-concealing that harbors in the sense that it releases the open that emerges, i.e., the free. For if, in Heraclitus's saying, κρύπτεσθαι is awarded to φύσις, then we must notice that κρύπτειν means to conceal in the sense of a harboring. However, 'to harbor' says not only to take away into inaccessibility, concealing in the sense of hiding something and making it disappear. 'To harbor' is to take away in the sense of a bringing under the protection of something. To harbor is, at the same time, also a preserving. Thought otherwise, emerging now shows itself at the same time as the release of what has been safeguarded into the free of the en-joining. The saying φύσις κρύπτεσθαι φιλεῖ—"emerging to self-concealing gives favor"—gradually reveals the sense that we would detect sooner if we were to let the meanings of harboring and preserving sound from out of the middle word of the saying, κρύπτεσθαι. Insofar as emerging gives favor to self-concealing, it does not cease to unfold as what it is: namely, as emerging. Rather, in the giving of such favor, φύσις possesses its perpetual inception; accordingly, emerging, above everything else that appears—that is, above any and every being—has already appeared. With regard to beings, and especially with regard to the objects that human exploration seeks to assay, φύσις is what never conceals itself, but is rather what has always already emerged. But this emerging itself rests [140] in the play in which emerging bestows to self-concealing the favor to remain the protector of the former's essence. Only when we think the saying in terms of how its three words are combined, do we think it as the saying of a thinker who is an inceptual thinker.

According to Plato it is difficult to behold the "essence of things" (i.e., the ἰδέα), not because the essence of things hides itself, but rather because the eyes of the human are clouded. The essence of things by no means hides itself, but is rather what is properly luminous and shining. It speaks against everything that has been thought about the essence of φύσις, and even more so against the essence of the ἰδέα (which is only a last echo of inceptual φύσις), if one says that φύσις "likes to hide." What is meant is: from the eyes of the human. However, this appears to be the case, since humans only seldom and with great difficulty grasp the essence of things. In the above-mentioned translation, one attributes a mood and an inclination to φύσις in its supposed incomprehensibility (of which there is no mention), instead of focusing on the human being and his distractibility; moreover, one asserts that that is the sort of thing that a thinker such as Heraclitus said. It is not necessary for φύσις to hide itself at all, since indeed, as the example shows, the ignorance of human beings ensures that they thrust their opinions in front of the vision of the always already unfolding emerging.

Heraclitus's saying says what it says about φύσις not in regard to its relation to the human's comprehension or non-comprehension of it, but rather in regard to the proper essence of φύσις. φύσις does not conceal itself from the human: rather, emerging preserves itself as emerging within self-occluding as its essential bestowal. That emerging 'is' a self-concealing in such a manner in no way means that φύσις hides itself, but rather that it reveals its essence precisely in emerging as a self-concealing. It is precisely because it is the essence of φύσις not to 'hide' itself that the conventional understanding [141] collides with this essence, and as a consequence of this collision solidifies its own conviction, which is understandable since, after all, one has created it for oneself. Because φύσις does not hide itself, but is to the contrary the simple emerging and the open, it is the nearest of the near.

§ 7. φύσις as the essential jointure (ἁρμονία) of emerging and submerging (self-concealing) in the reciprocal bestowal of its essence. Indication of the same in emerging and submerging. Fragments 54, 8, and 51

While emerging, as emerging, gives favor to self-concealing, self-concealing joins itself to emerging in such a manner that the latter can emerge from the former and, for its part, remain secured in self-concealing (and this means conjoined to it). φύσις itself, seen now in terms of the essence that the saying of fragment 123 names, is 'the jointure' in which emerging joins itself to self-concealing, and self-concealing joins itself to emerging. The Greek word for 'jointure' is ἁρμονία. When we hear this word, we think immediately of the joining of sounds, and take 'harmony' to mean that which is in 'uni-son.' However, the substance of ἁρμονία does not lie in the realm of sounds and tones. Rather, it lies in ἁρμός: i.e., in the joint, that whereby one thing fits into another, where both join themselves into the joint in such a way that that the jointure *is*.

However, because self-concealing is not something that lies outside of, and next to, emerging, and is not what is subsequently added and fitted onto it, and further, because self-concealing is what φύσις bestows from itself as that wherein it itself remains grounded, φύσις prevails here as the jointure (i.e., ἁρμονία), the joint in which emerging and self-concealing hand one another the bestowing of their essences in a reciprocal way. [142]

a) The inconspicuousness of the jointure of φύσις as the unique feature of its revealability. The originarily precious essence of pure emerging

In fragment 54 (which we treat as the third fragment), Heraclitus says the following about ἁρμονία, which is the φύειν of φύσις itself:

> ἁρμονίη ἀφανὴς φανερῆς κρείττων.

> Inconspicuous jointure, more precious than the conjoined that insistently pushes toward appearance.

φύσις is the inconspicuous. Emerging, as that which in the first place bestows the cleared open for an appearing, withdraws itself behind all appearing and every appearing thing and is not just one appearing thing among others. Consequently, within the narrower region of the visible, what typically (and often exclusively) attracts our attention is, for example, what stands in the light and remains accessible as illuminated; over against this, the brightness itself is the unimposing and self-evident medium to which we only pay attention (and then only in passing) when the illuminated object becomes inaccessible to us as a result of the onset of darkness. The human being then fashions a light for himself. As a result of such fashioning, the modern metropolis, even before the war, had already turned night into day by means of a technology of illumination, so that neither the sky nor the lights that belong to it can be seen. As a result of this lighting technology, brightness itself has become an object that can be produced. Brightness, in the sense of the inconspicuous in all shining, has lost its essence. However, brightness, in the sense of the pellucidity of the light, is grounded in the fact that, above all else, clearing and emergence (i.e., φύσις) unfold.

(The modern human is fascinated by this technological monstrosity of brightness; when it becomes too much, he uses the mountains or the sea as a palliative; he then 'experiences' 'nature', an experience that certainly [143] can become boring already on the first morning of the trip, whereupon he just goes to the movies. Ah, the totality of what is called 'life'!)

φύσις does not occur within what emerges and what has emerged in the manner of something that appears: rather, it is the inconspicuous in all appearing things. However, it is in no way 'the invisible,' as the previously mentioned philological translations erroneously suggest. φύσις is not the invisible—on the contrary, it is what is seen inceptually which, however, is for the most part never properly beheld. In order to represent here the relationship in question, take, for example, a room, which of course contains 'space.' However, we do not behold the space as such, but rather only the furnishings and whatnot (i.e., those things that appear as objects within that space). In the same way, we see the 'time' on the clock, but we do not truly behold it: rather, we have the digits and the hands in view and glean from them 'what' time it is. 'Space' and 'time' are in each case inconspicuous but also seen, though they are not beheld as concrete objects.

Therefore, it is not the case that the ἁρμονία of φύσις—i.e., the jointure as which φύσις unfolds—is ἀφανής (i.e., is something that 'does not come into manifest ap-pearance') because κρύπτεσθαι in the misinterpreted sense of the self-hiding belongs to it, but rather because φύσις, as the pure emerging, is more manifest than every manifest object: therefore, it remains and unfolds as the inconspicuous. As the inconspicuous, the jointure is κρείττων—"worthier," it is worth "more."

With this word, which names an intensification, we think immediately of the ζα in the word ζωή. We ask: in what respect is the jointure, as inconspicuous, worth "more"? Surely in respect to its essence, in respect to the emerging opening and harboring. In itself, and not only as some consequence or effect, the emerging as the inconspicuous is more disclosive and more revealing than any conjoined thing pushed forth [144] into appearance. What contains the more originary within itself does not require effects and activities, remains untouched by such 'doings' and their 'putting on appearances,' and shines from out of itself without contrived embellishments and trimmings and without imposition: this is, in its essence, the 'precious.' What is precious is intrinsically worthier than the prepared and arranged. The ἁρμονία ἀφανής is precious. The preciousness of pure emerging consists in its not entering into the appearance of the obviously contrived that pushes itself forward. φύσις is the inconspicuous shining. Within the inconspicuousness of emerging rests the guarantee that it, because it is not dependent on a presentation given to it, continually unfolds from out of itself without interruption into emerging and remains untouched by the vicissitudes of any particular appearing thing, and thus falls victim to a submerging "not ever" (μή). The μή in the naming of φύσις as τὸ μὴ δῦνόν ποτε names the κρείττων: the originary, innate, precious essence of pure emerging. The μή is said from out of an essential glimpse of the preciousness of φύσις, which, as emerging, bestows appearing, but which at the same time is not included with what appears. But the inconspicuousness of emerging rests in itself and does so only because in its very essence it gives favor to self-concealing.

b) The contra-tension and counter-tension as the essential moment of the jointure. Concerning the difficulty in thinking the counter-striving at one with the jointure: the difference between conventional and essential thinking. The jointure of φύσις and the signs of Artemis (bow and lyre). Note on fragment 9

ἁρμονία (i.e., the jointure) is there in the pure shining of its essence and lightens there unblemished: it unfolds there as what is most beautiful and as that wherein the emerging harbors itself, also unblemished, in the self-concealing, while at the same time self-concealing finds in the emerging the pure bestowing of itself. Thus, where emerging [145] gives itself to the essence of self-concealing, and self-concealing gives itself to the essence of emerging, each one goes toward what is contrary to it. Here, the going over-and-against within the favor of essential bestowal is, in Greek, τὸ ἀντίξουν. ξέω means to go back-and-forth over something, for example while in the process of working on something in order to smooth it out and bring out its form (such as in the grinding, abrading, scraping, and shaving of a stone). (ξέω, ξάω, and 'shave' are the same word). τὸ ἀντί-ξουν—the participial form of ἀντιξέω, to go toward and back—means: going-toward-and-against, as in the jointure of the essential joining of φύσις itself. Insofar as emerging joins to self-concealing as the bestowal of its essence, it goes toward what is opposed to it (namely, submerging); however, insofar as self-concealing joins to emerging, it too goes against what is against itself. τὸ ἀντίξουν prevails as the bearing that is over against, and yet toward, one another. By prevailing, 'it brings' emerging together with self-concealing. The Greeks called the bringing-together and bearing-toward of one to the essence of the other in the manner of a joining into the joint of the unity of essence συμφέρειν; the participle συμφέρον subsequently comes to mean what is 'beneficial' and helpful. Bearing-together in the sense of ἀντίξουν holds the self-joining in the unity of its essence.

Heraclitus says this in fragment 8, which we order as the fourth:

τὸ ἀντίξουν συμφέρον καὶ ἐκ τῶν διαφερόντων καλλίστην ἁρμονίαν.

Going-toward-and-against, a bringing-together; and from out of the bringing-apart, the one resplendent jointure.

The bringing-together, which is not a pushing together of things whereby the different is simply pushed toward the different and attached to it, but which on the contrary consists of a going-toward-and-against of what experiences and dispenses itself as essence, [146] brings together by joining into the joint. In fact, this bringing-together first enjoins the joint itself, thereby making its shining possible, and thereby bringing-apart, one from out of another, that which joins together, a bringing apart in the purity of the joint's self-dispensing opposition. However, where the reciprocal relation of φύσις and κρύπτεσθαι is thought as ἀντίξουν, we must always keep in mind that what is being thought is φύσις, and that emerging and submerging join themselves in a manner that goes both toward and against. Thinking this matter in a more originary way, we would even have to say that the essence of ἀντίξουν, συμφέρειν, and διαφέρειν are determined *from out of* φύσις, i.e., from out of its emerging, lightening essence. However, because some sensory and observable aspect is not being hastily posited here in place of beings as a whole, and because, to the contrary, thoughtful projection beholds being itself non-pictorially in its inceptually simple essence of jointure, conventional thinking is not able to think here the to-be-thought: for thinking would have to follow the ἀντίξουν/συμφέρον and take the going-toward-and-against as a bringing-together, and in so doing comport itself adequately toward the to-be-thought.[1] Emerging (i.e., φύσις) can only be thought as the above-mentioned jointure if thinking itself is compliantly joined to it and thinks the joining in the joint of the jointure, and thereby and exclusively knows already the inceptual disrupting dis-jointure. Conventional thinking, and particularly our modern thinking, is a thinking directed toward objects which seeks the defining characteristic of the truth of what is thought solely in what can be objectified. However, because it is the case that not just recent thinking, but rather all conventional thinking as such, is never able properly to accompany the thinking of φύσις, the difference between both ways of thinking must already have emerged for the inceptual thinkers. That conventional thinking is not able to carry out a thinking of φύσις is something that Heraclitus expresses clearly enough [147] in a saying that at the same time points to something that appears to be quite conventional, and in whose form the pure shining of φύσις most easily becomes delineated and visible. Fragment 51, which we place here as the fifth fragment, says:

οὐ ξυνιᾶσιν ὅκως διαφερόμενον ἑωυτῶι συμφέρεται · παλίντονος ἁρμονίη ὅκωσπερ τόξου καὶ λύρης.[2]

They do not put together how the self-differentiating should unfold in such a way that it (in the self-differentiating of itself) brings itself together with itself; the jointure (namely, the self-differentiating) unfolds drawing-back (-expanding back), as it (i.e., the unfolding) shows itself in the image of the bow and lyre.

---

[1] Regarding fragment 16, see below.
[2] [Diels supplies ὁμολογέει instead of συμφέρεται.—Ed.]

Instead of παλίντονος (which is used above), παλίντροπος is sometimes also used. It should be pointed out that the jointure in itself is at the same time both the turning-away-from-one-another into relaxed un-tensing, and the turning-back-toward in the sense of the tensing of what turns itself toward *un*-tensing. ἁρμονία thus does not consist merely in yoking together such that the drive to move apart from one another into un-tensing would be distinguished from it and, at most, what is conjoined together remains: rather, letting move apart into un-tensing belongs to ἁρμονία. When, therefore, παλίντονος ἁρμονίη is translated by the philologist Snell as "the joining of opposing tensions" [*Wider-Spännstigen Fügung*], it does succeed in bringing to mind Shakespeare's *The Taming of the Shrew*:[3] nevertheless, the translation is both grammatically incorrect and factually inaccurate. παλίντονος, which is a drawing-back, is the predicate of ἁρμονία: however, παλίντονος is not meant or named as what is of opposing tension in the sense of it being the object of a joining. It is not the case that an intractable 'opposing-tension' needs to be conjoined and compliantly join itself: rather, it should appear that the tensing-against-and-toward belongs to the essence of the jointure itself. The fact that another philologist finds this translation (which is untenable in every respect) 'vivid' casts a strange light on the alleged dependability of the translations of philologists. Equally strange is the fact that all [148] extant translations reproduce ξυνιᾶσιν as 'understand' which, although lexically correct, fails to hit upon what is said and thought by the Greeks. However, in order to find what is decisive in the translation, one only needs the literal rendering of the Greek συνίημι: 'I bring together'; the word means the same as λέγειν: 'to read,' 'to gather.' However, we all too easily render the phrase συμφέρειν (i.e., 'to bring together') as "to gather" in the sense of harvesting together, a bringing together as precisely a driving-together the resulting 'unity' of which is the outcome of this 'gathering.' In truth, however, the converse is the case: the gathering is determined from out of a previously beheld unity. 'To gather' means: to bring to appearance the unity that has already unfolded from out of itself; 'gathering oneself' means also to bring oneself together with a determinative unity that is not self-made and that therefore has previously addressed us. We should also not overlook the fact that in the words συνίημι and συμφέρω ('I bring/bear together') and λέγω ('I gather')—precisely because they are Greek words—there already resonates a reference to φύσις (i.e., the emerging, the beautiful), so that 'gathering' and 'bringing-together' have been thought, in a Greek way, the essential feature that we could call the letting-appear *from out of* the unity.

(Every etymology becomes a meaningless play with words if the spirit of the language from out of which the language speaks, i.e., the essence of being and of truth, is not experienced. The danger of etymology lies not in etymology itself, but

---

[3] Translators' note. Heidegger does not mention this play by name; rather, he writes "*so klingt das zwar gut nach* Shakespeare." We are assuming that it is *The Taming of the Shrew*, often translated into German as *Der Widerspenstigen Zähmung*, to which he is referring.

rather in the spiritual poverty of those who practice it—or, what amounts to the same, of those who seek to resist it. Thus, a philologist, with all due industriousness, can occupy himself for his entire life with the Greek language and command it, without ever being touched by the spirit of this language. On the contrary, he dutifully and conventionally allows his everyday world and the common way of thinking—even if modified 'historiographically'—to preside in place of the spirit of language.)

The saying of fragment 51 clearly indicates what can also be gleaned from [149] other statements of Heraclitus's: namely, that he knew of the difference between, and the manifest irreconcilability of, conventional thinking and essential thinking. One can see from this that the manifest irreconcilability with conventional thinking belongs to the very essence of essential thinking. The latter is, in its essence, entirely 'incomprehensible' to the conventional understanding. However, we would once again draw an all-too-hasty conclusion were we to maintain, as a result of the above, that anyone who states incomprehensible things is already thereby a thinker. Essential thinking is not incomprehensible because it is too complicated, but rather because it is too simple. Essential thinking is alienating not because what is thought by it lies too distant, but rather because it lies too near. The difference between conventional thinking and essential thinking is irresolvable. To know this and to know the reason for such irresolvability, and thereby to know the essence of manifest irreconcilability, are tasks that themselves belong to the knowledge of essential thinking. This difference is therefore expressed in various ways according to the fundamental position of a thinking within its history.

Seen from the perspective of conventional thinking—a perspective that is, for us, always the most familiar—every declaration of a thinker concerning the relation of essential thinking to conventional thinking is either taken as an arrogant dismissal of the ignorance of the masses, or as an irritated and petulant complaint concerning conventional thinking's 'deliberate' misunderstandings regarding the thinker, and by extension the aggression the mob feels toward the thinker.

The vehemence of the thinkers' comments regarding their relation to conventional thinking does not, in truth, arise from the minor irritation of one who is insulted merely as a result of a common lack of understanding. However, one can (because one can do this anywhere and anytime) very easily explain the defensive words of Parmenides, Heraclitus, Plato, Descartes, Kant, [150] Hegel, Schelling, and Nietzsche as resulting from anger: for, conventional thinking understands such an explanation most easily, and precisely thereby takes it to be the only true one. In truth, however, behind the thinkers' defensive words is concealed an entire range of connections whose essence has still not been questioned. What is at stake here is not the 'psychology' of the 'personality' of the thinkers and their particular way of responding to the public and its lack of understanding: rather, what is being questioned is the essentially manifold relation in which the human essence stands to the truth of beings. Phrased still more essentially: if conventional thinking conceives of beings and only this, and if essential thinking thinks being, and if the difference between being and beings is an essential difference—or, indeed, is the inceptual difference itself—then the rift between conventional thinking and essential thinking has its origin in the difference between being and beings. This means: the relation between common thinking and essential thinking is in no way only a question of the 'reaction' of the public to philosophy, nor is it a question of the reaction of philosophy to the public's reaction. Why do we say all of this during an elucidation of fragment 51? Because in this fragment the relation of essential thinking to common thinking is thought, and because a number of Heraclitus's fragments that say something about this relation have been handed down to us.[4] From the number of sayings alone it is evident that the above-discussed relation between conventional and essential thinking is something that must be thought essentially. What is also shown, through the haphazard scattering of such fragments through their customary sequence and arrangement, is that there is still no knowledge concerning their essential connectedness and the ground upon which such connectedness is based. Fragment 9, which [151] is so-named without regard for its proper content, reads:

ὄνους σύρματ' ἂν ἑλέσθαι μᾶλλον ἢ χρυσόν.

Asses may prefer chaff to gold.

The fragments of Heraclitus's enumerated above require a special elucidation because, up to this point, they have only been misused 'psychologically' to 'illuminate' the 'personality' of Heraclitus, and for characterizing the relation of the philosopher toward the public. In this, one forgets to consider whether perhaps a thinker such as Heraclitus was compelled by other reasons to speak out concerning this relation, just as one forgets to ask what is at stake in the fact that in the inception of Occidental thinking precisely this relation came to the word in unity with the inceptual thought that, in turn, bears all that is to come.

(In modern times one all too eagerly understands the words of Heraclitus's concerning the understanding of the mob in light of the rantings and ravings that Schopenhauer delivered during the previous century regarding university philosophy and its followers. With Schopenhauer—who was never a thinker, but merely a writer who obtained his thoughts secondhand from Hegel and Schelling and then trivialized them—grumpiness is *the* principle from which the relation of philosophers to the world is determined.)

Because the disparity between conventional and essential thinking is grounded in what each thinks, and because the disparity between what is thought in each, on

---

[4] Cf. fragments 1, 2, 9, 13, 17, 19, 29, 34, 37, 40, 72, 87, 97, 104, 108.

the one hand, and the to-be-thought, on the other, traces back to the difference between being and beings; because, moreover, this difference is operative everywhere in Occidental history but is the least questioned and least thought-through, and is never taken *as* the difference that it is; for all of these reasons, the insertion of numbered fragments into Heraclitus's thinking—that is, into that which he thinks [152]—must necessarily remain obscure. First we must learn what the to-be-thought is in Heraclitus's thinking. Therefore, the second part of the saying in that fragment that is numbered 51 is initially taken by us as the most important part. Here something essential is said regarding ἁρμονία, i.e., regarding the essence of φύσις:

παλίντονος ἁρμονίη ὅκωσπερ τόξου καὶ λύρης.

The jointure (namely, the self-differentiating) unfolds drawing-back, as shows itself in the image of the bow and lyre.

We spoke about the 'bow' and the 'lyre' at the beginning of this lecture course when we made reference to the goddess Artemis, whom we claimed to be the goddess of Heraclitus. Her essence shows itself in the bow and lyre. Now we learn that the essence of the to-be-thought, and thus of what Heraclitus thinks—namely, φύσις as ἁρμονία—reveals itself in the bow and lyre. Can we doubt any longer that Artemis is the goddess of Heraclitus? Will we recognize that Heraclitus, not as an Ephesian but as a thinker—and, indeed, as an inceptual thinker—is beckoned in his thinking by this goddess? The emerging that unfolds (in that it originates from self-concealing) brings itself into separation, in a way, from self-concealing. Emerging thereby appears to move away from submerging, and is thus determined by a closing-together and a self-closing, just as the one end of the relaxed bow springs away from the other so that the curvature of the bow (and thus the bow itself) disappears. Emerging, taken on its own terms, seems like the mere bending away from one another of the ends of a relaxed bow. In truth, however, emerging is what shows itself to us in the image of the tightened (and that means, at the same time, tensible) bow. It belongs to the essence of the bow that while the ends stretch away from one another they, at the same time and within this very stretching away, are stretched back toward one another. Emerging does not abandon submerging and unhitch it: rather, in emerging, emerging itself [153] submerges into self-concealment as the facilitator of its essence and yokes itself to it. φύσις is this moving 'away' and moving apart of self-opening and self-closing, as well as the 'return' of each into being toward-one-another. φύσις is the to-and-fro, the back-and-forth: ἁρμός/the counter-moving joining/ἁρμονία/'jointure.' But inasmuch as λύρα (the lyre) is named, the thinker, by means of a single image in which the bowed-ness and counter-striving are one with the jointure, grasps ἁρμονία, in which the special form of harmony appears. The goddess whose signs are bow and lyre unfolds herself only from out of the essence of φύσις, and compliantly joins herself to this. Therefore, she roams, as the huntress, the entirety of what we call 'nature.' We certainly must not think about the essence of 'tension' in modern dynamical and quantitative terms, but rather as the lightened apartness of an expanse that is, at the same time, held together. In emerging, emerging receives the self-concealing in itself, because it can emerge as emerging only from out of self-concealing: it draws itself back into this. Because emerging and self-concealing each bestow to each other the favor of essence, the jointure of self-concealing into emerging, which at the same time joins emerging into self-concealing, *is*. Emerging and self-concealing (i.e., submerging) are the same. However, according to our interpretation of the first saying, φύσις is precisely τὸ μὴ δῦνόν ποτε, the 'never submerging.' How can these two things square with one another? We must nevertheless question whether we are here justified in making the claim that they 'square' with one another, and thus make sense. φύσις is the never submerging precisely because it compliantly joins constantly to submerging as that from out of which it emerges. Without closure's bestowal and its continual essence, emerging would cease to be what it is. The 'never submerging' in no way means that in φύσις the relation to submerging is obliterated: rather, it means that this relation must constantly and inceptually unfold. The 'never submerging,' and precisely and solely it, must grant favor to self-concealing. [154] Were the 'never submerging' to deny favor to the self-concealing, it would be without that from out of which it, as emerging, emerges, and that in which it as 'the never submerging' can unfold. The 'never submerging' does not submerge, and indeed unfolds within self-closure. That self-closure necessarily unfolds within emerging by no means indicates that emerging 'submerges.'

(Were it to do so, its essence would of necessity decompose into non-essence. Were it the case that it could not bestow essence constantly, the 'never submerging' would still not even 'become' a mere submerging and revert to this.)

c) The inadequacy of logic (dialectic) in the face of the jointure thought in φύσις. The two-fold meaning of φύσις and the questionable 'priority' of emerging

If, however, emerging and submerging are in a certain manner the same, why then does the thinker always say φύσις when he thinks of this sameness? Why does he not say τὸ δῦνον, since within the essence of φύσις self-concealing has the same claim to essence as emerging does? And why, instead of τὸ δῦνον, is the opposite τὸ μὴ δῦνόν ποτε (i.e., emerging) used? In all of this, φύσις seems to have priority. However, this is merely an illusion that persists only so long as we think φύσις in a manner that disregards what comprises its essence (namely, ἁρμονία). Because φύσις is ἁρμονία, self-concealing is named within it as essentially equal. But then we could say τὸ δῦνον instead of φύσις, and thereby make it manifest that this submerging, as a going into concealing, is always already at the same time an emerging. Only the sun that, in emerging, both unfolds into its emergence and abandons that emergence, can submerge. Certainly—the sun involves both emerging as well as submerging, and we mean the latter as well as the former when we refer to the sun. The sun is so-named neither solely in relation to emerging nor solely in relation to submerging. [155] In the name φύσις, on the other hand, emerging has priority; but what this name names is essentially equally a submerging, and could indeed also be named according to it. If we nevertheless find priority given to the word φύσις, there must be a reason for this. Concerning the priority given to φύσις over κρύπτεσθαι, one can offer the following as a ground of explanation: emerging is the 'positive' and submerging the 'negative.' Everywhere and always the positive precedes the negative, not only, for example, in the ordering of affirming and denying, but rather in all 'placements' generally. Indeed, how could there be a de-nial without something first being placed before it, and thus a *positum* and a positive that the denial then re-places and dis-places? There is no beginning with dis-placement alone. The prefixes dis- and re- betray all too clearly here that the denial is dependent upon something that is already placed before it, and that it relies upon not only in every particular case, but also essentially. Only what has arrived and emerged can also go away and submerge. Because what displaces is in itself reliant upon something prior, placing-forth and placement, the position and the positive, retain an insuperable priority.

This is all clear enough and cleverly calculated. However, has the issue actually been *thought*? Is what we put forth concerning the relation and the essential consequences of placing-forth and displacement also valid for emerging and submerging? Placing-forth and displacing are, first of all, only ways that we bring beings before us and remove them. This placing-forth and displacing are the modes in which the action of presenting something, whatever it may be, moves. Placing and placing-forth are 'actions,' i.e., acts of thinking in the manner that 'logic' grasps and interprets 'thinking.' Does what applies to the behavior of human beings toward beings also apply to those beings themselves? Presuming it were indeed to apply to beings, would it therefore also apply to being? φύσις/κρύπτεσθαι are names for being. The persuasive argumentation offered with regard to the priority of positing over negating means nothing for the decision concerning the [156] relation of φύσις and κρύπτεσθαι. We speak while under the bewitchment of the blindly accepted omnipotence of 'logic' if we demonstrate the reliance of negation upon positing, and therefore unthinkingly assume that what applies to the ranking of formalized actions of thinking must also hold for the arrangement of beings and, further, for the essential arrangement of being (and this latter, indeed, already in advance). The very minimum that must here be required of a mindfully considerate thinking is that it at least ask whether what holds true for actions of thinking also already pertains to being itself, and indeed is even capable of pertaining to it: it must ask whether all thinking can only be thinking if it beforehand, and in the first place, is addressed by being. The competency of 'logic' to illuminate being itself is in every respect questionable.

However, one can raise the following obvious counterargument, which says in short: contesting the competency of logic for the illumination of the essence of being, or even calling it into question, is hypocritical—for in truth, any illumination of being that is articulated in propositions must proceed according to the rules 'of logic,' and must take place through actions of placement and displacement. One may respond to this objection in the following way: the actions of thinking in the sense of the placement of propositions may be necessary conditions for the execution of essential thinking and its saying: however, they are not thereby shown to be the 'sufficient' conditions and the originary bolstering support for this thinking. The claim that 'logic' is not competent to illuminate the truth of being says something other than the claim (supposed in the objection above) that the illumination of being can do without 'logic.'

The dismissal of the competency of 'logic' has the following purpose: to make clear that the actions of placing, placing-forth, and displacing, taken on their own as the actions that they are, can neither ground, establish, nor even constitute [157] or 'replace' the domain within which 'being' itself becomes clear. It is one thing to carry out thinking interpreted in terms of 'logic' (in the sense of the placing of the presentation of things) directly and ubiquitously, and another thing entirely to set forth blindly this 'logical' thinking as the guideline along which the question of the being of beings is placed and considered decided. The appeal to a ranking of priority between the 'positive' and the 'negative' is, in a manifold sense, 'logically' correct: however, it does not guarantee the relation to being itself, because it (and the mere pointing out of the formal representational placements) not only presupposes the relation of being to us, but also at the same time obscures and disguises it. The positing proposed by 'logic' is able to accomplish much within thinking, but this placing is not able to accomplish precisely that 'positing' that already lies in the so-called presup-positions, and it is in truth something other than a positing. Thus, in the very moment we clearly and distinctly interpret what emerges before and comes before as being presup-positions, 'logic' has already besieged and battered us with a blindness that can never be remedied by means of that which carried out the blinding itself (i.e., logic). Logic, as an authority over the decision concerning the essence of being, is not only intrinsically questionable and lacking a grounded competence, but this authority, and thus also the relation of the 'positive' to the 'negative,' is nowhere to be found in inceptual thinking. We force φύσις and κρύπτεσθαι into what is for them a thoroughly foreign relationship when we interpret the jointure, in and as which both are in essence united, as the chain of logical connection between the 'positive' and the 'negative.'

However, within the saying of the inceptual thinker, the name φύσις is obvious. Certainly, we must at the same time also consider and marvel at the fact that in φύσις, in emerging, ἀλήθεια is thought and is near. But through the presence [158] of the alpha-privative, it is shown within ἀλήθεια that in emerging the relation to concealing and concealment originally prevails.

On the way of such considerations we gradually arrive before an enigma that no 'logic' and no 'dialectic' (the hitherto greatest power of logic) has solved, precisely because they cannot solve it, since they are not able to look the enigma in the eye. The enigma is this: that φύσις names at once emerging in distinction to submerging (i.e., φύσις in its relation to κρύπτεσθαι) and *also* names the unified essence of the jointure of φύσις and κρύπτεσθαι.

What does this two-fold meaning of φύσις signify? For those of us who have not managed to escape the grasp of metaphysics and therefore of logic, therein lies ready a schema by means of which to grasp the enigma 'logically'—and through that very grasp to strangle it. Emerging and submerging stand in a relation (namely, a relation of φιλεῖν). They themselves are the links of the relation: the *relata*. φύσις is now the name for one of the *relata* and, at the same time, the name for the relation itself. φύσις is the relation itself and one of the *relata*. We can raise the following question to the enigma: why is it, and how does it come about, that something can and must be, at the very same time, the relation itself and one of the *relata* within that relation? To this question (which is posed within terms of the schema of logic), dialectic—the highest authority within metaphysical logic—might answer by pointing out that even thinking, precisely as the consummating act of the thinking 'I' (that is, the 'I' as the 'I think') has this essential character: that within the relation of the presentation of the object, it is at one and the same time this relation itself and one of the *relata* of the relation, specifically the 'I' that, in its representing, relates to the object.

However, we leave it entirely open here whether this dialectical-speculative answer born from out of the metaphysics of subjectivity is indeed an answer to the question raised by the above-mentioned enigma. For now, we observe only this: that φύσις [159] is in no way able to be compared with the 'I' and the 'representing I' (and thereby with subjectivity and consciousness), even though this equating in fact takes place when, for example, the famous saying of Parmenides's concerning the relationship between νοεῖν and εἶναι is interpreted in terms of the relationship between subject and object, or of consciousness and an object of consciousness.

Were we able to say straightaway what conceals itself behind the enigma of the essential two-foldness of φύσις, then we would already have stated the essence of the inception. But perhaps it already gives us enough to ponder if we can first arrive *before* this enigma and attempt to look straight at it.

Even if we no longer attend to the attempted equating of the connection between φύσις and κρύπτεσθαι, emerging and submerging, with the formal/thetical/logical relation of positive and negative, then there still remains a priority of emerging. However, it is also illuminating to us if we think emerging (in the sense of the self-opening of the clearing) from out of what is properly determined through this emerging: namely, from out of beings themselves, which appear into emerging. Because it appears—that is, because it attains to presence and is precisely thereby that-which-is—emerging 'dominates.' Seen from the perspective of beings, it is of course being in whose emerged light alone beings as such can come to presence. With this perspective, the priority of emerging is grounded upon the priority of beings. However, the question stands before us: why are beings decisive and not rather non-beings and, what amounts to the same, the 'nothing'? Why beings, and not rather nothing? Furthermore, apart from the question regarding the priority between that-which-is and that-which-is-not, could it not be the case that being itself unfolds as the prerequisite of the possibility of making a decision over whether or not there are beings?

[160] However, even this way of thinking—a way of retreat back to the priority of beings—does not allow us to find the grounding for the priority of being, and thereby the priority of emerging. Given this, we see that this justification on other grounds is not possible, since it already assumes the way of thinking characteristic of metaphysics, which questions being exclusively from the perspective of beings. By means of the metaphysical interpretation just executed above, we have already again taken being/emerging/φύσις for itself and have forgotten that according to the inceptual two-foldness, φύσις names at the same time the relation of φύσις to κρύπτεσθαι, and thus names φιλεῖν, the favor of the bestowal of essence in which the two join themselves together into their essence.

§ 8. The essence of φύσις and the truth of being. φύσις in view of fire and cosmos. ἀλήθεια thought in the μὴ δῦνόν ποτε (φύσις) as the dis-closing into the unconcealment of being. Fragments 64, 66, 30, and 124

a) Fire and lightning as the enkindling of the lightening. The cosmos as the fitting, inconspicuous jointure and the originary adornment. The same in fire and cosmos: Igniting and lightening of the decisive measure-dispensing expanses

We think φύσις inceptually only when we think it as that jointure (i.e., ἁρμονία) that joins emerging back into the sheltering concealing, and thus lets emerging unfold as what intrinsically derives from this sheltering concealing, and which we therefore more appropriately call 'revealing.' ἁρμονία joins and kindles revealing and concealing into the one-foldedness of its essence and is thus the enkindling itself. φύσις is the ἁρμονία, the jointure that joins emerging back into self-concealing and sheltering in such a way that lets emerging unfold as what lightens itself from out of this sheltering concealing. Emerging is, on account of this difference from self-concealing, [161] the revealing. ἁρμονία, thoroughly pervaded by the favor of the essential bestowal, joins and kindles revealing into concealing, and vice versa. Thus joined and kindled within the unity of the jointure, both are within the one-foldedness of their essence. Thus, φύσις is, as ἁρμονία, the enkindling of the lightening that itself unfolds simply in the unlightened. φύσις (thought now from out of its relational essence, and no longer as a 'relatum' of a 'relation') is the enkindling of the lightening, the enflaming of the flame. We must think φύσις as the flame and, at the same time, think the flame from out of the essential sway of φύσις. In doing so, we must voice the Greek word that corresponds to this: τὸ πῦρ, fire. Heraclitus uses this word, and uses it as the word that names the same as what φύσις names. Thus, here, where 'fire' is a foundational word of thinking, we must think the essence of so-called fire essentially and in the sense of essential thinking, and not according to any arbitrarily derived view.

Now, certainly the word πῦρ, in everyday speech, refers to fire in the sense of a sacrificial fire, to the fire of the funeral pyre, to the fire meant to give warning, or to a hearth fire, but also to the shine of torches, as well as to the glow of the stars. We think of the word ζάπυρος, which means "very fiery," and note that, with the ζα, emerging, coming-forth, breaking-through, and breaking-out are named. In 'fire,' the relations among what lightens, glows, blazes, and creates an expanse, but also among what burns up, collapses and sinks into itself, occludes, and fades, are all essential. Fire flames and is, in enflaming, the excising separation between the light and the dark: enflaming joins the light and the dark against, and into, one another. In enflaming, there occurs something that the eye grasps in a glimpse, something instantaneous and singular, which decisively excises the bright from the dark. The instantaneity of enflaming makes room for appearance over against the region of vanishing. [162] In particular, the instantaneity of enflaming lightens the region of all indicating and showing, but also lightens, at the same time, the region of directionlessness, rudderlessness, and absolute opacity. This flaming/excising essence that first bears light and dark toward one another and yokes them together is the defining essence of fire—an essence that no chemistry could ever grasp, because it must destroy this essence in advance in order to then make it comprehensible to itself. The fundamental essence of πῦρ, insofar as it stands for φύσις, in no way consists only in the mere radiance of the lightening or even in an indifferent dispersal of mere brightness: for, if conceived of in this manner, the φύσις-character of fire, and also the fire-character of φύσις, would not be adequately comprehended. The essence of fire assembles and shows itself in what we call 'lightning'. However, it now becomes necessary to think the essence of lightning from out of the above-mentioned connection. A saying of Heraclitus's can be helpful to us, if we observe that φύσις, as the enkindling jointure, and as the joining enkindling and the decisively lightening enacting, concerns beings as a whole. Heraclitus says the following in fragment 64 (which we rank as sixth):

τὰ δὲ πάντα οἰακίζει Κεραυνός.

But lightning steers beings as a whole.

Fire, as lightning, 'steers,' surveys, and shines over the whole of beings in advance and permeates this whole pre-luminously in such a way that, in the blink of an eye, the whole joins itself, kindles itself, and excises itself each time into its conjoinedness.

(To kindle means to catch and, through such catching, begin, i.e., to incept as the onefolding and the onefolded that enkindles itself as the lighting. Therefore, φύσις is not only the same in word as φάος (light): it is also the case that pure emerging and enkindling into the flame of the enflamed fire (πῦρ) are the same in essence, provided that we do not remain stuck on appearances, which only give us a preview in place [163] of a thoughtful experiencing of the pure shining of the enkindling one-foldedness in the lightening emerging.)

Thus, things are lifted out and set over against one another, thereby grasped and defined in distinction to one another. Fire is what strikes 'in a flash' in such a way as to brighten and excise in its striking. Fragment 66, which we rank as the seventh, says the following:

πάντα γὰρ τὸ πῦρ ἐπελθὸν κρινεῖ καὶ καταλήψεται.

All things, fire, ceaselessly advancing, shall (joining them) set out and lift away.

In the light of fire conceived in such a way, and thus in the emerging of φύσις understood in such a way, every appearance first appears within the conjoined boundaries of its form. Through the jointure, the whole of beings is opened up to its emerging, 'endowed' in a literal sense, without any connotation of decorating or embellishing. For φύσις is, as the inconspicuous jointure, the precious endowing, the clearing unfolding from out of itself. In this lightening jointure, beings appear and gleam forth. That particular opening up and unlocking and 'endowing' through which something is equipped such that it appears and shines forth in the conjoinedness of its jointure, we call 'decorating' and 'adorning.' With these terms, however, we are tempted to take 'decoration' and 'adornment' as something that is first attached to another, and by which this other is decorated and outfitted. However, the lightening letting-appear, in which something emerges into the conjoinedness into which it was sent, is no subsequent ornamentation or mere endowing in the sense of an outfitting. It is rather the originary decorating and adorning that can go without all embellishing, furnishing, and endowing in the vulgar sense, for it itself lets the fitting gleam forth. To open something into the splendor of its conjoined appearance—to 'endow' and thus to let arise—the Greeks called κοσμέω. κόσμος is 'adornment'; the word also means "honors," "distinction" thought in a Greek way: [164] appearing in the light, standing in the open of glory and splendor. When the word κόσμος is 'used' by a thinker, it surely names the to-be-thought. κοσμέω—"to adorn"—then certainly does not mean to outfit any old existing thing, nor to embellish the entirety of beings with a 'decoration' (something of which the human is hardly capable). "Adorning" (κοσμέω) and "adornment" (κόσμος) will then no doubt be said of being itself. Therefore, we cannot impose here our own idea of 'cosmos,' picked up from one place or another, onto the inceptual word of the thinker. Furthermore, we should avoid assaulting this thinking with ideas about any particular 'cosmology': rather, we must think the word from out of its essential unity with φύσις/ἁρμονία/μὴ δῦνόν ποτε. But even if we do so, κόσμος does not mean only the entirety of beings, but rather the jointure of the conjoining of beings, the adornment in which, and from out of which, beings gleam. This adornment, thought here in its essential sense and, at the same time, in the simple style of the inceptual, is the adorning that inceptually adorns, giving the splendor of the joints and what has been conjoined, letting them gleam and light up. This adorning does not come about as the consequence of a subsequently conjoined decoration: rather, it is, as the originary letting-gleam-forth into the splendor of emerging, solely and suddenly the adornment that strikes like lightning into the unadorned. Such lighting places into the light (and thus also produces and provides) the dark and what is opposite to the lightening. We often speak about jewelry being 'flashy' and say that a precious stone itself 'flashes,' but we do not consider the possibility that the flash itself is the originary adornment and unfolds as the precious. This originary adornment is the adornment that ordains the fitting. This adornment, thought thusly as the lightening jointure—and thus as φύσις/ζωή/ἁρμονία—is the adorning fire itself: lightning. κόσμος and πῦρ say the same.

Once we have seen these simple connections, at least some of the preconditions have been met in order [165] for us to consider the main features of that saying from which we already previously analyzed an essential word for the sake of illuminating the essence of φύσις. The fragment in question is fragment 30, in which the word ἀείζωον, which we discussed above, is said. We order the saying as the eighth, and it reads:

κόσμον τόνδε, τὸν αὐτὸν ἁπάντων, οὔτε τις θεῶν οὔτα ἀνθρώπων ἐποίησεν, ἀλλ'ἦν ἀεὶ καὶ ἔστιν καὶ ἔσται πῦρ ἀείζωον, ἁπτόμενον μέτρα καὶ ἀποσβεννύμενον μέτρα.

This adornment mentioned here, the same in all that is adorned, is neither something produced by gods nor by human beings (anyone), rather it was always and is (always) and will be (always): (namely) fire perpetually emerging, the expanses (clearings) igniting themselves, the expanses extinguishing (occluding) themselves (into the clearingless).

Here κόσμος is named in an exemplary sense as that adornment whose adorning, whose lightening jointure, unfolds in everything that is adorned. The one singular originary adornment is to be distinguished here from everything adorned. By 'everything adorned' we mean the conjoined that is in each case brought into appearance by intrusively 'establishing' itself into appearance and semblance (i.e., ἁρμονία φανερή), in distinction to the inconspicuous jointure (i.e., ἁρμονία ἀφανής). In comparison to the latter, every appearing, apparent, and present conjoinedness of beings as a whole is merely something protruding into the foreground, by which the pure jointure is covered over and is thus, in a way, distorted through the rigidified conjoinedness. The intrusive semblance may still captivate and enchant our understanding. The adorned may therefore be what is most beautiful, which is mentioned in fragment 124 (which we number as ninth) and which we connect to fragment 30:

ὄκωσπερ σάρμα εἰκῆ κεχυμένων ὁ κάλλιστος κόσμος.

Just as a heap of randomly poured-out things is (yet) the most beautiful adornment.

[166] When we consider the merely appearing adornment directly, our consideration is constrained to it, and we never become aware of the singular adornment. The latter does not let itself be removed from the adornment that is given. It is beheld only when we look toward the inconspicuous jointure. Regarding the inceptual adornment, Heraclitus says that it is neither made nor produced by a god nor by a human being. φύσις is above gods and human beings. Every metaphysical consideration, which likes to base itself upon God as the first cause or on the human being as the center of all objectivity, fails when it attempts to think what is dispatched to thinking in this saying. Before all beings, and before every genesis of beings from beings, being itself unfolds. It is not made, and therefore has no determinate beginning in time and no corresponding end to its duration. The one singular κόσμος that is thought in essential thinking—i.e., the inceptual adornment—is so different from the modernly conceived or popularly imagined 'cosmos' that we are unable to articulate any adequate measure for this difference. What is here called 'cosmos' is not some vague burbling of mists and forces out of which gods and human beings 'evolve.' Resistance to this conception is necessary, for it represents the unspoken and unreflective understanding still held by most people today. If God was designated by biology as a 'gaseous vertebrate' during the preceding century, then such a designation is at least an honest

articulation of what one actually means when one thinks that it is possible to 'explain' 'the world,' beings, or even being by means of a so-called biological-scientific worldview. Whether one explains God as a gaseous vertebrate, or whether one thinks (in accordance with present-day physicists) that the 'essence of freedom' can be 'explained' with the help of atomic-physics and its statistical method, the two in principle amount to the same. κόσμος, thought in the thinking of the inceptual thinker, [167] has nothing to do with a 'cosmology.' When, conversely, 'cosmological' doctrines subsequently latch themselves onto inceptual thinking, we must not present the inept behavior of those who are no longer thinkers in place of the thoughts of the thinker. For the time being, and presumably always, one is more likely to grasp what has been thought by the thinker according to the dictums of the thoughtless, and thus with the least struggle, than to decide to experience within the thoughts of the thinker the to-be-thought, which even for the thinkers never presents itself as something simply graspable.

(We are inclined to say that the originary adornment, the lightening joining of the joint of emerging, is nothing 'temporal,' but is rather 'eternal.' Indeed, Heraclitus says ἦν ἀεί: the adornment always already was; the ἀεί also obviously holds true for the ἔστιν and the ἔσται, the "is" and the "will be." Here the three temporal determinations—past, present, future—are named. More precisely: the way in which κόσμος unfolds is determined with regard to these. It unfolds at all times. It endures always. The always enduring is the eternal in the twofold sense of the *sempiternitas* and the *aeternitas*. In these, metaphysics recognizes the proper essence of eternity, which is not the result or consequence of an unbroken duration, but rather is itself the ground of such duration, insofar as it is the *nunc stans*, the enduring now. Strictly thought, both conceptions of eternity are undergirded by the same determinations and, as is obvious when considering the naming of *nunc stans*, they are purely temporal determinations. The 'now' is a temporal aspect, and the permanence of enduring and presencing is no less so. One can indeed equate eternity with timelessness, but one must nevertheless know that in so doing one conceives of eternity always from out of time. The designation of eternity as timelessness leads to the misunderstanding that time is excluded from the essence of eternity; that, however, is not the case. Rather, the fundamental essence of metaphysically conceived [168] time, the 'now,' is absolutely presupposed within the metaphysical concept of eternity, and that means that the essence of time is employed in an exemplary sense. If we absolutely must employ a temporal characteristic here, then we name the originary adornment 'the pre-temporal,' and indicate thereby that κόσμος is more originary than every temporality, and that indeed the temporal grounds itself in it, which is only possible if κόσμος is 'time' itself, this word certainly being understood in an inceptual sense. The thus named temporality does not let itself be grasped or interpreted from within the horizon of the heretofore Occidental presentation of time.)

The unfolding adornment, which comes before all that can be made and produced, and in whose radiance gleams the clearing of all that is lightened, is πῦρ ἀείζωον, the perpetually emerging fire. After and on account of all that was said regarding φύσις, ἁρμονία, and κόσμος, it is now no longer within our power to intend with the word 'fire' anything arbitrary, incidental, or familiar. Then again, we should also avoid believing that we have already thought of everything and thus in fact think what this word says within the saying of Heraclitus's. Fortunately, this saying, which names φύσις as κόσμος and this latter as the perpetually emerging fire, contains a determination of this 'fire,' to which not only we *may* adhere, but to which we perhaps *must* adhere prior to any attempt to think it:

πῦρ ἀειζωον, ἁπτόμενον μέτρα καὶ ἀποσβεννύμενον μέτρα.

Fire perpetually emerging, the expanses igniting themselves, the expanses extinguishing themselves.

πῦρ is named here together with μέτρον. One translates μέτρον 'correctly' as "measure." But what does "measure" mean here? What is the meaning of μέτρον thought in a Greek way? In what manner does an essential relationship exist between μέτρον and πῦρ, and thus also between μέτρον and φύσις/ἁρμονία/κόσμος? [169] This is no longer a serious question for the modern imagination, for whom φύσις is simply 'nature'; Heraclitus gratuitously calls it "cosmos." "Nature"/"the universe"/"cosmos" moves within the harmony of the spheres. Thus, it is 'perfectly natural' for this 'world'—that is, of 'fire' and 'global conflagration'—to flare up and burn away 'in accordance with measure and law.' Indeed, to 'nature' belongs natural laws, the measures according to which natural processes proceed. 'Naturally' one cannot demand that people in the sixth century BCE construct 'nature' with mathematical precision by way of infinitesimal calculus. However, they do already articulate, albeit very roughly and imprecisely, the thought that the cosmos moves and behaves 'according to measure.' Certainly, that is a first step in the grand advancement in the understanding of nature. How baffled would an inceptual thinker be if he were to discover that modern natural science in this way still concedes to him, albeit arrogantly, a small spot in the light of its peculiar sun. Philology (a compatriot from another discipline) also eagerly reinforces natural science's patronization of this thinker by itself translating Heraclitus's saying in philological terms. The 'authoritative' philological additions, and thus those additions by which all others are 'measured,' translate as follows: "eternally living fire, glimmering according to measure and fading according to measure" (Diels-Kranz), and "perpetually-living fire, flaring-up according to measure and extinguishing according to measure" (Snell).

In the face of these translations, I ask: where in the Greek text does "according to measure" appear? For all eternity, ἁπτόμενον will never mean glimmering or flaring-up: rather, ἅπτω means to rivet, to attach, to pin on; however, it is also used by Heraclitus (as comes to light from fragment 26) to mean the striking of fire, that is, of light. To strike the light means: to make light, to let become bright, to lighten, to endow light. Now, when there is talk of the adornment here, which as fire itself is nothing made nor makeable; furthermore, when this adornment is not drawn from something other [170] that determines and rules it in some manner; if precisely the adornment is the inceptual unlocking, how then could this adornment inflame "according to measure"? Within the train of thought characteristic of a theological/metaphysical 'cosmology,' one may see evidence here for proof of God: however, in the saying of Heraclitus's, there is no such thing. Moreover, it is utterly linguistically impossible to translate ἁπτόμενον μέτρα as "glimmering according to measure." Anyone who does so retreats into the Old Testament in lieu of attempting to think the phrase in a Greek way. Moreover, such translations and interpretations do not make the least attempt to bring the word μέτρον into an essential relationship with πῦρ, i.e., κόσμος, i.e., ἁρμονία ἀφανής, i.e., φύσις.

τὸ μέτρον means "the measure," and the word signifies also that "measurement" whereby and whereupon, for example, weights and lengths are measured. However, in the saying of Heraclitus's, μέτρον certainly does not mean any old ruler by which things are measured. What is "measure"? Why is a ruler a μέτρον? Because with it length can be measured. What is measurable by measures and other measurement tools is itself the genuine measure: it is what is capable of being measured across and measured through—i.e., the di-mension. The fundamental meaning of μέτρον, and thus its very essence, is the expanse, the open, the sprawling and widening clearing. For the Greeks, μέτρον θαλάσσης does not mean "the measure" or the "scale" of the sea, but rather the expanse of the sea, the "open sea" itself. The inceptual adornment—φύσις as lightening jointure—ignites and lights the expanse in whose open that which appears first disperses into the conjoined expanse of its appearance and its distinctive look. However, because κόσμος (i.e., the inceptual adorning) is the emerging itself, this igniting and lightening of the expanses *is* in such a way that it constitutes the proper essence of κόσμος and bestows to it its essence. The perpetually emerging ignites for itself the emerging expanses that are essentially proper to it and that emerge within it owing to its character as emerging. However, because φύσις is essentially equal to the self-concealing (i.e., self-occluding), [171] this fire is precisely what occludes the expanses and thus conceals all dimensionality in which something can arise and presence as something appearing. Fire thus occludes, just as with the flash of lightning (and only with it) obscurity and darkness come to light and luminance for the first time in the suddenness of its extinguishing: namely, as the darkness that the lightning lightens. μέτρα are thus the measures in the originary sense of the emerging and self-occluding expanses into which a human perspective may first enter, and to which it may open itself in such a way as to be able to see the measure (i.e., the 'span') in which a being appears as such. The perpetually emerging fire does not conform itself 'according' to measures: rather, it gives the measure in the correctly understood sense of μέτρον. The inceptual adornment, κόσμος, is the measure-giving; the measure that κόσμος gives is κόσμος itself as φύσις. It bestows, as φύσις, "a measure," an expanse. κόσμος, as perpetually emerging, can only bestow these measures because "fire"—i.e., πῦρ (φάος) as φύσις—unfolds in itself as the favor in which emerging and occluding reciprocally grant their essential ground.

b) ἀλήθεια as essential inception, and as the essential ground of φύσις. The essential relation between unconcealment and self-concealment in φύσις, thought inceptually. ἀλήθεια as the unconcealment of the self-concealing

τὸ μὴ δῦνόν ποτε—"the not ever submerging": thus sounds the first saying of Heraclitus's to which we attempt to listen. We have asked what this means. The answer has now been won, at least with regard to some principal features. τὸ μὴ δῦνόν ποτε is φύσις: this is the reciprocal favor of emerging and self-occluding; this favor is the ἁρμονία ἀφανής, the inconspicuous jointure that shines over all things. It shines thusly only because it, as the precious, is the originary adornment: ὁ κόσμος ὅδε—"this adornment," the one thought in that thinking that thinks φύσις. This κόσμος, as the perpetually [172] lightening inconspicuous jointure, is 'the fire' that gives measure to all coming-forth and all submerging. τὸ πῦρ ἀείζωον is τὸ μὴ δῦνόν ποτε.

But why is the perpetually lightening-joining emerging called in the first saying by the name "the not ever submerging"? Because the saying is spoken in the manner of a question which, while asking about what unfolds as the essence of φύσις, also at the same time asks it in such a way that the essence of φύσις is seen with regard to τίς—"someone." πῶς ἄν τις λάθοι;—"how may anyone be concealed (from it)?"

The never submerging is questioningly beheld as what decides on the possibility and impossibility of being-concealed: namely, the concealability and non-concealability of that being whom we address as τίς ("someone") and not as τί ("something"). The first saying names φύσις in its relation to τίς: the saying is the questioning regarding this relation. The question of 'who' is meant by this τίς, this "anyone," had to remain open. Certainly, it is natural to think of human beings here, especially since the question of the saying and the saying itself are bespoken by a human being to other human beings. However, because the human being who speaks here is a thinker, and because Artemis and Apollo are near to this thinker, it could be that his saying is essentially a dialogue with the gods—that is, with those who peer in. In that case the saying, which says "someone" (i.e., τίς), could also mean the gods. From another saying (fragment 30) we hear: οὔτε τις θεῶν οὔτε ἀνθρώπων ἐποίησεν—"neither some god nor some human being has produced 'the adornment' (i.e., φύσις)": rather, gods and human beings—indeed, anyone who is a being that is addressable by the question 'who are you,' whoever that may be—is such that, according to the saying, he is not able to be concealed from the perpetually emerging.

No one can be concealed before φύσις. Anyone who *is*, insofar as that one *is*, must thus be such that he emerges against the [173] emerging itself, and comports himself emergently toward φύσις. Everyone who *is*, as someone, does not merely occur as a being within the clearing (of being). Such a one not only stands 'in' the clearing, as does a rock or a tree or a mountain animal: rather, such a one looks into the clearing, and this looking is one's ζωή—"life," as 'we' say. But the Greeks thereby think emerging as being. The one who looks, in an essential way, into the clearing is lightened into the clearing. That one's standing is an emerging-projecting into the clearing.

(ἔκ-στασις—"eksistent" in the just-mentioned sense: only a being who *is* such that it, not being able to conceal itself, comports in an emergent way toward φύσις can—precisely because it has emerged in such a sense—reflect upon itself and thus be itself, that is, be a self as the sort of being that we would address with the τίς— 'someone.')

The saying questions the relation of φύσις (that is, of κόσμος as the inceptual adornment) to gods and human beings. The emerging adornment is 'above' them because gods and human beings, insofar as they are, only are in that they emerge into the open, and in such a way as to never be able to be concealed from it.

Only those whose essence cannot remain concealed over against φύσις are beings in such a way that they correspond in their being to emerging. The corresponding bearing of φύσις to φύσις must have in itself the essential features of emerging, self-opening, non-self-occlusion, non-self-concealment. Non-self-concealing is self-revealing abiding in revealing and unconcealment—or, as the Greeks said, in ἀλήθεια. We render this term as "truth." However, we see now, in our first attempt to think the first saying of Heraclitus's, that ἀλήθεια is thought in the saying, though it is not named in it.

ἀλήθεια—revealing into unconcealment—is the essence of φύσις, of emerging, and is at the same time the fundamental feature of the way that anyone who himself *is*, be he a god or a human being, comports toward ἀλήθεια in such a way as to not [174] be a λαθών—i.e., one who conceals, hides, and occludes oneself—but rather one who reveals. Every being who is addressable only by the 'who are you' and the 'who are you all,' and never with the 'what is that' or 'what is that thing'; everyone only addressable by the 'who' is a being only insofar as they are in ἀλήθεια—unconcealment.

If we think the first saying of Heraclitus's more inceptually in view of unconcealment and revealing, then it appears that in the essence of φύσις, and in the essence of those who correspond revealingly to it, ἀλήθεια prevails as the originary unifying ground. To be sure, this is not articulated in the saying, nor in any other sayings of Heraclitus's. This is also not said by either of the other inceptual thinkers, Anaximander and Parmenides. All the same, based upon the proper essence of ἀλήθεια, it is necessary to note that precisely because ἀλήθεια has still not been named inceptually, and indeed remains the unsaid, it is that from out of which inceptual thinking speaks when it speaks inceptually.

In view of what is unsaid and still unsayable, the first saying of Heraclitus's is a question. πῶς—how may anyone who revealingly, and thereby in accordance with his essence, opens himself and peers into emerging, be concealed from emerging? Is it not the case that for each person who revealingly comports himself thusly, the essence to which he comports himself is always already emerging, and in such a way that it must be addressed as the never submerging?

πῶς—how is it possible within the realm of emerging, and of the openness to emerging of the human and godly essences, that someone could be concealed within this realm, and thereby be locked out of emerging and at the same time have its essence hidden from itself? πῶς—how can it be possible, since φύσις prevails and human beings and gods reveal themselves to φύσις? [175]

τὸ μὴ δῦνόν ποτε πῶς ἄν τις λάθοι;

Before the not ever submerging, how is it possible for anyone to be concealed from it (given that ἀλήθεια unfolds in the never submerging and in the essence of every τίς)?

However, we also heard this: the essence of φύσις is never a pure emerging that arises groundlessly as though out of the nothing. φύσις κρύπτεσθαι φιλεῖ— "emerging grants favor to self-concealing." If, however, ἀλήθεια is the essential ground of φύσις, then only now do we understand the name ἀλήθεια as unconcealment, re-vealing. ἀλήθεια unfolds from out of concealment and within sheltering. ἀλήθεια is, as its name says, no mere openness, but is rather the unconcealment of self-concealment. ἀλήθεια has for a long time and exclusively been translated and thought in terms of what we now call by the name "truth."

Metaphysical thinking knows truth only as a characteristic of cognition. It is for this reason that the clue just provided—namely, that "truth" in the sense of ἀλήθεια is the inception of the essence of φύσις itself and of the gods and human beings who belong to it—remains strange to such a viewpoint. Indeed, it is even preferable and crucial that we retain this strangeness and not hastily talk ourselves into believing that the meaning of ἀλήθεια is 'self-evidently' not a mere achievement of cognitive faculties (as metaphysics has hitherto thought), but is rather the fundamental feature of being itself. It remains strange to us, and must remain strange, that truth is the inceptual essence of being, and thereby the inception itself. If, however, as we have previously noted, the inception is not what is behind us; if, rather, the inception is what has already overtaken us as the all-unfolding that catches and draws to itself in advance, only first approaching us as that which unfolds in advance, then we ourselves—and, indeed, the present age of the Occident—are in need of an inceptual transformation that would leave behind [176] every other turning point (be it Copernican or otherwise) in the history of thinking. The historical essence of Occidental humanity is in need of a prolonged transformation so that it may enter into its inception and learn to recognize that a consideration on 'the essence of truth' is the essential thinking within the inception of being itself, and only this.

Along with this experience comes at once another: namely, that the knowledge of the truth and of the true is of an inceptually simple sort that remains decisively divorced both from the reckoning of mere logic and from the hollow dizziness of a mystical profundity. But we cannot extract this knowledge regarding the essence of truth historiographically from the text of the first thinker of the ancient Greek world as though from some transcript. If we ourselves have not come to the nearness of being through prior inceptual experiences, then our hearing remains deaf to the inceptual word of inceptual thinking. Supposing, however, that we learn to heed what is essentially the to-be-thought, then the inceptual thinker and his sayings speak another language. Some may remark in regard to this event [*Ereignis*] that modern conceptions and a peculiar philosophy are being interpolated into earlier thought. Some may indeed see it that way. But this is merely a method of self-soothing to compensate for one's own triviality, about which not one word more should be spoken.

But what if our attention is freed from all prior metaphysical thinking and is thereby free for the inceptual? Then we grasp the substance of a saying of Heraclitus's that contains the clue regarding how the now stated essence of φύσις and ἀλήθεια communicates itself to those who hear it.

If now, however, the essence of φύσις is granted to it by self-occlusion; if unconcealment is grounded in a self-concealing; if this belongs to the essence of being itself, then φύσις can never be thought inceptually so long as we do not think [177] and consider self-concealing as well. In that case, being and truth can never be experienced and disclosed in such a way that one simply enunciates and, as it were, conceives them. The thinker who thinks φύσις must ensure that its essence is thought and spoken of as that which articulates itself in the saying φύσις κρύπτεσθαι φιλεῖ.

c) On the hearing and saying of being in inceptual thinking: λόγος and signs. The signs of Apollo as the self-showing of φύσις. Fragment 93. On the truth and the word of beyng in Occidental history

The previously discussed sayings signify that φύσις is διαφερόμενον ἑωυτῶι συμφερόμενον—that which pulls together with itself while pulling asunder. This essence of φύσις, the inconspicuous jointure of favor, appears in the bow and lyre, the signs of Artemis. Apollo, the brother of the goddess Artemis, bears the same signs. He is, along with his sister Artemis, *the* god of Heraclitus. A saying is preserved in which the thinker names this god himself, a naming that makes him visible in his essence. Heraclitus states here in what manner Apollo is the one who peers in and appears, and how he, in his appearing, beckons toward being. The god himself must, insofar as he is a god, correspond to being (i.e., to the essence of φύσις). Fragment 93, which we take as the *tenth* saying, reads:

ὁ ἄναξ, οὗ τὸ μαντεῖόν ἐστι τὸ ἐν Δελφοῖς, οὔτε λέγει οὔτε κρύπτει ἀλλὰ σημαίνει.

The supreme one, whose place of the intimating saying is Delphi, neither (only) reveals, nor (only) conceals, but rather gives signs.

λέγειν is here clearly used as the opposite of κρύπτειν and thus means 'revealing' in contrast to 'concealing.' [178] We have here the simple confirmation of our interpretation of the fundamental meaning of the word λέγειν in the sense of "to harvest" and "to gather"; thought in a Greek way, 'to gather' means to let appear that One in whose oneness is gathered what is essentially together in itself and forgathered from itself. 'Forgathered' here means: to remain held together as one within the originary oneness of the jointure. It is because the calling and saying word has, as word, the fundamental feature of making manifest and letting appear, that the saying of words can for the Greeks be named a gathering, λέγειν. This is why with Parmenides, the other inceptual thinker, νοεῖν is the grasping of the One together with λέγειν.

It is only because being is experienced as jointure and φύσις, and because the saying word is recognized as the fundamental way of hearing being, that saying itself must, given its character as the opening relation to the oneness of the jointure, be grasped as a gathering (i.e., as λέγειν). If we fail to bear all of this in mind, then it can never be grasped how 'harvesting' and 'gathering' could constitute the fundamental feature of saying. λόγος—another foundational word of Heraclitus's—thus means for him neither "doctrine" nor "talk" nor "meaning," but rather the self-revealing 'gathering' in the sense of the originary self-joining oneness of the inconspicuous jointure. λόγος/ἁρμονία/φύσις/κόσμος all say the same, though in each case from out of a different originary determination of being. We learn here first to anticipate in which way the inceptual thinker is able to behold and articulate the richness of the simple. In the previously mentioned saying, λέγειν is the opposite of κρύπτειν. Both belong within the essential region of making manifest and letting appear. However, an even more originary letting appear, behind which every λέγειν and κρύπτειν as such already lags behind, is σημαίμειν: "to give a sign."

The extant translations (and that also means interpretations) of Heraclitus's saying regarding Apollo are so thoughtlessly [179] senseless that they can presently be skipped over. The saying says that the god gives the intimation of what is always indispensable, i.e., the essential. This, however, is φύσις, which is in itself at once emerging and self-concealing. If the god would only reveal emerging or only conceal self-concealing, he would thereby continually and thoroughly miss the essence of φύσις. On the contrary, he is able neither only to reveal nor only to conceal, nor can he simply do one and then the other: rather, he must accomplish both originarily in an originary oneness. That happens, however, insofar as he gives signs. What, then, is a sign? Something that is shown and thereby revealed: however, this something that is revealed is of the sort that it points to something not-shown, something non-appearing, something concealed. To give signs means: to reveal something which, by appearing, points to something concealed, an operation that thereby both conceals and harbors and thus lets what is harbored emerge as such. The essence of the sign is this revealing concealing. The essence of the sign is not, however, pieced and patched together from out of both of these functions: rather, the showing of the sign is the originary way in which what is only later and elsewhere separated—namely, revealing itself and concealing itself—preside inseparably. To show in the manner of the sign, however, means to make visible the essence of φύσις in a way that accords with that essence and corresponds to the favor prevailing in φύσις. φύσις itself is the self-showing that essentially shows itself in signs.

Certainly σῆμα/σημεῖον/σημαίμειν must be thought here in a Greek way and with reference to φύσις and ἀλήθεια. Parmenides speaks, in his fragment 8, of the σήματα of being, about which extant interpretations spread a certain unsurpassable nonsense. 'Signs,' thought in a Greek way, are the self-showing of emerging itself, to which this self-showing belongs and which is removed as far as possible from all 'ciphering.' 'Signs,' thought in a Greek way, are nothing made or thought-up, as are, [180] for example, 'numerals' and 'ciphers' in arithmetic, which designate something with which they 'actually' have nothing to do. It is the province only of contemporary thinking and its metaphysics, and of the latter's intrinsic and now manifest decline, to misunderstand what is thought and said in essential thinking as a mere 'cipher' for something entirely different and to misjudge in every respect all originary unfolding of truth in the sense of clearing and revealing. It is the unstoppable consequence of Nietzsche's metaphysics, which holds the 'truth' only to be a 'value' and one cipher among others, that one misunderstands all philosophical thinking as a script of ciphers. Such thinking achieves the utmost distance from the essence of truth, and the only thing that remains for such straying is for it to write its own 'logic.'

The true in the inceptual sense of the unconcealed does not have the nature of mere clarity of explication and explicability. To the same degree, the true is not the unclear in the sense of an inexplicable and ciphered profundity. The true is neither the one-dimensionality of mere arithmetic nor the 'profound' dimensions hidden behind a theatre's curtain.

The true is the unsaid that remains the unsaid only in what is strictly and properly said.

To think essentially: this means to listen to what is unsaid in the consideration of what is said, and thereby to come into unanimity with what in the unsaid keeps its silence before us. So long as the word remains conferred upon the human as the fundamental property of his essence, the human cannot escape the unsaid.

τὸ μὴ δῦνόν ποτε πῶς ἄν τις λάθοι;

The word wherein the essence of the historical human conveys [*übereignet*] itself is the word of beyng. This inceptual word is safeguarded in poetry and thinking. In whatever way the fate of the Occident may be conjoined, [181] the greatest and truest trial of the Germans is yet to come: namely, that trial in which they are tested by the ignorant against their will regarding whether the Germans are in harmony with the truth of beyng, and whether they are strong enough in their readiness for death to save the inceptual in its inconspicuous adornment from the spiritual poverty of the modern world.

The danger in which the 'holy heart of the people' of the Occident stands is not that of decline: rather, it is that we, bewildered, shall yield to the will of modernity and race into it. In order to prevent this calamity from happening, we are dependent, within the coming decades, upon those thirty- and forty-year-olds who have learned to think essentially.

[183] LOGIC
Heraclitus's Doctrine of the *Logos*

Summer Semester, 1944

[185] Preliminary remark

The simple aim of this lecture is to arrive at originary 'logic.' 'Logic' is originary when it consists of the thinking 'of the' Λόγος, when the originary Λόγος is thought and is present in and for this thinking. Such has transpired in the thinking of Heraclitus. Our simple aim is thus to think-after what Heraclitus says about the Λόγος. These statements will become clearer in what follows.

[186] FIRST SECTION

Logic: its name and its matter

§ 1. The term 'logic'

a) The logic of thinking and the logic of things

'Logic'—this term is commonly understood to be 'the doctrine of correct thinking,' and has been so understood since time immemorial. Still today, occupying oneself with 'logic' means: learning to think correctly by informing ourselves about the structure, form, and rules of thinking, memorizing these and applying them in given cases. In an admittedly somewhat colloquial expression one says: "this person does not have a logical bone in his body." Usually, two things are meant by this: on the one hand, it means that the ability to think correctly is an innate part of human nature, that it is part of embodied human life, and that correct thinking should result from out of itself naturally. On the other hand, the saying also means that the human must be taught 'logic,' and that through a specialized form of education it must become incorporated so that his thinking lives and exists from out of 'logic,' and is thereby correct at any given moment. According to this view, as soon as the human has become familiar with logic and is at home in it, he can easily recognize in each particular case what is 'logical' and what is not. One says: "that is logical," and one thereby means: this clearly results from the given situation and from commonly known prior facts. The 'logical' is thereby the consistent, i.e., that which corresponds to 'logic.' But with this use of 'logic' we are not so much referring to the lawfulness and orderliness of thinking, but rather to [187] the inner consistency of a matter, a situation, a process. Here, things in themselves have an innate 'logic,' their own 'logic.' We are thus only thinking 'logically' in the properly understood sense when we follow and think the logic innate to some thing.

That is why we will never learn 'to think correctly' so long as we only take note of the structure and rules of thinking and, as one says, 'learn them by heart,' without proceeding from out of the innate logic of a thing and allowing ourselves and our knowing to be guided by it. Many a person seemingly possesses 'logic,' but still never thinks a single truthful thought. Now, granted, truthful thoughts are rare.

The human 'thinks' often and about many different things: however, the thoughts thus produced are not necessarily reliable. True thoughts, which are quite rare, do not arise out of self-produced thinking, nor do they reside in the things themselves, like a stone in a field or a net in the water. True thoughts are thought *toward* the human and directed toward him, and only when he is in a correctly thoughtful disposition—i.e., when he is in a state of practiced readiness to think what approaches him as the to-be-thought.

The term 'logic' therefore reveals itself to us through a strange ambiguity. On the one hand, it means the logic of thinking; on the other hand, it means the logic of things; on the one hand, it refers to the regulatory dimension of the conduct of thinking; on the other hand, it refers to the structure of things themselves. Initially, we do not know from where this ambiguity of 'logic' and the 'logical' arises, nor in what sense it became necessary and why it has established itself as something common and familiar in which we scamper about thoughtlessly, tossed this way and that. In most cases, certainly, we understand the term 'logic' exclusively in the sense of a doctrine of forms and rules for thinking.

This is a strange explanation of 'logic' and the study of 'logic.' If one understands it as the doctrine of thinking, then one should also like to hold the opinion that [188] everything depends upon not only learning the rules of thinking set out by logic, but also how to apply them correctly. But apply them to what? Obviously to the experience, observation, and treatment of things, matters, and humans. However, how are we to apply our thinking to matters if we do not correctly know these matters and things with regard to their own innate 'logic'? Supposing, however, that we are always familiar with the 'logic' of matters themselves and with the 'logic' of the realm of things, for what reason would we then still need to apply the rules of logic to things in the sense of a doctrine of thinking? We think 'logically' when we think 'factually' and 'properly.' But when and how do we think 'factually'? On what path and by what instruction do we learn to think this way? To what extent must we think from out of matters and things? What kind of 'must' comes upon us here? Does it arise from a demand that was formulated by someone during some era to think 'objectively'? But only 'subjects' can think 'objectively,' i.e., in a manner corresponding to 'objects.' Objectivity as an ideal only exists in the realm of subjectivity, wherein the human understands himself as a 'subject.' And yet, is the demand for objectivity readily the same as what we are here calling 'the factual'? How could that be, if it were true that everything objective were only the particular way in which the subjectivity of humans 'objectifies' matters, i.e., throws them up as opposite, counter-posing objects? How could that be, if the 'objective' does not yet penetrate into the realm of 'things themselves'? Once again we ask: why and how must we think from out of matters and things themselves? What kind of a necessity is it that determines our thinking here, determining it in such a way that, without such determination from out of the matter, thinking has not yet become thinking? What is going on with the human that he feels compelled by this necessity to think factually, where this means to think at all? What is at stake in the fact that the human can [189] withdraw himself from this demand, can evade it, pass it by and misunderstand it, in order then to stray into defenselessness and find himself in a state of neglect?

From where and how, finally, is the demand addressed to the human that he think things, and do so in a way proper to those things themselves? Does the human still have an ear that can hear this address? Do *we*? Do we understand the language of this address? Do we have any connection to the word that is brought forth into language in this address? *The word*—what is that, anyway? What does it mean to answer to a demand that determines our essence? Are these questions that were posed just now perhaps the essential questions of 'logic'? 'Logic,' as one says, is the doctrine of correct thinking.

Thinking correctly, thinking from out of the matter itself, and thinking at all are all necessary: however, *learning* to think is the highest necessity, and not simply for the sake of avoiding mere errors in thinking. Thinking is a necessity so that we may thereby correspond to a perhaps still-hidden determination of the historical human. Perhaps it is the case that, for a long time, all futurity has rested solely upon whether this ability to correspond and to think is bestowed to the historical human, or whether it remains withheld from him. 'The historical human': this refers to that particular humanity toward whom a fate is intended—namely, as the to-be-thought. But who today and in the coming days is better able and suited to receive the gift of thinking than the 'nation of thinkers,' that nation about whom a particular person who left this nation felt compelled to say that it is the "holy heart of nations"[1] and that from out of it comes a "counsel" that "surrounds kings and nations"[2]? All poetry and play, all building and construction, all care and action, all fighting and suffering, lose themselves in the confused, the dull, the coincidental, and the purely calculated, so long as the simple luminosity of thinking is not there, a luminosity from out of which [190] world and earth appear and can remain as a sign of the true.

But how shall we find the luminosity of thinking, if we do not allow ourselves to be led onto the wide path of thinking and slowly learn to think?

Perhaps there is indeed something even more preliminary: namely, that we must first learn how to learn and learn the ability to learn. In fact, before this preliminary condition there is one even more preliminary: namely, that we ready ourselves to learn how to learn. What does it mean to learn? A single definition cannot answer this, but it can give us a clue: to learn is to knowingly appropriate something according to instruction and hints, in order to give it away as the property of knowledge without losing it and thus becoming impoverished in the

---

[1] Hölderlin, *Werke*, IV, 129.
[2] Ibid., IV, 185.

process. Learning is directed toward the knowing appropriation of the possession of knowledge. But this possession does not belong to us: rather, we belong to it. We must first learn how to learn. Everything must be preliminary, decidedly anticipatory, and slow if the true, as the singular fate, shall be able to approach us and our descendants without our already calculating when and where and in what form this event [*ereignet*] shall come to pass. A generation of the slow must be awakened if the rush for action and quick fixes, along with the greed for immediate information and cheap solutions, is not to carry us away into the void or force us into the flight toward merely conventional thinking and believing—a flight that is simply an escape that can never be, nor become, an origin.

b) ἐπιστήμη and τέχνη in relation to modern science and technology

To think is a necessity, and learning to think even more so. Do we learn this through 'logic'? What does thinking have to do with 'logic'? What does this term even mean? What is it, precisely, to which the term 'logic' refers? 'Logic': perhaps a half-understood [191] task that has been led astray and never originarily taken over by the historical human? In that case, the term 'logic' and its use would only be a stopgap measure for us, used to hint at something else by way of a reference to something long known, thereby admitting that we are just beginning our journey toward that something else, and are still at great remove from it. If that is the case, then we must surely, and for that very reason, first gain sufficient clarity about 'logic,' both the name and the thing itself.

'Logic'—we know and use other terms like this, such as 'physics' and 'ethics.' These are abbreviations of the corresponding Greek words λογική, φυσική, and ἠθική. Before and above all three of these words must be placed the word ἐπιστήμη, which we initially translate as "knowledge." λογικόν/λογικά names all that is pertaining to λόγος. In a corresponding way, φυσικόν/φυσικά names all that belongs to φύσις. In the very same way, ἠθικόν names all that pertains to ἦθος. 'Logic,' understood as the abbreviated expression of ἐπιστήμη λογική, is the knowledge of what pertains to λόγος. But what does λόγος signify here?

Before we answer this question, it would be good to elucidate the word ἐπιστήμη first. This we shall do in a three-fold respect and with a three-fold purpose. To begin with, this elucidation will set out to experience what that particular Greek word means that we also find in the two corresponding Greek terms ἐπιστήμη φυσική and ἐπιστήμη ἠθική. Second, the elucidation of precisely this Greek word will prepare us for the elucidation of λόγος and what it names. Finally, the elucidation will help us provisionally learn how to consider what it means that the word and the matter of 'logic' originate in the Greek world.

What does ἐπιστήμη mean? The corresponding verb is ἐπίστασθαι, which means to place oneself before something, to linger with it and stand before it, so that it may show itself within its own aspect. ἐπίστασις also means the action of lingering before something, attending to it. This attendant lingering before something, ἐπιστήμη, yields and entails that we become, and then are, acquainted [192] with that before which we stand. Thus acquainted with the matter in front of which, and toward which, we attentively and lingeringly stand, we are able to stand before it. Being able to stand before a matter: this means to understand it. We thereby translate ἐπιστήμη as "to-understand-something."

Very often one translates the word as "science," inadvertently (and thus also imprecisely and only provisionally) meaning contemporary, modern science. This modern science is in its innermost core of a technical essence, which is becoming increasingly visible in the course of contemporary history. Our assertion that contemporary science is a necessary consummation of modern technology is, by necessity, an alienating claim. This alienation would persist even if we were able to say outright of what the essence of modern technology consists. However, this cannot readily be said, in part because this essence still remains partially concealed, and also in part because what can already be illuminated about the essence of modern technology cannot be transposed into a few sentences. Only one thing can be indicated given even minimally attentive thinking: namely, that the sciences of inanimate and animate nature, and also the sciences of the historical and its works, are ever more clearly developing themselves in a manner akin to how the contemporary human uses explanations to gain mastery over the 'world,' the 'earth,' 'nature,' 'history,' as well as all else, in order to then use these explained sectors according to plan (or need) for a securing and bolstering of the will to become master of the world in the sense of ordering it. This will is the ground and essential domain of modern technology: a will which, in all planning and examining and in all that is willed and attained, only wills itself, all the while equipped with the ever-increasing possibility of this self-willing. Technology is the organization and the enactment of the will to will. The varied forms of humanity, [193] peoples, and nations—these groups and the individual members of whom they are comprised—are everywhere only what is willed by this will, and not themselves the origin and caretaker of this will. Rather, they are merely its often unwilling enactors.

What is the purpose of this reference to modern technology and the thoroughly technological character of modern science? It is supposed to lead us to a consideration of whether we are permitted in translating the Greek word ἐπιστήμη (i.e., "to-understand-something") with the word "science." If by this word we mean only modern science and only in an approximate sense—a state of affairs that certainly suggests itself, albeit through a lack of reflection—then the translation is incorrect. Nonetheless, there remains something truthful in the rendering of the Greek word ἐπιστήμη with the German word "*Wissenschaft*" ["science"], and precisely when we are thinking of the technological character of modern science.

Therefore, modern science and the Greek ἐπιστήμη do indeed have a connection to one another. Certainly. Regarding the translation of ἐπιστήμη with the German word *"Wissenschaft"* ["science"], one could easily make reference to the oft-mentioned fact that Occidental and modern history both trace back to Greek antiquity, and that this lineage is particularly pronounced in the Occidental approach to cognition and knowledge. Where would the Roman, the medieval, and the contemporary scientific attitudes be without the ancient Greeks and without the possibility of an ever-renewable dialogue with them? How would matters stand, if the ancient Greeks had not occurred? What is at stake with the enigma of the past, of the having-been? The having-been is something entirely different from the merely bygone.

We today—i.e., we of the contemporary era—eagerly seek to root out even the darkest recesses of bygone days: however, because we go about this task by way of the discipline of historiography, we are only fleetingly acquainted with the indestructible nearness of the having-been. Perhaps historiography, as a kind of technical mastery of bygone history, is precisely the barrier that the contemporary human [194] has erected between the having-been and his own, simple wonderment. As those who have reached a later point in history, we presume ourselves to be further along than the having-been, whereas in fact the having-been simply and purely surpasses us and will continue to do so until one day we learn to intuit that the hidden secret of our essence is awaiting us in the having-been, and only as such is present to us. But how can this happen, if we still do not yet quite know what the present is? How can this come about if we spend all of our time calculating back-and-forth between the bygone, what will soon be bygone, and what has been bygone for ages? This also occurs when we make the Greek word ἐπιστήμη German by translating it with the German word *"Wissenschaft"* ["science"].

If we now assert that ἐπιστήμη may indeed be translated as "science," taken in its modern technical essence, then we are thinking of something more than just the oft-cited historical connection between modern 'culture' and the ancient Greeks. We are thinking of something even more essential and significant, something the ground and consequences of which have not even been intuited, let alone clearly apprehended: namely, that already in the Greek experience of the essence of knowledge and of "science," ἐπιστήμη is itself intimately related to τέχνη, if not simply the same thing. But what does τέχνη mean? Given the few aforementioned indications regarding our understanding of ἐπιστήμη, we will avoid attempting here to illuminate the essence of the Greek τέχνη by means of notions about modern "technology." The proper path actually leads in the opposite direction. However, this is more easily said than done. We ask again: what does τέχνη mean?

Let us stick to the original meaning of the word. This path that leads through the illumination of the root meaning of words and expressions is full of peril, and this is something that holds true also for all future cases of the same. The mere command of language usage and the consultation of dictionaries do not suffice to enable us to follow this path. What more is required cannot be extensively discussed here. But he who attentively [195] thinks along with us will one day notice and recognize that we are not just skimming off random meanings of mere words in order to then construct a philosophy and declare that the insight gained into the matter through the word is exhaustive and sufficient. What is a word without the connection to what it names and to what comes to presence in the word? We must avoid all empty and coincidental etymologies, for they degenerate into frivolous play if what is named by the word is not first thought and continually reconsidered, slowly and at length, and continually examined and reexamined in its word essence.

REVIEW

1) The intimate connection between thinking and things. Logic, pure thinking, and reflection

'Logic' is the term for 'the doctrine of correct thinking.' It represents the inner structure of thinking, its form, and its rules. 'To practice logic' thus means: to learn to think correctly. When is thinking correct? Apparently when it unfolds in accordance with the forms and rules established by logic, thereby corresponding to 'logic.' Thinking is correct when it is 'logical.' One says that this or that thing is 'completely logical,' but by that one does not make reference to a thought process and its validity, but rather to a situation (a process or state of affairs) that has arisen with consistency from out of a given set of circumstances. This 'consistency' consists of the proper course of events belonging to the circumstances obtaining to the matter. Accordingly, what is 'logical,' what is 'consistent,' and generally what is correct lie not in our thinking, but rather in things. We speak of an inner 'logic of a thing.' Therefore, we are only thinking logically, i.e., correctly, when we think 'factually' from out of and with regard to the matters themselves. But how can our thinking be 'factual' if it does not involve itself [196] with matters and attend to their minutiae? Thus, the correctness of thinking is once again dependent upon our thinking and the proper involvement of thinking with things. Therefore, there exists a two-fold 'logic': a logic of thinking that states how thinking properly follows and pursues things, and a logic of things that shows how and in what sense things have their own, internal consistency. Things do not appeal to or address themselves toward us if we ourselves do not intend our thoughts toward them. Our thinking, however, remains adrift and becomes dissolute if it is not first addressed by things and beholden to this address. It is strange how here the logic of things and the logic of thinking, like thinking and things themselves, are drawn into each other, with one returning in the other and one making a claim on the other. It would be stranger still if the claim through which things and thinking reciprocally make a demand on one another did not arise from out of either things or thinking. It would be enigmatic indeed if it proved to be the case that this claim occurs in the things themselves and has always and in advance arrived for the human, even though he is not attentive to the arrival or the origin of this claim.

Perhaps this is already a sufficient hint that neither the logic of thinking nor the logic of things, or their reciprocal coupling, constitute essential logic. In this case, the origin and foundation of correct thinking, and even of thinking as such, would remain hidden from us. It would then be the case that we would not even understand, nor be able to observe in even a remote way, the character of that demand under which we stand when we attempt to comply with the conventional demand to think correctly. Perhaps the human, ceaselessly and resourcefully thinking up new things, has been for a long time already living in a state of disregard toward thinking, and precisely because he has become fixated on the idea that thinking is only a kind of calculating. This idea is surely as old as essential thinking itself, an idea by [197] which we may someday see that thinking itself runs astray in its proper essence and thereby also constantly errs.

This is why the incorrectness proper to thinking never consists in the fact that in a given sequence of thoughts—for example, in a deduction—a mistake is being made. Rather, it is thinking itself that makes an error in regard to its own essence and essential origin. Could this mistake regarding its proper essence be the reason for the incorrectness proper to thinking? If so, then surely the task of thinking correctly and learning to think correctly leads to other higher—and perhaps even the highest—matters.

(Perhaps this state of being mistaken in its own essence is a special endowment that characterizes the origin and determination of thinking and only thinking, an endowment that must not be regarded as mere lack, but rather as a bestowal of that through which authentic decisions are decided, if, moreover, deciding belongs to dividing, which in turn belongs to differentiation. Differentiation is present only where there is difference. But, indeed, how could a difference ever reveal itself if it were not accompanied by differentiation and a readiness for it? Differentiation: is that not a fundamental feature of thinking? Whence does thinking get this fundamental feature?)

But does 'logic' as the doctrine of correct thinking offer the guarantee that through it we will learn to think? How do things stand with 'learning,' anyway? If 'to learn' means 'to apprentice oneself,' and if all 'teaching' and 'learning' remain essentially distinct from what belongs to the realm of mere training, drilling, and cramming; further, if 'to learn' means to 'apprentice oneself' (i.e., to be lingeringly underway within learning), then in every learning there already pervades a form of thinking. That being said, we who are here claiming this to be the case certainly cannot yet say what this thinking is. But if, in truth, there is no properly understood learning and teaching without thinking, then every sort of learning to think as a process of learning [198] is already a thinking in which thinking as such, and only thinking, is thought.

But does this not all come down to the fact that in the process of learning to think, what is thought 'of' and thought 'about' is thinking? It appears so. For 'logic,' as the doctrine of correct thinking, is, after all, a thinking about thinking. Certainly, this thinking 'about' thinking is a rather contrived, almost unnatural activity. Thinking about thinking—this seems to be something warped and distorted by which thinking bends back towards itself and abandons its straight course. Bending back means reflecting. Reflection inhibits action and causes indecision. And thinking about thinking: is that not the very paradigm of reflection? That is like a reflection on reflection: it circles emptily around itself and detaches itself from all matters and things. Furthermore, thinking about thinking is unusual and foreign to natural thinking and is an esoteric pursuit through which it is difficult for us to find a point of reference or a lead-line. As a thinking about thinking, 'logic' is a total abstraction. Is there actually a type of learning in it through which we learn to think? For surely all learning necessitates simple, straight paths on which what is to be learned encounters us in an unmediated and clear way: learning necessitates a slow start and a step-by-step progress without bends or entanglements. Thinking about thinking—what could be more entangled and enmeshed than this? That is why the often anxious 'normal understanding' has given voice many times to its suspicion regarding logic and its use. It is said that if thinking itself is to be learned properly, and if thinking correctly always means 'thinking factually,' then we are most assured of learning to think through the thinking interaction with the things and matters in question. We learn how to think historiographically through the historiographical sciences. Where is there really a need for logic? [199] We learn how to think physically through physics. We thereby learn each type of factual thinking through the matters and things themselves.

However, here we do not want to learn how to think historiographically, nor biologically, nor physically, nor even scientifically, economically, nor artistically: here we 'only' want to learn how to think. 'Only thinking'? What are we thinking when we are 'only' thinking? 'Only thinking'—is this somehow less than thinking factually, because it is lacking a matter? Or is 'only thinking' more than all factual thinking? Because it is freed of all objects, is it pure thinking? But what does thinking think, and in what direction does it think, when it is 'only' thinking? Logic, as the doctrine of correct thinking, surely refrains from references to specific subject matters. It only deals with thinking itself. Only thinking and only learning to think is what we would like to learn here. That is the matter of concern here and now, and indeed exclusively: namely, that we must first make an effort to learn this learning to think. Thereby, the question of what logic is capable of, and what logic is, becomes inescapable. What in the world does 'logic' have to do with thinking?

2) Return to the Greek context at work in the naming of the words ἐπιστήμη λογική: ἐπιστήμη and τέχνη

The name 'logic'—i.e., the matter and the contours of its essence—originates with the ancient Greeks. If indeed there is something within Occidental history that was present to the ancient Greeks and still remains present to us, it is 'logic,' even if we do not yet recognize this. 'Logic' is the shortened term for λογική (λογική, λογικά—that which pertains to λόγος). Before λογική is ἐπιστήμη: we translate that phrase as the science of λόγος. We know other, corresponding terms: ἐπιστήμη φυσική (i.e., the science of φύσις and that which belongs to φύσις), and ἐπιστήμη ἠθική (i.e., the science of ἦθος and that which concerns the ἦθος).

[200] Before we elucidate what the word λόγος means in the term ἐπιστήμη λογική, we will first designate the meaning of the general term ἐπιστήμη. ἐπίστασθαι means to place oneself before something, to stand before it in such a way that through and for this standing-before, something shows itself, and does so specifically to us (as medium). To stand before something means: to allow something to be shown to oneself, to be able to stand before that which shows itself in a manner that accords with what, and how, that which shows itself *is*. To be able to stand before a matter means to understand it: accordingly, ἐπίστασθαι comes to mean 'to understand something.'

If we are within our rights in translating ἐπιστήμη as "science" (and we are indeed permitted to do this), then the reason for this is that what we have come to know as "science" is in the ground of its essence designated and determined by ἐπιστήμη, i.e., the understanding of something.

Although modern science seems distant from the Greek ἐπιστήμη in time, scope, and in the manner of its organization, execution, and validity, the core of modern science is ἐπιστήμη, and in such an originary way that what lies as a dormant seed within ἐπιστήμη only begins to see the light of day in the form of modern science. This is what we call the essentially technical character of modern science. So, does that mean that the Greek ἐπιστήμη already has a connection to 'technology'? Certainly; however, not to modern machine technology, but to what is named by the Greek word τέχνη. But what does τέχνη mean?

§ 2. Logic, ἐπιστήμη, τέχνη. The related meanings of ἐπιστήμη and τέχνη. An analysis regarding the questionable relationship between thinking and logic

a) τέχνη, φύσις, and ἐπιστήμη. τέχνη (to bring forth, to place-forth) and φύσις (to emerge from out of itself) in their relation to unconcealment. [201] A rejection of the interpretation of τέχνη and ἐπιστήμη in terms of the differentiation between theory and practice

What does τέχνη, which we say has the most intimate relation to ἐπιστήμη, mean? τέχνη is related to the root word τέκω/τίκτω, commonly translated as "to create." What is created is τὸ τέκνον, the child; τίκτω means to create—indeed, it means to beget as well as to bear, but for the most part it means the latter. In our mother tongue, this bearing-creating is expressed by the beautiful and not yet fully comprehended turn of phrase 'to bring into the world.' The proper and most concealed Greek meaning of τέκω is not 'making' or 'manufacturing,' but is rather the bringing-forth of something into the unconcealed by the human so that it may presence there in the unconcealed as something that has been thus brought forth, so that it may shine out of the unconcealed and 'be' in the sense that the Greeks understood it. ὁ τέκτων is the one who brings forth, the one who places-forth and sets-forth something in the unconcealed and sets it into the open. This setting-forth in the manner of bringing-forth is carried out by the human—for example, in building, hewing, and molding. ὁ τέκτων lies in the word 'architect.' Something issues and projects-forth from the architect, who is the ἀρχή of a τεκεῖν and who guides it—as in, for example, the bringing-forth of a temple.

All bringing-forth in this larger and richer sense of setting-forth into the unconcealed (properly understood) moves and persists in the realm of unconcealment, which is the realm of all possible realms and is that in which the human stands and falls, walks and rests, climbs and plunges, erects and destroys. This bringing-forth is essentially different from 'what is brought forth' by 'nature.' To be sure, we say that 'nature' brings-forth plants and animals. But this 'bringing-forth' is not the characteristically human activity of setting-forth and setting into the unconcealed. 'Nature,' especially if we think it in the Greek way as φύσις, is the self-emerging and self-occluding. Given that this is so, we can easily see that φύσις [202] as emerging and occluding stands in relation to unconcealment and concealing, and in a certain sense is unconcealment and concealing themselves, so long as by φύσις we think (as is necessary) 'nature' in a more originary sense than we are used to (i.e., only as a special realm to be differentiated from history). These connections between φύσις as emerging into the unconcealed, and unconcealment itself, never became clear and grounded in Greek thinking itself. Indeed, they are still not fully thought through today. The relationship between φύσις and τέχνη and the connection of both to unconcealment has yet to be illuminated. But, rooted in this connection is the uncanny enigma that for the modern human there is a fate concealed within modern technology, one to which he will never be able to respond properly through the merely purported mastery of technology. But what, now, is τέχνη in relation to τεκεῖν, to "bringing-forth"?

τέχνη is what pertains intimately to all bringing-forth in the sense of human setting-forth. If bringing-forth (τεκεῖν) is a setting into the unconcealed (i.e., the world), then τέχνη means the knowledge of the unconcealed and the ways of attaining, obtaining, and implementing it. The essential feature of bringing-forth is τέχνη, and the essential feature of τέχνη is *to be* the relation with unconcealment and to unfold that relatedness. Thus, τέχνη does not mean a type of activity in the sense of an effecting of bringing-forth, but rather a preparing-beforehand and keeping ready of the respective realm of the unconcealed into which something is brought forth and set-forth: namely, what is to be set-forth. This preparing-beforehand and keeping-ready of the unconcealed (ἀληθές)—that is, of the true—is τέχνη. If we call this particular residing within the true by the name 'knowledge,' taken here in a far-ranging and rich sense, then τέχνη is a form of knowledge in the broad sense of illuminating, of making 'light.' The conventional translation of τέχνη as "art" is wrong and misleading, especially when we understand 'art' [203] in the way it is meant in the common pairing and differentiation 'art and science.' But even if we take 'art' in the broadest sense of 'skill,' the essentially knowledge-based (and thus Greek) dimension of τέχνη is thereby still not expressed, and the sense of proficiency and dexterity predominate. How exclusively the Greeks think a dimension of knowledge within the word τέχνη is exhibited by the fact that it often means something like 'cunning,' which in our language originally meant something like 'knowledge' and 'wisdom,' without the additional connotations of the deceitful and the calculating. On the other hand, it would be erroneous if we were to think that ἐπιστήμη–τέχνη, as a type of 'knowledge,' were to account for, as is commonly said, the theoretical side of 'practical' doing, making, and executing. One may see how crooked and confused the thinking of this view is if one looks to the fact that, for the Greeks, 'the theoretical' (i.e., θεωρεῖν) is the highest form of action itself. Of what use, then, is our thoughtless and groundless differentiation between the 'theoretical' and the 'practical'? The still-veiled essential feature of the essence of ἐπιστήμη and τέχνη consists in their relation to the unconcealment of what is and what can be.

ἐπιστήμη, the understanding-of-something, and τέχνη, the knowledge of something, are so near to one another in essence that very often one word stands in for the other. This was already the case in the ancient Greek world: indeed, it is through ancient Greece that an essential connection between all knowledge and τέχνη is founded. The fact that now, at a turning point of Occidental fate—if not the Occidentally determined fate of the earth as a whole—τέχνη in the form of modern mechanized technology is becoming the admitted (or the not yet fully admitted) fundamental form of knowledge as a calculating ordering, is a sign whose immediate interpretation cannot be dared by any mortal. The 'philosophies of technology' now running wild are all only the spawn of technological thinking itself or, at best, mere re-actions against it (which amounts to the same). [204] At the moment, we can only make a supposition regarding what surely gives more than enough to think about: namely, that the fate of humanity and of peoples is intimately rooted in the particular relation of the human toward the respective appearing or self-withholding essence of unconcealment—that is, of truth. Whether and how the true is fatefully sent is grounded in whether and how the truth itself shows itself in its essence. If we consider that the essence of truth first opened itself for the Occident in general, and then decisively for the ancient Greek world, we then recognize to what extent the fate that unfolded in the ancient Greek world is nothing bygone or antiquated, and also nothing 'ancient,' but is rather something still undecided and still approaching us toward which we the Germans—preeminently and, for a long time also, probably alone—can and must direct our thinking. I say 'thinking': this is why it is necessary to learn how to think. Does 'logic' help in this regard? Once again we ask: what does 'logic' have to do with thinking? Why does thinking find itself subject to the laws of 'logic'? We are in the process of elucidating this term in its totality.

b) Logic as ἐπιστήμη λογική in connection with ἐπιστήμη φυσική and ἐπιστήμη ἠθική. On the dominance of reflection

'Logic' is the shortened expression for ἐπιστήμη λογική, and now means: having an understanding of what pertains to λόγος. And what does λόγος now mean? We let the question stand once more and linger first with the historical 'fact' that the name and matter of ἐπιστήμη λογική arises in connection with two other names and matters—ἐπιστήμη φυσική and ἐπιστήμη ἠθική—and in a manner that becomes historical.

ἐπιστήμη φυσική is the understanding of what belongs to φύσις or, more precisely, to the φύσει ὄντα. These are those particular beings that, emerging and submerging on their own accord, safeguard arising and vanishing: heaven and earth, the stars, the ocean, the mountains, rocks and waters, plants and animals. [205] If we thus understand the emerging and the emerged as what presences and appears in the broadest sense, then even humans and gods belong to φύσει ὄντα, insofar as they appear and presence, decay and disappear, peer into the unconcealed and withdraw themselves. ἐπιστήμη φυσική—that is, physics thus understood—is the knowledge of beings as a whole, in all of their guises and stages, in terms of their first and simplest connections. This 'physics' is not only substantially wider in scope than what we think of as 'physics' today (i.e., the mathematical, experimental knowledge pertaining to the laws of motion of material points of mass in space and time). ἐπιστήμη φυσική also thinks in a completely different way than the modern science of physics—indeed, in a completely different way than all science. ἐπιστήμη φυσική thinks beings as a whole, and thereby also beings in general, with an eye toward what is common to every being insofar as it is, can be, must be, or is none of these. What is common, proper, and ownmost to all beings is 'being.' 'Being'—the emptiest word which, it would appear, makes us initially not think much at all. Being—the word from out of which we nevertheless think and experience everything, and the word through which we *are*. When will we finally have the 'courage,' for once, to think genuinely and tenaciously what would come to be if we (i.e., humans) could not think and say 'being' and 'to be'? The ἐπιστήμη φυσική of the ancient Greeks is a way and an attempt to understand beings as a whole with an eye toward being, an attempt to place themselves before beings and stand before them so that these beings may show themselves in their being. The entirety of Occidental thinking has not moved beyond this attempt—at most, perhaps, it has deviated from it.

The third term, ἐπιστήμη ἠθική, designates the understanding of what belongs to the ἦθος. The word ἦθος originally means dwelling, sojourn. Here, in the term ἐπιστήμη ἠθική, τὸ ἦθος is meant in a simple way. So understood, it means [206] the sojourn of the human, the residing, the 'dwelling' of the human in the midst of beings as a whole. The essential feature of ἦθος, of this sojourning, is the way in which the human holds fast to beings, and thereby holds himself, keeps himself, and allows himself to be held. The understanding of ἦθος, the knowledge of it, is 'ethics.' Here we take this word in a very broad and essential sense. The conventional meaning of 'ethics' as a moral doctrine, a theory of virtue, or even a doctrine of values, is only a consequence, mutation, and aberration of the concealed, original meaning. Moreover, whereas 'physics' thinks about beings as a whole, 'ethics' only regards one being—namely, the human—set apart from the others. However, the human is here not regarded as a separate solitary being, cut off from beings as a whole, but rather precisely in view of the fact that he, and he alone, abides in beings as a whole, relates to them, and thereby consummates and maintains this relation from either a particular grounding or groundlessness. τὸ ἦθος is the comportment of the human's sojourn in the midst of beings as a whole. In this sense, even the knowledge of 'ethics,' although surely in a different way and approach, is oriented toward beings as a whole: in this case, the human is in one respect the center, though in another respect, not. Hidden within these connections is the essence that is both proper to, and characteristic of, the human, an essence which we could call 'eccentric.' The human *is*, dwelling in the midst of beings as a whole, without, however, being its center in the sense of a ground that mediates and upholds it. The human is in the center of beings but is not that center itself. ἐπιστήμη φυσική and ἐπιστήμη ἠθική are an understanding of beings as a whole, a whole which shows itself to the human, and to which the human relates by holding himself to it and sojourning in it.

From these short references to 'physics' and 'ethics' we may surmise that now the aforementioned [207] 'logic,' the ἐπιστήμη λογική, in some sense also connects to beings as a whole. Here, also, the remarked-upon essential feature—i.e., the understanding that it somehow concerns beings as whole—is grounded in that on which ἐπιστήμη λογική draws: namely, λόγος.

REVIEW

1) Logic as the reflection about reflection without an attachment to things. On the power of the self-reflection of subjectivity and pure thinking (Rilke, Hölderlin)

In this lecture on logic, we would like to set out to learn how to think. However, so that right at the beginning of our efforts a certain illumination already brightens this path, we must at least have provisional knowledge of what, through its traditional transmission (to which we are all knowingly or unknowingly subject), we understand as 'logic.' What is 'logic'? What is it that is signified by this Greek name? What does it mean for the fate and course of thinking itself that, from long ago (although *not* from the inception), 'logic' appears in Occidental thinking as the doctrine of correct thinking? Early on, 'logic' is regarded as the ὄργανον, the tool and the equipment, as it were, with which thinking is handled. Since then, one finds it proper that thinking belongs under the province of 'logic,' as though this belonging together of 'thinking' and 'logic' had been eternally written in the stars.

Nevertheless, one is not entirely certain about the authoritative role accorded to 'logic.' Occasionally a suspicion regarding 'logic' arises, even if it is only a suspicion regarding its usefulness (which, admittedly, remains only a superficial suspicion): for something can be without usefulness, thus being useless, and can nevertheless [208] still have *being*—indeed, it can even be the case that the useless has infinitely more being than all that is useful combined. Behind the suspicion that logic is, in a practical sense, useless, owing to the fact that we always only learn correct thinking through contact with things and never through an 'abstract' logic—behind this fear of the uselessness of logic there nevertheless remains a more serious concern.

The concern is this: that logic, as the doctrine of proper thinking, is itself a form of thinking. To 'study logic' therefore means to think about thinking. Hereby thinking bends back toward itself and becomes reflection. Since logic thinks about thinking and thinks about it in general, and since the thinking which is the object of this thought has no reference to an object determined in terms of its content, and thereby remains a pure thinking that dissolves into itself, logic as the thinking about pure thinking is not only reflection, but is rather the reflection about reflection, a reflection that whirls away into emptiness like a hollow vortex without an object or a connection to things. Logic: a thinking about thinking (i.e., reflection)—a detour into utter entanglement. If already within the context of dealing with things a thinking about them easily hampers action and decisiveness, what then would be the consequences of a thinking about thinking? Reflection, the bending-back toward oneself, is, as one says, 'egocentric,' self-centered, self-absorbed, 'individualistic.'

But is this due to reflection? It is possible for a group of people to be focused upon itself as a group, as an association, as a coalition—i.e., reflection. A people can be focused on itself and only itself—i.e., reflection. Indeed, even all of humanity on earth could be focused back upon itself—i.e., reflection. Does reflection cease to be reflective, reflected, and self-absorbed when many people reflect together instead of a loner only by himself reflecting about himself and his 'I'? But how could this be, if in fact the totality of humanity on this earth reflecting upon itself constitutes the most monstrous case of reflection, and if, [209] in this reflection, the abstract and abstraction have become the uncanny itself? Has the human already escaped reflection when, for example, as a Christian he thinks of his god? Or is he thereby only concerned with his own salvation? But how could this be, if only with and through this type of self-concern and this form of self-encounter the power of subjectivity's self-reflection has been released into modern world history and has become hardened in it? Then Christianity, with its belief in, and teaching of, the τέχνη-like notion of Creation (regarded metaphysically), is an essential reason for the rise of modern technology, and also plays an essential role in the formation of the dominance of the self-reflection of subjectivity. As a result, it is precisely Christianity that is unable to overcome this reflection. What else could be the cause of the historical bankruptcy of Christianity and its church in the modern era of world history? Is a third world war needed in order to prove this?

The matter of reflection is a peculiar one, and it is not settled with the simple suspicion that reflection is allegedly only a 'solipsistic' circling of the individual around itself. Through such a suspicion, the essence of reflection is not recognized, nor are the distortions of its essence averted. Perhaps reflection belongs to the essence of the human. Perhaps the harm of reflection does not lie in the bending-back as such, but rather in what is being bent-back toward, and in that toward which the essence of the human is inclined. But perhaps it is not only that the essence of the human is essentially turned toward something. Perhaps it is even the case that the essence of the human is in itself re-flection, an originary turning-toward that is a re-turn that also entails within itself that the reversal and the inverted become stronger and gain the upper hand. Then what one would otherwise call and understand as 'reflection' would only be a particular variation of reflection: namely, the reflection of subjectivity in which the human conducts [210] himself as the self-regarded subject, accepting all beings only as 'objects' and as the merely objective. This kind of reflection, thought as the essence of the modern human (i.e., as the inner structure of the subjectivity of the subject), is consummately articulated poetically, and at the same time experienced in regard to its metaphysical dimension, in Rilke's eighth *Duino Elegy*.

From this elegy it becomes clear that Rilke's poetry, notwithstanding other differences, still belongs in the same realm of the same stage of Occidental metaphysics as what is given voice by Nietzsche's philosophy. That Rilke was both able and compelled to speak the eighth *Duino Elegy* also bears witness to the greatness of his inner tact in regard to the boundary set for the poet. That he was able to stay within the limits of this boundary and bear the room to maneuver afforded by his position is more essential than any overly effortful and purely deliberate breaking of these boundaries.

If there is to be at all a kind of 'overcoming' of modern forms of reflection (i.e., the reflection of subjectivity), then it is only possible through another type of reflection, even though it may initially appear that this is the very height of madness: namely, to attempt to reflect oneself out of reflection by way of reflection! But if 'reflection' is always a manner of thinking, then the proper reflection belonging to the essence of the human could only consist of a corresponding thinking. Then we would have to learn to think, even if we thereby run the risk of creating the impression that when we think-after thinking, this thinking is simply circling around itself with neither goal nor ground.

Mindful of this danger, we nonetheless attempt to learn how to think: every meditation on every sentence is already that attempt at learning, one that does not only begin, for example, once we have moved beyond these apparently only introductory lectures. Learning how to think—only thinking and nothing else besides. What are we thinking when we are 'only' thinking? When we are only thinking, we embark down the path toward what, for thinking, is the to-be-thought. [211] This shows itself to us when we are only—and that means, *purely*—thinking. This means that, as long as we are thinking about particular matters and within the confines of a particular subject matter, we remain on one level (i.e., we remain merely on the surface). In thinking about specific matters, we do not proceed toward what opens itself in and to pure thinking, opening itself to it because it is intended for thinking and only for thinking. For then pure thinking inclines itself toward, and opens itself to, its own depth, and finds within this depth enough of the to-be-thought—and only there finds, inclined toward this depth, what is deepest.

Thinking would thus not at all be an occupation that immanently circles itself, an occupation for the benefit of which a matter must be identified and offered up to it as an object so that thinking may have a hold and a ground. In this case, all of these solid foundations that present the objective to subjects would be merely surface aspects and superficial levels that hide from the human the profound depth into which thinking itself, as thinking, opens itself: for, as the thinking that it is, it is in itself, and not retroactively, oriented toward what is deepest, and is attracted by it and taken up into a relation with it. In one of his short odes that serves as a prelude to his hymnal and elegiac poetry, Hölderlin says the following:

> Whosoever has thought what is deepest, loves what is most alive.
>
> (Socrates and Alcibiades)

We are tempted to think that "what is deepest" allows itself to be identified, so that we may then use thinking, among other things, in order to make it an object of understanding. But what is deepest only comes about *when* we have *already* thought, and simply *only* thought. However, he who has already thought has also already ceased to think—how shall the deepest then still open itself? The Greek thinkers already knew all of this, albeit differently and better. Whosoever has thought is not at the end of thinking and finished with it: rather, whosoever has thought is only beginning [212] to think, and *only* to think. The more purely the human has thought, the more decisively has he arrived on the path of thinking and remains one who thinks, in the very same manner that someone who has seen the right way has only just begun to see. Strange, how here the end is actually only the beginning. Whosoever has thought and thus has only first begun to think, and is thus *in* thinking and operating from out of it, has in this way, and only in this way, already thought what is deepest, which never exists somewhere apart.

"Whosoever has thought what is deepest, loves what is most alive." This makes it sound as though the love for what is most alive is a consequence of thinking, as though this love activates itself once thinking has been consummated. Yet, the truth is otherwise: it is rather the case that thinking is itself the love, the love for what is "most alive," for that in which all that is alive has gathered itself in life. Love—a kind of thinking? Or, indeed, is thinking a kind of love? We are told that love is a 'feeling' and that thinking is without feeling. Psychology clearly differentiates between thinking, feeling, desire, and 'classifies' these as 'psychical phenomena.' One also thinks—and, from a certain perspective, justifiably—that thinking is cleaner and more precise the less it is affected (i.e., polluted) by moods and feelings. If, however, thinking is ever able to lead to love, then it would surely have to be a thinking in the proper mood and therefore an 'emotive' thinking, a thinking with 'emotions,' i.e., 'emotional thinking.' However, how can this be if what is deepest is only reachable in thinking and if it only opens itself to thinking? Does everything not then depend upon *only* thinking, upon thinking *purely*, in order to assure that the to-be-thought approaches thinking?

We now say Hölderlin's saying aloud with the emphasis suggested by the structure and rhythm of the verse itself:

Whosoever has thought *what is deepest*, loves what is *most alive*.

However, given the mysterious inexhaustibility of such lines, which always speak above and beyond the poet, it is good if we also occasionally emphasize it *thusly*:

[213] Whosoever has *thought* what is deepest, *loves* what is most alive.

"Thought" and "loves" are in such immediate proximity that they are effectively the same, though not, of course, as an indistinct monotony, but rather as a conjoined simplicity whose unity as thinking and life is named but nevertheless remains unsaid.

2) ἐπιστήμη λογική, ἐπιστήμη φυσική, ἐπιστήμη ἠθική

The thinking named here, and perhaps only provisionally intuited, is that thinking which we are trying to learn by learning 'thinking *as such*.'

Can this be accomplished through 'logic'? What is 'logic'? It is the ἐπιστήμη λογική: the science of λόγος and what pertains to λόγος. ἐπιστήμη means: the understanding of something. At the time of the formation and development of 'logic' in ancient Greece, the word ἐπιστήμη had the same meaning, or was closely related to, τέχνη. We translate τέχνη as "knowledge of something."

This mention of the kinship, and perhaps even sameness, of the meaning of the two Greek words ἐπιστήμη and τέχνη does not yet amount to much. But if we consider that ἐπιστήμη is the historical origin of Occidental science and of the Occidental forms of knowledge in general, and that in its modern guise it has become entirely ubiquitous, then the reference to the kinship between ἐπιστήμη and τέχνη gains in importance. Behind this fact, which bears upon the history of a word, there lies hidden the predestination of the technological essence of Occidental knowledge, for whose development the Judeo-Christian understanding of Creation, specifically in the form of late-Greek and Roman terminology, plays a decisive role.

Before we now elucidate the term ἐπιστήμη λογική and the matter it names, we must attend to the fact that this term appears at the same time alongside two others: ἐπιστήμη φύσική and ἐπιστήμη ἠθική. How does this fact bear upon our understanding [214] of what ἐπιστήμη means? The name means an understanding that pertains to beings as a whole. φύσις, understood properly, does not only include that which, in distinction to history, we call 'nature': for history also belongs to φύσις, as do the human and the gods. φύσις means beings as a whole. ἐπιστήμη φύσική, certainly in distinction to modern physics, is the knowledge of beings as a whole.

By contrast, ἐπιστήμη ἠθική now does appear to bring forth a separate, or in any case particular, region of beings. The word ἦθος means dwelling, sojourn. We say: the dwelling of the human, his sojourn amidst beings as a whole. ἐπιστήμη ἠθική, 'ethics,' thought essentially and expansively, seeks to understand how the human abides in this sojourn amidst beings, thereby upholding himself and abiding. The word ἦθος refers to the bearing of all conduct obtaining to this sojourning amidst beings. 'Ethics' does not concern the human as a separate matter among other matters: rather, it regards the human in view of the relation of beings as a whole to the human, and of the human to beings as a whole. The human is thus, in a certain sense, in the middle of beings as a whole, but not, however, in the sense that he is the middle itself of beings such that he would be their sustaining ground. In any case, ethics—even though, like ἐπιστήμη φύσική, it deals with the human, albeit from a different perspective and in a different way—is concerned with beings as a whole.

Now, how do matters stand with regard to the third ἐπιστήμη that is named next to physics and ethics—namely, ἐπιστήμη λογική (i.e., logic)?

[215] c) λόγος and ἦθος. The universal role of λόγος as *ratio* and reason in the determinations of the human essence and its consequential consummation in the "will to power" (Nietzsche)

In the term ἐπιστήμη λογική, the word λόγος means something akin to "assertion": λέγειν τι κατά τινος—"to claim something about something," and at the same time to hold fast to it, thereby establishing it and showing it. The essential feature of λόγος, of making an assertion, lies in saying in the sense of a making apparent of something that each time allows a particular being to be seen and grasped in the manner that it is. Saying brings and places what is said, and what is shown through the saying, before us, presenting and delivering it to us. The essential feature of λόγος, of the assertion, is not, therefore, a saying in the sense of a speaking and of making a verbal statement. This is already implied by the fact that the Greek word λόγος, and what it actually means, does not have anything directly to do with language and discourse. What this means for the essence of λόγος, the insight into its essence, and also for the misapprehension of its essence (and consequently for the origin of 'logic' and its role and limitations), will reveal itself to us in what follows. Above all we will have to consider when and how the words λέγειν and λόγος arrived at the undeniable meaning of saying and asserting, even though the original meaning did not include a connection to saying and language.

However, first it is still necessary to bring the designation of logic as ἐπιστήμη λογική—the knowledge pertaining to that which belongs to asserting—into its correct connection with the given designations of 'physics' and 'ethics.'

Physics and ethics both have, albeit in different ways, the fundamental feature of an understanding about beings as a whole. They are oriented toward this one whole, they are *versus unum*, universal in the simplest sense of the word. Physics and ethics are each an understanding of beings as a whole. Does this also apply to 'logic'? If so, in what sense? [216] As a human activity, λόγος—assertion, judgment—only appears in one particular region of beings: namely, in the region of the human, but not, for example, in that of plants, stones, or even animals. Assertion is thereby not like what may be encountered everywhere in every being, and thus also continuously and universally in beings. This statement applies also to ἦθος which, as the abiding of the human's sojourn amidst beings, only pertains to the human. However, ἦθος pertains to the human in just such a way that he, *in* ἦθος and through it, stands in relation to beings as a whole, and in such a manner that, reciprocally, the whole of beings addresses itself to him alone. Could not something similar apply also to λόγος, since as assertion it is a behavior of the human that can relate itself to all beings and somehow also always beings as a whole, especially and particularly when the assertion hits upon the unsayable? For the unsayable and unutterable is what it is, as the no-longer-sayable and the no-longer-utterable, owing to its relation to asserting. However, λόγος does seem to be constituted differently than ἦθος. Asserting can perhaps relate itself to all beings; but asserting, taken strictly for itself, is only a particular and isolated activity among the totality of activities that comprise the bearing of the human sojourn amidst beings. Seen from this perspective, λόγος is only a special case among the other possible human activities.

λόγος, as the activity of asserting, belongs to ἦθος, which is the bearing that pervades all behavior. Hence ethics, as the knowledge of human behavior in relation to this bearing, is the more expansive knowledge that includes logic within itself. 'Logic' is, as it were, a particular kind of ethics, that of assertoric behavior: logic is the ethics of λόγος, the ethics of asserting. If this is the case, then any justification for equating logic with the other forms of knowledge (i.e., physics and ethics), or even placing it above them, falls away. The human, insofar as he is seen and thought with regard to his universal relations and modes of behavior [217] toward beings as a whole, is determined by ἦθος. That is why we would be justified in saying that the human is that particular being amidst beings as a whole whose essence is characterized by ἦθος.

However, in light of the form of the human essence just now delineated, we come upon something strange: namely, that in the Greek world, and throughout the entirety of Occidental history following upon it, the human is defined as τὸ ζῷον λόγον ἔχον, that living being who has as its defining characteristic both saying and asserting. This determination of the human essence with an eye toward λόγος gets its character through the differentiation of the human from the animal, and thereby within the context of the life of living beings in general. The animal is, with respect to λόγος, ζῷον ἄλογον, the living being without λόγος. However, α- (i.e., "without") does not mean here an absence, a lack, and a going-without. Indeed, going-without is only present where the absent as such has become recognizable through a desire for it. The animal is entirely excluded from λόγος, no matter how 'intelligent' animals may be (and no matter how eager modern psychology is, in a strange misapprehension of the simplest connections, to research the 'intelligence' of animals). The human is characterized by λόγος: it is the human's most essential possession.

Following what was elucidated above, one might rather expect a characterization of the human essence that reads thusly: ἄνθρωπος ζῷον ἦθος ἔχον, the human is that living being whose ownmost and most distinguishing characteristic is ἦθος. However, instead of this, λόγος is now seen to have the undeniable primacy over ἦθος. The essence of the Occidental human finds itself being imprinted upon by the character of ζῷον λόγον ἔχον. The Roman re-articulation of this—which is something more than just a translation into Latin—reads: *homo est animal rationale*, the human is the rational living being. If we pay attention to the relation of *ratio* and λόγος to thinking, and the equating of both, then we could also say: [218] the human is the thinking animal. If we understand thinking to be the form through which knowledge (i.e., ἐπιστήμη and τέχνη) carries itself out, then the human is the cunning, clever animal. With an eye toward this essence of the human, and from within the perspective of modern metaphysics, the young Nietzsche precociously caught sight of and verbalized an outline of his later metaphysics of the will to power. In the summer of 1873, the twenty-nine-year-old Nietzsche wrote an essay entitled *On Truth and Lie in an Extra-Moral Sense*. This essay would be published for the first time only later (in 1903) as a part of his literary estate.[1] The essay begins with the following excerpt:

> In some remote corner of the universe, poured out into countless flickering solar systems, there was once a star on which some clever animals invented knowledge. It was the most arrogant and dishonest minute of 'world history'; but, still, it was only a minute. Once nature had drawn in a few breaths, the star solidified, and the clever animals had to die.

To what extent Nietzsche, in his later metaphysics, holds fast to this conception of the human, while at the same time radicalizing his thoughts regarding the over-human, cannot be elucidated presently. It is enough if we can initially and approximately see that, from the beginning of Occidental metaphysics on through its consummation, the essence of the human is understood in relation to λόγος, and λόγος is interpreted as thinking. In what sense this characteristic of λόγος is to be understood; to what extent λόγος thereby remains ambiguous; what all of this means for history and the essence of the Occidental human and for the manner in which he exists historically: all of this can only be alluded to here in an inquiring way. 'Logic' forms itself and its history in accordance with the fate from out of which λόγος unfolds (and does not unfold) its essence in the history of the Occident and of the world.

[219] REVIEW

3) On the dominance of reflection and subjectivity. The question concerning the depth of pure thinking and the re-turn (Rilke, Hölderlin)

The prior session attempted to discuss three things: two relating to thinking, and the third on the doctrine of thinking (i.e., logic as ἐπιστήμη λογική).

---

[1] Nietzsche, *Werke*, X, 189 ff.

Thinking was characterized, on the one hand, with regard to reflection, and on the other hand in relation to its own depth. We today only know reflection in the form of the reflection belonging to subjectivity. That is why we fear, with the equally common equating of subjectivity with the I-hood of the singular 'I,' that reflection is the breeding ground of individualism and egoism. However, an argument against this is the fact that not only individual people may be carried away by, and entangled up in, this essence of reflection as a form of selfish obstinacy, but also entire groups, federations, nations, peoples—indeed, even all of humanity on earth. Reflective self-referentiality need not necessarily hit upon a singular, separate 'I,' but it does always hit upon a self. But the 'I' and the self are not the same. Not only is there an I-self, but also a you-self [*Du-Selbst*], as well as a we-self and the you-self [*Ihr-Selbst*]. For each particular essence of reflection, what is decisive is how the self-hood of the self is determined, and vice versa.

To be sure, every thinking thinks its thoughts in such a way that thinking itself is thereby also thought, and that what is thought about, and thought with, refers back to the one who is thinking. How else could it be that what is thought about is also what is intended for us to be thought about? But the question remains how what is thought about is being thought about—if, for example, only as a thing or an object. The question also remains how the one thinking knows himself in this—as only, for example, an 'I' or a subject. If it is only as such, then all reference back to what is representationally set-before [220] ends already with a subject oriented toward itself, and then it is indeed the case that all representation, imagining, and bringing-before-oneself resemble a capturing of objects in snares that have been set out. And then Rilke, in whom the age of consummate subjectivity poetizes its own end, can say the following in these strangely fitting yet nevertheless profoundly errant lines at the beginning of the eighth *Duino Elegy:*

> With full gaze, the animal sees
> the open. Only our eyes are,
> as if reversed, entirely like snares
> set around it, blocking the freedom of its out-going.
> What *is* outside, we know only from the animal's face.

Let us reflect on what announces itself in these words: "What is outside, we know only from the animal's face." 'The creature'—that is, in this case, the animal, and in no way the creation of God as conceived of by Christianity—alone sees the open. The human, however, gathers knowledge of the open from the animal. This thought is not only mentioned in passing within this elegy. Rather, it everywhere bears Rilke's true poetry. It contains a decision concerning the thinking of the human as subject, whose essence is now being made true in a world-historical sense. Those of the contemporary era, instead of ceaselessly blathering about this poet, should for once earnestly think-after such a thought as the above, in order to recognize in it a consummation, finally brought to word, of an approaching errancy whose origin lies in a misapprehension of the essence of reflection and, thus, of thinking. When determining the essence of reflection, we must first ask from where and back to where and in what way thinking is bent back into itself, so that it carries within itself the fundamental feature of a re-turn.

So that we may nevertheless find the proper 'perspective' regarding all of these questions concerning the character of reflection, it is necessary first to pay some attention to the dimension into which thinking as thinking reaches, and within [221] which, and through which, it wields itself. It is necessary to consider the depth proper to pure thinking, from which thinking itself first receives the seal of its essence. We usually only think 'depth' in contrast to height, and therefore in the direction of downward and the below. But the essence of depth is otherwise. For example, we speak of the 'deep woods.' Depth is the self-opening concealing expanse that continually points to an ever more lightened concealment and gathers itself therein. The quoted words of Hölderlin should only be a hint, and not the answer, to the question concerning the depth proper to pure thinking.

He who has thought *what is deepest*, loves what is *most alive*.

The exegesis of this line can be briefly summarized in the resonant, albeit different, intonation:

He who has *thought* what is deepest, *loves* what is most alive.

Whosoever *has thought* is thinking for the first time, in the very same way that whosoever *has seen* sees for the first time. The perfect case is the proper present, and the proper present is the future. Authentic thinking is true loving and the coming-to-be at home in the essential ground of all relations: re-turn. Only when thinking has thought what is deepest—that is, only when it has begun to think and continues to think the essential and singular to-be-thought—does the re-turn proper to thinking, i.e., the originary reflection, come to itself and come into play originarily.

4) Logic as the doctrine of the assertion (concept, judgment, inference). λόγος, *ratio*, reason: on the universal meaning of logic in the determination of the human essence. The equating of thinking and logic as the origin of Occidental fate

Do we now experience something of the depth allotted to thinking and about the reflection originally proper to it, [222] or anything essential about the essence of thinking, through logic, which since antiquity has been known as the 'doctrine of thinking'? What is logic? We find the doctrine of thinking under the name of ἐπιστήμη λογική: the understanding of λόγος. This name is no mere label, behind which something other than what it says is concealed. Through this name 'logic,' it is decided that thinking is thought as λόγος, with λόγος being understood in a very particular way. But this is not at all self-evident. In this equating of thinking and λόγος, the origin of an Occidental fate conceals itself: it conceals itself there inconspicuously, without noise, fanfare or hawkers, so that it appears—and for millennia has appeared—as though there is nothing remarkable there. Moreover, ἐπιστήμη λογική—i.e., logic—is also named in connection with two other manners of ἐπιστήμη: ἐπιστήμη φυσική and ἐπιστήμη ἠθική. Each of these are, albeit in different ways, oriented toward beings as a whole. 'Physics' and 'ethics' unfold a knowledge directed toward the universal. Does this also apply to that particular understanding that deals with λόγος? λόγος is for 'logic' the λέγειν τι κατά τινος— that is, the asserting of something about something. λόγος is understood in Roman and medieval terms as *enuntiatio*, assertion; at the same time, it is understood as *propositio*, a placing-before, a statement, i.e., *recta determination iustorum*, the correct determination of what is right, *iudicium*, judgment: λόγος is assertion, judgment. The elements of a judgment are concepts. Judgments themselves are related to one another in the form of inferences ('deductions'). Logic, as the doctrine of the assertion—that is, of judgment—is at the same time the doctrine of the concept and the inference. Judging/asserting is certainly not a special mode of human behavior: it is only one among many possible others. 'Ethics,' however, elucidates the modes of human behavior, all of which arise out of the unity of the human abiding in the sense of his sojourning amidst [223] beings—in short, the ἦθος of the human. It is in this way that we can understand 'logic' as a branch of ethics. It is the ethics of the behavior of asserting. Thus, in distinction to ethics and physics, 'logic' is missing the feature of the universal.

According to the above-mentioned determination of the human essence from out of ἦθος, the definition of the human should be ἄνθρωπος ζῷον ἦθος ἔχον— the human is that living being that has ethics and is distinguished by it. However, the determination of the human essence, according to the Greeks, is otherwise:

ἄνθρωπος ζῷον λόγον ἔχον—the human is that living being that has λόγος and is distinguished by it. According to this, should not 'logic,' as the science of λόγος, have a distinguished character, one that is equal to that of ethics and perhaps even above it?

The 'definition' of the human essence is as follows: the human is that living being that has λόγος, as pronounced by the character of the human whose fate is the Occidental and Occidentally determined world history of humanity. We know the Greek definition in later formulations: *homo est animal rationale*, the human is the rational living being. λόγος becomes *ratio*, and *ratio* becomes reason. The defining characteristic of the ability to reason is thinking. As the *animal rationale*, the human is the thinking animal. In Rilke's words: the animal that sets snares for things, lying in wait for them. We could say that the above-named definition is the metaphysical determination of the human essence: in it the human, who is subject to the sway of metaphysics, speaks its essence. In recent times, Nietzsche, the last thinker of metaphysics, has taken up this determination of the human essence: the human is the clever, discerning animal. A treatise by the twenty-nine-year-old Nietzsche, first written in Basel in 1873 but not published until 1903 after his death, begins this way:

> [224] In some remote corner of the universe, poured out into countless flickering solar systems, there was once a star on which some clever animals invented knowledge. It was the most arrogant and dishonest minute of 'world history'; but, still, it was only a minute. Once nature had drawn in a few breaths, the star solidified, and the clever animals had to die.

But this interpretation of the human was, for the later and authentic Nietzsche, only a half-measure. Later he would oppose it with his doctrine of the eternal recurrence of the same. Around the time that Nietzsche was writing his *Zarathustra* and getting closer to his one, unique thought of the will to power (every thinker only thinks one thought); around this time Nietzsche recognized that the human up to this point, the *animal rationale*, was indeed an animal, but the "animal" whose essence "has not yet been established." The task is therefore to understand decisively the essence of the *ratio* that determines the animal human, and according to the direction already set out step-by-step in contemporary thought. The essence of reason—and that means, subjectivity—is not mere thinking and reason, but rather the will: for in the will as self-willing, the positioning of the self toward itself first consummates itself as subjectivity. According to Nietzsche, however, the will is a will to power. The human is that animal who is determined through the thinking will to power, and is only thereby established in its metaphysical essence. This willing animal—the human—is, according to Nietzsche, the "animal of prey." How close this is to Rilke's snare-setting, ambushing animal! The human thus conceived, and therefore willed and also self-willing, goes beyond the prior human, the merely clever animal. As he who goes beyond the prior human, the future human of metaphysics is 'the over-human,' the human as the human of the will to power.

[225] When λόγος has turned into *ratio*, and *ratio* into reason, and reason into a thinking will, and when this will as the will to power determines the essence of the human and even beings as such and as a whole, then 'logic' as the doctrine of '*logos*' has a universal meaning equal to that of physics and ethics.

§ 3. Logic and λόγος.
The discipline and the matter.
Logic and Occidental metaphysics

a) The origin of the three-fold division of logic, physics, and ethics as the scientific disciplines comprising philosophy, and the fate of Occidental metaphysics

The three terms 'logic,' 'physics,' and 'ethics' name three manners and directions of understanding beings as a whole. Did these three directions of universal knowledge come together by happenstance, or do they originate in a concealed togetherness that entrusts them to one another? We intuit something of this togetherness, even if we do not yet see clearly where it originates or on what it is grounded (i.e., where the unity of these three directions of knowledge has its starting point, its 'principle'). If these three terms—and most importantly, what they name—belong together in a unity, then this unity contains a structure and an arrangement. Only with this structure and arrangement in mind can the tripartite division be executed.

Regarding the provenance of this tripartite division, we have the report of Sextus Empiricus, a philosophical writer who lived around 200 AD. In his work, *Adversus Mathematicos*, Book 7, § 16, he states the following:

ἐντελέστερον δὲ [λέγουσιν τὰ μέρη τῆς φιλοσοφίας] ... οἱ εἰπόντες τῆς φιλοσοφίας τὸ μέν τι εἶναι φυσικὸν τὸ δὲ ἠθικὸν τὸ δὲ λογικόν· ὧν δυνάμει μὲν Πλάτων ἐστὶν ἀρχηγός, περὶ πολλῶν μὲν [226] φυσικῶν [περὶ] πολλῶν δὲ ἠθικῶν οὐκ ὀλίγων δὲ λογικῶν διαλεχθείς· ῥητότατα δὲ οἱ περὶ τὸν Ξενοκράτην καὶ οἱ ἀπὸ τοῦ περιπάτου ἔτι δὲ οἱ ἀπὸ τῆς στοᾶς ἔχονται τῆσδε τῆς διαιρέσεως.

However, more thorough [i.e., accomplished] are those who say in regard to philosophy (naming the parts of it) that the one part [i.e., what comprises it] is that which belongs to φύσις, the other part, however, that which concerns ἦθος, and the other part, ultimately that which concerns λόγος. Among those who speak this way, Plato is the one through whom the possibility actually arises [i.e., to look in a unifying way toward all three of these aspects], insofar as he fostered discussion of many things pertaining to φύσις, but also much pertaining to ἦθος, and not least of all of that which pertains to λόγος. However, the above-mentioned classification is most explicitly apparent [i.e., named in terms and defined and codified] in the followers of Xenokrates, and those who come from the Peripatetics, and in addition but less so, also those who come from the Stoa.

As a three-fold division, the three terms 'logic,' 'physics,' and 'ethics' comprise the decisive division of philosophy, and have done so since Plato. According to the account cited above, Plato himself did not establish this trichotomy, but his thinking with regard to λόγος, φύσις, and ἦθος opened new viewpoints and connections whose unity can best be grasped in the three-fold division, and whose unity is sought to be grasped above all when the task is to make what has been thought in advance by the thinker solid and graspable for cognition and the scrutiny of science. This happens each time the thinking of a thinker is granted the highly ambiguous fate of being processed scholastically in a so-called 'school,' and being passed on in this state of concretion and ossification. According to Sextus's account, Xenokrates—or, more precisely, his followers—explicitly established the above-cited three-fold division of philosophy. Following Speusippus [227], Xenokrates became the second head of the 'Academy' founded by Plato, and served as its head for two decades. It is difficult to say anything certain regarding the essence of this inceptual founding by Plato. At its core, it was based upon a cult of the Muses, and it cultivated philosophy, through lectures and conversations, as the core of the other forms of knowledge (i.e., mathematics, astronomy, natural science). The Academy was neither merely an association of scholars within an organization of scientific research, nor was it a 'school of wisdom.' It must be said, however, that since Plato's founding of the Academy, and since the corresponding founding of the 'Peripatetic School' by Aristotle, that thinking which only now is given the distinguishing title of φιλοσοφία entered into a privileged relationship with what we call 'the sciences.' This intertwining of philosophy with the sciences becomes, from that time on, determinative not only for 'philosophy itself,' but also for 'the sciences.' Since that time, the attempts to think philosophy as a kind of 'science'—namely, as the most universal, the most stringent, or the highest 'science'—arise again and again. In these attempts, however, lies the danger of measuring what is more originary than every kind of science (in the sense of τέχνη) by what has first arisen from out of this origin. The curious situation that comes to pass is that the thing which is only the consequence of a prior ground and, as such, can only be a consequence of it (namely, 'science'), overpowers the ground (namely, philosophy), thereby inverting the relationship between ground and consequence. What is dependent attempts to subdue and master that on which it depends. Concealed herein lies a strange fate: namely, that since Plato and Aristotle, the thinking called 'philosophy' has failed to return to its own essential grounding in order to receive from it—and only from it—the imprint and secret of its essence [228]. This self-estrangement of philosophy has the consequence that when one wishes to avoid an equating of philosophy and science, philosophy is then characterized from a perspective foreign to it: namely, as a form of 'art,' i.e., as a kind of 'poetics.' One speaks of 'conceptual poetry' and 'poetic philosophers.' Philosophy is regarded as a kind of profession of faith or as a 'world view.' To think philosophy only as philosophy and to follow this thinking where it necessarily leads is too daunting and difficult for the world to attempt: for the thinking that is concealed in 'philosophy' is set apart from everything discussed above, including 'science,' as though separated by an abyss. It will necessitate a long journey in order to free authentic thinking, which curtly and emphatically we call 'thinking *as such*,' from common misapprehensions.

However, because philosophy since Plato has at the same time also been divided into disciplines and remains so divided (in the same manner as the sciences), the impression is solidified that what has been divided into disciplines is, in its essence, as concrete and unambiguous as the disciplines themselves are rigid and unquestionable.

But let us not recklessly deceive ourselves about what hides itself in the validity of such a division into disciplines and the roles thereof. What is this, precisely? Namely, that through the notion of a discipline, a set of possible questions and with them directions and ways of possible exploration are determined with a certain finality. The objects of inquiry occupied by the discipline are thereby held captive by the discipline. The matters investigated by and through the discipline can only announce themselves insofar as the discipline and its methodological apparatus allows. The discipline and its validity remain the decisive authority regarding whether and how something may become a possible object of scientific inquiry, as well as its suitability for becoming an object for research. The reigning disciplines [229] are like sieves that only allow precisely determined aspects of things through. What belongs to 'a matter' is decided not so much by the matters in question, their ground, and their 'truth,' but rather by the discipline into which they remain committed as an object of that discipline. The shackling of questions and directions of inquiry by disciplines, and the division into disciplines, also applies to the sciences and Occidental philosophy (owing to their constant proximity), and this not only in cases where such philosophy is conveyed as a doctrine in a scholastic manner, but also (and in particular) when it unfolds and consummates its fate as metaphysics in the originary thinking of thinkers. Even Kant was fond of invoking the three-fold division of philosophy. He thus begins the preface to the

Groundwork for the Metaphysics of Morals, published in 1785, with the following sentences:

> Ancient Greek philosophy was divided into three branches of knowledge: physics, ethics, and logic. This classification fits the nature of this manner of inquiry perfectly, and one cannot improve upon it, except perhaps to add the principle upon which it is based, in order to, on the one hand, thereby assure oneself of its comprehensiveness, and, on the other hand, in order to be able to determine the necessary subdivisions correctly.[1]

Now, surely that which, according to Kant, still needs to be added to this classification—namely, the 'principle' of classification (i.e., that from which it proceeds and in its necessity is shaped and sustained)—is the most difficult. Whether and in what way Kant himself found this principle, and whether and in what way this principle was exhibited in the metaphysical systems of German Idealism, cannot be expounded upon here: for something else is more pressing. [230]

b) Logic and the inhibiting of the unfolding of the essence of the Λόγος

In order to attain the correct insight into the essence and meaning of logic, we must consider that the 'revolution' of thinking brought into philosophy by Kant was carried out in the realm of logic. Before even diving into the matter, we can already see this in the titles of his three main works: *Critique of Pure Reason*, *Critique of Practical Reason*, and *Critique of Judgment*. At issue in each case is reason, i.e., *ratio*, i.e., the faculty of judgment, i.e., thinking, i.e., a doctrine of reason, i.e., 'logic.' The decisive step in thinking undertaken by Kant—a thinking about whose essence and scope he also possessed a clear knowledge—is the step away from a prior logic toward a new 'logic' that he named "transcendental logic." 'Logic,' in various extended forms and permutations, thus becomes the core of thinking immediately following Kant, specifically in the metaphysics of Fichte, Schelling, and Hegel. Indeed, the entirety of thinking between 1790 and 1830 is deeply determined by Kant's new 'logic.' The meaning of Kant's thinking for Heinrich von Kleist, both in a positive and a negative sense, is well-known. Even Goethe's thinking, in those occasional moments when it brushes up against philosophy (in odd ways), only attains its proper lucidity and sharpness from

---

[1] Kant, *Werke*, IV, 243.

Kant's *Critique of Judgment*. (One can say this also of Schiller's thought.) The twenty-six-year-old Hölderlin, under the sway of Kant's and Fichte's philosophies (on account of having attended their lectures in Jena), writes the following to his brother on October 13, 1796: "You *must* study philosophy, even if you don't have any more money than what is needed to buy a lamp and oil, and no more time than those hours between midnight and the cock's crow."[2]

[231] In the age of this kind of thinking, the matter and even the term 'logic' attained a new dignity. This is made apparent by the fact that Hegel changes the name of the highest level of his thinking, and that of Occidental thinking in general, from 'metaphysics' to 'logic'—more precisely, to *Science of Logic*. In the 'logic' thought by Hegel, absolute reason (i.e., pure consciousness) attains its own, pure essence. Prepared by Leibniz, established by Kant, fueled by Schelling, and developed by Hegel into an absolute and a system, this 'logic' could be called 'metaphysical logic.' All new thinkers who think along the lines of this new logic continue to hold fast to the memory of the old 'logic' and its beginning in Greek thought, while also attending to the differences and distance of this new 'logic' to that of the Greeks. Thus, Kant states the following in the preface to the second edition of the *Critique of Pure Reason* (1787):

> That logic has taken this straight path (namely, that of a science) since time immemorial can be seen in the fact that since Aristotle, it has not been allowed to take one step backward. . . . Nevertheless, it is strange that until now it has not been able to take a step forward, thereby remaining to all appearances closed and perfected.[3]

In writing this, Kant clearly knew that this appearance was deceptive, and that logic was not only capable of taking a step beyond Aristotle, but that it had in fact already done so in his own 1781 work *Critique of Pure Reason*. From these observations, we can surmise that within Occidental thinking, 'logic' was more than just an academic discipline for the scholastic training of thinking. Before all else, 'logic,' at times explicitly and at times implicitly, is the path and dimension [232] of metaphysical thinking. It establishes and builds the fundamental bearing of the Occidental human amidst beings as a whole. And how could it be otherwise? For the human receives the imprint of his essence from the determination ἄνθρωπος ζῷον λόγον ἔχον—the human is the living being that has a λόγος. Should not λόγος, and with it 'logic,' therefore remain essential for the human? But how does 'logic' understand λόγος? If 'logic' is the doctrine of thinking, and if 'logic' sustains and directs the true authentic thinking of the thinkers, then it must surely understand λόγος as thinking, as the capacity for thinking, as *ratio*, as

---

[2] Hölderlin, *Werke*, II, 379.
[3] Kant, *Werke*, III, 13.

reason. 'Logic' is the metaphysics of λόγος. As metaphysics, logic has decided in what way and how λόγος should be a topic and object of thinking for itself: in other words, it has made a decision regarding the essence of λόγος itself. However, is it ultimately self-evident that 'logic,' although it gets its name from λόγος, also primordially and sufficiently experiences, captures, and grasps the essence of λόγος? Or is what is entitled 'logic' only given that name because λόγος is here being understood in a very particular way: namely, one giving rise to the idea that through 'logic' λόγος is truly understood? Could it not be the case that it is precisely 'logic' that makes an error regarding the essence of λόγος? Could this error not have led to it being precisely 'logic,' already with its name announcing itself to be the knowledge of λόγος, which nevertheless enacts a misapprehension of λόγος? And could it not be the dominance of 'logic' that keeps every originary consideration of λόγος at bay, since surely any other consideration of λόγος other than the 'logical' one must doubtlessly appear as unfitting? Not one reason can be marshaled that could guarantee 'logic' as being the single fitting and originary consideration of λόγος. On the contrary, we have reason to believe that 'logic' has not only inhibited the unfolding of the essence of λόγος, but has also prevented it and continues to do so.

[233] REVIEW

The dominance of the discipline over the matter, and logic as the grounding essence of Occidental philosophy as metaphysics

The term 'logic,' and with it logic itself, both appear in the trinity of 'physics,' 'ethics,' and 'logic.' This trinity is neither an arbitrary listing of a certain established ἐπιστήμη in connection with others, nor did it rise to power at an arbitrary time in the history of thinking. The trinity points to a three-fold division. Fundamental to classification is an orientation toward a totality. That is why the concept of classification arose at a time when thinking began to think the to-be-thought in accordance with a single, all-dominant perspective. This happened when Plato, while reflecting on beings as a whole, began to think what one now calls the theory of 'the ideas.' Here is certainly not the place to elucidate what this expression means. It is presently only important to grasp that Plato is the thinker who thinks beings as a whole from the perspective of 'ideas,' and that it was in his 'Academy' that, according to the report by Sextus Empiricus, the three-fold classification was established.

('Logic' has only existed since Plato. At first glance, this sentence sounds like a purely historiographical statement concerning the provenance and age of 'logic.' However, this sentence says something about our own history and, accordingly, our still unassailable relationship to what most concerns logic—namely, λόγος. In order to understand this, it is necessary to first remember a process that conceals itself in the dominance of Occidental science.)

With the classification of philosophy into 'physics,' 'ethics,' and 'logic,' a division into disciplines is performed. With that begins a process whose consummation is the mastery of the discipline over its own content. What belongs to the 'matter' of the discipline is not so much decided by the object of inquiry itself and the law of its [234] essence, or even its own concealed essential ground. What belongs to the 'matter' of a discipline is decided by precisely *those* perspectives and directions of inquiry that the discipline prescribes, for the purpose of its own furtherance, as the only possible way of objectifying the matter in question.

What does this say about 'logic' and its concern, λόγος? For one thing, it means that 'logic' is constantly practiced from out of a distinction to other disciplines, and through this interdependence is itself no longer free in the scope and manner of its inquiry. It also means that logic itself only allows λόγος to enter the picture in a way that is consistent with the procedural dictates of logic. For logic, λόγος is λέγειν as assertion, judgment; it is the operation of *ratio*, the activity of reason: 'logic' is the doctrine of reason. The mastery of the discipline over the matter elucidated by the discipline reinforces itself not only in the sciences, but foremost in philosophy itself, which is exclusively sought and developed from out of proximity to the sciences, and as a science itself.

(Since Aristotle and Plato, philosophy is ἐπιστήμη ζητουμένη, "the sought-after science." This appellation is not a statement of fact, but rather the determination of an essence: to be what is sought for as that which is evolving into an absolute knowledge of metaphysics. Such knowledge must be cultivated as the first science. In that lies the task of modern thinking: to elevate philosophy to the level of an absolute science capable of departing from its former name of philo-sophy (in the sense of a love for knowledge) by becoming the absolute scientific knowledge.)

The primacy of the disciplines within philosophy also remains intact when thinkers of the highest ranks, in simple amazement at the self-evident, ponder matters outside the norm and thereby go against the common opinions held in the discipline. It is in this light that Kant begins the preface to his [235] *Groundwork for the Metaphysics of Morals*, published in 1785, with the following sentences: "Ancient Greek philosophy was divided into three branches of knowledge: *physics*, *ethics*, and *logic*. This classification fits the nature of this manner of inquiry perfectly. . . ." These sentences of Kant's make it clear that he sees the 'nature of this manner of inquiry' pertaining to philosophy in the same way as the two Greek thinkers through whom the three-fold classification was prepared, and in whose schools it was established: namely, Plato and Aristotle. Through them, thinking becomes metaphysics. However, since it was created later, neither Plato nor Aristotle knew or used the term 'metaphysics,' even though it expresses the essence of their thinking and all that comes after it. The exact wording of the term 'metaphysics' already indicates that it concerns a type of 'physics' in the previously elucidated sense. 'Physics' is thereby the understanding of beings as such and as a whole. In its later meaning, the term *meta*-physics thus elucidates what 'physics,' in its essence, is. μετά can and does mean here: beyond something, for example, stepping beyond something, executing a stepping-beyond. 'Physics' executes the stepping-beyond of a given being to what determines beings as such and as a whole: namely, being. Because physics in its original intent thinks of being from out of beings, thereby thinking-over to what is distinct from beings, physics as such is meta-physics. Conversely, all metaphysics is in its essence 'physics': for beings, beyond which metaphysics inquires as to their grounding essence, are determined from out of φύσις, which leaves open to what extent the essence of φύσις is experienced in this process.

If 'physics' is essentially meta-physics, and if the 'ethics' that is achieved and developed through the above-mentioned classification is just as universally oriented toward [236] the whole of beings, only from a different perspective, then ethics also thinks meta-physically: for, it inquires about the being of that particular being the human, insofar as the human sojourns amidst beings and comports himself in relation to beings as a whole. This comportment is later called 'morals': it concerns itself with moral customs, which are governed by the moral law. This is why Kant, when he is reflecting upon the essence of ethics (i.e., moral philosophy), at times calls it simply "the metaphysics of morals." All of this allows us to presume that 'logic,' which springs from the same classification as physics and ethics, also belongs to such a meta-physics: namely, the metaphysics of the assertion, of making a judgment, of the faculty of judgment—that is, of reason. Indeed, Occidental 'logic' achieves its consummation in the system of metaphysics, specifically, in that of Hegel's. And not only that. Hegel even names the foundation and core of the system of metaphysics "logic," and understands it as the absolute, self-knowing science of reason. Metaphysics is, in the very core of its essence, 'logic.' Because Occidental thinking as metaphysical thinking is in its ground the unfolding of 'logic,' it (particularly that of the current era) executes its most essential steps in the realm of 'logic,' which in turn thereby evolves and molds itself into its predetermined essence. However, the consummation of metaphysics as absolute logic in Hegel's system only became possible with the philosophy of Kant. Nevertheless, the decisive moment of Kantian thinking remains the step away from a prior logic and its role in philosophy toward a new logic, one that Kant calls "transcendental" logic, but which we could also call 'metaphysical logic.' That Kant's metaphysical thinking is everywhere logic—that is, the doctrine of reason, of thinking, and of judgment—is signaled by the titles of his three main works, *Critique of Pure Reason*, *Critique of Practical Reason*, and *Critique of Judgment* (that is, of aesthetic and teleological reason). The word 'critique' [237] in these titles does not mean 'to find fault with.' Here the word 'critique' means something along the lines of the original meaning of the Greek verb κρίνειν, from which it originates. κρίνειν means: to draw out, to bring out, to distinguish and draw out the contours of what encloses something in its essence and dignity. In the titles of Kant's works, the word 'critique' means the drawing out, the defining and distinguishing, of the essence of reason.

[238] SECOND SECTION

The reclusiveness of the originary Λόγος and the paths to approaching it

§ 4. Preparation for the listening to the Λόγος

a) On the meaning of λόγος as speech, saying, and assertion. The necessity of a renewed questioning concerning the inceptual meaning of the Λόγος

We ask: what does λόγος mean? This oft-used word, and also that which it names, remain obscure. Nevertheless, 'logic' already emerged with the Greeks. Aristotle is called the "father of logic," and with some justification. (The previously cited words of Kant also come to the same conclusion.) But if 'logic' is itself mistaken in how it understands the essence of λόγος, then must the Greek thinkers themselves already have been mistaken in their understanding of the essence of λόγος? Are we even justified in suspecting this? Are we latecomers now going to presume that we ourselves are more knowledgeable than the Greek thinkers who, in thinking through and from out of their language, should, after all, be those who alone know what λόγος is? Plato and Aristotle are indeed the thinkers through whom the thinking of the Greeks consummated itself, and they are the thinkers whose thinking has become the symbol for Greek thinking as such and for Occidental thinking more generally. However, the Greeks had already thought before Plato and Aristotle, and one of these 'pre-Platonic' thinkers had even already thought about λόγος. However, even this does not guarantee that λόγος was being experienced in its true essence. The more originary a thinker thinks, the more distant he is from what remains for thinking the [239] to-be-thought, and the more he knows himself to be at such a distance. But suppose that the distance that opens itself here in such thinking were precisely that deepness in which what is deepest could suddenly be thought after all? These considerations attest to only one thing: that the essence of 'logic' and its demand to grasp λόγος are questionable. This is true, however, because the essence of λόγος remains obscure. In fact, it could even be the case that λόγος itself, from out of itself and on its own accord, casts obscurity around its essence. If so, the common determination of the human as ζῷον λόγον ἔχον would evince a strange constitution, and we would have to seriously doubt the privilege of 'logic.' It would no longer be enough to appeal to Aristotle as the 'father of logic.' Now, after two thousand years, the time would finally have arrived to ask about the mother of logic. She seems forgotten and unknown. But perhaps the origin of logic lies neither with the father, nor with the mother, nor with them both. What is λόγος itself? To what extent do the essence of thinking, and the doctrine of thinking, derive their determination from it? What is λόγος, such that thinking, and only thinking, properly belongs to it? For that matter, what is thinking? For logic, λόγος is assertion; as assertion, it belongs to saying; saying is speech and language; λόγος is an occurrence of language: λόγος is, thereby, the word. All of this is already familiar enough to Occidental thinking. Nevertheless, we must impress upon ourselves that λόγος neither means "word," nor "speech," nor indeed "language." This is already evident in the fact that the fundamental meaning of the Greek word λόγος can in no way mean the same as "speech" and "language," and in fact does not even point toward anything linguistic or language-like. At the same time, it is equally certain that λόγος and its attendant verb λέγειν already meant something akin to "speaking" and "saying" very early on for the Greeks. These are two inarguable facts that we must face. In their co-existence, these two facts conceal something enigmatic.

[240] Unnoticed for two and a half thousand years, this enigma is situated in a strange historical background. Supposing, however, that precisely in these millennia a peculiar imprinting of the essence of λόγος is the concealed ground of the Occidental history of this time-period, then a consideration wishing to inquire about a turning-point of this history of logic as the doctrine of λόγος must first recognize and acknowledge the enigma as such.

We present the riveting nature of this enigma once more: λόγος and λέγειν mean speech, word, and saying. At the same time, the meaning of λόγος and λέγειν is not at all related to anything language-like or to any linguistic activity. How do λόγος and λέγειν then come to mean speech and saying? To what extent, and why, is the originary essence of the word λόγος lost in this meaning? What is at stake in this disappearance of the originary meaning? Wherein lies its ground? Is this reclusiveness of the originary meaning of the Λόγος—i.e., the reclusiveness of what is named by it—permanent, or is it rather the inconspicuous portent of a long-awaited return? So long as we only begin to ask a small number of these questions—and we cannot even speak yet of an adequate answer—we can never achieve an understanding *of the* λόγος from which 'logic' gets its name, but which since the onset of 'logic' has also been in its ward. Without asking these questions, we will never attain knowledge of the fact that the Greeks themselves struggled in their thinking with what they called λόγος, nor of how that struggle occurred. Without such knowledge, we will never recognize what remained unthought in the Greek thinking of λόγος and why it had to remain unthought, nor to what extent what is unthought is still preeminently the to-be-thought remaining for Occidental thinking.

Thus, the next question is as follows: what is the inceptual meaning of the Greek word λόγος? With this question, we are already asking another: namely, what is λόγος? To answer this question, we will limit [241] ourselves to the consideration of three references that may give us important information about the history of the word λόγος. These references have been chosen so that they primarily reveal the vibrancy of the word. At the same time, we will thereby also come to know the difficulty of bringing something essential of what is named by the word λόγος into view.

(The questioning directed toward such foundational words must prepare itself for the strange eventuality that, through the course of questioning, the relationships posited at the outset will change. At first it appears as though information about the word is being sought. Those who are seeking this information alter and control this word and the history of its meaning. In this case, it is we who are thus manipulating the word. But suddenly it is revealed that, in fact, *we* are the ones being manipulated by the word and that which it names, and that we were being manipulated even before we began on our present course of elucidation. Because it is the case that, in the guise of an apparently merely historiographic consideration, the history of a word can become something entirely other—and I say explicitly that it 'can' become so, not that it 'does' become so—an interjection to clarify our present undertaking and its limits is necessary.

It remains outside the task of this lecture to present a historiographical summary of all the various meanings of the word λόγος. And, of course, there will be differing opinions regarding the import and value of such investigations into the history of words and the history of concepts, all depending upon what one expects from a historiographical survey of the past and the representation of what has been handed down. In any case, the productivity and compactness of any investigation into the history of a concept depends upon whether the one investigating orients his thinking toward what is named by the word being addressed, and whether or not he is adequately prepared for the thinking-through of the thing in question and its thing-ness. Of what does such preparation consist? It consists of experiencing the essential realm from out of which the word, now being taken on its own, is spoken. At the same time, to this preparation also belongs [242] the realization that everything depends upon whether or not the one investigating directs his thinking into the essential realm of the word and picks up a directive from within it, or whether he only 'lexicographically' collects the places in which this word appears in order to bring these places together, as if an understanding of the word, its meaning, and the thing meant by it results on its own accord from the mere conglomeration of these places. Behind the history of such foundational words—a history which, notwithstanding historiographical recalculation, is only known in a few respects—another history conceals itself, one that cannot be reached by any historiographical inquiry and that no human thinking can reach on its own if it is not first offered to the human. But, even then, the human can and will err in the reception of this offering.)

b) Access to the hearing of the Λόγος. The hearkening listening to the Λόγος as an entryway into authentic knowledge. Fragment 50. The question concerning the originary concordance (ὁμολογία). References to fragments 32 and 112

What does λόγος mean? We can gather the first clue from a few sayings of the thinker Heraclitus, who also bears the epithet 'The Obscure.' What Heraclitus calls the Λόγος, and what he thinks with this word, is the most obscure of all that is obscure pertaining to this thinker. One often thinks that the obscurity belonging to a thinking only lies in the fact that conceptual clarity has not yet been achieved and has yet to be consistently mastered. But, regarding the to-be-thought, the obscurity lies within this itself. However, considered in this way, the essence of obscurity remains, for the most part, misunderstood. In an everyday sense, the obscure is the absence of light; the obscure hardly exists. In fact, the obscure is always something other, and always something more. The obscure can be the light that drives toward darkness. But the obscure can also be the brightness that keeps to itself. The obscure can also vacillate between [243] these two ways of being. If this vacillation calcifies into indecision, then the obscure is always the obscurity of confusion. However, the authentically obscure is all of this together in such a way that the inner gravity of its essence is suspended in the very obscurity that is also the brightness that keeps to itself. The thinking of Heraclitus's is authentically obscure in such a way. Given this, how can the saying mentioned here presume to give illumination and to offer up a straightforward enlightenment?

The first of the sayings that we are choosing to assist us in elucidating the word λόγος in Heraclitus is fragment 50, which says:

οὐκ ἐμοῦ, ἀλλὰ τοῦ λόγου ἀκούσαντας ὁμολογεῖν σοφόν ἐστιν ἓν πάντα εἶναι.

In a provisional but already clarifying translation, this means:

If you have listened not merely to me, but rather have listened to the *Logos* (in obedience to it, hearkening to it), then knowledge (which subsists therein) is to say the same as the *Logos*: one is all.

We will attempt to elucidate this saying by making reference to other sayings in which the same is thought, though from other perspectives, and in which, most importantly, the word λέγειν is used.

We will initially leave the word λόγος, which bears the weight of fragment 50, untranslated. In considering the saying, we will for now only focus upon the relations named within it, so that our considerations may not wander in the realm of indeterminacy. Stated plainly, λόγος is: ὁ λόγος, the Logos; at stake here is a kind of "listening"—ἀκούειν, more precisely, a kind of having-listened-to-before, namely, to the Logos. Therefore, the Logos, which is heard and which can be heard, is a form of saying, an utterance: for the listening of the human that is meant by the saying is directed toward sounds and voices. However, the saying of Heraclitus's begins with a sharp οὐκ, with a "not" that [244] rejects something, namely, something concerning human listening. οὐκ ἐμοῦ—you should not listen to me, to this particular human being and my speeches, simply in order to then report that you have heard Heraclitus.

οὐκ ἐμοῦ—you should not listen to me, says Heraclitus. It is also strange that the thinker begins with a "not" and a "no." Perhaps it is the lot of thinkers to always be forced to begin that way, with a rejection and with resistance, so that the "yes" they perhaps say does not immediately fall into the category of that to which the human listens in his everyday life (e.g., in idle talk, in cinema, and on the radio). However, the "not" and "no" with which the saying of Heraclitus's begins is, strictly speaking, not really so negative, and is not an utterance of mere resistance: it is perhaps rather a pointing toward a detaching and a jumping off.

οὐκ ἐμοῦ, ἀλλὰ τοῦ λόγου ἀκούσαντας

Have you not merely listened to me, but rather (ἀλλά) listened to the *Logos*?

According to this, the *Logos* is something audible, a kind of speech and a voice, but clearly not the voice of a human, which speaks through audible noises. Who is speaking as 'the *Logos*'? The *Logos*—what kind of voice is that? If not a human one and therefore not an audible one, is it then an inaudible voice? Does such a thing exist? Moreover, can one listen to such a thing? Wanting to listen to what does not make a sound: is that not like wanting to build castles in the sky? 'To listen'—that means to apprehend something by means of the ear. For example, we listen to the noise that enters the ear. But, distinct from such an effortless and will-less hearing is the hearing in the manner of an attending to something whereby we, as the saying has it, are 'all ears.' Or, does language, whose veiling is more enigmatic than its revealing, say that we are 'all ears' precisely because we have now forgotten about 'being all ears' and have forgotten about our actual ears, and are purely engaged in attending-to, in which the mere apprehending of something is no longer what is essential? Rather, does the essential lie in the process whereby that which we are apprehending takes us along with it and accepts us? Attending-to does not depend [245] upon what is presently in the ear. What has just been heard and what can be heard are already passed over by the attending-to. Attending-to even exists, indeed exists in its purest form, when nothing that could be heard approaches us, i.e., when nothing is audible. This attending-to that does not yet 'hear' anything we call 'hearkening.' It appears that in this hearkening we are putting particular strain on our ears and our hearing. And yet, what would all of this hearkening be were we not already able to hearken to an appeal that is still preserved for us and sustains itself? What would such hearkening and hearkening-toward be, and how would it awaken, if we were not already obedient to what is able to, and indeed does, come forward to meet us? What would all human listening in the sense of a perceptual apprehension of noises, tones, and sounds be without a listening in the sense of an obedient relation to what can be encountered, and without that listening mentioned in the adage which says, "He who does not wish to listen, must feel"? But how can anything at all approach us within an obedient relation to what is to be encountered, without what is approaching us already having us, insofar as we somehow already belong to it? Would then a listening (i.e., a hearkening) be an obedience to something to which we already belong by virtue of our listening to it, an obedience that has nothing in common with subjugation, since this originary listening is nothing other than the being open to the open—in other words, freedom itself? But, if this is the case, who *are* we? Who is the human? The human is the essence that is alone open to the open, and only because of this openness can the human also close himself off from the open in a certain way: namely, by allowing what is to be encountered in it only to be an object, an objectified thing, and thereby through his calculating and planning lie in wait to ambush it. Who is the human if an originary obedience belonging to his essence determines him as vigilant, and if all discord stems from a lack of such vigilance? This question besets us here.

Nevertheless, even more important than this question, and even more important than answering it quickly, is that we first experience [246] and learn to think through something as simple as the difference between listening as the sensual perception of acoustic sound and noise by the ear, and attending-to as hearkening, and this latter as a hearkening vigilance and obedience. This hearkening listening is the authentic listening, which is not missing from other types of listening, even mere acoustic listening, but is instead simply forgotten by us. That is why, when we proceed to understand the acoustic physiologically and psychologically from a technical and scientific perspective, the whole matter gets turned upside down: for then we erroneously think that listening by means of the corporeal listening apparatus is authentic listening, and that listening in the sense of obedience is 'naturally' only a transposition into the spiritual and 'naturally' can only be taken metaphorically.

(In the realm of technical research, one can find much, and much of use. For example, one can state and demonstrate that periodic fluctuations of air pressure at a certain frequency are perceived as 'tones,' without these fluctuations ever achieving a pure sine curve in their form. Proceeding from such discoveries regarding hearing, a program of research can be built up and established which eventually becomes the sole purview of specialists in the physiology of the senses. There is, by contrast, perhaps little that can be said about essential listening: however, what can be said directly concerns every human. It is not important here to engage in research, but rather to be thoughtfully vigilant to what little can be said, most importantly because the consideration of the hearkening listening must immediately recognize that to authentic listening also belongs the following: that the human can err in listening and often does not hear what is essential. But even this is only possible for the human because he, as obedient in the manner elucidated above, already belongs to something else and never belongs to himself.)

If the ears do not directly belong to hearing (in the sense of hearkening) and to obedience, then the relationship between hearing and the ears is indeed a peculiar one.

[247] We do not listen because we have ears: rather, we have and can have ears because we listen. However, we humans are only able to listen—for example, to the thunder of the heavens, to the rustling of the woods, to the flowing of a spring, to the tones of the harp, to the clattering of motors, and to the noise of the city—insofar we belong, or do not belong, to all of this. We have ears because we can listen in a hearkening way, and through such hearkening are allowed to listen to the song of the earth, its shudders and shakes, a song that nevertheless remains untouched by the colossal noise that the human is now causing upon earth's battered surface. Being able to listen to the song of the earth demands that our listening be a sensual one dependent upon tools of sensual perception (i.e., the ears). Listening and listening are therefore not the same. Mere acoustical listening is not ἀκούειν, neither in the sense of listening to a speech being delivered, nor in the sense of a hearkening listening to the Λόγος. What is 'the Logos'? Heraclitus does not say anywhere in the sayings remaining for us. Presumably he never said it in the manner of an explanation and the determination of a concept. Nevertheless, Heraclitus says enough about λόγος, even in just the saying that we have already cited. We must only properly think-after what he says. Heraclitus says:

> If you have not merely listened to me, but rather have listened, hearkening, to the Λόγος, thereby becoming and being obedient, then . . . .

What happens then? σοφόν ἐστιν—"then (an initiation into) authentic knowledge is." σοφόν: originally, σοφία had the same meaning as τέχνη—to know one's way about something, to know its message, namely, the message a matter gives, and thus knowing what has been messaged to the human. σοφός sits within φιλόσοφος—σοφία sits within φιλοσοφία. However, in Greek, σοφόν is also always an echo of σαφές, which means luminous, manifest, radiant. σοφόν ἐστιν—the knowing/knowledge *is*, and this means always and most importantly for the Greeks that what-is-to-be-known stands σαφές (i.e., luminously manifest before us). We also attempt to elucidate σοφόν, [248] as understood by Heraclitus, with reference to fragments 32 and 112, about which we surely cannot provide a thorough interpretation here. Fragment 32 states:

ἓν τὸ σοφὸν μοῦνον λέγεσθαι οὐκ ἐθέλει καὶ ἐθέλει Ζηνὸς ὄνομα.

The One—which is the sole to-be-known—withholds itself from being said, while at the same time offering itself up as the sayable, in the name of Zeus (i.e., of 'life,' that is, of that which emerges luminously).

From this saying, we can first conclude that λέγεσθαι/λέγειν is unambiguously related to ὄνομα: noun, name, naming. However, in order that we may properly heed the word ὄνομα (i.e., name) and not understand it in an empty and damaged way, we must ponder an aspect of its meaning that can still be seen in the expression 'to have a recognizable name,' 'to have a reputation.' Here, name has the sense of *renown*, thought in an elevated sense, and not as mere fame. To have a name for oneself, to be known for it, thus means: to stand in the light, to be illuminated by it. Naming is illuminating, a bringing into the light, a bringing into the unconcealed. It is from this meaning that ὄνομα (i.e., name), as still remains to be shown, enters into a connection with λέγειν, i.e., a "saying" in which the merely linguistic and grammatical are not of primary importance. Later, of course, ὄνομα becomes a grammatical term that designates the substantive (i.e., the noun) in distinction to ῥῆμα, the verb. Presently, however, we will pay attention to τὸ σοφόν—the authentic to-be-known and the knowledge of it.

Knowledge—τὸ σοφόν/ ἡ σοφία—is: to know what has been messaged, to stand within it. This knowledge is in itself already an authentic readiness to act and to do, one grounded upon an attending-to. In fragment 112 it is stated:

καὶ σοφίη ἀληθέα λέγειν καὶ ποιεῖν κατὰ φύσιν ἐπαΐοντας.

And so authentic knowledge consists in saying and doing the unconcealed, from out of an attending-to, along and in accordance with that which, in emerging from out of itself, shows itself.

Knowledge is, authentically and in itself, λέγειν καὶ ποιεῖν—we translate this initially as: 'saying' and 'doing' (i.e., word and deed). We will, however, leave it [249] open if the saying is thereby already properly thought: for we do not yet know to what degree λέγειν means something like "saying," nor do we know what "saying" is, and we are only beginning to ask. Most importantly, however, we are attentive to the fact that knowledge, as the standing-within-the-message—a standing that both says and does—sways and weaves within an attending-to that is κατὰ φύσιν, i.e., that is along with, and in accordance with, what shows itself from out of a self-emerging. According to this, the hearkening relation (i.e., listening) is somehow oriented toward φύσις. Yet, can one 'listen to' φύσις? From fragment 50 we have already gleaned that if there is to be a knowledge it is necessary to listen to the Λόγος. According to fragment 112, listening is oriented toward φύσις. Could it be the case, then, that the Λόγος has more of an essential relationship with φύσις than with speech, language, and enunciating?

In the obedient relation to the Λόγος lies the *initiation* into authentic knowledge. We add the explanatory word 'initiation' in order to indicate that this knowledge is not simply made and arranged by the human, but that it comes to him, namely, through a hearkening to the Λόγος. But wherein does this authentic knowledge exist, when it *is*? Heraclitus says: ὁμολογεῖν σοφόν ἐστιν.

ὁμολογεῖν—Heraclitus places that wherein authentic knowledge exists before σοφόν ἐστιν. Moreover, the ὁμολογεῖν in which λέγειν and λόγος are named comes, through this combination of words, into close proximity to the Λόγος: ἀλλὰ τοῦ λόγου ἀκούσαντας—ὁμολογεῖν. What does the verb ὁμολογεῖν mean? Literally, and essentially, it means: to say the same as what another says. This could mean: to repeat, in a simple and unreflective way, the exact wording of what someone else has said. But it is precisely this that ὁμολογεῖν does not mean, from which fact, if we are keenly attentive to it, we can already recognize that *this* λέγειν, this saying, and λέγειν in general cannot have their essence in linguistic expression and utterance. ὁμολογεῖν—saying the same as someone else—does not only signify that one person says the same thing as another, so that [250] somewhere and at some point two identical opinions exist. Rather, ὁμολογεῖν means: to stand equivalent to what another has said, to admit to it, and thereby to concede and agree to what has been said. ὁμολογεῖν is an acknowledging in such a way that what someone else has said shows itself, by virtue of showing itself, as something requiring concession and agreement. To concede and to acknowledge what someone else has said is therefore already a concurrence with the other. ὁμολογεῖν is the conceding, acknowledging concordance. Concordance, therefore, does not consist in the same opinion existing in both the one and the other, but rather in the fact that one human and the other, as distinct individuals, are in agreement with each other in acknowledging that the same thing addresses them both. ὁμολογεῖν— to say the same as another. Every sameness, and above all the sameness of ὁμολογία, is grounded in difference: only what is different can be the same. It is by virtue of its differing from the same that the different itself remains self-same. Upon the self-same and its sameness, both the difference of the different, and the sameness of the same, depend. A sentence applies here that has barely been thought through, but must now be spoken, owing to the fact that it belongs to 'logic' properly understood: the more originary the sameness of the self-same, the more essential is the difference within sameness, and all the more so the sameness of the same. ὁμολογεῖν σοφόν ἐστιν: authentic knowledge consists of an acknowledging, conceding concordance.

However, if we are to think this concordance properly, there is still an ambiguity that must be clarified. On the one hand, there belongs to concordance that with which—and that means, with *whom*—the concordance is such; and, on the other hand, there belongs that about which the concordance is concerned. Concordance can arise concerning a myriad of things: it can be about this or that matter, this or that circumstance, this or that task, this or that behavior. A concordance that, from this perspective, already appears manifold, can at the same time also be further differentiated [251] by the fact that it is a concordance between humans who, on the basis of precisely this concordance, may stand in greater proximity or distance to one another. But perhaps the human does not only stand in concordance with other humans. Perhaps there is a concordance in which the concern in relation to which the concordance exists is the same as that through which the concordance occurs. Such a ὁμολογεῖν would then be a distinguished one. And should not a concordance be a distinguished one precisely where it constitutes essential knowledge, i.e., τὸ σοφόν? With what is this ὁμολογεῖν in concordance? Heraclitus tells us: τοῦ λόγου ἀκούσαντας—in the obedient listening to λόγος lies that knowledge that is in concordance ... with what? With what else but with λόγος itself? Can there be a more originary ὁμολογία than the one with λόγος itself? Obviously not. Here, λέγειν is of the kind that says the same as what the *Logos* says. But what is ὁ λόγος, "the *Logos*"? Heraclitus does not outright say: yet, he nevertheless does say by stating that authentic concordance exists when it is a concordance with "the *Logos*."

ὁμολογεῖν σοφόν ἐστιν ἓν πάντα εἶναι.

Out of an obedient listening to the Λόγος is the knowledge that consists of saying the same as the Λόγος: one is all.

REVIEW

1) λόγος as assertion about beings by way of the idea (εἶδος), and the category in metaphysical thinking (Plato, Aristotle, Kant)

In the previous sessions, an attempt was made to shed some light on the origin of 'logic' from several different perspectives. This was attempted with the aim of thereby making discernible [252], at least in some provisional way, in what way logic is concerned with λόγος: not, however, for the sake of 'logic' or the discipline thereof, but rather for the sake of the Λόγος. In order that we might gain a commensurate relation to the Λόγος, we began with considerations concerning 'logic.' We nevertheless remain far removed from a knowledge about the essence and scope of the origin of 'logic.' For now, we can only remark that in accordance with the origin of 'logic' as the science of λόγος delineated above, logic takes up λόγος itself according to particular perspectives, only then to investigate λόγος in its various forms within the strict limitations set out by those very perspectives. The particular perspectives according to which logic thinks about λόγος derive from the origin of 'logic.' For 'logic' owes its essence and its existence to the classification of knowledge and the knowable that became necessary within the context of Platonic and Aristotelian thinking. This classification yields the three 'sciences' of physics, ethics, and logic. Even Kant still claims that this classification is proper to the nature of the matter. If we were now to construe that particular thinking from out of which this classification had to arise as 'metaphysics'—more precisely, as the decisive beginning of metaphysics, a notion that can for now neither be fully explored nor expressly justified—then logic is, to put it succinctly, nothing more than the metaphysical consideration and explanation of λόγος. At first, this assertion does not say much. In fact, at first it only replaces one still unclear thing (i.e., the essence of logic) with another equally unclear thing (i.e., what is now called 'metaphysical consideration'). This determination of logic as the metaphysics of λόγος does not in fact bring clarity, but passes itself off as information only from out of a place of perplexity. But this perplexity in which we now find ourselves is unavoidable: for what metaphysics is can in large part only be illuminated through a clarification of the essence of 'logic.' At the same time, the opposite also holds true: what 'logic' is can only be clarified from out of the essence of metaphysics. [253] We move, therefore, in a circle. As soon as thinking enters into such a circular path, it is often—though not always—a sign that such thinking can abide in the realm of the essential, or can at least draw nearer to its outer precincts.

For the moment, we will stay with the sentence that at first may remain a mere allegation: logic is the metaphysics of λόγος. We take this sentence as a somewhat unmediated signpost, one that is almost forcefully erected, serving to guide our thinking toward the thought that logic considers λόγος from a particular perspective, namely a 'metaphysical' one. What this means, however, must allow itself to be merely provisionally indicated without our losing ourselves in an expansive elucidation 'concerning' metaphysics. This is indeed possible, but only with a number of reservations, and in such a way that much remains unclarified.

For 'logic,' λόγος is assertion—λέγειν τι κατά τινος, asserting something about something. In order that something may be asserted about something, the thing about which something is being asserted must already, for its part, be addressed—namely, as what it is. As assertion, λόγος is *in itself* (i.e., taken in a more originary way) the addressing of something from out of an orientation toward what is addressed. Something will appear as what it is, provided that the 'is' and 'being' can somehow be experienced as the activity of appearing. The aspect something provides is how it appears and shows itself, the look and appearance that it gives. What appears over there—for example, that house—shows itself in the aspect and look of 'house' and 'house-ness,' and *is* thus *a* house. As another example: what appears *here* shows itself as the look of a book and book-ness, and *is* thus *a* book. The look in terms of which something appears as what it is thus contains the 'what-being'—i.e., the being of beings—of that particular being. Plato was the first to think the being of beings from out of the look of what appears and as [254] this look. In Greek, 'look' is εἶδος–ἰδέα–'idea.' The look wherein it is discernible what a house is—not this or that particular house, but rather what a house is in general—is something not at all sensory, but rather something extrasensory. To think beings from out of the idea, and thus from out of the extrasensory, is the distinguishing characteristic of the thinking that is given the name 'metaphysics.'

If we make the assertion 'this house is tall,' then already lying at the ground of this assertion is the address to what it is, i.e., the εἶδος of a house. In Greek, λόγος does not only mean to address (i.e., λέγειν): rather, at the same time and often more importantly, it means what is being addressed by the address. τὸ λεγόμενον—that which is addressed—is nothing other than the look, εἶδος, ἰδέα. In a certain sense, then, εἶδος and λόγος mean the same. In other words, the λόγος embodied in addressing and asserting is understood from the perspective of the ἰδέα: λόγος, taken as assertion, is that particular understanding of λόγος that is found in the thinking that thinks beings from out of ideas—that is, that thinks them metaphysically. The λόγος thought by logic is thought metaphysically: logic is the metaphysics of λόγος.

Previously, it was only superficially shown that logic, along with the other two disciplines of 'philosophy' (physics and ethics), arose from out of the horizon of Platonic thinking. Now we recognize the meaning of this origination from out of Plato's thought for logic and λόγος. The determination brought about by Plato of the what-being and the being of a being as εἶδος and ἰδέα is the preliminary step for the possibility of comprehending λόγος as the address of something in its what-being. This determination brings itself about in such a way that beings themselves are projected onto being by way of beings, and the being of beings is thought as the most universal of all beings. To think the being of beings in such a way is the defining characteristic of all metaphysics. As long as metaphysics, in whatever form it may take, continues to rule over Occidental thinking in its ground—and this [255] is indeed still happening at the present moment—λόγος and every question concerning λόγος will be mastered, but thereby also limited, by 'logic.'

How decisively λόγος is circumscribed by its being thought in terms of address and assertion, both at the beginning of metaphysics and also in all later metaphysics, can be seen in one case that we have not yet sufficiently thought through, but by which today we are so dominated that it seems to be the most self-evident thing in the world. This case in question consists of the fact that those particular determinations of beings in which they show themselves according to their most universal look are, as the essential features of the being of beings, called 'categories.' The Greek word κατηγορία means "assertion"; in fact, by virtue of its stem and composition, this word is closer to that meaning than is the word λόγος. κατ-αγορεύιν means: to attribute something to someone of which they are the cause and of which they are guilty, and to do so in public, in the marketplace or during a judicial proceeding, so that this attribution as pronouncement makes known an accusation or state of affairs. κατηγορία is assertion in the sense of an emphasizing, informing, disclosing pronouncement.

κατηγορία is assertion in the preeminent sense. λόγος also counts as assertion. However, λόγος and κατηγορία do not quite mean the same thing. By contrast, Aristotle certainly recognizes (and we suppose Plato does as well) that in every λόγος in the sense of a commonplace assertion, κατηγορία prevails: in all sorts of assertions about all manner of possible and impossible things there prevails a singular, preeminent assertion. In what way?

In order to see this, we must now commit more decisively to the step already taken during the previous general identification of the 'idea.' When we say 'this tree over there is healthy,' then, in saying 'this tree over there,' what is already being said, though not aloud, is '*this*, presencing from out of itself.' [256] When we say 'is healthy,' then we are also saying, though not aloud, 'is constituted in such and such a way.' 'To be constituted' and 'presencing from out of itself' are both necessarily and in advance already being said in the λόγος about this tree: for were this not said—or, in this case, thought silently—then we could neither say 'this tree over there' nor 'is healthy.' Similarly, 'presencing from out of itself' and 'to be constituted' are also said in the assertion 'this house over there is tall,' and so on for all similar assertions. All commonplace asserting rests and sways in such preeminent assertions in which, for example, presencing-from-out-of-itself, being-constituted, being-related, etc., are said. These things that are spoken about are the fundamental features of being: namely, that being from which every being has its origin, its γένος. Plato calls these fundamental features of the being of beings the γένη or εἴδη—the highest ideas. Why should this preeminent saying in which a fundamental feature of being comes to appearance—ἐμφαίνεται, as Aristotle says—and which also bears all common asserting, not also contain the name of essential asserting, κατηγορία? That is how κατηγορία becomes the name for the being that is asserted in every λόγος about any being whatsoever. 'Being'—the fundamental feature of beings, is called 'assertion,' i.e., that which has been asserted. Something thoroughly estranging reveals itself here. Category and *logos* have an essential relationship that the Greek thinkers neither illuminated nor even justified. Plato and Aristotle simply move about in the tracks of this relationship between λόγος and category. Why this was possible, and even necessary, is something that we will someday have to ask when an insight into the essence of λόγος has become a pressing necessity for us.

If for now we only think-after the relationship between category and λόγος in a provisional way, we learn to understand what is otherwise incomprehensible: namely, that the highest determinations for [257] beings are called 'categories,' that is, 'assertions' in the already elucidated sense. The name and the matter 'category' later formulated itself, in part, along the lines of an inversion, so that the term 'category' only designates a superficial 'schema' and 'pigeonhole' to which and in which something can be said to belong. Since Plato and Aristotle—that is, since the beginning of metaphysics as the fundamental feature of Occidental thinking—it remains the task of this thinking about beings as a whole to create a doctrine of categories in accordance with which the most universal determinations of being— that is, categories—may be ordered. However, only seldom in the history of metaphysics does the relationship between category and *logos* in the sense of assertion and judgment become visible.

It is no coincidence that in Kant's thinking, in which metaphysics undergoes its last decisive shift, this relationship between category and assertion comes to light once again. It appears Kant's choice that "the logical function of the understanding in judgment" (that is, λόγος as assertion) serve as the "guiding thread for the discovery of all pure concepts of the understanding"[1] (that is, of the categories) is arbitrary, and many of his readers and critics agree on this point. But this fact, that λόγος becomes the guiding thread for the establishment of the categories, only makes visible something already at work since the beginning of metaphysics: namely, that logic is the guiding thread, and in fact the authentic horizon, of metaphysical thinking. This role accorded to logic was beyond question for Kant, which is why he himself never pondered the connection between λόγος and κατηγορία, or even the origin and reason for this connection. But logic can only be the guiding thread and the horizon for metaphysical thinking because, for its part, logic is nothing other than the metaphysics of λόγος, with this understood as assertion in its authentic sense—that is, as κατηγορία understood as ἰδέα and εἶδος. [258] If one accepts metaphysics as the highest form of the deepest thinking, a conclusion that tradition has made inescapable, then the essence of λόγος must be thought the deepest in 'logic,' especially if the latter is the metaphysics of λόγος. Seen in this way, pre-Platonic thinking becomes pre-metaphysical thinking, the kind of thinking that is still incomplete and is still on its way toward metaphysics. What the pre-Platonic thinkers said about λόγος can only be thought from out of

---

[1] Kant, *Werke*, III, 89–92.

later metaphysics. This is the situation that came to pass, and it is still happening now. Indeed, we even have metaphysics and its thinking about λόγος to thank for the fact that any sayings from the pre-Platonic thinkers, and particularly those of Heraclitus's, remain for us at all.

2) The return to the pre-metaphysical Λόγος through λόγος as assertion. Fragment 50

However, on the path that our attempts to think the essence of the Λόγος traverse, another course of action is necessary. We do not take 'logic' to be a divinely granted, definitively decided doctrine of λόγος that can, at most, only be modified. Our questioning through logic toward the Λόγος is, more precisely, a questioning regarding how it has become possible that λόγος as assertion ascended to the role of a guiding thread for the discovery of the foundations of beings in metaphysics. We think-after whether, and how, the Λόγος was thought before the emergence of 'logic' within metaphysics and before metaphysics itself. When we seek to understand what a pre-Platonic thinker (namely, Heraclitus) thought about the Λόγος, then we leave aside the metaphysical understanding of λόγος. At first, this closing-off of the horizon of metaphysical understanding is merely something negative. In addition to this negative move, we will also need a horizon in which what Heraclitus says about λόγος becomes visible, [259] graspable, and sayable. However, there is little that can immediately be said about this particular horizon of consideration. Within it we will surely come upon an enigma. To take hold of this enigma is alone what matters. The enigma consists of the following: namely, that from early on for the Greeks, λόγος meant "to say" and "to speak," but that, at the same time, this was not the original meaning of λόγος. Indeed, even around the time that the metaphysical understanding of λόγος had already coalesced, something of the original meaning remained within the concept of λόγος.

At the present moment, it is not important that we solve this enigma of the ambiguity of λόγος: rather, it is only important that we first recognize this enigma and allow ourselves to be guided by it.

We will now hear a few sayings of Heraclitus's that speak of λόγος, and that have been placed into a specific order. The first is fragment 50, which says:

οὐκ ἐμοῦ, ἀλλὰ τοῦ λόγου ἀκούσαντας ὁμολογεῖν σοφόν ἐστιν ἓν πάντα εἶναι.

(In the provisional but nevertheless already clarifying translation, we will leave the decisive word Λόγος untranslated for now; the fact that we are translating the other word that also echoes Λόγος—namely ὁμολογεῖν—with "to say" is not meant to convey anything decisive yet about the essence of the Λόγος.) The translation is as follows:

> If you have not listened merely to me, but have listened (in obedience to the Λόγος) to the Λόγος, then knowledge (which subsists therein) is to say the same as the Λόγος: one is all.

This saying speaks of a listening. This listening, in order to be a proper one, should not be directed toward the vocalizations of the thinker, but rather toward the Λόγος. Therefore, and inarguably, Λόγος, because it is related to a listening (i.e., to something that can be listened to), is indeed a kind of saying and a kind of word. From out of this proper listening to the Λόγος emerges and exists rigorous [260] knowledge—σοφόν. This rigorous knowledge exists because it is grounded upon a relation to the Λόγος—it is grounded in ὁμολογεῖν: we are translating this 'literally' as 'to say the same as what the Λόγος says.' It would be difficult to argue that here the Λόγος and ὁμολογεῖν are not being thought from out of the realm of saying and listening. But what is it that one calls saying and listening? Listening is a matter concerning the ears. Whosoever has ears to hear, hears. But what are the 'ears'? The ears, when considered solely in terms of their anatomical and physiological presence, do not perform or cause hearing, not even when we understand listening merely as the hearing of noises and sounds. Apprehending cannot be detected anatomically, nor can it be proven physiologically, or even grasped biologically. What would the ear and the entire hearing apparatus be without the ability to apprehend? Listening understood as the perception of noises always takes place on the basis of that listening which is a listening to something in the sense of a hearkening. Our hearkening, however, is always in and of itself already in some way a hearkening to what-is-to-be-heard, either prepared for it or not, and in some way obedient to it. The 'ear' that is necessary for proper hearing is this obedience. That which can be heard, that to which one actively listens, need not be anything akin to sound or noise. What makes up this obedience cannot easily be said. From the saying of Heraclitus's we only learn that knowledge emerges from out of the hearkening listening to the Λόγος, which in distinction to the human speech of the thinker is not an auditory phenomenon. And this knowledge consists of ὁμολογεῖν—saying the same as another, which here means, saying the same as the Λόγος. Saying the same here does not mean simply to parrot, but rather to say something again so that the same is said in a different way, and in such a way that what is said after what is first said succeeds and 'follows' it: that is, it is tractable, a follower, *obedient*. Perhaps that is how obedience subsists in ὁμολογεῖν: namely, in a following, tractable saying-after. But what is being said in this saying-after, which is said to be authentic knowledge?

§ 5. Three paths toward answering the question: What is the Λόγος?

a) The first path: the Λόγος as One and all. Access to the Λόγος (as being) through the ἓν πάντα εἶναι in fragment 50

Clearly, the Λόγος does not say anything arbitrary or desultory. Rather, it says something about 'all': namely, that it is 'one.' It is not possible to speak of anything beyond the 'all.' And one cannot say something simpler about something than what has been said: namely, that it is one. The Λόγος thus simultaneously says something far-reaching and something simple.

How easily this sentence allows itself to be pronounced: one is all! In this dictum, the fleeting superficiality of vague opining meets the hesitating caution of questioning thinking. The attempt to explain the world hastily with a formula that is everywhere and always correct can make quick use of the sentence "one is all." However, the first steps of a thinker—the steps that are decisive for the entire fate of thinking—can also be concealed in this saying. How may *we* now—*we* who are unprepared and who have grown even more clueless through the accumulation of varied historiographical knowledge—how can we approach this ἓν πάντα εἶναι, this 'one is all,' directly, in order to wrest from it a 'sense' that is easy for *us* to grasp and, in the event that such a sense does not offer itself up, to pin one onto the saying ourselves?

ἕν—"one." What does this mean? Numerically, it means 'one' instead of 'two' or 'three.' Or, does ἕν not mean the numeral or the number one, but rather "the one" which we think when we say: "one and the same"? But even here it is not readily apparent what the "one" means, given that it is meant to convey something different than the word 'the same,' which has been added to it. ἓν πάντα εἶναι—"one and the same is all." Does this perhaps mean: all is the same? Does 'one and the same,' when said of all, mean the effacement of all difference? All—πάντα—would then be comprised out of [262] that which has no differentiation. But this would be the indifference that belongs to the emptiness of nullifying nothingness. Or, does ἕν mean neither the one of the numerical one, nor the one of sameness, but perhaps rather the one in the sense of unifying, which is called such because it unifies and unites? If so, how and from what perspective can this unifying one be thought? Is the unifying of πάντα, a unifying that unites all, itself something seperate from 'the all'? If so, then πάντα, the all, would not be everything. The unifying one would then stand over against the all and would preside over it. ἕν would be the one and πάντα the other, and then they would be two and not ἕν, not one.

Or, is ἕν the one in the sense of a unifying that, as the unifying of all, unifies itself with what has been united in such a way that it cannot be said to wrap itself around it or be above it, but rather incorporates itself into, and binds itself to, what has been united? How shall we then think this unifying one?

Or, does ἕν, the one, mean something like the one, the singular, which excludes all else, but that excludes in such a way that it still precisely thereby manages to include the other (πάντα)? In this case, a simple uniting of the manifold would not merely be a holding together of multiplicity, but rather the unity that originally retains all in its 'unifying.'

How obscure and without toehold remains the ἕν for a thinking sufficiently conjoined to it, even though it is so easily pronounced. Perhaps we should not differentiate the various meanings of ἕν—the numerical one, the one of sameness, the one of the unifying oneness, the one of singularity—and exclude them from one another through an either/or dynamic. Perhaps all of the above-named meanings of ἕν are thought in the ἕν that Heraclitus thinks. But, if this is the case, the question is only intensified for us: in what oneness, and in which *One*, are all these different meanings of ἕν themselves united? It is easy to see that all the questions concerning the possible meanings of ἕν return when we attempt also to think πάντα in a correspondingly clear, concrete, and concise way. [263] Does πάντα only indicate the all in the sense of a somehow concluded summation of the possible many? Is the 'all' only an accumulation of the various and the differing? Is the 'all' the totality of the real and possible multiplicity of things? Is the 'all' the whole of the many sorts of divided and divisible parts? Of what does the wholeness of the whole consist?

What can we add to the determination of the recent popular conception of 'wholeness,' if the oneness and essence of the One remain indeterminate? It is easy to say that the totality determines the parts and their divisibility in the process of classification, and that this totality is thereby not simply the result of an accumulation of pieces. It also makes some sense that the manner in which the quantity of pieces comprise a sum is different from the manner by which the totality alone predetermines the way in which its divisions and parts are joined. This difference between sum and totality, already familiar to thinking, does not offer up much help as we try to think πάντα, the all, in its relation to ἕν in the midst of all this generality and indeterminateness.

Given what has now been said about ἕν and πάντα, we can see that these words presumably name something essential, but at the very same time remain ambiguous and hollow, and are often only enunciated as 'empty words.' Again and again, thinking attempts to gain some clarity and grounding in regard to ἕν and πᾶν, in order to help with the sentence ἕν πάντα εἶναι. And, again and again, these attempts break apart only to find themselves in new and different iterations. It suffices here to point to the single term 'pantheism' in order to bring to mind the various attempts to experience and to think in a way that clarifies ἕν πάντα εἶναι, and thereby to divine an explanation of the totality of the world. The strangely indistinct and futile nature of these attempts cannot be denied. However, it is now also time to inquire into the reason for this undeniable fact. [264] The reason for it is that thinking forgets—and until now has forgotten—that it must first seek out the mode of measure from which the dangerously innocuous words ἕν and πάντα receive what is nameable and determinable in them.

ἕν and πάντα are named in what we hear from out of λόγος itself, and that is: ἕν πάντα εἶναι, one *is* all. In being, and as being, the One unites the all that is. The all consists of beings, the being of which has its essential feature in the ἕν. How can we ever find our way toward a proper gasp of ἕν and πάντα if we do not clearly and precisely think that within which they show and unfold? πάντα (as beings as a whole) and ἕν (as the essential feature of beings) show themselves and unfold in being. But, surely we must first ask how being, εἶναι, is thought in ἕν πάντα εἶναι, or even how it must be thought in accordance with Heraclitus's manner of thinking. If we do not undertake to think εἶναι, being, in accordance with the manner of Heraclitus and inceptual Greek thinking—or even just intuit the direction and breadth of this thinking—any attempt to think and thereby also experience ἕν and πάντα in thinking will be in vain.

Let us now be attentive to the entirety of the saying, which speaks of the proper listening to λόγος:

οὐκ ἐμοῦ, ἀλλὰ τοῦ λόγου ἀκούσαντας ὁμολογεῖν σοφόν ἐστιν ἕν πάντα εἶναι.

We recognize that the saying concludes with the word εἶναι. But εἶναι (being), which is the last in the word order of the saying, remains the first of all words in the totality of the saying—the first, that is, according to the rank and dignity and expansiveness of saying. However, the saying of Heraclitus's does not speak of being, but rather of λόγος and ὁμολογεῖν. And precisely ὁμολογεῖν, the obedient saying of which comprises authentic knowledge, says the same as what λόγος says. λόγος says ἕν πάντα εἶναι—always presuming that λόγος is a saying and only that. ἕν πάντα εἶναι is heard in and from out of a hearkening-listening [265] to λόγος. ἕν πάντα εἶναι comes from out of λόγος. It is that which can be heard through a listening to λόγος, and is thereby what is gleaned from λόγος. But how can ἓν πάντα εἶναι be derived from λόγος, if it does not belong to it? How can ἓν πάντα εἶναι belong to λόγος, if λόγος itself does not safeguard ἓν πάντα εἶναι within itself? And how can it preserve it within itself if it itself does not measure up to, or equate to, ἓν πάντα εἶναι? But, what can λόγος itself still be 'outside of' and 'apart from' ἓν πάντα εἶναι? πάντα, as the whole of beings, unfolds in being. At the same time, and emphatically, ἓν unfolds as the essential feature of all beings that are in being. Therefore, λόγος, which can be heard in ἓν πάντα εἶναι, cannot unfold as anything other than as being itself. However, given the exegesis up to this point, λόγος is, if nothing else, that which *says*, i.e., it is the word and the word-sense of the word. By contrast, ἕν, πάντα, and εἶναι have nothing λόγος-like (i.e., word-like) about them (in the above-specified sense): rather, at most they are what is said in λόγος. However, as long as we continue to think in this way, we are only unhesitatingly delving deeper toward that particular determination of λόγος established by 'logic' through its thinking of λόγος as assertion, and more generally as 'saying,' with logic thereby purporting to know what 'saying' is. Moreover, we find this determination of λόγος to be quite obvious, for it is indeed the case that already early on for the Greeks λέγειν and λόγος meant "to speak" and "to say." But in contrast to all of this, the fact reveals itself that, in the saying of Heraclitus's, ἓν πάντα εἶναι somehow and undeniably derives from λόγος itself. λόγος itself must therefore let ἕν, πάντα, and εἶναι each unfold in itself and all together in their relations to one another. λόγος itself must prevail in the way of their unfolding, and thereby in the unfolding of the One, the all, and of being.

Perhaps the time has finally come to ponder the fact that what reveals itself from out of λόγος—and perhaps reveals itself *as* λόγος itself—is the ἓν πάντα εἶναι. Perhaps this, and only this, gives us [266] the correct clue for grasping the essence of the Λόγος, purely based upon what it itself allows us to hear about it. Is it not perhaps time to set aside all of our customary perspectives and opinions belonging to all later and thoroughly metaphysical interpretations of λόγος?

What, then, does ἓν πάντα εἶναι say to us when, in this audible form, the Λόγος itself emerges and, in showing itself, makes itself heard? What, then, does ἓν πάντα εἶναι say to us about the Λόγος itself, if we ponder this and hold fast to it? If we now attempt to glimpse the essence of λόγος from out of ἓν πάντα εἶναι, we will surely recall that ἓν πάντα (εἶναι) has remained thoroughly ambiguous. Most importantly, however, we have abstained from also including the indeterminate ambiguity of the third word, εἶναι. Nevertheless, the following thing remains graspable even given the incomprehensibility of ἕν, πάντα, their relation, and the foundation thereof—namely, that which here is being called the unifying and uniting of the all, i.e., the unifying and uniting of what *is*, of the entirety of beings. The unifying and uniting in reference to beings as a whole—i.e., beings as such— must then also be the foundational character of the Λόγος, provided that ἓν πάντα εἶναι, as that which can be heard, becomes audible from out of, and as, the Λόγος.

b) The second path: access to the Λόγος through the original meaning of λέγειν. The Λόγος as harvest and gathering

Now, what does λόγος/λέγειν properly mean if, as we contend, the word originally did not have anything to do with saying and asserting, speech and language? λέγειν—*legere* in Latin—is the same word as our word 'to read' [*lesen*], but not that particular 'reading' which we immediately associate with script and thereby with the written word and, by extension, with speech and language. Henceforth, we will take *lesen* in a much broader and also more original sense as meaning [267] 'to harvest,' such as 'to harvest the ears in the field,' 'to harvest the grapes in the vineyard,' and 'to harvest wood in the forest.' λέγειν, to harvest; λόγος, the harvest. The same way that the Greek word λόγος means λέγειν and λεγόμενον, the German word *die Lese* means, on the one hand, the carrying out of the harvest—for example, the currently ongoing harvesting of wine grapes—but also, on the other hand, that which has been harvested in the sense of the particular yield of a harvest, such as, for example, when we speak of a variety of wine made out of grapes harvested late in the season (i.e., *Spätlese*).

(Alas—if only after all perspectives and consequences the attempt to think through the essence of λόγος purely in accordance with the above meaning of λέγειν would succeed in unfolding the region of thought that it indicates!)

Little is accomplished, and even less is gained, by merely indicating the visually verifiable root meaning of λέγειν in its correspondence to the German word *lesen* in the sense of harvesting. It is much more important that we now illuminate this kind of harvesting according to its essential features. It is also important that we attempt to clarify λέγειν and λόγος from within the horizons of Greek experience and thought, using harvesting thought in this way as a guide. We thus ask two things:

1. Of what does harvesting consist?
2. In what way does harvesting, properly understood as λέγειν, give us a clue as to how the Λόγος can be thought insofar as it discloses itself as ἓν πάντα εἶναι?

Regarding the first point. What is 'harvesting'? To harvest is to take and to pick up from the earth: it is the act of bringing-together and laying-together, and in such a way that it is λέγειν, gathering. However, what has been picked up and laid together in the harvesting is not simply brought together in the sense of an accumulation that may someday be finished. Harvesting finds its end only in that very act of picking-up that preserves what has been taken and brought in. Harvesting is at the same time a picking-up in the sense of a taking-up from the earth, a picking-up in the sense of a conserving: only in this does harvesting come to an end. But regarded properly, harvesting does not end with this picking-up and bringing-in that conserves. [268] In fact, proper harvesting begins from out of this picking-up that conserves, insofar as harvesting is oriented from the beginning toward such a bringing-in and conserving, and is constantly determined from out of it. Harvesting contains safeguarding within itself as its prevailing fundamental trait. At the same time, there is yet another feature of harvesting that must be examined. Harvesting is not a haphazard and slipshod snatching-up, hastily moving from one thing to the next. Rather, the taking-up and bringing-in of harvesting is always a careful drawing-in. But this only becomes possible on the foundation of a prior, prevailing drawing-out, a drawing-out whose breadth and limitedness are granted by what is in need of being conserved, and concerning which care must be taken. All of the above-named features and relations must be thought as one if we wish even to approximate a thinking of harvesting in its full sense.

Instead of 'to harvest' [*lesen*] in the sense just illuminated, we could also say: 'to gather' [*sammeln*]. This word is even more unambiguous in relation to what is now being meant by the word *lesen*, for otherwise we are prone to understanding *lesen* as 'reading,' thereby associating it with 'script.' On the other hand, this talk of 'gathering' all too easily seduces one to take 'harvesting' in a superficial way as a mere bundling together. The harvest, however, is the drawing-in/drawing-out gathering, whose gathering is already being held together by what is to be conserved and has been designated as what is to be conserved. That is why all proper gathering must already have pulled itself together: that is, it must have already gathered itself and be forgathered in its determination. In the harvest, this originally gathered for-gathering prevails toward what is to be conserved. For-gathering, so understood, is the originary gatheredness and 'gathering' that already prevails in every gathering that takes up.

Today, this wonderful word 'for-gathering' is only known to us in its very limited and everyday meaning. Presently, however, we are thinking it in the just elucidated sense of the harvest, and in doing so we are most attuned to gathering now not meaning a mere additive bringing-together, [269] but rather the originary gatheredness of what is to be conserved, from out of which all gathering springs up and in which it remains held, i.e., for-gathered, i.e., gathered from out of originary gathering and secured within it. If we think this 'forgathering' that prevails throughout and within all gathering and harvesting, then we grant this word a unique dignity and determinateness. Forgathering is the originary retaining within a gatheredness, a retaining that first determines all drawing-out and drawing-in, but also is that which allows all scattering and dispersal. Forgathering, thus understood, is the essence of harvesting and of the harvest. The harvest and the gathering, thought in this way, are more originary than what is scattered and the act of dispersal. Just as all 'concentration' is only possible from out of an already prevailing and concentrating center, so too is all typical gathering sustained and conjoined by a forgathering that thoroughly prevails in the totality of drawing-out, picking-up, bringing-in, and drawing-in—i.e., what is here being called 'gathering.' Indeed, at first it is not so easy for us to think 'gathering' in its fullest, originary, origin-creating sense, on account of our being accustomed to thinking—when we think of it at all—only of a retroactive pushing and driving together of something that has been dispersed.

Regarding the second point enumerated above: when we attempt to think harvesting and the harvest, gathering and forgathering, in the sense just elucidated, then perhaps we may eventually come to intuit the originary essence of the Λόγος, and that means to think its essence as one with what the early thinkers of the Greeks named when they used the name φύσις/ἀλήθεια. From the saying of Heraclitus's we learn that λόγος unveils itself as ἓν πάντα εἶναι, as the all-uniting One. It is hardly necessary now to call special attention to the fact that the Λόγος, thought as the originary harvest and forgathering, cannot unveil itself as anything other than [270] the all-uniting One. But, with all of this we are only at the beginning of the attempt to think the Λόγος. Only one thing has been established thus far: namely, that the common meaning of λέγειν and λόγος—that is, in the sense of assertion, saying, speech, word, and word-meaning—does not allow the originary essence of the Λόγος to appear. We can, however, already see the following as well: that the common meaning of λόγος as speech and assertion is not suited to making the essence of λόγος, which has been shown to be harvest and gathering, accessible and understandable. However, it is very possible that a way may reveal itself that allows us to see how the common meaning of *lesen* as a taking-up and grasping of writing and the written word, speech and the spoken word, originates from out of the originally thought λέγειν: reading as gathering.

REVIEW

1) Expanded reconsideration of λόγος within the horizon of the meta-physical doctrine of ideas and of the to-be-thought pre-metaphysical essence of the Λόγος as the naming of being

Logic thinks λόγος as the assertion. In an assertion, something is being addressed as something. That in terms of which the particular thing is even capable of being addressed constitutes what is addressable about that thing. What something is— i.e., the what-being of something (for example, the house-ness of a house, the blooming of a blossom)—is conceived of by Plato as the ἰδέα, the look, the visage, which reveals the thing in question in such a way that through this it shows itself in its what-being. However, these 'visages' of things and of particular beings are, when judged from the perspective of their visibility, not visible in a sensible manner—they are not sensible visages, but are rather supersensible. If one calls the sensible, taken in its widest sense, the 'physical,' then the ideas, as the supersensible visages of beings, are meta-physical.

To conceive of λόγος as address, from the perspective of the ideas, is to think λόγος metaphysically. Therefore, we designate [271] the logic that thinks λόγος in such a way the metaphysics of λόγος. Usually, logic is understood to be the doctrine of thinking. Logic is indeed the doctrine of thinking, in the deeper sense of it keeping open the horizon of the 'metaphysical' that is proper to Occidental thinking: for the λόγος of logic characterizes and sustains the differentiation of the supersensible and the sensible, thereby defining what is possible within metaphysical thinking. The addressing of something as something makes it so that I, through the addressing, take something as something, and consider it as something. "I consider something to be something," in Latin, is *reor*. The corresponding faculty of considering something as something is *ratio*. One translates this word as 'reason,' and equates reason, *ratio*, and λόγος in their meanings. If we say that 'the logical,' 'the rational,' and 'the reasonable' are the same, then we are not only saying that three different sounding words are the designation for the same meaning, but also that in 'λόγος,' '*ratio*,' and 'reason,' the unfolding of fate, and the entirety of the history of Occidental metaphysics, are present. To consider something as something, and to pass it off as something, is judgment. Judgment constitutes the essence of thinking, understood metaphysically. Thinking thus interpreted as 'logical,' as λογικῶς, and as related to λόγος as assertion, is the essence of *ratio*, i.e., of reason. According to the demonstrated connection between κατηγορία, λόγος, and ἰδέα, Kant still determines the essence of reason to be the faculty of ideas, i.e., the faculty that thinks the ideas and, from such thinking, governs all other thinking. In such a manner, logic becomes the doctrine of reason, just as now in all metaphysics λόγος is grasped as the assertion and as the faculty of reason understood in terms of the ideas. Said otherwise, all thinking from the perspective of (and as a product of) ideas is enacted according to the guiding principles of λόγος understood in terms of logic. That is why logic, as the 'doctrine of reason,' is the inner core of the thinking of ideas—that is, of metaphysics.

[272] However, if the innermost fate of Occidental history according to its course heretofore were grounded in metaphysics, and if this fate were to hold a transformation of this history inside itself, then metaphysics, as the foundation of this history, would first have to be affected by this transformation. Were it to be necessary to help thinking bear out the fate of this transformation, both now and in the future, if solely in a way that only prepares with an eye toward this transformation of the fate of the Occidental human, then a consideration of this Occidental fate would first and incessantly have to ponder the innermost essence of metaphysics: that is, it would have to ponder the essence of 'logic.'

The question raised previously—'What is metaphysics?'—became a significant predicament from which thinking could no longer hide, no matter how unprepared and almost helplessly it wrestles with the way this question can first be posed and thus become elevated to a question-*worthy* question. In relation to this question, it must come to pass—and the first tentative steps of this have already been taken—that somehow logic and its essence are brought to language. However, to bring the essence of logic to language means to think-after what λόγος is. To think-after what λόγος is does not mean to locate a concept about λόγος, but rather to question-after the Λόγος itself, to embark down the path toward it in order to let a relation of the Λόγος toward us become possible. If we attempt this, then surely we cannot hold ourselves solely to what logic thinks about λόγος: for logic thinks it metaphysically, thereby preventing any progress toward the foundation of metaphysics, and that means any progress toward that realm in which the fate of metaphysics, and with it Occidental history, decide themselves. But is logic the only—and more importantly, the *originary*—knowledge of that for which it is named (i.e., λόγος)? Supposing that the Λόγος did not become [273] the λόγος of logic overnight and without reason, we must think-after what the essence of the Λόγος has revealed of itself before the beginning of metaphysics. We thus question the thinker who thought the Λόγος before Plato and Aristotle, and who perhaps thought it so essentially that the word 'λόγος' remains the foundational word of his thinking. This thinker is Heraclitus.

We will first think through fragment 50, paying attention to what the Λόγος named in this saying of Heraclitus's itself offers up to an attentive, hearkening listening. That which can be heard from out of the Λόγος states, said in human words: ἓν πάντα εἶναι.

(As an aside, it is once more worth recalling that the young Hölderlin inscribed the Heraclitean λόγος "ἓν πάντα" into his university friend Hegel's guest-book in the following form: Εν και παν. At the same time, it must be pointed out that one and a half decades later, the same Hegel used a saying of Heraclitus's regarding the Λόγος as a maxim at the beginning of his work *The Phenomenology of Spirit*, a work that founds the absolute metaphysics of Spirit and at the same time, from a certain perspective, consummates Occidental metaphysics altogether. This saying will also be elucidated in what follows.)

According to the saying of Heraclitus's, ἓν πάντα εἶναι becomes audible from out of the Λόγος. Approaching this from the outside, we initially attempted to grasp in a more stringent way the first two words, ἕν and πάντα, in their possible meanings. In doing so, each time we hit upon a strange ambiguity pertaining to ἕν as well as to πάντα. However, the matter had to be put to rest with a simple enumeration of the various meanings of "one" and "all," for these words do not provide us with any guidance as to how their respective, various meanings can be thought coherently, or even any guidance to think in what sense πάντα (i.e., the all) is, in effect, ἕν (i.e., one). But it almost appears as if this strange indeterminacy [274] of ἓν πάντα εἶναι is what continually assures that this phrase becomes the guiding thought for all thinking about the entirety of beings.

In the previous lecture, a step was taken whose style, path, and direction did not achieve a sufficiently clear concurrence, as was evidenced by the voicing of various concerns and questions. The main cause for this lack of clarity is surely the obscurity and remoteness of the matter itself. The indeterminacy also surely arises from various unavoidable issues of presentation. However, it arises just as much from the fact that we are unable to keep everything that has been preliminarily elucidated in the previous lectures present in a uniformly immediate way. The attempt will therefore be made once again, by way of an extended review, to clarify the step already taken, thereby recalling the entirety of the venture and running the risk of repeating what has already been said (and thus, when measured against the progress of reflections, of not moving forward). In all thinking it is more favorable if we march in place and think ever more clearly, rather than hastily moving from one unclear thing to the next just for the sake of progress. Because the goal of the thinking that is being practiced here pertains to what, at the ground of its truth, is the simple itself, this venture is in all respects difficult for us. To think and to say the simple *simply* would certainly be easy if the simple were the same thing as what, without much effort and at any time and in any situation, is the familiar. Perhaps, however, it is precisely the familiar that is essentially misleading and which, for all its apparent straightforwardness, is the tangled, or perhaps even the entangled.

In these lectures, and under the aegis of the term 'logic,' we are attempting a consideration. To consider means to hold oneself up to the demand of meaning and to linger under its roof. ('Meaning': the true in which all rests and sways.) [275] 'To consider' here is nothing other than an attempt to learn thinking through a 'logic.'

The traditional meaning of logic concerns λόγος. It grasps λόγος as assertion. In the realm of this determination the essence of λόγος unfolds into *ratio*, into judgment, into a thinking from out of, and in accordance with, ideas. In unison with the unfolding of λόγος as assertion into reason, the essence of the idea also changes. The way in which Plato thinks the ἰδέα is different from the way in which Augustine grasps the *idea*. Descartes thinks the idea still differently, as do Leibniz, Hume, Kant, Hegel, Nietzsche, and modern world consciousness in general. Nevertheless, within these differences, the same is thought. In the modern world consciousness, with which we either knowingly or unknowingly concur and which we carry with ourselves, the entire history of the idea and its changes, but also the history of λόγος and its changes, are present. Only when we represent the history of the idea and of λόγος in a merely historiographical way are Plato, Augustine, Descartes, Leibniz, Kant, and all the others mere names for something bygone on which we nevertheless wish to dwell, or to which we wish to remain connected. But if we do not think some historiographical bygone, but rather think what *is*, then what was thought by Plato and the thinkers who followed him is *immediate presence*—and not just any random one, but rather the one that right now in world history is the concealed, sending fate. In order to learn to experience this and only this, we learn to think. And in order to learn to think, we must, however, proceed from the doctrine of thinking that reigns all around us: namely, 'logic.' This means: we must be attentive to how 'logic' thinks λόγος.

We say: logic thinks λόγος metaphysically. However, it is metaphysics that has given the historical world of the Occident and our fate its character, and it is also metaphysics that, as what shapes and joins, remains the authentically present. [276] The presence of this present does not depend upon whether we as a whole, or a single one of us occasionally—or, indeed, the human at all—takes notice of the presence of history. By contrast, however, the power and scope of our knowledge and ability to know depends upon whether what is present in history still approaches us, or whether it has already begun to withdraw from us. The power and scope of our knowledge of the true is perhaps only an unprepossessing, yet nevertheless integral and necessary stone or beam in the arch of the bridge into the future. The question regarding the status of metaphysics and its essential core— that is, the question regarding the status of 'logic' and the λόγος as thought by it—is only yet another form of the question concerning that about which metaphysics is asking when it asks what beings are. The question "what are beings?" looks out toward being for the answer. How matters stand with being itself, however—how it unfolds and presides in its truth—is a question never asked by metaphysics because it is incapable of asking it, and need not ask it in order to remain metaphysics. Metaphysics, in the face of the question of being itself, can only differentiate it from non-being. The question concerning being itself is, at the same time, the question concerning non-being and the nothing. However, the question concerning being itself and the nothing goes infinitely deeper, reaching essentially different realms than the question "to be or not to be" as it is commonly known and understood in relation to the passage from Shakespeare's *Hamlet*, insofar as one usually only relates being and non-being to the continuance or ending of human life.

We are now asking whether or not the originary essence of the Λόγος has come to light in metaphysics. Why do we ask the question in this way? At first glance, and initially, we ask it in this manner because, before the beginning of metaphysics, the Λόγος was experienced and thought in a different way. The legitimacy of this must, for now, remain mere conjecture, for it is offered within the unceasing dominance of metaphysical thought, [277] with its control over the interpretation of the entire history of Occidental thought, including pre-Platonic thought.

Supposing now that Heraclitus is, in truth, a pre-metaphysical thinker, and supposing that he thinks the Λόγος differently, why are we then reaching so far back into the history of Occidental thought with our question? Why do we not simply posit a determination that is contrary to the metaphysical interpretation of λόγος and of thinking, given that there is the occasion, or even the necessity, for doing so? Of what concern to us is the 'historically' far-removed, pre-metaphysical essence of the Λόγος? To these questions one should answer thusly: whether or not the pre-metaphysical essence of the Λόγος immediately concerns us, whether or not it already concerns us now, and whether or not it will one day again concern us remains, at present, a matter of indifference.

However, it could happen that in the pre-metaphysical essence of the Λόγος something pushes forward into the light and becomes present, something that not only concerns us, or only some other race of humans, or only a particular realm of beings (for example, nature or art, or perhaps the order of society, or technology), but which, rather than concerning beings, concerns being itself, from out of which every particular being receives its truth and untruth. It could then certainly also happen that because of this it no longer remains a matter of indifference how the historical human and the future human think of being and 'about' it, nor does it remain a matter of indifference if we and they—that is, if those who will come to stand before what is to come—have ever thought such a thing solely in view of the truth of being, and whether we and they will reflect upon it and are inclined to think it. If it is the case, as we began to intimate in the previous lecture, that the pre-metaphysical Λόγος is not an activity of human saying and asserting regarding which 'theories' and a 'doctrinal system' were erected in logic (theories about which hardly anyone cares); if, moreover, it is the case that 'the Λόγος' [278] is somehow the same as the one being that prevails in all beings; and if, furthermore, all that has been given the name of the Λόγος were to shine through all historiographical masking of history and remain present and be the present as the same (i.e., as being), then perhaps there would exist also for us a sufficiently pressing reason to ask about the Λόγος as it was thought pre-metaphysically: for in this Λόγος, the to-be-thought for all thinking both hides itself and shows itself, presuming always that nothing higher, nothing more originary, nothing more present, but also nothing more inconspicuous and indestructible, can be thought than beyng itself.

The λόγος of what is commonly called logic is, as assertion and saying, an activity and a faculty of the human. This λόγος belongs to that which, among beings, is called the human. The Λόγος of which Heraclitus speaks, as harvesting and gathering, and as the all-uniting One, is not some quality or condition obtaining to beings. This Λόγος is the originary forgathering that safeguards beings as the beings that they are. This Λόγος is being itself, within which all beings unfold. To think-after this Λόγος is surely no longer logic in the conventional sense. At the same time, we will hold onto the term 'logic,' but in doing so we will now understand it to mean something more provisional: namely, a consideration of 'the Λόγος' as which being inceptually announces itself, thereby revealing itself as the originary to-be-thought. To engage oneself with 'logic' now means only this: to learn to experience the authentic to-be-thought, i.e., being itself. Indeed, even more provisionally, it now means to prepare the possibility of becoming open to this to-be-thought so that it (i.e., being) would perhaps at some point grace us with a configurable relation between itself and us, and grant us the furthering of this relation, thereby coming upon us as we are in the constitution of our essence, and thereby bringing about and leading into a transformation of that essence. So understood, the term 'logic' heralds a more originary task, one that appears only to contain the inconspicuous to which we [279] will barely manage to measure up for a long time yet. For, what matters in this process of learning to think is taking only a few steps, perhaps even only one step, which will then unlock for us the realm of the to-be-thought and the correct pathway to it. This more originary logic, as the consideration of the originary essence of the Λόγος, is essentially without doctrinal content: it is impoverished when compared to the richness of learnable propositions, information, systematicity, and the succession of theories of metaphysical logic. This more originary logic is merely the unceasing practice of—or perhaps even just the preparation for—taking a simple step in one's thinking into the realm of the authentic to-be-thought. Logic in this more originary sense pertains to that particular 'activity' that is at the same time a 'letting be': namely, a letting unfold of being from out of its own truth.

On its own, the contemporary human is not able to enact such a thinking activity. Indeed, the contemporary human cannot even find or invent a consideration of it, if the traces of such a thinking do not already address him and if he does not agree to enter into a conversation with this address. This possibility surely presumes the experience of history not as consisting of the bygone, and also not as that which has been handed down, out of whose ridges and valleys certain peaks of 'greatness' stand out. History is, in itself, the pre-articulated conversation of the essential with itself. The question nevertheless always remains whether and how the human enters into this conversation.

c) The third path: access through the λόγος of the ψυχή. Fragment 45. The question concerning ὁμολογεῖν

Initially, and above all, what matters now is to think-after, in a more proper way, the Λόγος as thought by Heraclitus along the lines of the already elucidated essential features of the 'harvest' and the 'for-gathering.' In order to do this, it is necessary to elucidate still other sayings of Heraclitus's that deal with the Λόγος, though admittedly to do so only from within the limits set by the task of making the pre-metaphysical essence [280] of λόγος visible. Fragment 50, which has already been discussed, tells us the following:

The sole relation proper to the Λόγος that arises from out of a hearkening listening to the Λόγος can itself only be a λόγος, a λέγειν. It is ὁμολογεῖν—that is, to harvest the same thing that 'the' Λόγος harvests as 'the' harvest. That now means: to gather oneself toward the same as what the Λόγος, as the forgathering, holds gathered in and toward itself. The way in which the human gathers himself toward the forgathering is different from the way in which the Λόγος is, in itself, the for-gathering. This difference makes possible a sameness of λέγειν, which, even given this difference, concerns the same Λόγος. Who executes the gathering and the harvesting in the sense of ὁμολογεῖν? Obviously the human: for the saying of Heraclitus's speaks to the human.

If, however, the human himself is the λέγων—i.e., the one who harvests, the one who gathers—then he can only take over and complete that particular harvesting that harvests the same as what is harvested by 'the' Λόγος if he himself, in his essence, somehow 'has' a λόγος—that is, if the essence of the human is such a harvesting. The human is ζῷον—a living being, a being that is determined by life. But what does 'life,' ζωή, mean? When thinking this word,[1] the Greeks, in a way similar to their thinking of φύσις, think of the 'emerging-from-out-of-itself' which is always, at the same time, a 'return-back-into-itself.' Emerging opens itself to the open, keeps it, in a certain sense, and maintains itself in the open and in this way contains the open within itself. Since time immemorial, the essence of life thus experienced, and the essence of that which lives, have been distinguished by the ψυχή: we say 'soul,' and call what is alive 'ensouled.' ψυχή means a small puff of air, a breath. However, here we are not thinking of breathing merely as the movement and functioning of the organs dedicated to it, but rather as a breathing out and in. Insofar as ψυχή as breath [281] should now designate the essence of what is alive in all of its demeanors and behaviors, breathing cannot mean the mere drawing-in and expulsion of air. Were we to take it only as such, we would at best be thinking of breathing and the organs dedicated to it in a causally scientific way as a fundamental prerequisite of the living and its existence, but not as the omnipresent, essential feature of the entire essence of what is alive. Rather, that drawing-in and drawing-out called breathing is the essential feature of the living: namely, that it emerges into the open, and by emergingly going out into the open enters into its characteristic relationship with the open, thereby bringing the open into that relationship and referring the open back to it. The essence of the ψυχή thereby rests in the emerging self-opening into the open, an emerging that each time takes the open up and back into itself, and in this manner of taking upholds itself and abides in the open. ψυχή, ensoulment, and ζωή, "life," are thus the same, provided that we also think ζωή in a Greek way. This demands that we think ψυχή and ζωή from out of what the Greek thinkers called φύσις, in which they think the being of beings in general. All that exists 'lives' insofar as it *is*, and as something living, it is in some sense ensouled, though in a different manner in each case. This now means: the emergent relationship to the open and the openness of the open are determined in different ways, all according to the kind of 'living being,' and also the other way around.

Based on ζωή and ψυχή, one can see that the living can *be* in a way conforming to the self-opening emerging, and thus itself be a self-opening as a drawing-out-drawing-in, in the manner of the already described 'harvesting' and 'gathering' (i.e.,

---

[1] See *The Inception of Occidental Thinking* in this volume.

of λέγειν and λόγος). ζωή and ψυχή, the living, can thereby have a λόγος. If the living being has a λόγος, then the drawing-out and drawing-in—i.e., the relationship to the open—is determined as 'harvesting' and 'gathering.' If that is so, then the living being *is* in the manner of the human: the 'harvesting' and 'gathering,' the λέγειν of the human, is ὁμολογεῖν. This emergent and thus unfolding being— i.e., the human—is open to the Λόγος.

[282] Does Heraclitus tell us something about the living being called 'the human' from this perspective (i.e., from the perspective of λόγος)? Heraclitus says enough. But what does he say? What does he who expressly demands the ὁμολογεῖν of the human say about the ψυχή of the human? A saying that is counted as fragment 45 states:

ψυχῆς πείρατα ἰὼν οὐκ ἂν ἐξεύροιο, πᾶσαν ἐπιπορευόμενος ὁδόν · οὕτω βαθὺν λόγον ἔχει.

The outermost extremities of the soul you will surely not be able to find on your course, even if you were to wander down every single path—so far-reaching is its harvest (gathering).

According to this, the ψυχή, the essence of the living being 'the human,' has a λόγος, and this λόγος is βαθύς—"deep"; indeed, it is "deep" in an exceptional sense. As previously mentioned, for the most part we understand the deep only as the opposite of what is high (and, correspondingly, height). In that sense, the deep contains within itself an orientation downward. However, that is not the essential thing regarding βαθύς. We speak of a 'deep woods'; even Homer already uses this turn of phrase in the *Iliad*.[2] The deep is the far that entirely reaches into the concealed, and thereby it is somehow that which gathers. In what way can a λόγος be deep? Harvesting and gathering draw out. Indeed, this drawing-out even determines all gathering drawing-in and what is able to be drawn-in. The drawing-out is the reaching into the farness, from out of which harvesting first allots the gathering. The λόγος of the ψυχή is, as λόγος, deep, and in such a way that this depth consists in the drawing-out reaching to the far, from out of which the gatheredness of what is to-be-gathered determines itself. Insofar as the soul has such a λόγος, the drawing-out reaching into the farness belongs to its self-opening and taking-up-taking-back. Whereabouts this reaching-far reaches, there the ψυχή as ψυχή has its outermost extremities, through which it is open for that toward which its λόγος, as such, intimates.

[283] Fragment 45 reads: ψυχῆς πείρατα ἰὼν οὐκ ἂν ἐξεύροιο, πᾶσαν ἐπιπορευόμενος ὁδόν · οὕτω βαθὺν λόγον ἔχει.

---

[2] Homer, *Iliad*, Φ 573.

The outermost extremities of the soul you will surely not be able to find on your course, even if you were to wander down every single path: so far-reaching is its harvest (gathering).

From this saying we can initially and generally surmise that the soul—namely, the soul of the human, who is here being addressed in regard to his course through the soul—has a λόγος: the human is a ὄν λόγον ἔχον. In this saying we hear, almost verbatim, the essential differentiation of the human that is determinative for all later metaphysics, according to which the human is ζῷον λόγον ἔχον, that (particular) living being that has a (i.e., the) λόγος. However, in the interpretation of this definition of the human, λόγος is thought as *ratio*—that is, as reason—in the sense of the faculty to think ideas, to make judgments based upon concepts. Now, what could be more natural than the desire to attempt to find this later, metaphysical definition of the human in the above-cited saying of Heraclitus's? Indeed, this particular attempt to interpret the saying would have some standing and weight. However, it will not be attempted here: not because one would like to avoid interpreting the metaphysical understanding of the human essence back into the thought of Heraclitus, but rather because one still understands the word λόγος used in this saying superficially and in a metaphysical sense. For the saying speaks about the λόγος of the human soul from another perspective, insofar as it would like to express that this λόγος which the human soul has is 'deep.' However, one immediately refuses to think-after the essence of the depth of the human λόγος further. One therefore goes no further than taking this utterance of Heraclitus's merely to be a comment on the fact that the human soul is difficult to plumb, owing to its depth. And because one already and in every case thinks 'λόγος' metaphysically here, one ends up with an interpretation of this saying that [284] is forged by common usage. However, it is due to the uncommonness of this interpretation that we mention it here. It is uncommon because it has something to teach us.

Interpreted metaphysically and logically, λόγος means: assertion, judgment, or also 'concept,' insofar as one understands the concept as the coagulation of a certain comprehension, i.e., a certain judgment. Instead of using the terms assertion and judgment to describe the foundation of logical thinking, one can also just say 'thought,' and thereby understand λόγος to be 'thought,' albeit not as a thought-activity of the soul, but rather as what is thought in this activity: the thought as what gives meaning in thinking. λόγος as assertion/judgment/comprehension is thus equated with 'concept' and with what has been conceived (i.e., with meaning). Armed with this logical and metaphysical conception of λόγος, one can easily face the saying of Heraclitus's and give to it an interpretation that, above all, makes immediate sense to the modern human. If we equate λόγος with concept, then with this quote Heraclitus wishes to say with his saying that the concept of the soul is so deep that all attempts to plumb its depths in the sphere of the 'psyche' (that is, of psychology) must fail, for they can never reach the boundaries of the soul and that which, in bounding and surrounding the soul, also 'defines' it. The saying of Heraclitus's is therefore taken as the earliest testament to the difficulties of psychology and psychological self-observation. There is even a work about "General Psychology" that takes this saying of Heraclitus's in the just touched-upon sense as its motto on the title page. The author of this work, Natorp, was also, at the time of its writing, an accomplished expert on Greek philosophy.

But in this saying, Heraclitus does not wish to say anything about the limitations and difficulties of psychological research. Such claims are altogether impossible, given that for the early Greek thinkers—and indeed, for all of the ancient Greek world—something like 'psychology' was entirely foreign. This is not meant as [285] a denigration of 'psychology,' but merely as an indirect reference to the fact that psychology, in essentially arising out of Christian thinking, is of one and the same metaphysical origin as modern historiography and technology, and is only today entering upon the path toward unfolding its historical determination and toward becoming that which, at its very core, it is: namely 'psychotechnics.' However, if in the above-cited saying of Heraclitus's the first word to be heard is ψυχή, and if we translate this word as 'soul,' thereby thinking it as the Greeks did, and if we do not interpret the word λόγος that is named in the saying as 'meaning' and 'concept,' then we keep away from all 'psychology' and thus remain open to thinking this saying in harmony with fragment 50, which has already been elucidated.

REVIEW

2) A reconsideration of fragments 50 and 45. The Λόγος as the self-disclosing all-uniting One and the original meaning of λόγος and λέγειν. The Λόγος as the for-gathering that dispenses the origin and thereby retains it

In order to approach what Heraclitus thinks in regard to ὁ Λόγος (i.e., the Λόγος), we have taken two paths, and have chosen a saying by Heraclitus, fragment 50, as the first guideline. We have done so because, in this saying, Heraclitus names the Λόγος from a perspective out of which it becomes apparent that the Λόγος itself announces itself and, in doing so, allows its own essence to be heard: ἓν πάντα εἶναι—one is all. This is revealed by the Λόγος. It can only reveal this when it itself *is* what opens there: for the Λόγος cannot be something 'in addition to' the One and 'in addition to' the all, if it itself 'is.' Then again, it must at least be on par with, or even perhaps surpass, what it announces and offers up and opens, for the ἓν πάντα εἶναι depends upon the Λόγος to become audible. [286] In this ἓν πάντα εἶναι, 'the Λόγος itself' shows itself, and indeed *as* the Λόγος. For ἓν πάντα εἶναι contains the following: namely, that the One as the uniting all—i.e., the being of all—constitutes the being of beings as a whole. The Λόγος itself is the all-uniting One. According to the saying of Heraclitus's, this is precisely what the human should authentically know: it is the to-be-thought that is before all else, in all else, and beyond all else.

One of the paths we have taken leads to the following realization: the Λόγος is the self-announcing all-uniting One. The Λόγος is the uniting of all. Based on this, what is now called 'Λόγος'—namely, the uniting One—is fundamentally different in its meaning from λόγος as thought by 'logic' when it thinks it as 'assertion' and 'saying,' as 'speech' and 'word,' as 'judgment' and 'reason.'

But precisely that which, according to the saying of Heraclitus's, the Λόγος reveals about itself—namely, that it is the uniting unifying—precisely this self-announcing essence of the Λόγος corresponds in an originary and exact way to what the word λέγειν actually and authentically means. To show and to highlight this original meaning of λόγος and λέγειν is the other path that then meets the first one in the same. λόγος and λέγειν mean "to harvest," "to gather," that is, to unify and to unite.

Now, the result of the preceding elucidation of ἓν and πάντα is that the essence of the One and the all, and thereby also of unifying and uniting, cannot be precisely defined. At the same time, however, it was still possible to determine that what remains consistent throughout is what is named with the words 'to gather' and 'to harvest.' That is why, in order to gain a proper insight into the essence of the Λόγος, everything depends upon grasping the essence of 'harvesting' and the 'harvest,' gathering and the gathering, more clearly, more completely, and in a more fulfilled way.

[287] We initially attempted this through an elucidation of that particular 'harvesting' that we encounter as a human activity, e.g., 'harvesting ears of grain,' 'harvesting grapes,' 'harvesting wood.' We thereby discover that to harvest is to pick up from the earth, a picking-off of grapes and berries from the vine. This picking-up and picking-off enacts itself as a bringing-together. We are inclined already to take this to be gathering. To be sure, this initially mentioned activity is that dimension of gathering that is apparent to the eye, the appearance through which 'harvesting' and 'gathering' show themselves. However, are we allowed to stop at the appearance and to take what appears in it to be the essence of gathering and harvesting? Obviously not. Moreover, we cannot immediately and exclusively take this superficially and thereby incompletely grasped harvesting and gathering as the essence of the harvest and the gathering, at least not if the

harvest (i.e., the Λόγος) is to be thought as what constitutes the being of beings in general. Even if Heraclitus did not say more about the Λόγος and its essence as the harvest and the gathering (which for various reasons we may presume), it is necessary for us to think the essence of harvesting and gathering more emphatically. Why? Because we are assuming that the thinkers at the beginning of the history of Occidental thinking thought such things, and thought them in such a way that their thinking still continues to think beyond our thinking in new ways, which is why we may never catch up to that particular incipient thinking. Or is this assumption perhaps arbitrary? Is perhaps the assumption that the be-ginning of Occidental thinking shelters within itself the fate of Occidental history, thereby predetermining the truth of this history, untenable? Is the assumption that this beginning is of such dignity also untenable? I think not. Concerning earlier thinkers, we can only attempt a conversation that corresponds from a distance if we presume and recognize [288] that what the beginning of thinking once (in the past) began is once more (in the future) to come toward the human, owing to the fact that what is always already there in advance, thought in this double sense, is always 'in front' of human musing and activity. History, in its hidden course, is not progress from an inception to an end, but is rather the return of what is always already there in advance into the beginning. That is why in this particular case, which concerns the need to think the Λόγος in the manner of Heraclitus (i.e., as being itself), we cannot think the essence of λέγειν (namely, harvesting and gathering) essentially and richly enough. In addition, the other namings of being that are executed in the inceptual thinking of the Greeks give us enough guidance to define the essence of the Λόγος, in the sense of harvesting and gathering, in a manner proper to this essence. We should therefore not be content with the superficial characteristics of the initial understanding of 'harvesting' and 'gathering' as a human activity, thereby equating this activity of gathering solely and categorically with picking-up and carrying-together. Picking-up in the sense of taking something up and carrying-together is grounded in something other which, as the ground, also constitutes what is essential in the essence of 'harvesting' and 'gathering.' The strange thing regarding the essential constitution of harvesting (taken as a whole) is this: that it itself can only be what it is when it not only carries together what lies before it, but also when it pulls itself together into itself (i.e., 'concentrates' itself) and orients itself in all of its phases toward what has been determined in advance by harvesting and gathering. But this is a picking-up in the sense of a conserving. And conserving, for its part, is grounded in a sheltering. This, in turn, is a watching over something that at the same time harbors it. In 'picking-up' as a conserving, that which belongs to gathering in an essential (and not a retroactive) way is pre-served in advance. That is why gathering and harvesting are in their innermost core a preserving conserving. In this, gathering itself is entirely gathered into its own essence, a situation we call 'for-gathered.'

[289] This forgathering, thought from out of the conserving preserving, is, as the originary sheltering gatheredness of gathering, the essence of gathering. And from this, drawing-in, as what holds together and joins taking-up and bringing-in, first gets determined. For its part, drawing-in is itself (according to its own possibility) grounded in a drawing-out that opens and allots to the drawing-in its domain, extent, region, and possible directions. The characteristic of drawing-out found in harvesting is now completely and properly determined by that which, as a preserving and conserving, necessitates all expansive drawing-out. In order that we may gain the proper (i.e., essential) perspective on the essential constitution of gathering and harvesting (the latter still understood as a human activity), we should avoid pondering the single steps undertaken in gathering which, when viewed from the outside and due to their temporal order, appear as a progression. Seen from this perspective, harvesting commences with a picking-up from the earth and ends with the storing of what has been gathered in a silo or container, so that therein a conserving may take place—a conserving which, when seen from this perspective, no longer has anything to do with the activity of gathering as a bringing-in; that is why it appears as though conserving and sheltering do not at all belong to 'gathering.'

Nevertheless, safeguarding and preserving have everything to do with 'gathering' and 'harvesting.' What would a gathering be, if a conserving and safeguarding did not first preside as the ground of the determination of harvesting and as the predisposing of all its essential traits? The fact that this occurs last within the temporal order of provisions and steps required for the execution of gathering does not go against the essential law according to which the safeguarding and conserving come before the very possibility of gathering and must, in fact, already have belonged to the human if his gathering is to have a goal, a direction, an expansiveness, and thereby an essential space.

[290] (The order proper to the essential structure of gathering and harvesting is one distinct from the order of the particular succession of steps for the execution of this or that gathering and harvesting. Regarding the essential structure of gathering and harvesting, and thereby regarding the sustaining foundation of its essence, we recognize that all gathering and harvesting is grounded in a conserving which, in turn, is grounded in a sheltering. Sheltering is the authentic harvesting, insofar as in it a selecting takes place of that toward which drawing-out and drawing-in become and are determined. In turn, selecting is grounded still more originally in an electing of what is itself the elected, i.e., the rare, i.e., what is from beginning to end the unique because it remains as the One which, as such, unifies: that is, it has originally for-gathered everything from out of itself into the keeping safe of the elected.)

We may verify what has been said about gathering as a human activity if we turn our thoughts to another realm of human gathering—if, for example, we consider the gathering (i.e., the collecting) of art. We easily recognize how decisively the essence (and the distortions of the essence) of gathering are rooted in the fact that conserving, along with safeguarding, are essentially grounded in the necessity belonging to gathering, grounded in fact in what is to be conserved in such a gathering/collection of artworks. It remains to be asked what is properly maintained through this conserving of the artwork. All conserving, and the 'gathering' suspended within it (in both the limited and more expansive senses of a bringing-together), determines itself from out of the manner and essentialness of what is here to be sheltered. What is to be sheltered in the conserving of artworks lies in the movement of what is, in each case, given historically as essential and inessential in art—that is, in the particular historical disclosure of art's essence itself, which rests on co-founding and erecting the historicity of history, through the way in which the artwork sets the truth of being to work.

[291] In the wake of such considerations we may surely and easily recognize that the opinions regarding what is properly to be sheltered in the gathering of art diverge widely and perhaps even culminate in a never before acknowledged lack of counsel, given that presumably the historical peoples are without counsel when it comes to the essence and the parameters of sheltering and of forming and the reciprocal relationship of the two. Now is not the occasion to engage in further elucidations on this matter. We should solely focus our attention on the fact that mere gathering (the so-called curatorial enterprise), without the gatheredness of the historical human toward the inner forgathering and saving of his own essence, is not true gathering, and that the essence of gathering is in no way exhausted in a hasty bringing-together and amassing.

It should be noted in passing that, for some time, those who think-after these things have noticed that the obsession with mere curatorial gathering of antiquities shares a peculiar reciprocal relationship with the steadily increasing unfolding of technology. It has hardly been considered what essential connections determine this reciprocal relationship.

(Perhaps these essential connections arise from out of the still-concealed yet originary belonging-together of the λόγος of 'logic'—which has fallen away from the originary Λόγος—and τέχνη, both of which in their interdependence co-determine the essence of metaphysics, which is, in turn, the origin of modern historiographical/technical thinking and willing.)

In considering the essence of gathering and of the harvest by way of the example of the human activity of gathering, it was at first important to recognize that all harvesting and gathering are grounded in the for-gathering according to which we understand the gatheredness of all steps and stages of harvesting into the safeguarding sheltering. 'Harvest' and 'gathering' are, in an essentially originary way, for-gathering in the now defined sense. However, that which up to now we have said and have attempted to think about harvesting and gathering [292], should not only and primarily apply to the human activity of gathering, but should rather show us the foundational features of what characterizes *the* harvest and *the* gathering that Heraclitus simply names ὁ Λόγος, with which word he names being itself, the One that unifies all beings. ὁ Λόγος is the originary, origin-dispensing for-gathering that remains retained within the origin and which, as such, is the essencing of being itself.

It thus appears that Heraclitus took the essence of harvesting and gathering from human activity, and then carried it over to the being of beings as a whole. In Greek, such a carrying-over is called μεταφέρειν. The signifier for the being of beings as Λόγος would therefore be a metaphor. In this metaphor lies the perhaps oft-practiced, part conscious and part unconscious, but in any case perhaps unavoidable tendency of carrying the characteristics and forms of human ways and demeanors over to the world in its entirety. By means of this manner of projection, the world is presented in 'human' terms. This manner of thinking is called anthropomorphism. Therefore, if 'the Λόγος' means the being of beings, it would also only be a making human of the world. Perhaps we should not wonder about this: for it is often claimed that less developed peoples, in distinction to those who are more 'advanced,' are more familiar with the metaphorical way of thinking, since the impetus behind this manner of thinking arises out of a unique lack of criticalness that characterizes 'primitive' thinking.

Now, is the characterization of the being of beings as a whole as Λόγος merely a carrying-over of the characteristics of human behavior into the ground of the essential? We do not want to rush to judgment, for the question concerning wherein human gathering and harvesting are themselves grounded has not yet been answered, and in fact has not even been posed. It remains open whether human λέγειν in fact presupposes the relation to the Λόγος in the sense of being, and receives its proper possibility of essence from 'the Λόγος.'

[293] (If this were indeed the case, then it would be difficult to speak of a carrying-over of 'human' traits to the fundamental feature of the being of beings as a whole. Perhaps it is not even permissible to force the question hovering here into a crude either/or that wishes to express itself in the following formula: either all of the traits that the human purports to find in being are abstracted from the image of the human, or the form of the human is only one among many different appearances of being. In the latter case, being would need to be recognized purely as itself, and indeed through the human. But how could this occur if the human were not formed by way of the image and the appearance of being, and in such a way that the human, from out of himself, allows being to approach him? In that case, the following either/or—namely, either everything is only human images and productions, or everything is only a copy of being—would not apply. Furthermore, the relation of being to the human would be the originary relation, insofar as it characterizes being itself, but also because it belongs originally to the essence of the human. Moreover, being itself could not be experienced without a more originary experience of the essence of the human, and vice versa. This more originary experience would then be that in which being and the essence of the human have their truth (i.e., the truth of their relation). In that case, the true would

be above being and deep within the human essence and would preside over the relation of both as their origin. The reference to these connections, which have heretofore hardly been thought through, should only make us aware that being itself can in no way be grasped like a thing or an object, not because it still remains too distant from the human, but rather because it has already come too close to him. Moreover, it should make us aware that the human can only gain the distance necessary to grasp being by retreating from being back into his own essence, which is not the same at all as retreating away from being. That is why the relations touched upon here were still engaged with one another [294] in an oddly veiled play even back at the beginning of Occidental thinking when being itself was first properly named. For we who have come later, this is a warning to be aware that, also and already for the first thinkers, the saying of being was full of enigmas. From out of this we derive the suggestion that when we think-through what is said by the early thinkers, we should rather, and more stringently than before, pay attention to their path, thereby paying attention to the relation to being and, only from out of this relation, to being itself.)

In terms of the manner by which it shows itself to us immediately, gathering and harvesting may be a human activity. Initially, this only means that a human activity is a way of being human, the being of which would remain withdrawn from the human were the latter not at all capable of thinking and experiencing 'being.' That which manifests itself to us through traits of being human need not also have its essential origin in these manifestations. Out of this, at least, arises the possibility that the essence of gathering and harvesting may indeed initially be experienced by us through our activity pertaining to them, but that they nevertheless originate elsewhere, and are also bound and structured elsewhere. Such a bond announces itself in fragment 50. We will therefore follow fragment 50 and be attentive to the fact that here Heraclitus specifically determines the relationship of the human to the Λόγος as ὁμολογεῖν. Out of this arises something decisive: namely, that the human himself must have within himself a λέγειν and a λόγος, a harvesting and a gathering, which have gathered themselves toward the harvest and the forgathering that constitutes the essence of being. However, should it be the case—and this can hardly be doubted—that the relation of the human to the Λόγος, and thus to the being of beings, were the highest possible relation in which all other human relations to humans and things are grounded, then this relation (i.e., ὁμολογεῖν) should in fact carry and sustain the essence of the human. The human himself, then—as the very being that he is—must 'have' a λόγος in the core of his essence which, as this λόγος, is itself 'the relation' to 'the Λόγος' in the sense of the being of beings.

[295] According to the Greek conception, the human is a ζῷον, a living being. The essence of what is alive, however, is the ψυχή, the soul. The essence of the human—that is, the ψυχή—must therefore have a λόγος, in order for ὁμολογεῖν to be possible. Presumably, this human λόγος must be a distinguished one, if the

relation to 'the Λόγος' is to show itself and unfold within it in a unique way. In fragment 45 we experience what Heraclitus thinks about the relation of the essence of the human (i.e., of the ψυχή) to the Λόγος (i.e., to the being of beings):

ψυχῆς πείρατα ἰὼν οὐκ ἂν ἐξεύροιο, πᾶσαν ἐπιπορευόμενος ὁδόν · οὕτω βαθὺν λόγον ἔχει.

§ 6. The absent presence of the Λόγος for the human and the indication of the objectless region of the originary Λόγος

a) The harmony of fragments 50 and 45. The homological relation of the λόγος of the soul to the Λόγος. ὁμολογεῖν as the self-gathering toward the originary forgathering of the Λόγος of being

To what extent are fragments 50 and 45 in harmony with one another such that, in a certain sense, they complement each other? This question may be answered by way of a brief, prescient observation.

Fragment 50 is about λόγος in the sense of being itself, but at the same time it is also about ὁμολογεῖν. Through ὁμολογεῖν, the λέγειν that is essentially proper to the human, and thereby also the λόγος that the human 'has,' are determined. This harvesting and gathering should be a hearkening one, and thereby a compliant self-gathering that joins itself to the originary for-gathering, a for-gathering by way of which 'the Λόγος' holds the essence of the human gathered toward itself, preserving within itself as *the* Λόγος the hearkening belongingness of the human to being, [296] a preserving that simultaneously gives and withholds according to measure. Said simply: fragment 50 is about the homological relation of the human λόγος to *the* Λόγος. In this saying, the relation of being itself to the essence of the human is thought, and in such a way that the essence of the human is not only one reference 'point' while '*the* Λόγος' is the other, but rather in such a way that the essence of the human exists and is grounded precisely in the relation of being to the human. The human, as the one who gathers in a hearkening way, is 'gathered toward' being:

that is, the human is open to being, and is so on account of being. Only insofar as the essence of the human in this gathering depends upon, and is based upon, being, can the human relation to being also be un-gathered, dis-sipated, and a-stray, i.e., bewildered by confusion. Strictly speaking, metaphysics in truth only knows the question concerning the relation of the human (as *one* being among others) toward beings as such and as a whole; the modern iteration of this question is the one concerning the relation of the subject to the object. However, the subject–object relation is grounded, in all ways, in the metaphysically ungraspable relation of being toward the human essence. Moreover, this relation is not properly thought or inquired into in pre-metaphysical thinking, however abstractly experienced and named it may be. Perhaps metaphysics and its entire history bears this fate within itself: namely, that it is only through metaphysics and its history that the differentiation of being and beings is at all brought to light in order to be experienced and questioned someday as this differentiation, a questioning in which being itself first approaches thinking in its question-worthy truth and transforms thinking itself.

Heraclitus's saying, numbered as fragment 50, deals with the homological relation of the human λόγος to *the* Λόγος. To what extent is fragment 45 in harmony with fragment 50? Fragment 45 does not mention [297] '*the* Λόγος'; by contrast, it mentions "a" λόγος, specifically, a "deep" one that the human soul "has," and evidently 'has' as a foundational aspect of its essence. The saying (fragment 45) says that the furthest extremities of the soul, to which in its reaching the soul essentially extends, cannot be detected by the human, owing to the fact that the λόγος of the soul is an exceptionally "deep" one. Even though the relation of the human essence to *the* Λόγος is not addressed in this, we may nevertheless presume that 'the Λόγος' referred to is that toward which the soul, in its extending, directs its outermost extremities. However, how is it then possible, as stipulated in fragment 50, for the human himself to hearken to and submit to the Λόγος, if 'the Λόγος,' as fragment 45 suggests, is undetectable by him? The two sayings do not appear to be in harmony, for indeed they contradict one another insofar as they make contradictory statements regarding the relation of the human λόγος to *the* Λόγος.

In order to see more clearly here and, most importantly, to grasp the proper content of fragment 45, a more extensive elucidation is needed. It is clearly stated: the ψυχή—namely the one of the human, who traverses it—has a λόγος, indeed, a "deep" one. To what extent can the ψυχή as such have a λόγος? To what extent is a λέγειν, in the sense of the designated gathering and harvesting, possible in the ψυχή, so that even the ψυχή itself, by way of the λόγος that it 'has,' first arrives in the authentic realm of the possibility of its essence? What is the ψυχή if we think it from out of that along with which it is constantly named, and if we thereby think in a Greek way all that is to-be-thought, leaving aside modern conceptions of the 'psyche' and also the allegedly well-known, primitive ideas about the 'soul' (of which ethnology and anthropology believe themselves to have accounts)? To think the ψυχή in a Greek way means: to think its essence from out of its belongingness to ζωή and φύσις, to 'life' and 'nature.' However, referring the ψυχή [298] back to ζωή and φύσις would also not bring us into proximity with what is essential, if at the same time and before all else we did not also think ζωή and φύσις in a 'Greek' way. If we are everywhere emphasizing that what is named in these foundational Greek words should be thought in a 'Greek' way, we are not being driven by the intention of accurately reproducing a past world in a historiographical way: rather, in the constantly emphasized 'Greek,' we are simply seeking what is the hidden essential, i.e., what bears and decides both our history and the history of the future. The fundamental feature of φύσις and ζωή is an emerging from out of itself that is, at the same time, a self-occluding withdrawal back into itself. Under the protection of these names, Greek thinking, experiencing, building, and dwelling in beings already possessed something in advance, something that at some point only those yet to come will found and build into the immovable truth to which, as the proper ground, what is named in the foundational words φύσις, ζωή, and ψυχή already makes reference in inconspicuous ways. That is why we today, no matter how often we repeat these foundational words, only have preliminary names with which to make what is essential in φύσις and ζωή visible, albeit in a distant and faint way. And in order to assure even this, what is precisely not necessitated is a broad marshalling of learnedness and the display of partially understood connections within intellectual history, but rather only the ever newly begun and ever-simpler consideration of, and thinking-through, what sounds-forth in these foundational words like a prelude. What we initially hear there is always the same and, indeed, almost monotonous. Yet, it is the foundational tone of the inceptual thinking of the Greeks. In the thinking through of foundational words we continuously experience the limitations of thinking, but also the pent-up grace of the still-buried treasures of our own language. The latter is not ours as our tool: rather, we are the ones to belong to it as those who are either at home in it or made homeless by it. If we therefore now attempt to clarify the translating interpretation of the foundational words φύσις and ζωή, then we will easily [299] find ourselves off-track, while nevertheless perhaps still, at the same time, providing a rough clue to be subsequently taken up by a recapitulating thinking-after.

If we are attentive to the fact that φύσις means the emerging that from itself is a withdrawing into itself, then the two determinations are not only to be thought as simultaneous and existing alongside one another, but rather as designating one and the same fundamental feature of φύσις. φύσις contains within itself the following dimensional character which must, nevertheless, be thought of as one with the above: namely, that φύσις is the arising-from-out-of-itself and the self-occluding. Therefore, 'dimensional' does not simply mean the extent of a thing, the way in which, for example, we could speak of the breadth of a wall: rather, the dimensional is in itself self-opening and self-occluding. What has the characteristics of φύσις—i.e., the 'natural'—is thereby never something with the characteristics of an object which is the source of object-like effects in other objects. φύσις is also not 'nature' in the sense of the lawfulness of what appears and the unity of what appears in its objectivity. On the contrary, in order even to think φύσις in a remotely adequate way, we must exhort ourselves to experience everything with an eye toward the extending, occluding self-opening in such a way that everything pervaded by φύσις weaves and unfolds in such relations.

By virtue of being conditioned by Roman and Latin thought, predicated as it is on nouns and the relations between them, and also by virtue of being conditioned by modern scientific thought, predicated as it is on objective, functional relations, we today are virtually excluded from the possibility of thinking-after being inceptually, and that means thinking it in the sense of φύσις in the manner that the Greeks did. Moreover, even Goethe's view of nature is of no help to us here. Though such a view is in some ways in contrast to the mathematical and physical objectification of nature in the manner of Galileo and Newton, it is nevertheless thoroughly grounded in the modern metaphysics founded by Descartes and, above all, Leibniz, and thus remains separated by a chasm [300] from inceptual, Greek thinking. The decisive justification for these sentences, by means of which we distinguish the essence of φύσις from all later thought and the concepts of nature developing from it, can surely only be provided if we show to what extent the essence of truth, under whose law the thinking of φύσις stands, is fundamentally different from that particular essence of truth that determines metaphysics and the metaphysical views of nature. According to its originary meaning, φύσις is not at all the name for nature in distinction to history: rather, it means the being of beings, but not from the later perspective that interprets all beings naturally, or even biologically.

However, what has been said about the inceptual name φύσις also applies to the word ζωή, which we translate as "life." Accordingly, what is alive also has the characteristic of emerging and arising-from-out-of-itself at one with the corresponding and oppositional characteristics of withdrawing-back-into-itself and self-occluding. Similarly, the word ζωή has the same breadth of meaning as φύσις, such that ζωή also can become the name for being. However, we are here asking about the essence of ψυχή. Previously, we said: to think ψυχή in a Greek way means to think its essence from out of its belongingness to ζωή and φύσις.

But what do we encounter as the main characteristic of ψυχή according to the meaning of the word? The word means puff, breath, the breath of life. Is it merely a coincidence that, when the soul slips away, we say that the breath of life has expired and the light of life has been extinguished? Why is it that we consider both 'breath' and 'light' as having the same relation to the fundamental characteristic of the living thing? Light is the lightening—it is that which lightens and opens, and which, as the bright, holds open. Breath, grasped broadly and properly enough as not being limited to air, is the drawing-in and drawing-out, the emerging into the open and the pulling back in of the open. In fact, if we think of air as ether, then 'air' and 'light' coincide. However, for our belated thinking they only coincide [301] because they are one in their concealed essence: they are one and the same with 'life' and φύσις.

The soul—i.e., that which animates—is the essence of the living thing insofar as 'ensoulment' means precisely this: that through it a being arrives and abides in such a manner of being that, as emerging, it unfolds into the open and, thus unfolding, gathers the open and what is encountered in the open to itself. However, due to a long tradition of thinking, we are certainly conditioned (and, for yet different reasons, also hastily inclined) to imagine any self-referential entity both as being a subject and as having the characteristics of an 'I,' whenever there is talk of a living thing that references itself and other things back to 'itself.' The point of reference, so to speak, into which the relation that we call 'toward itself' flows, is known as the 'I,' and the 'I' is like a point or a pole or a center. It is not by accident that Leibniz, who imagines every being as having the characteristics of a 'subject' or an 'I,' speaks of the singular, self-contained beings as the 'metaphysical points' that are then at the same time determined as the 'inner' over against the 'outer.' Accordingly, what pertains to the 'soul' is considered to be what is 'inner' and 'internal.' Furthermore, unmediated, intuitive opining (and this is true even for the Greeks) posits inner organs such as 'the heart' (καρδία—poetic form, κραδία) and 'the diaphragm' (φρήν, φρένες–φρονεῖν, φρόνησις) as the seat of fluctuations in the mind's disposition, and of the mind in general. However, we must slowly learn to differentiate between what, on the one hand, intuitive imagining often prematurely grasps and at which it ultimately arrives, and what, on the other hand, is in truth meant by thinking and knowledge. The reference to this difference does not, however, mean that the intuitive and imagistic shall be pushed out over time in favor of the non-intuitive and non-imagistic. On the contrary, it means that everything imagistic and every image only appears and is brought into appearing from out of the non-imagistic, which beckons to the image. The more originarily and essentially the non-imagistic presides, the more it beckons to the image, and the more image-like is the image itself. [302] We easily recognize that the differentiation between the intuitive imagistic and the non-intuitive non-imagistic goes together with, and even coincides with, the differentiation between the sensible and the not-sensible (i.e., the non-sensible and the supersensible). However, this is the differentiation upon which all metaphysics is based. The question nevertheless remains—or, to be clearer, the question must first be asked—where this differentiation originates and to where it leads. The question thus posed concerning this differentiation and its essential origin directly addresses the origin of the imagistic and the non-imagistic in their interrelationship, as well as the foundation of this relationship itself.

If we now think a few more steps ahead, we can easily see to what degree the question concerning the origin and the difference between poetic saying and thoughtful saying lurks in the background of the question concerning the origin and the difference between the imagistic and non-imagistic, insofar as poeticizing (not to mention the other forms of art) is an imagistic saying. However, poeticizing is precisely not merely a sensible saying: rather, it utters a meaning, the same way in which thoughtful saying is not without images, but is rather imagistic in its own way. From this it becomes clear that we cannot easily categorize the essential difference between poeticizing and thinking as belonging to the difference between the imagistic and the non-imagistic and, by extension, the difference of both of these from saying.

On what detour do our thoughts now find themselves? We are supposed to be concerned with the ψυχή, and yet we find ourselves now talking about the essential difference between poeticizing and thinking. But the view being indicated here, as we shall soon see, only has the appearance of a detour. For, we found ourselves on the path that led toward a consideration of the difference between the imagistic and the image-less because, for the sake of the essence of ψυχή being indicated—that is, for the sake of the drawing-out into the open which is at the same time a drawing-in— we were attempting to detect the relation between this drawing-out-with-itself and this withdrawing-back-into-itself, and thus detect the being of the self (and in so doing [303] determine the essential core of ψυχή). Such an approach does not immediately succeed. Perhaps the essential core of ψυχή, and thus of breath essentially grasped and understood as the drawing-out drawing-in, lies neither in an outside and an external, nor in an inside and internal, but perhaps rather in an intertwining that could be called 'intimacy,' assuming that we leave aside everything psychological, subjective, experiential, and emotional that is associated with the term.

How shall this circuitous and admittedly clumsy reflection eventually lead to the fundamental essence of the ψυχή, about which even the Greeks were only barely able to think clearly? In this essence of the ψυχή we should initially only observe this one thing: namely, to what degree the ψυχή, in accordance with its essence, can have something like a λόγος. For this is stated in fragment 45: the soul ... not only has a λόγος, but indeed has a deep one. If we understand λόγος to be judgment and assertion, then it remains utterly incomprehensible how precisely the ψυχή relates to λόγος, and relates to it in such a way that it is a matter of λόγος and its depth when the outer extremities of the soul cannot be found. If, however, we understand λόγος as λέγειν in the sense of harvesting and gathering, and if we think gathering from out of its essential characteristic and thereby beyond its superficial attributes, then it no longer appears estranging when the saying of Heraclitus's reflects on the ψυχή (i.e., the drawing-in drawing-out into the open) as being determined by λόγος (i.e., by gathering). Perhaps, then, this λόγος is not only one among many characteristics of the ψυχή, but perhaps it is even the ground of the essence of the ψυχή that is being discussed here (i.e., the human ψυχή). But before we specifically determine this essential connection between ψυχή and λόγος, let us consider what else the saying of Heraclitus's says about the ψυχή and in what way the saying speaks about it.

ψυχῆς πείρατα: τὸ πεῖρας means the end, the extremity, that whereby something finally ends and 'ceases' and where something [304] else begins. However, 'extremity' and cessation are themselves determined from out of that whose end they bring about. A piece of wood or a stone end in different ways and have different endings than, for example, a downpour of rain; different still are the endings of a tree, or of an animal. No living being ends at the limits of its corporeal surface—this is not the limit circumscribing the living being. But the endings of that which, like the soul, is in itself an emerging drawing-in drawing-out, must surely have this character of reaching-out into the open; the πείρατα are the outermost extremities in the strictest sense of the word, which here means the ways and paths of going-out. The word πεῖρας appears in the plural form. The ψυχή has several, indeed, many extremities, many paths of going-out, all of which are meant. Every perceiving, every visualization, every willing and every remembering, every be-thinking, every be-holding, is a striving, a movement toward . . ., the being underway of a way; but also, every involving oneself with something, every sojourning, is a pause on the treading of paths. However, all going, in turn, is only what it is within and on the basis of a barely intuited and determinate dwelling of the human whose site conceals itself. There is everywhere, in all that is thoroughly pervaded by the soul—i.e., in all doing and letting, all bearing and enacting, all musing and striving, all falling and ascending—a reaching-out toward the extremities. However, Heraclitus says to the human whose soul—that is, whose unfolding life—is named here, 'you cannot find the outermost of this going-out and reaching-out, even if you were to tread every single path.' That there is still specific talk of "paths" here only confirms what was just now said: namely, that we should not grasp the extremities as object-like ends and boundaries akin to a wall or a room-divider, but rather that we should pay attention to the way-like and path-like nature of everything that is determined by the soul. But even this does not suffice if we fail to think the way-like and path-like as the Greeks did: namely, as the going-out into the open, as the going-through in the manner of a going-forth that enacts itself in going and gathers [305] what presences and is encountered. The "ways" are the paths for the courses of the unconcealing emerging and the concealing returning-into-itself. But why is it that the human cannot find the outermost extremities of his essence? Because the λόγος of the human soul is so "deep"—οὕτω βαθὺν λόγον ἔχει.

Much was said about the essence of this deep already at an earlier point, and as we can now see, it was done so in anticipation of this saying of Heraclitus's. The essence of the deep does not lie in it being the opposing category to the high. The essence of the deep lies in a concealed reaching into a still unmeasured farness of concealment and occlusion. Therefore, we do not translate βαθύς as "deep," but rather as "far-reaching" and "having reached far," phrases which, like all words of translation, need an accompanying interpretation in view of that in reference to which they are being said. βαθύς—having reached far, far-reaching—is being said about the λόγος of the human soul.

In the soul of the human—i.e., in the essence of the human—there unfolds a far-reaching harvesting and a gathering that has reached far. Whereabouts this gathering, which draws-out and draws-in, reaches; what this gathering in its essence actually shelters (i.e., as safeguarding and sheltering)—or rather, what it does not shelter and, in a certain sense, omits and passes over and loses—the human being cannot discover through its going along the paths of the soul.

However, does fragment 50 not state that the λόγος of the human soul is ὁμολογεῖν, and that this consists of a 'listening to' the Λόγος itself? Does this not clearly state of what the 'termination' of ψυχή consists? The soul as that drawing-in drawing-out 'terminates there,' i.e., it goes 'out' to the other, 'over' to the other, where this 'termination' ['*Aufhören*'] is a 'listening to' ['*Hören auf*']—i.e., the ὁμολογεῖν as the self-gathering toward the originary gatheredness. Does this not then name the outermost reaches of the wanderings of its paths? Does this not state how deep the human λόγος is? The Λόγος as being itself [306] is surely and obviously that deep into which the far-reaching λόγος of the human soul points. So, how can fragment 45 state that it is precisely because of this far-reaching λόγος of the human soul that the human is unable to find the outermost reaches of his own essence, even if he were to traverse all paths? In ὁμολογεῖν; in the self-gathering harvesting of λόγος; in the self-gathering toward these, 'the Λόγος' *is*, i.e., it is present. Thus, in ὁμολογεῖν, precisely that toward which the essence of the human proceeds is found, and in such a way that all of its extremities terminate exactly there and gather themselves to the Λόγος as the originary for-gathering. However, according to fragment 50, ὁμολογεῖν neither happens on its own, nor does it happen constantly. Human listening does not easily gather itself toward the Λόγος: rather, it tends to run astray and disperse itself in such a way that it predominately listens to human speech and human utterances. If this were not so, Heraclitus could not specifically point toward the ceasing of the mere listening-to and listening-in-on of human speech in favor of engaging in a gathering of itself toward the Λόγος. Therefore, the λόγος of the essence of the human does not arrive at the outermost extremities of the soul easily: it does not arrive of itself or through itself, even though it, as λόγος, points toward that to which it alone, as λόγος, corresponds. Indeed, precisely when the human—entirely from out of himself and on his own initiative, selfishly and under his own authority—goes along all of his paths and seeks only along these paths, does he not arrive at the outermost extremities or follow the far-reaching λόγος.

If we reflect upon these considerations correctly and often, we must then infer that, through his λόγος, the human can be related to the Λόγος in ὁμολογεῖν, but that this is not always the case and, indeed, is so perhaps only rarely. Therein lies the strange fact that 'the Λόγος' in the sense of the originary for-gathering—that is, the Λόγος of being itself—presences to the human and that the human is nevertheless turned away from it. For the human, the presencing λόγος [307] is thus at the same time an absent one. Thus, what presences, which properly awaits the human, can also absence. What presences need not be present, and what is present need not thereby already be what presences. The human, by clinging only to what is present, can misjudge what presences, and in that misjudgment, lose it entirely. Therefore, precisely what concerns the human soul in its ground (i.e., in its own λόγος) authentically and essentially, and therefore constantly—namely, the Λόγος as being—precisely this would presence toward the human and its dispersal onto its selfish paths, but at the same time would be absent and remote and therefore foreign. But perhaps we are here developing arbitrary trains of thought of which Heraclitus himself was not aware. Where in the cited fragment is there mention of presencing, absence and presence, or of the relationship between presencing and absencing, or of the difference between presencing and presentness (which are usually one and the same for us)? It is indeed the case that nothing concerning this is to be found, at least not *in* the text. But perhaps what 'stands written' in such a text by such a thinker is always what is present and not what presences. Perhaps a thinker also thinks more than what he knows, thinks he knows, and speaks about. Perhaps this 'more' is what brings the thinker to think and what first thinks him. Perhaps we must concede to a thinker that this is indeed the case, if we at all and in advance are to take him seriously as a thinker.

REVIEW

1) The λόγος of the ψυχή as the gathering toward the originary, all-preserving gathering. The erroneousness of psychological views. Fragments 45 and 50. References to fragments 101 and 116

This lecture on 'logic' dwells upon an interpretation of what Heraclitus says about the Λόγος. In this way, we are thinking the essence of λόγος in a more originary way. We are thereby following a more [308] originary 'logic.' We are thereby also learning to think in a more originary way. Perhaps in taking this path we will succeed in taking one step in our thinking, though even this one step may still be rather clumsy. Compared to the deluge of results and information that the sciences pour out on a daily basis, what our attempt at thinking accomplishes seems pitiful. It appears as though we are not moving about within any clearly defined domain. And not only does it appear this way—it is indeed the case. The thinking being undertaken here is without a domain. Nevertheless, it moves toward one single place. It appears as though this thinking is of no immediate use to us. And not only does it appear this way—it is indeed the case. This thinking is useless and, in that sense, it is unnecessary. Nevertheless, the unnecessary is the most necessary: it is fulfilled through the essential need and necessity of the human essence, and is thereby unavoidable. In the event that this domain-less and useless thinking now and then brushes against the essential, it could lead us onto the path toward a mindful consideration. It is then up to us whether or not this mindful consideration endures.

Since time immemorial, it has been noted that Heraclitus speaks of λόγος. The ordering of the remaining one hundred and thirty fragments familiar to us today even counts the first and second fragments (of this ordering) among those utterances concerning λόγος. However, we purposefully do not begin our interpretation with fragments 1 and 2. By contrast, we place fragment 50 at the center and move fragment 45 into its vicinity. We will initially ask about the inner connection between these two sayings. We will now hear them anew and add the translation which in the meantime has become clearer:

Fragment 50: οὐκ ἐμοῦ, ἀλλὰ τοῦ λόγου ἀκούσαντας ὁμολογεῖν σοφόν ἐστιν ἓν πάντα εἶναι.

If you have listened not merely to me, but rather have obediently regarded the originary forgathering, then (the) knowledge (which subsists therein) is to gather oneself toward the forgathering and to be gathered in the 'one is all.'

[309] Fragment 45: ψυχῆς πείρατα ἰὼν οὐκ ἂν ἐξεύροιο, πᾶσαν ἐπιπορευόμενος ὁδόν · οὕτω βαθὺν λόγον ἔχει.

On your course, you will surely not be able to find the outermost extremities of the drawing-in drawing-out, even if you were to wander down every single path: so far-reaching is its gathering.

Fragment 50 speaks of the relation of the human to 'the Λόγος.' This relation has the way of ὁμολογεῖν. Thus, a λόγος appertains to the human, whose λέγειν reaches all the way to 'the Λόγος.' The human λόγος stands before the claim which 'the Λόγος,' as it speaks-out, makes. In order once again to drive the point home expressly, we are now differentiating, based on the two fragments, what had already become capable of being differentiated based on fragment 50 alone: namely, we are differentiating between 'the Λόγος' as such (that is, the Λόγος *simpliciter*) and the human λόγος. The Λόγος is the originary forgathering, the being of beings as a whole. The human λόγος is properly the self-gathering toward and into the originary forgathering.

In distinction to fragment 50, fragment 45 does not speak of 'the Λόγος' to which the human should attend. However, it does state expressly that the human 'soul'—that is, the human in his essence—has a λόγος. This λόγος, as a faculty proper to the human, is surely one and the same as that from out of which, and in which, the particular ὁμολογεῖν of which fragment 50 speaks fulfills itself. However, at the same time fragment 45 also states that the human λόγος, owing to its 'depth,' prevents the human from reaching the outermost extremities of his essence.

According to this saying (fragment 45), the human is thus incapable of taking the measure of the vast dimensions of his own essence. However, the other saying (fragment 50) demands precisely this: that the human take measure of his own essence by gathering himself in this measuring by reaching beyond himself and joining himself to the Λόγος, therein achieving the gathering of his essence in the Λόγος, i.e., in the originary forgathering.

[310] Thus, the two fragments are irreconcilable. However, the difficulty that has now arisen in thinking fragments 50 and 45 as one falls away if we understand the oft-cited fragment 45 as it is popularly interpreted: for in this case, the fragment provides no basis for thinking what is said in it together with what is said in fragment 50 in the manner just attempted. The popular interpretation and application of fragment 45 is of interest to us, however, because in it the unbroken and commonly accepted power of the metaphysical interpretation of λόγος can be seen particularly clearly. In pondering the popular interpretation of fragment 45, we have a good opportunity to separate ourselves from the metaphysical interpretation of λόγος, or, at least, to attempt this separation.

The popular interpretation of the entirety of fragment 45 hinges solely upon the meaning given to a single word that appears in the saying—namely, the word λόγος. Because one is long accustomed to understanding λόγος as assertion and judgment, this results in a meaning for this word that makes the entire saying intuitive to the understanding. Thus, λόγος is unreflectively understood as assertion, as judgment. In a judgment, something is taken as something. For instance, we make the judgment that "this thing is a house." The thing that is encountered is taken in by the grasp of representation, it is grasped by this representing apprehension. The thing comes to be conceived by way of the representation 'house.' The assertion "this thing is a house" proves itself to be the activity of conceiving: the assertion is ultimately the con-cept. λόγος, as assertion, is the concept. Through the concept of something, we are able 'to think something' regarding the object. Therefore, the object has something that is accessible to thinking and understanding, something understandable. The object, through its concept, thus has a 'meaning' for us: λόγος is thus the 'concept' and the 'meaning' of something. Because λέγειν is understood as asserting, and this, in turn, is understood as pronouncing, λόγος is at the same time that which has been pronounced, [311] i.e., 'the word.' The word 'house' is the name for the 'concept' 'house'; the name 'house' has the 'sense' and the 'meaning' of 'house.' The entire metaphysical interpretation of λόγος moves about within this equivocation of λόγος with 'concept,' 'meaning,' and 'word.'

In fragment 45, Heraclitus speaks of the human soul having a λόγον βαθύν: in terms of the analysis of λόγος offered immediately above, that would now mean a "deep meaning," a "deep concept." If one understands λόγος thusly as concept, and understands what Heraclitus is saying in the same vein—namely, that a deep concept corresponds to the soul—then in one fell swoop everything else that is said by the saying becomes understandable. Because the concept of the soul is deep, making the soul itself difficult to grasp, in exploring it one does not reach the boundaries with whose help one could delineate (or, said with a Latin word, 'define') its borders. According to this interpretation of fragment 45, Heraclitus wishes to say that the soul, as an object of human exploration, is difficult to examine and that psychological research of it is particularly difficult. In this way fragment 45 has become a commonly used slogan with which one, channeling the authority of a thinker from the most ancient time, announces and assures the difficulty of psychological research.

As commonly understood as this interpretation of Heraclitus's saying may be, it is absurd. It is sufficient here to call attention to two things that make it impossible to understand the saying in this common way.

First, neither Plato nor Aristotle, nor even the early thinkers of the ancient Greek world, were aware of something like 'psychology.' The prerequisite for the possibility of any psychology is the positing of the human as a being that knows itself, wills itself, and more precisely, a being that is sure of itself and assures itself. So understood, the human is experienced as 'subject' and the world is experienced as 'object.' The notion that the human is a 'subject'—and, moreover, the notion of subjectivity in general—is foreign to the ancient Greek world. Consequently, not only is there in fact no 'psychology' there, but something like that cannot exist in the ancient Greek world [312], and most certainly not at the beginning of its history and its thinking. The treatise by Aristotle entitled περὶ ψυχῆς, *De Anima*, is not psychology: rather, it is concerned with the essence and stages of what is alive. But it is also not biology: it is rather a metaphysics of what is alive. However, is there not another saying of Heraclitus's that in one stroke disproves what was just said about psychology (i.e., that it is an impossibility in the ancient Greek world)? One possibility that comes to mind is fragment 101, which consists of only two words: ἐδιζησάμην ἐμεωυτόν. Snell translates it as: "I have investigated myself." That is taken to mean: I have attempted to examine the state and operations of my own soul through self-observation, thereby turning myself into the object of investigation. This translation is readily understood to speak from out of the context of the modern relationship of the human to himself, which as a subject has his own essence within his self-consciousness, and through this self-consciousness makes himself 'conscious' of his own self, all in order to be assured of this self by the awareness thus achieved, and from out of this assurance to undertake the securing of the world for the human subject and to use human subjects in the service of this securing. Someday the psycho-technical testing of the 'human material' that is to be employed in this perception of the self will be just as necessary as the inspection of a machine before its first use. It is not a matter of chance that, for a long time, America has been undertaking psycho-technology on a large scale. In contemporary thinking, the relationship of the human to himself is understood psychologically: that is, as the self-consciousness of a subject. It is from out of the context of this understanding of the human and his relationship to himself that one translates fragment 101. However, this translation not only carries the modern understanding of the essence of the human back into early Greek thinking, it also neglects to ask whether this saying of Heraclitus's [313] should not first be thought from out of the context of his own thinking. Lastly, it must also be noted that the verb δίζημα properly and simply means 'to seek something.'

However, 'to seek something' in no way means the same thing as 'to examine something' or 'to search something thematically,' thereby 'researching' it. 'To seek something' initially and simply means 'to seek after it in its place and to seek this place.' Thought in a Greek way, ἐδιζησάμην ἐμεωυτόν means: "I have sought after myself." The thinker has sought after himself, but not as one who is singular, special, and individuated. If that were the case, he would have understood himself in his subjective condition as an isolated subject, which would subsequently be dissected with an eye toward discovering the conditions of its soul. The thinker has sought himself as the human. He has sought after the human on the way to the question: to where does the human, as human, belong? Among beings, where is the place of the human? Whence is the placeness of the place of the human determined? The thinker is seeking the human: he thinks toward where the human stands. This seeking is separated from a psychological examination of the human soul by an abyss. Such a seeking can never be 'psychology,' for psychology, like any science, must presuppose that its object is given and that the place of its essence is accounted for, or that it remains unimportant within the realm of psychological questioning. Fragment 101 can therefore not be marshalled as evidence that Heraclitus harbored a special interest in psychological self-observation. The same is also true of fragment 116, which we shall not examine further at the present time. It can be shown without difficulty that fragment 101, when thought in a Greek way, is in simple harmony with fragments 50 and 45, but also with the other fragments that address λόγος.

Because psychological thinking is foreign to Heraclitus, the content of fragment 45 is as little related to the psychological examination of the soul (in particular, [314] the difficulty of finding a fitting 'concept' for the essence of the human soul) as is the content of fragment 101. The other reason why the common interpretation of fragment 45 is invalid consists in the fact that the word λόγος, which appears in this saying, does not mean 'concept,' and therefore also does not mean 'sense/meaning,' owing to the fact that λόγος *cannot* mean this. The word only gains this meaning based upon Plato's metaphysics through Aristotle. If in the saying of Heraclitus's, λόγος cannot mean 'concept,' then it is also impossible for the saying to be speaking about the difficulty of finding a fitting concept of the soul.

However, it is admittedly true that Heraclitus says that the human ψυχή has a βαθὺν λόγον, a "deep" λόγος. After all that has been said, we must now attempt to understand the λόγος named here from out of the originary essence of λέγειν in the sense of gathering and harvesting. However, we will first ask: what is the ψυχή such that it can even have a λόγος in the sense of gathering? We will think the ψυχή with an eye toward what is named in those words that are often said in conjunction with it: namely, φύσις and ζωή. The fundamental feature of what these words name is the emerging into the open which is at the same time the returning-back-into-itself of self-occluding. If we attend to the root meaning of ψυχή, according to which the word means "breath," and if we take breathing to be the fundamental feature of ζωή (life), then breathing is the drawing-out drawing-in. However, insofar as ψυχή does not mean the narrow reference to air nor the actions of the lungs and breast; insofar, too, as ψυχή does not mean a distinct and separate process within the living being or the activity of the organs responsible for breathing, but rather means the essential state of what is alive; insofar, finally, as ψυχή is understood as the essence of what is alive: in light of all of this, the word names the drawing-in drawing-out self-opening for what approaches the human and directs itself toward the human's essential core. We are elucidating the essence [315] of the ψυχή in service of the question regarding in what way the ψυχή could have something like a λόγος.

In this series of lectures, we are solely attempting to think-after the one thing that Heraclitus—a thinker standing at the beginning of Occidental thinking—says about λόγος. Heraclitus speaks of the Λόγος, and of the human λόγος. ὁ Λόγος is the originary, all-preserving forgathering. The human λόγος is the self-gathering toward the originary forgathering. The human gathering toward the originary forgathering occurs in ὁμολογεῖν. With this exegesis of the Λόγος and of λέγειν, we remain outside of the common, metaphysical interpretation of the Λόγος as thought by Heraclitus.

2) A reconsideration of the harmony of fragments 50 and 45. The drawing-in drawing-out of the λόγος of the ψυχή as the relation to beings as such and as a whole. The absent presence of the Λόγος for the human

Following the teachings of Heraclitus, we will now attempt to make clearer in what way the human λόγος can be related to the Λόγος, and that means above all how the Λόγος, from out of itself, takes up the human λόγος into a relation with itself so that the human, for his part, approaches the Λόγος by way of a λόγος. However, underlying the question of the relation of human λόγος to the Λόγος is the assumption that the essence of the human can even have a λόγος, and that it indeed does so. The essence of the human as a living being is ψυχή. We translate this as "the soul." According to fragment 45, the human ψυχή has a λόγος, indeed, a 'deep' one. We say: a λόγος that has reached far, because it is far-reaching. However, the same fragment also says that the human λόγος, precisely by virtue of its far-reaching manner, prevents the human from reaching the outermost extremities of his essence, i.e., it prevents the human from going through and beyond these extremities to reach that to which fragment 50 says he is related [316] as soon as his λόγος is an authentic one, i.e., as soon as his λόγος is such a one that corresponds to the proper essence of 'the' Λόγος, and in the manner of ὁμολογεῖν.

If we think fragments 45 and 50 together, something irreconcilable results. The same human λόγος that, according to fragment 50, is determined to be ὁμολογεῖν, and is thus determined to enact the self-gathering that goes forth toward the Λόγος, is the same λόγος that, according to fragment 45, prevents the human from even reaching the extremities of his essence, thereby preventing the human from achieving the proper relation to the Λόγος. Moreover, it is precisely owing to the far-reaching character of the human λόγος that the human fails to gather himself into the farness of the Λόγος. All of this is strange and enigmatic, and not only for our understanding which, due to some kind of disinclination, does not immediately seek to resolve into harmony what appears to be irreconcilable. What is strange and enigmatic probably conceals itself in the essence of the human himself.

When we say here the 'human himself,' of course we mean the essence of the human as experienced in a Greek way, according to which the human himself is precisely not himself in a distinguished and singular sense, such as when we think this 'self' in a Christian sense, or as a subject according to modern metaphysics with its subject–object relation. What is enigmatic about the Greek essence of the human is even more mysterious than we think, which is why, for example, once we discount contemporary interpretations and leave aside our psychological understanding of the human, we realize we know next to nothing about the poetic truth of the tragic poetry of Aeschylus and Sophocles.

In order that we may now gain a little more clarity regarding the relation of the human λόγος to the Λόγος thought in the manner that Heraclitus thinks it—and, above all, so that we do not everywhere erase what is enigmatic—we must first ask the preliminary question: in what way can the ψυχή of the human have something like λόγος at all? As long as we think what is named by ψυχή, "the soul," in a contemporary [317] psychological way, and as long we understand the human metaphysically as 'substance' or as a 'subject' (which are in their essence absolutely the same); as long as we understand the human as 'self-consciousness,' as 'an individual with reason,' and as a 'personality'; as long as all of this is the case, the question that has been posed here lacks any proper ground and domain whatsoever. By contrast, if we are to think ψυχή in a Greek way from out of φύσις and ζωή, then we begin to see it as that drawing-in drawing-out in which what is alive is suspended, oscillating in various possible relations to 'beings.' In view of the ψυχή as the drawing-in drawing-out, we then see that it is indeed possible for a λέγειν, a gathering, to preside therein. Indeed, we reach the insight that through λέγειν, provided that it (as λόγος) has gathered itself to the Λόγος in ὁμολογεῖν, the drawing-in drawing-out, and thus the soul (and with it the essence of the human), first receives the proper and singular farness of its reaching and attaining. Thinking in a more originary way, we must even say: the drawing-in drawing-out not only absorbs λέγειν (i.e., gathering) into itself as the appropriate way of executing the drawing-in drawing-out, but that, in fact, this drawing-in drawing-out is itself first grounded within λόγος as the self-gathering toward the Λόγος. It is only through λόγος that this drawing-in drawing-out (i.e., the ψυχή) becomes and is the relation to beings as such and as a whole.

But how shall this same λόγος of the human ψυχή, which transports (one could even say 'throws') the human foremost into his own essence, also bring it about that the human fails to reach his own essence, or even the extremities of it?

When looked at from the perspective of human λόγος, this λόγος, while existing in relation to the Λόγος, nevertheless cannot reach it. When looked at from the perspective of the Λόγος, the Λόγος is somehow present to the essence of the human, while not being properly present to the human. For the human λόγος, the Λόγος is something akin to an absent presence. Measured by the yardstick of conventional 'logic,' which is [318] at the same time the yardstick of 'dialectics,' an absent presence is an obvious contradiction and is thereby impossible—or, at the very least, it can be disposed of through a 'sublation.' But Heraclitus knew nothing of a sublating dialectics, on account of the fact that the modern essence of consciousness as absolute self-consciousness was as foreign to him as the modern internal combustion engine would be to the Greek builder. To interpret Heraclitus dialectically is even more untenable than interpreting Aristotelean metaphysics with the assistance of the medieval theology of Thomas Aquinas. Now, it is certainly the case that, in view of Heraclitus's doctrine of the Λόγος, we do not at all see how and in what way he thinks something like an absent presence: for in the sayings of Heraclitus's that have been quoted, there is no direct mention of it. That is why the very first task must now be to find out whether and how Heraclitus speaks about the strange relationship of the human λόγος to the Λόγος. In fragment 72, Heraclitus speaks precisely of this.

b) The two-fold relation of the human to beings and to being: the forgotten, concealed presence of being in the everyday use of λόγος. Fragment 72. References to fragments 16, 45, 50, 101, 43, 118, 30, 64

Heraclitus knows of the enigmatic absent presence of the Λόγος for the human. For us, it necessitates only the care of thinking-after in order to recognize this, thereby leaving the knowledge of this thinker in that state of vibrancy through which it will live on, undamaged by human forgetfulness. The saying of Heraclitus's that is numbered as fragment 72 states the following:

ὧι μάλιστα διηνεκῶς ὁμιλοῦσι λόγωι τούτωι διαφέρονται, καὶ οἷς καθ᾽ ἡμέραν ἐγκυροῦσι, ταῦτα αὐτοῖς ξένα φαίνεται.

That to which they are most turned, while carrying out λόγος (bearing it), is (precisely) that from which they rend themselves asunder—[319] whatever they encounter daily, (precisely) that appears foreign to them.

And so we see that, upon an initial reading of this saying, it seems to say the same thing twice. However, this only appears to be the case. Owing to the καί, it seems as though two versions of the same thought, distinguished only by vocabulary, have been pushed together. Behind this superficial appearance, however, a meaningful difference conceals itself, the thinking of which is important for a more profound knowledge of the Λόγος.

First of all, attention must be drawn to some wordplay in the first part of the saying that is nearly impossible to replicate in our language. This wordplay, if we are able to hear it, passes along to us an essential insight. In the first part of the saying two words appear that both begin with δια and that are both linguistic variations of the same verb. We are referring here to διηνεκῶς and διαφέρονται, which are both word forms that belong to διαφέρειν; however, each says something different according to the different meanings of δια. One meaning of δια is "through something": for example, διαφαίνω/διαφανές, to shine through, to radiate forth through everything. Moreover, there is, for example, διαφέρειν: to carry through something, bearing it incessantly; we say, "carrying out." In some way, those who carry out linger with and safeguard what is carried out. We translate διηνεκῶς as "bearing." Bearing is the designation for a lingering with something, especially when this something has the character of ὁμιλεῖν, which we understand to be the somehow intimate attitude of being turned and disposed toward something. However, if we are intimate with a matter, it does not yet mean that is it opened up for us in its essence. On the contrary, that the matter under consideration remains concealed in its manifold essence is, in some sense, the prerequisite for being intimate with something. However, that toward which the human is most turned in the manner of bearing is "the Λόγος"—that is, being. With this, Heraclitus is saying that what is continually and most present for the human is the originary forgathering: namely, being itself.

[320] However, Heraclitus says this in order then immediately to say, and in starkest opposition, the following: τούτωι διαφέρονται—"from this (i.e., the Λόγος) they rend themselves asunder." Here, δια does not mean "through something" in the manner of a carrying out that maintains, makes an effort, and is

sustained (as was the case with διηνεκῶς). Rather, δια is now being used in the sense of "asunder," as indicated by the corresponding noun διαφορά, the bearing apart from one another, rending asunder from one another: rupture, strife (ἔρις); διαφορά then also means dissimilarity and difference more generally. But in the state of being-asunder and being-opposed that belongs to things that have been differentiated from each other, a relationship still unfolds between them: namely, a relationship of difference. Insofar as the human rends himself asunder from the Λόγος, he moves himself away from it in such a way that the presence of it that is turned toward him appears as though it were absent. The human turns away from what is turned toward him. In this turning away, what is present absences, but it can only absent itself as what is present. Therefore, διαφέρεσθαι, the rending-itself-asunder, is never a severing in the sense of a separation of things. The Λόγος presences toward the human, but insofar as he strays from it, it does not appear for him. In a certain sense, the Λόγος does not show itself at all and is akin to nothing: namely, the nothing of beings which, of course, remains fundamentally different from the nothing of beyng. Accordingly, Heraclitus thus knows very well, in his own way, of the strange and for the most part dominating absencing from the human of the continually presencing being. This—namely, the Λόγος as the originary for-gathering—holds the essence of the human toward itself in advance as somehow gathered. The forgathering Λόγος is therefore that which incessantly presences toward the human, '*the* present' in an extraordinary sense: it is that which, in remaining turned toward the human, emerges (φύσις), and which in another fragment Heraclitus therefore calls τὸ μὴ δῦνόν ποτε[1]—the not ever submerging, the always and forever emerging. In reference to this latter point, fragment 16 states: τὸ μὴ δῦνόν ποτε πῶς ἄν τις λάθοι; [321]—"How could a human ever conceal himself from the always and forever emerging thing?"[2] The human—that is, the being that carries out λόγος—cannot do this: rather, as saying 72 (which must now be elucidated) says at its beginning, the human must be turned toward the Λόγος, bearing it most of all.

The second part of the saying is joined to the first by a καί. We translate καί not merely as "and," but rather as "therefore also." This indicates that we take the first part of the saying as the grounding for what is, in the second part, the essential consequence, and which, as what has been grounded, itself shines a light for our understanding back onto the grounding ground.

In both the first and second parts of fragment 72, there is talk of a relation belonging to the human. The first relationship that is named consists of διηνεκῶς ὁμιλεῖν, a turning toward that bears. It is also stated toward what this relation stands: namely, it goes toward the Λόγος. The relationship named in the second part of the

---

[1] Translators' note: We have supplied the ποτε, which is missing in the German volume.
[2] See *The Inception of Occidental Thinking* in this volume.

saying is καθ᾽ ἡμέραν ἐγκυρεῖν—the everyday encountering of.... The exact object of this encounter is not named: rather, it is only expressed by way of the neuter plural ταῦτα. That toward which the human is incessantly turned, ὁ Λόγος, this 'singularity,' must therefore be something other than the 'plurality' the human encounters daily. The human thereby lingers within two relationships, and does so constantly. However, at one and the same time, that toward which the human is turned in the manner of bearing remains mostly absent from him, and that which the human encounters daily remains foreign to him, so that he does not know how to make use of it, and therefore simply does not. What he encounters daily is nothing for the human, so to speak. How are we to understand this? For, day in and day out, the human relates to things and other humans—that is, he relates toward what *is* and what he takes for, and refers to, as beings: τὰ ὄντα. Beings: this is clearly what is meant by ταῦτα. But how can Heraclitus then say that what the human [322] encounters daily is foreign and unfamiliar to him? For surely the human knows his way about in the everyday and what is encountered within it. Indeed, the human is so accustomed to the everyday that, for him, it is the ordinary. But, how can what is familiar and ordinary be extraordinary and estranging, such that its extraordinary and estranging elements are overlooked in favor of the ordinary? Moreover, where and in what way is the ordinary still given, when what is encountered daily is strange and out of the ordinary? Beings, things, and human beings of near and distant places: these are beings for the human. Of course, beings that 'are' in this way do not approach the human in terms of the 'is,' i.e., in terms of being. It is enough that beings show themselves and remain: that is sufficient for the human in order to be able to function and work within beings, in order to move things along and set them up according to his needs. The human in his everyday life need not concern himself with the fact that beings 'are,' and that they, as the beings that 'are,' are determined by being. However, the human encounters beings every day; but the being of beings remains foreign to him. We say (i.e., we see it and say): the weather is bad; it even suffices simply to say 'bad weather.' We are not concerned at all with the 'is,' not even when we experience it and see: the weather is good. Good or bad weather—perhaps—but we cannot make use of the 'is.' But 'is' nevertheless remains one of the names of being.

The being of beings—ὁ Λόγος—which forgathers and keeps safe every being regarding the fact that it is, and that it is in such and such a way, is therefore named in the first half of the saying as that from which humans rend themselves asunder and what remains foreign to them. Because the everyday relation to the Λόγος (i.e., to being) prevails in this particular way, and because being itself is, so to speak, away, the human, as stated in the second half of the saying, is also estranged from beings in their being. Nevertheless, the beginning of the saying states that the human is ceaselessly turned toward the Λόγος μάλιστα διηνεκῶς (i.e., bearing it most of all).

[323] The human constantly relates himself to beings, and thus also to being, but he also constantly forgets the being of beings, to which he remains referred

despite all of this forgetting, and which nonetheless constantly shines toward him, even though he pays no attention to this shining or even this light. For how else but through this relation to the Λόγος could the human even know beings and be able to say 'is'!

In all "relating to" and "residing with," this ambivalence prevails: namely, that the human knows beings and forgets being. In all of his daily hustling and bustling, the human everywhere reaches into beings; in all of his paths and meanderings, he hits upon them. However, he does not reach to the extremities, does not reach that to which they extend, and does not reach that toward which—beyond his dispersal toward beings—he is already forgathered, and toward which his λόγος properly, and with a constant bearing, turns: namely, the Λόγος, i.e., being.

If we now attend to this essentially ambivalent relation of the human to beings and to being—namely, that the human always knows beings while at the same time forgetting being—then it becomes clear that, within this ambivalence, insofar as it exists, the irreconcilable is reconciled in a certain way. That is why, in fragment 45, Heraclitus can indeed say that the human does not reach the outermost extremities of his essence, but rather that, in not thinking being, he remains confined within his relation to beings. However, because the human himself nevertheless remains turned toward being even amidst his forgetfulness, the human λόγος is a 'deep' one that remains pointed toward that which commonly conceals itself from it and is, as it were, absent. The depth of human λόγος consists of the relation of this λόγος to *the* Λόγος. In all of the human's relations to beings, what remains far-reaching is the manner in which he remains constantly turned toward being, even though this turning-toward remains concealed and forgotten. Insofar as the drawing-in drawing-out (i.e., the soul of the human) has such a far-reaching λόγος, the living being that is the human is distinguished from all others. The human, in his place amidst beings, is not only bound to, and under the sway of, beings [324], but is also directed toward being and addressed by it. It is because this manner of far-reaching presides in the essence of the human that that to which it points can also become capable of being apprehended by him.

Although the human, usually and on his own accord within his everyday activity and comportment, does not get to the outermost extremities of his essence, the possibility nevertheless remains for him to apprehend the Λόγος, which remains, despite everything, an absent presence. Indeed, the human must listen to the Λόγος if a proper knowledge of beings is to sustain and guide him. Fragment 50 can say what it says not only without regard for what is pronounced in fragment 45; in fact, fragment 50 must pronounce what it does because it concerns that of which fragment 45 speaks: namely, the dispersal into beings that turns away from being. The two fragments are thus not only not irreconcilable, but in fact necessarily belong together. Fragment 50 tells us in what way the human λόγος is deep and in what manner it is far-reaching. Fragment 45 says why it requires what fragment 50 subtly declares, when it demands a compliant listening to the Λόγος.

In being turned toward beings—perhaps even being lost and enslaved to them—the human forgets about being, which nevertheless constantly addresses him in its absence, without him paying it any heed. The human thereby stands in an ambivalent relation to beings and being. But, perhaps it is a bit hasty to speak of ambivalence here, for this designation can easily call to mind a lack of harmony. Perhaps we should speak more carefully of a two-foldedness, rather than of an ambivalence. The two-fold allows the double to exist. In thinking the two-fold we are not attempting to think of the double as ambivalence and opposition in order then to think this opposition as a contradiction to be sublated into a higher unity. This two-foldedness is the sign for the extraordinary position of the human amidst beings. [325] This unusual position of the human essence presupposes an unusual site that must be a place the human cannot easily find, so that he must set himself underway toward it and must ask about the place in which he sojourns in accordance with his essence. Only when the place of this ambivalent, two-folded sojourn of the human within beings is found does it become evident that, and in what way, it is necessary for the human to listen to the Λόγος. But, at the same time, the opposite also holds true: only when the Λόγος itself has become perceptible does it lighten in such a way that the essential place of the human becomes discernable. The one belongs with the other. The essential place of the human is in the region of the Λόγος. By 'region' we initially mean the lightened, cleared area, out of which and within which something can approach and bring itself toward the human. This lightened area, this region, contains and preserves and forgathers the essential place of the human within itself. 'The Λόγος' is, as will become clearer in what follows, the region in which the human has his ambivalent, two-folded sojourn, insofar as he, turned toward being, relates to beings, gives himself over to them, and forgets being.

In fragment 50, the thinker Heraclitus says: you should not listen to me, but should rather, in a hearkening way, obediently join yourself to the Λόγος. From this we can deduce that it is the task of the thinker to point toward the Λόγος, thereby intimating that one should not pay heed to he himself or his language. The thinker himself is unimportant. Nevertheless, the thinker claims about himself (in fragment 101): ἐδιζησάμην ἐμεωυτόν—"I have sought after myself." If the thinker of fragment 50 demands that he himself not be taken seriously, then fragment 101 cannot mean that the thinker has thoroughly researched himself in the manner of a self-important vivisection. The saying can only have wanted to say: I have sought the essential place of the human. However, this means: I have [326] attempted to attend to the Λόγος itself, toward which all human sojourning amidst beings remains forgathered. This essential forgathering of the human essence toward the Λόγος—that is, the turn toward being itself—does not preclude, but rather includes, the fact that the human within his relation to beings wishes to cling solely to them, and often holds fast only to them. The human surely pays little mind (and what mind he does pay he does not do so expressly) to the fact that it is being and only being, insofar as it is what is thought by the human and remains for him the to-be-thought, that first lets beings be accessible and approachable for the human. The human finds in beings what is sufficient for him, in the way in which they display themselves to his most cherished needs and wishes, almost appearing to supplicate themselves to him. And it is from these beings, appearing to impose themselves on the human, that he believes to have taken the measure of his thinking and doing. However, insofar as being itself is the only measure of beings, and the human indeed forgets being, he is mistaken in his measure and presumptuously mismeasures. Within the ambivalent and two-folded sojourn of the human, this presumptuous mismeasurement comes to dominate.

If the human is to be able to attend to being and perceive the Λόγος, then the flames of this presumptuous mismeasurement must constantly be extinguished in advance. (In Greek, "beyond" something, "namely and essentially beyond measure," is ὑπέρ. It is from ὑπέρ that ὕβρις derives.) Regarding all of this, Heraclitus states (in fragment 43):

ὕβριν χρὴ σβεννύναι μᾶλλον ἢ πυρκαϊήν.

(The) presumptuous mismeasurement it is necessary to extinguish, even before (the) conflagration.

This saying becomes clearer to us, if we do not take it as a moral directive, but rather take what it names—i.e., the blazing flames of this presumptuous mismeasurement—and think it back into the already defined essence of the human. (ψυχή—ζωή—πῦρ—φάος—φύσις; see αὔη, "dry fire"; see fragment 118.) The drawing-in drawing-out is borne and channeled through a λόγος, a gathering that is far-reaching in such a way that its expansiveness is determined by the Λόγος (i.e., being), which is initially and most [327] often absent, but is at the same time always presencing. By way of that λόγος which the human soul has, the essence of the human is forgathered in a manner that reaches out toward being, is opened and cleared for it. However, the light of this clearing is darkened by the blazing flames of presumptuous mismeasuring, which only ever derives its measure from beings. The restive flickering of the flames of ὕβρις tears apart the gaze, the posture, and the comportment of the human, thereby tearing apart the gathering while fostering the dispersal through which he misplaces the extremities by which he, in following the far-reaching λόγος, arrives at being by letting it be the sole measure. The flickering and thus darkening fire of presumptuous mismeasuring stands in intimate connection with the calm light of the lightened and the open, into which the soul reaches through its λόγος. Even if we do not yet grasp this connection with sufficient clarity here, it should nevertheless be mentioned in view of what follows. The light, the calm, and the measure belong together with the dark, the flickering, and the presumptuous mismeasuring. This connection clarifies for us the essence of the

'Λόγος' as soon as we are led, by way of other sayings of Heraclitus's, to grasp in one essential glimpse the fundamental features of being as experienced in a Greek way.

(Regarding the connection between fire, light, and measure, see fragment 30. Regarding the relationship of the One (which, as being, unites all beings) with light and what lightens, see fragment 64.)

When fragment 45 says that the soul of the human has a far-reaching λόγος, and when fragment 72 says that humans are most of all turned toward the Λόγος in a manner that bears, the two fragments say the same and designate that in which the drawing-in drawing-out (i.e., the soul) is engaged. Because the soul of the human has a far-reaching λόγος that has reached far—which, however, as dictated by the necessity of ὁμολογεῖν, points [328] to the Λόγος and is both sublated and grounded within it—we will only ever experience, know, and consummate the essence of human λόγος to the degree to which the Λόγος itself presences in the human's compliant attendance to it.

For the sake of all further efforts to think-after λόγος as Heraclitus conceived it, in order to thereby arrive at an originary 'logic,' we must heed the directive that arises from out of what has already been said: namely, we must attempt to formulate a definition of the essence of the Λόγος to the highest possible degree of precision before turning to the human λόγος. But how are we to direct our gaze toward the essence of the Λόγος if the human λόγος, by which we are carried and led, is not executed properly in the manner of a ὁμολογεῖν? We cannot take 'the Λόγος,' which is being itself, and the essence of the human and his λόγος, as two separate objects cut off from one another and placed somewhere with the purpose of examining each on its own, the way in which we bring an object of scientific research before ourselves. Moreover, the preceding should have made it increasingly clearer that everything rests upon the relation of the Λόγος, as which being itself unfolds, to the human λόγος, and vice versa. Speaking accordingly, we should not speak about a relation of the human λόγος to the Λόγος—for, indeed, the human λόγος and the Λόγος are themselves already relations. A relating is a form of harvesting and gathering—λέγειν. In Greek mathematics, the word λόγος still retains its original meaning of 'relation.' The relation between the human λόγος and the Λόγος is therefore not a relation between things or objects, but rather the relation between relations, i.e., pure relation without origin, and only this. However, because we are accustomed and even constantly pushed toward always thinking objects in object-like relations, a proper sojourn into the λόγος-like relation to the Λόγος is initially, and for a long time, difficult for us. More difficult still [329] is the proper thinking of this relation from out of it. We can never obtain this thinking, which is the only proper and true thinking, by way of various presuppositions and deductions: rather, we may only just prepare it. In the same way that the interpretation of a poem can never bring about the hearing of its poetic word by force, the interpreting of a saying and sentence of the thinker can never place us immediately into that thinking.

How then are we to prepare the ὁμολογεῖν as the proper relation of human λόγος to the Λόγος?[3] The preparation contains two elements: namely, that we prepare ourselves for the exemplary λέγειν that takes place, so to speak, as ὁμολογεῖν, and that this λέγειν is itself prepared as λόγος for the presencing of the Λόγος. But this preparation would have to remain in vain in all respects, as long as it remains confused about what characterizes the presencing, and thereby the arrival and the manner of address, of 'the Λόγος' as such. The very first effort in this preparation of ὁμολογεῖν, an effort that precedes and even guides all else, must therefore orient itself toward knowing what is in accordance with the presencing of 'the Λόγος' as such—that is, toward knowing the region from which it comes and out of which it approaches human λόγος. Human thinking, if it does not wish to cling obstinately and blindly to an isolated opinion, must thoroughly examine the entirety of what displays itself as the λόγος-like relation to the Λόγος within the realm of human experience and tradition.

[330] c) The apparent contradiction between the Λόγος understood as gathering and understood as what has been 'separated.' Fragment 108. πάντων κεχωρισμένον as the distinct, to-be-thought determination of the Λόγος as ἓν πάντα, and as the object-less region of the Λόγος

Even a thinker of the stature granted to Heraclitus cannot free himself from the task of listening to what others (before him and along with him) have said about that of which proper knowledge (τὸ σοφόν) consists, i.e., that which first and foremost is properly to-be-known and the fundamental features thereof. We have some evidence to support the hypothesis that Heraclitus knew of the thinking of Anaximander, and himself thought from out of this knowledge. From fragment 50 we learned that proper knowledge (τὸ σοφόν) consists in ὁμολογεῖν. However, now we are engaged in preparing this ὁμολογεῖν as the possible λέγειν of the human, and this means, at the same time, preparing the human for it. How shall we gather ourselves toward the Λόγος—how shall we go toward it and stretch ourselves out to it, if we do not know what characterizes its presence? Heraclitus's efforts were directed toward precisely this proper knowledge and anticipatory foreknowledge that precedes thinking. This is clearly stated in fragment 108:

---

[3] See German page 353 and following.

ὁκόσων λόγους ἤκουσα, οὐδεὶς ἀφικνεῖται ἐς τοῦτο, ὥστε γινώσκειν ὅτι σοφόν ἐστι πάντων κεχωρισμένον.

As many λόγοι as I have (already) heard, none of them have ever reached that from out of which they become acquainted with the fact that the proper to-be-known, in relation to all beings, unfolds from out of its (own) region.

The general and approximate content of this saying states that what matters to Heraclitus is to determine what characterizes the properly to-be-known. However, according to fragment 50, that toward which this proper knowledge gathers itself is ὁ Λόγος [331] which, according to the same saying, is the One that originarily forgathers all. Now it is said of this that it is πάντων κεχωρισμένον. Diels translates this as: "what is separated from everything," or, "what is set apart from everything." On top of this, another translator even manages to render the κεχωρισμένον, which he has translated as "the separated," with the Latin "*ab-solutum*," which means what has been ex-cised and ab-cised from everything. According to this, 'the Λόγος' that Heraclitus names is the 'absolute,' by which metaphysics understands the highest of beings that exists on its own, and is thus the ground and origin of all other beings.

Ever since the Christian interpretation of metaphysics, which is nevertheless still operative even in the *Anti-Christ* of Nietzsche's (albeit in the manner of a dependent and reactionary counteracting), 'the absolute' is equated with God as the creator of the world. This 'absolute,' thought in a Christian way, is conceived theologically, dogmatically, and in a Trinitarian way as the unity of the Father, Son, and Spirit. The second personage of this divinity is, according to the first sentence of the Gospel of John, the Λόγος, of which is said:

Ἐν ἀρχῇ ἦν ὁ λόγος, καὶ ὁ λόγος ἦν πρὸς τὸν θεόν, καὶ θεὸς ἦν ὁ λόγος. οὗτος ἦν ἐν ἀρχῇ πρὸς τὸν θεόν. πάντα δι' αὐτοῦ ἐγένετο, καὶ χωρὶς αὐτοῦ ἐγένετο οὐδὲ ἓν ὃ γέγονεν.

According to the translation of the Vulgate this means:

In principio erat verbum, et verbum erat apud Deum, et Deus erat verbum. Hoc erat in principio apud Deum. Omnia per ipsum facta sunt: et sine ipso factum est nihil, quod factum est.

In the beginning was the Word and the Word was with God and God was the Word. That was in the beginning with God. All is made through it (him), and without it (him) nothing is made that is made.

At this point we will pay less attention to the fact that here λόγος is understood as *verbum* and Word, although it should not be forgotten that this Word is the second personage of the divinity, and that this Word then became human in the guise of the savior God. We will also not follow up on that particularly modern opposition [332] to these initial sentences of the Gospel of John that is spoken of in Goethe's *Faust*: namely, that in the beginning was not 'the Word,' but 'the Deed.' We will now only pay heed to the fact that here 'the Λόγος' is of equal stature with the highest cause of all that exists and all that has been made, and that this highest of beings, the Λόγος, appears in metaphysics as the absolute. And, corresponding to the manifold exegesis of the absolute, the Λόγος is interpreted at times as the Word, at times as world-reason, at times as the 'meaning' of the world, at times as the 'law of the world,' and at times as 'absolute Spirit.' If we consider that, over centuries this equating of the Λόγος with the absolute has calcified itself slowly within metaphysics, then it is not surprising that in the saying now cited, the Greek word κεχωρισμένον is interpreted as 'the absolute.'

However, no matter how unanimous the tradition of metaphysics might be, no matter how unassailable the power of its thinking, and no matter how little we may actually intuit of pre-metaphysical thinking, we must nevertheless attempt, with an eye toward what is singular and incomparable in the beginning of Occidental thinking, to prevent the hasty retroactive application of metaphysical conceptions onto 'inceptual' thinking, and instead attempt to hear what is said in this saying from out of itself and the realm of its saying. Heraclitus thinks-after how the to-be-known unfolds in σοφόν (i.e., in authentic knowledge and precisely as this knowledge) and thus how it unfolds toward ὁμολογεῖν and thereby the human λόγος; moreover, Heraclitus thinks-after how it unfolds in relation to the whole of beings. What is properly the to-be-known is 'the Λόγος.' If human λέγειν is to pay it heed and gather itself toward it (and to be able to do just this), then 'the Λόγος' must on its own accord forgather this human gathering within itself and be present in the whole of beings as the originary forgathering of beings. For even if 'the Λόγος' expressly addresses the human λόγος, this in no way means [333] that the human is thereby being addressed as a being that has been separated off: for the human only is human on the basis of human λόγος, and in the manner that he constantly comports himself toward beings as a whole by way of this λόγος. Because the human λόγος is addressed by the Λόγος, beings as a whole constantly address the human, and the presence of the Λόγος in beings as a whole ceaselessly unfolds for him in his relation to them. Of course, these relations are not expressed thematically in early thinking. We today, however, are long accustomed to experiencing and interpreting the relation of the human to beings and being from out of the subject–object relation. This is why it remains difficult for us, in every sense, to elucidate the presence of the Λόγος pre-metaphysically. The Λόγος is the sheltering forgathering which, as the One, unites beings as a whole, thereby shining as being through beings as a whole, allowing this whole to appear in its light.

However, fragment 108 says of 'the Λόγος' that it is πάντων κεχωρισμένον, which means, according to the conventional translation and interpretation, that it is separated from everything, severed from it, ab-cised, *ab-solutum*. We shall presently allow this metaphysical elucidation to be put to rest and will only call attention to the following: namely, that it refrains from bringing the character of the absolute into any sort of connection with the essence of the Λόγος, i.e., with the Λόγος in the sense of the originary sheltering forgathering.

Let us here think the Λόγος in this originary sense and thereby consider that it is precisely this sense that, according to fragment 108, should come into knowledge in regard to the Λόγος (i.e., in regard to πάντων κεχωρισμένον). If this is so, then what is said about the Λόγος can only be brought together with the originary and sheltering forgathering with great difficulty, or, in fact, not at all. Given all that has been said already about the Λόγος, we had to expect the following as its distinguishing characteristic: namely, that as the forgathering that shelters the totality of beings and the human in particular [334], it is related to beings, and therefore does not exist separately somewhere in the manner of a thing in itself. How could the Λόγος as the One, originary, all-uniting singularity unfold if it were cut off as something separate? Perhaps, however, the saying offers up to thought the notion that the Λόγος, even though it remains essentially related to the whole of beings as the sheltering forgathering, nevertheless remains independent of beings and rests within itself. But, in that case, the determination that it is 'separated from', 'cut off', and 'absolute' is erroneous and meaningless, for it says nothing regarding what is decisive: namely, that (and how) the originary sheltering forgathering is related to beings as a whole, and how within this relation, and by virtue of it, it nevertheless rests in itself. Given this, πάντων κεχωρισμένον must mean something else, if indeed it is the characteristic determination of the Λόγος understood as ἓν πάντα εἶναι.[4] If we prepare ourselves to translate and think πάντων κεχωρισμένον independently of the conventional interpretation and free it from metaphysical ways of thinking, then something astounding indeed results: namely, that what is properly to-be-known, the πάντων κεχωρισμένον, contains within itself precisely what is asked for.

It is not necessary for us to impose upon the decisive word κεχωρισμένον a meaning thought up specifically for it. It is only necessary that we keep the word free of the meaning that is conventionally, tritely, and superficially ascribed to it, and allow it to retain the dignity of a word spoken by a thinker in order to name what is properly to-be-known. κεχωρισμένον belongs to χωρίζω/χωρίζειν, which one translates as 'cutting-off', 'separating', and 'moving-away'. Given these words, one only thinks of the moving away of one thing from another, thereby paying attention neither to what belongs to moving away and what lies at its foundation, nor to the fact that in the translation as "separating" and "cutting off" one hears not the faintest glimmer of the Greek word's meaning. However, this meaning points to precisely what lies at the

---

[4] Translators' note: The German edition has ἓν πάντα ὄν, rather than ἓν πάντα εἶναι, here. Given that the phrase ἓν πάντα ὄν occurs nowhere else within Heidegger, nor does it occur within Heraclitus's writings, we have replaced ὄν with εἶναι.

foundation of all putting away and cutting off, [335] which is why even the often-correct translation of χωρίζειν as "separating" and "cutting off" nevertheless remains untrue, insofar as it does not allow what is named by χωρίζειν to appear.

In the verb χωρίζειν lies ἡ χώρα, ὁ χῶρος, which we translate as: surroundings, surroundings that enclose, that make room for and guarantee a sojourning. The nouns χώρα/χῶρος trace back to χάω (from which χάος is derived): 'yawning,' 'gaping,' 'opening up,' 'self-opening'; ἡ χώρα as the surroundings that surround is then "the region." We understand this to be the open area and the expanse in which something takes its sojourn, wherefrom it arrives, escapes, and responds. ἡ χώρα, as the region, can also be named, in an imprecise manner of speaking, "the place." However, 'region' and 'place' are not the same. For "place," the Greeks have the word τόπος. That is the site at which something comes forth, is present, and persists. The place is always in an area, and around it are the surroundings that arise from out of the surrounding area. We speak of the 'heavenly firmament,' and could only with great difficulty substitute this with the 'heavenly place.' In the Tyrolean vernacular, there exists the expression 'lacking a region,' which means not having a clear shot. When we say, 'in the region of Mt. Feldberg,' we mean neither 'in the direction toward' nor the exact location of Mt. Feldberg, but rather that surrounding, self-opening and forth-coming expanse that grants places and directions. The open expanse is not, however, the emptiness of a container, but rather the restrained open, the open that retains much, and properly, on its own accord, delineates itself, but whose boundaries are themselves of a regioning nature (i.e., of such a nature as to reach far). Because regions, so understood, always surround places and grant them and thereby first allow the founding and occupation of places, it is, from a certain perspective, the essential feature of a place, its locality. This and only this is the reason that χώρα can also mean place in the sense of a site that has been occupied, a location that has been made use of in accordance with particular measurements and demarcations. In the localities [336] themselves and the way in which they contain the surroundings, the concealed joining and shaping of the region comes to the fore, without it expressly becoming an 'object.' The objectlessness of the region is the sign of its superior, and not inferior, being.

Now, it is neither an exaggerated demand, nor something violent, if we understand the verb χωρίζειν from out of χώρα. Then it says: to bring into surroundings that surround, into a region, and from out of this region to allow to presence. That which is brought into and located in such a surrounding expanse can be regarded as separated off given two conditions: namely, that it is compared to something that exists in another area, and that in this comparison only differences are taken into account. In doing so, only what has been excised becomes visible. Separating, cutting-off, setting-off, and excising are possible essential consequences of the region and what is surrounded by a region. In accordance with a strange habit of thinking that erupts everywhere and at all times, and which itself is deserving of a more thorough elucidation, we forget, for example, that through the separating and placing into a region, with the cutting-off and moving-away of it, that which has been moved away always unfolds toward other things from out of its region, and into the region of the other objects. We only pay attention to the things themselves and their different, given localities, as though these were also something thing-like, present-to-hand, and capable of being differentiated. However, it is always the case that a κεχωρισμένον is, according to its essence, first and foremost not only something that has been moved-away, but is rather what appears from out of a (and indeed its) region. In order to get the above-named essential connections into proper view, more is needed than merely to trace, in an argumentative way, cutting-off and separating back to their preconditions. Thinking in this way, one could simply say that even in the separating of one thing from another there remains a relation between the two: namely, that the one is bound to the other—for how could [337] things that have absolutely no relation even be cut off from one another? The '*away* from one another' of things is still, and necessarily, a relation of being 'toward one another.' διαίρεσις, as the Greeks already knew, is still, and always, σύνθεσις. Nevertheless, as we have said, for the understanding of the Greek essence of χωρίζειν and κεχωρισμένον, formally empty argumentation like the following does not suffice: even separating is still a connecting and relating. It is much more important that we bring into view what is properly essential to regions and regioning so that we may think χωρίζειν and κεχωρισμένον exclusively with regard to these.

d) The Λόγος as the regioning presencing in which and from out of which everything presences and absences, and the originary difference between beings and being

Ultimately, however, the understanding of fragment 108 necessitates one other, and more essential, step: for κεχωρισμένον is not here being said about any random thing. In fact, it is not even being said about a thing at all—it is neither said of a being, nor of beings as a whole, but rather of the Λόγος itself, which is the originary sheltering forgathering of beings as a whole. In a word, it is said of being. The Λόγος is λέγων: forgathering, uniting, retaining beings as a whole and granting their sojourn. It is not the case that the Λόγος is all of this additionally: rather, the Λόγος *is* all of this by virtue of being *the* Λόγος. In order to recognize that with this essential look at the Λόγος we arrive at the essential connection between the Λόγος and χώρα in the sense of "region," we need only to continue on in this vein without being prejudiced by common interpretations and translations. However, since the task is to think being itself, we must not now think of merely spatial relations. χώρα is the self-opening, approaching expanse. It is now said of the Λόγος that it is [338] κεχωρισμένον. Translating this as 'cut-off,' 'detached,' or 'absolute' is not only incorrect because thereby no attention is paid to the χώρα in κεχωρισμένον, but also because such a translation takes it as a given that the word κεχωρισμένον is to be thought passively, and that what has been separated and detached has fallen victim to a separating and a detaching. If, however—and of the following there can be no doubt—πάντων κεχωρισμένον is said of the Λόγος, and if the latter unfolds as λέγων as the originary sheltering forgathering, then κεχωρισμένον cannot be taken in a passive sense, but rather needs to be understood medially. The Λόγος is, as λόγος, πάντων κεχωρισμένον: it is the all-surrounding region which, in relation to the whole of beings, is open for all and encounters all; it is the presence into which everything and all is forgathered and preserved, and from out of which—as *the* region *simpliciter*—everything emerges and receives its coming forth and submerging, its appearing and disappearing. The πάντων κεχωρισμένον said of the Λόγος does not mean what has been moved-away and separated from everything: rather, it means the presencing, self-approaching bringing in the manner of the sheltering forgathering that is toward everything and which, as such, is the ground of everything. As the originary sheltering forgathering, the Λόγος is the regioning encountering presence in which what passes-forth and passes-away presences and absences.

It is only now that one can, and indeed must, also look toward the other essential moment that is said in the here quoted πάντων κεχωρισμένον: namely, that the Λόγος, as the regioning presence in which everything presences and absences, regions from out of itself, and can never be derived and reached from out of singular beings, or even from out of the totality of beings.

It is here that *the* originary difference between beings and being presides.

However, this difference between being and beings is decidedly not a separation and cutting-off. Admittedly, the thinking of the thinker has heretofore never thought about this difference, which is [339] even 'the difference' as such. We are still almost entirely without the perspective and ways of seeing that would allow us to espy its essence, even though the difference between beings and being is for the human the nearest of the near, while remaining, however, for human conceiving, the most distant. However, Heraclitus, and also the other early thinkers, intuit the enigmatic nearness of being, which is present but at the same time also absent.[5]

It may still be the case that the elucidation of πάντων κεχωρισμένον (fragment 108) attempted here appears arbitrary and estranging. For anyone who insists upon the metaphysical interpretation of pre-Platonic thought, this impression cannot be obviated. Nevertheless, two things must be pointed out here, which any independent verification of what has been delivered here must take into account. First, the elucidation of πάντων κεχωρισμένον is not simply derived from out of these two words, but rather is accomplished in light of all the sayings that have been handed down to us by Heraclitus. Second, the given elucidation does not rely

---

[5] See fragment 72.

solely upon Heraclitus, but also ponders what the other two early thinkers, Anaximander and Parmenides, say about the being of beings. All of this cannot be presented here. However, it is the case that two other sayings by Heraclitus are cited, sayings that, while they may appear similar to fragment 108 in their language and content, what is thought in them seems to point to other perspectives.

[340] REVIEW

3) The ambivalent two-fold of turning-toward and turning-away as the relation of the human to being and beings. The rupture in the two-foldedness of the two-fold and the relational rule of λόγοι. Fragment 72. References to fragments 50 and 108

We now consider fragment 72. Incidentally, it should be remarked that we use the term 'fragment' solely in deference to the conventional designation. In this case, 'fragment' is the designation for a philological and literary term. Otherwise, as happened in the earlier lectures,[6] the words of Heraclitus's cited in each case would be named a 'saying.' Given this, we must surely take care not to treat the thoughtful sayings of Heraclitus's as a form of 'aphorism.'

By considering the guiding notion of saying 72, we will try to gain some clarity for ourselves regarding how and in what sense the Λόγος, according to the knowledge granted by Heraclitus, is constantly present to the human, while being at the same time for the most part absent. To this strange presence of the Λόγος, humans correspond through their own, strange relation to the Λόγος. Humans are toward the Λόγος in an exceptional way: they are the most turned toward it. At the same time, however, they are turned away from it, insofar as they rend themselves asunder from that toward which they are most turned. The saying states this in its first part:

ὧι μάλιστα διηνεκῶς ὁμιλοῦσι λόγωι τούτωι διαφέρονται . . .

That to which they are most turned in a manner of bearing—namely, the Λόγος—is precisely that from which they rend themselves asunder.

---

[6] See *The Inception of Occidental Thinking* in this volume.

The διά, named twice but each time with a different meaning, determines the structure of what is thought. What is constant through and through is at the same time, in its constancy, like something broken, although not interrupted or shattered. If instead of the Λόγος [341] we say 'originary forgathering,' and by this think being, then the first part of the saying can be rewritten as follows: the human is turned most of all toward being, from which and toward which he always relates, though in such a way that he is normally turned away from it. When we hear for the first time this reference to this strange relation of the human to being, it seems as though we cannot think anything about it, as though at stake here were something that thinkers once thought about in distant speculations. But it is precisely the fact that we are of this opinion that serves as the most pressing proof that what is said about the relation to being presides and dominates everywhere within us. Indeed, it is because we are the most turned toward being in a manner that is the most bearing that we understand being automatically, so to speak.

After all, who fails to understand what is said when someone in the course of speaking uses the word 'is'? While we do understand the word 'being,' we nevertheless do not turn ourselves more toward what is thereby understood. Of course, it is different with beings as a whole, which presence everywhere. But with 'being'? This mountain, which either *is* or *is not*, addresses the human: but the 'is' itself does not. This river, which either *is* or *is not*, besets the human: but the 'is' itself does not. This human, who either *is* or *is not*, concerns the human: but the 'is' itself does not. This god, who either *is* or *is not*, rules over the human: but the 'is' itself does not. The mountain, the river, the human, the god: certainly, all of this, and yet still more, concerns us. We treat the 'is' like an unimportant add-on, if we pay attention to it at all. Nevertheless, the 'is' names being. How would matters stand if the human were not turned toward being before all else, and turned toward it the most? How would matters stand if the human were not standing in the presencing of being? What, then, would happen to the mountain that either *is* or *is not*, or the river that either *is* or *is not*, or the human that either *is* or *is not*, or the god that either *is* or *is not*? Without being, what would all aggregations and throngs of beings amount to? Still, the human remains mostly turned away from being itself, without thereby [342] effacing the presencing of being. What is the essential consequence of this turning-away? And what, at the same time, ineluctably comes with it?

Heraclitus speaks of this in the second part of saying 72, which he begins with καί:

καὶ οἷς καθ' ἡμέραν ἐγκυροῦσι, ταῦτα αὐτοῖς ξένα φαίνεται.

Therefore also that (i.e., the many various things), they encounter daily.

Here, Heraclitus is not speaking of the singularity of being, but rather of the plurality of beings: every day the human encounters the manifold of beings, pursues it, dissolves himself within it, and loses himself to it. But how can Heraclitus say that beings appear foreign to the human? Are beings not something familiar to the human, something that he commands, something that he knows his way around in and within which he establishes himself? Certainly. But with regard to what the thinker alone is considering here—with regard, that is, to the Λόγος (i.e., to being)—beings are precisely that which, for the human, nevertheless remain foreign, notwithstanding the obtrusiveness, rashness, and familiarity of them, as well as their usefulness, fruitfulness, and, lastly, their charm and stability. For, beings would only be familiar, and only *be* the beings that they are—namely, beings as such—if being itself were present within their being and were nothing other than that presence. For example, consider how familiar the contemporary human is with the machine, how familiar to him the operation of the technical apparatus is, so much so that he often encounters it as though it were a living being. But who knows what the machine is? Who knows what technology is? Who intuits something of the essence of the machine, of the being of this being, given the prominence of the inexorable machine-essence? Even if a few individual humans intuit something, from a distance, of this essence and its history (i.e., its fate), this knowledge and what is known within it remain nothing more than a fleeting inanity over and against the obtrusiveness and unconditionality of the everyday rush forward. The human is so helpless in the face of being itself that he rejects 'being' and 'is' [343] as mere husks of words in favor of the supremacy of beings. However, this rejection always only and ever occurs, knowingly or not, thanks to the presencing of being. The human carries out the relation to being, insofar as the human *is*.

In the first part of the saying, Heraclitus speaks of the relation of the human to being. The relation is ambivalent: it is an anterior turning-toward that remains at the same time, and more predominately, a turning-away. In the second part of the saying, Heraclitus speaks of the relation between the human and beings. This relation is also ambivalent, for it is a constant encountering that is not a knowing: it is a countering that is nevertheless a passing-by. This ambivalence in relation to beings is, however, only the essential consequence of the ambivalence in relation to being. Because the latter, although present, nevertheless absences, it appears as though only beings stand in the foreground, as though being had sunken and disappeared.

However, the relation of the human to being does not stand beside the relation of the human to beings. They are not two, separate relations, one to being and the other to beings. Rather, there exists one relation which is, nevertheless, characterized by a singular two-foldedness: namely, that the human relates to beings while standing in the presence of being, and that he encounters beings in the light of being. This simple two-foldedness from out of which, and in which, the human relates to beings while standing amidst them is nonetheless, in each of its two folds, at the same time constantly ambivalent. The sojourning of the human amidst beings is characterized by an ambivalent two-foldedness.

A different manner of thinking may be able to illuminate the saying of Heraclitus's. It is not being asserted that Heraclitus explicitly thought and said all of this. But if we think through what was just said, and continue to think through it in the days to come, then what is obscure, inceptual, and far-reaching in the saying can emerge to us, and the saying may indeed come to address us for the first time.

[344] There is no other way to gain clarity regarding the presence of the Λόγος for the human. If, however, all 'logic' originates from the human relation to the Λόγος, and if 'logic' dominates the sojourn of the modern human within beings, then we will one day have to think-after the Λόγος in a more originary way—more originarily even than Heraclitus did—in order to find our way about within 'logic.'

Once we have finally experienced and thought through saying 72 for ourselves, it will show itself to us as the first, distant glimmer of a knowledge regarding being and the relation between the human and being.

The ambivalent two-fold of the relation of being to beings is the sign of the unusual position of the human amidst beings. In the 'two' of 'two-fold,' and in the 'ambi' of 'ambivalent,' a rupture is announced. In accordance with our habituation to metaphysical thinking, we are here easily inclined initially and solely to think of a division into two parts, to take up this division as an 'opposition,' and then to bend what is oppositional into its proper form through dialectics. However, the two-foldedness of the ambivalent two-fold is first to be thought in the direction of the rupture that rips open, and in the direction of the open in which the essence of the human, in the manner of this ambivalent two-foldedness, is folded and gathered, but at the same time also dispersed. (The ambivalent two-fold, the simplicity of the two-folded: the difference.)

Listening to saying 72 should give us some assistance in our attempt to think-after the relation of human λόγος to the Λόγος.

The ambivalent two-foldedness of the human sojourn amidst beings is unusual, not to say uncanny. This sojourn presupposes a place whose place-ness is not easily found by the human. That is why he must set out to seek for, and inquire about, this place of its essence.

We are concerned with the relation of human λόγος to the Λόγος. Said more precisely, human λόγος is not [345] one link of this relation while 'the Λόγος' is the other link. Rather, human λόγος is itself the relation, and the Λόγος is, also, the same relation. It is not a relation between two λόγοι: rather, they *themselves* are the between and the in-between, within which everything between and relational has its essence and its relational rule. However, given a provisional understanding and an introductory manner of speaking, there is at first no other way to speak about the relation of human λόγος to the Λόγος. The Greeks themselves, and even Heraclitus, never had the proper words and the proper saying for this originary relatedness.

Such a saying only comes to language if the beyng to be thought here has come into its word. One day—and we know not when—beyng will come into such a word, for beyng is everlasting, and also on its way into its own truth: for this fatedness of beyng into its truth is beyng itself in its inceptuality.

From saying 72 we learn that the relation of human λόγος to the Λόγος is ambivalent and that, overall, the sojourn of the human amidst beings is characterized by an ambivalent two-foldedness, which is why the ὁμολογεῖν that is demanded in saying 50 never approaches the human directly, on its own accord, in a simple, one-folded way. The human must send himself into an authentic standing-forth within this ambivalent two-fold and prepare himself for such a standing-forth.

ὁμολογεῖν is the self-gathering gatheredness toward the originary forgathering—i.e., toward the Λόγος. However, the possibility of such a self-gathering toward the Λόγος requires some form of knowledge of the Λόγος. Presumably, such a knowledge is of a specific kind, and not simply a mere familiarity. Even if such a familiarity could be expressed in a sentence, such a sentence and its mere understanding would still not be the knowledge of how the human is to gather himself toward the Λόγος, and how he should remain in the presence of the Λόγος.

[346] What does the thinker say about the Λόγος? To be gathered toward it is τὸ σοφόν: authentic knowledge. Heraclitus speaks of this σοφόν repeatedly, even in that saying (saying 108) that says something distinctive to us about τὸ σοφόν, and thereby something about the Λόγος.

Here, Heraclitus says:

ὁκόσων λόγους ἤκουσα, οὐδεὶς ἀφικνεῖται ἐς τοῦτο, ὥστε γινώσκειν ὅτι σοφόν ἐστι πάντων κεχωρισμένον.

A commonly accepted translation (by Snell) renders it thus:

Though many words have I heard, none of them go so far as to recognize that the wise is something set-off from all (*ab-solutum*).

According to this, what is authentically to-be-known is πάντων κεχωρισμένον. One translates, and thus understands this, in the sense of "what is separated from everything," what is "cut-off from everything." For what is thus ab-cised, which is cut-off from all and is thereby also independent of it, the term 'the absolute' practically imposes itself upon it. With this term, metaphysics accounts for the highest of beings which, as the ground and cause of all beings, undergoes manifold interpretations which, in turn, are thoroughly determined by the Christian world-view (be it in affirmation or rejection), and which are nevertheless modified in accordance with the way the world is experienced and grasped. A certain preliminary sketch of this metaphysical thought of the 'absolute' is already given in the beginning of Occidental metaphysics in the thought of Plato, and especially in Aristotle. Plato knows of the ὑπερουράνιος τόπος, the place that exists above the heavens; and in the final book of his *Physics*, Aristotle thinks the unmoved mover, presiding and unfolding in its own, particular place.

A path is thereby delineated for metaphysics, along which the relationship of the absolute to the world is thought to be one of causation, of making things and sustaining them, and thus as a relationship of conditioning. The absolute is the unconditional thing. Because of the fact that, in modern metaphysics—namely, in the metaphysics of Kant, prepared by Descartes and Leibniz—conditioning and its conditions have been understood transcendentally and in regard to consciousness, [347] the essence of the thought of the absolute and its conditioning relationship to the world remains unchanged. That this is so can be seen clearly in German Idealism, in which the foundational thought of contemporary metaphysics (i.e., the Kantian thought of the transcendental) undergoes a peculiar melding with the speculatively considered Christian interpretation of the world. The relationship of 'conditioning' is so familiar to us that it never occurs to us even to inquire after the origin and essence of this relationship. It also plays a decisive role in an unexpected sphere, but one in which, by all rights, we should expect it if we in fact know anything at all about the essence of metaphysics: namely, in the metaphysics of Nietzsche, which itself is a metaphysics of values.

Even these roughly hewn observations and remarks suffice in order to make us at least more cautious and thoughtful regarding un-reflected translations and interpretations of the Heraclitean πάντων κεχωρισμένον in the sense of the absolute as thought by metaphysics.

Nevertheless, this only remains a preliminary attempt as we now, along with Heraclitus, think-after how σοφόν (i.e., the to-be-known in authentic knowledge) unfolds in such authentic knowledge (i.e., unfolds in ὁμολογεῖν, and thus in human λόγος) and how it unfolds in general in relation to beings as a whole.

[348] THIRD SECTION
Retreat into the originary region of logic

§ 7. On the illumination of being, experienced through inceptual thinking. Fragments 108, 41, 64, 78, 119, 16, 115, 50, 112

a) The 'steering vision' and the jointure (ἁρμονία) of the originary forgathering. γνώμη and the Λόγος as the unifying One in the advising, counseling presence of the originary sheltering forgathering

In saying 108, τὸ σοφόν, the authentically to-be-known, is determined as the regioning countering presence in which everything presences. In saying 41, σοφόν is expressed even *more* decisively in its uniqueness, while at the same time being described in such a way as to allow us a new look at the essence of the Λόγος. Saying 41, whose linguistic form is debatable, is captured in the following formulation:

ἓν τὸ σοφόν, ἐπίστασθαι γνώμην, ὁτέη κυβερνᾷ πάντα διὰ πάντων.

One, the sole One, is that which knows, (and to know means) lingering steadfastly before γνώμη, which steers all things through all things.

If we initially only state the content of the saying in a calculating and superficial way, we again find that the to-be-known—i.e., τὸ σοφόν—is the One (i.e., ἕν) which relates itself to the πάντα. However, there is no mention of the Λόγος and its λέγειν. In fact, in this saying we hear words [349] that before now we have not heard. The saying speaks of γνώμη and κυβερνᾶν. It sounds strange that the to-be-known—that is, the Λόγος—is itself γνώμη, a word that we could initially and in a lexically correct way translate as "cognition." If we were to understand the Λόγος in accordance with the accepted interpretation of it as reason and "world reason," then the equating of the Λόγος and γνώμη, "reason" and cognition, would not pose the least difficulty. However, ὁ Λόγος is the originary sheltering forgathering. Yet, it is said of γνώμη that it steers. 'Cognition' as such does not 'steer,' insofar as 'steering' is an activity and a practice, whereas 'cognition,' in principle, remains 'theoretical.' This is what has led one translator to translate γνώμη as "the insightful will."

It is therefore a matter of some luck that two sayings of Heraclitus's have been preserved for us, one of which (namely, fragment 78) gives us the opportunity to reflect upon γνώμη and its essence. The other saying (fragment 64) tells us something about κυβερνᾶν, steering.

Fragment 78 states:

ἦθος γὰρ ἀνθρώπειον μὲν οὐκ ἔχει γνώμας, θεῖον δὲ ἔχει.

The sojourn—namely, of the human (amidst beings as a whole)—may not have γνώμαι: the godly, however, does.

In accordance with our earlier elucidation of 'physics,' 'ethics,' and 'logic,' we do not translate ἦθος as "moral disposition," but rather as "sojourn" in the sense of dwelling amidst beings.

It is precisely this meaning that the word ἦθος also exhibits, and indeed most expressly, in another fragment of Heraclitus's (fragment 119), which states: ἦθος ἀνθρώπωι δαίμων. This can be translated as: "For the human, his character is his daemon." This translation surely thinks along lines that are modern, psychological, and characterological. The thought that, for the human, the inheritance of his disposition is what goads, drives, and stalks him may [350] be in some sense correct, and it certainly provides ample opportunity for mindful consideration. But this is not a reason for such a thought to be interpreted, without further ado, back into Heraclitus's saying. Certainly, fragment 119 is to be counted among the most essential of all that have been handed down to us, and perhaps it could be sufficiently elucidated after an interpretation of Heraclitus's thought as a whole has been completed. However, this indicates that fragment 119 must be thought together with that particular saying that I have named on another occasion as the first, and upon which any attempt to think-after the thinker Heraclitus as a whole must be grounded. (That is fragment 16.[1]) Fragment 78 states: the sojourn of the human

---

[1] See *The Inception of Occidental Thinking* in this volume.

amidst beings has no γνῶμαι. Properly understood, γνώμη means a particular manner of disposition: namely, one that allows beings to be encountered and become visible. γνώμη is a mood of the mind, thought of as a fundamental mood. However, "manner of disposition," "constitution," "mood," and "fundamental mood" are all also contemporary conceptions, not far removed from the so-called 'mental states' that we dissect and examine psychologically. However, even if we do not think the essence of 'constitution' and 'mood' psychologically, but rather hold fast to what is ecstatically-disclosing and actively open within them, we must nevertheless take care not to translate γνώμη as one of these terms. The meaning of the word γνώμη is so rich and multifaceted that it contains all that we name as 'constitution,' whereby we are not equating disposition with the capability of sensation in a reductive way. Rather, we mean any kind of disposition to which one is disposed, so that γνώμη can mean decision and conviction, and also determination and vision. Any attempt at translation here risks a one-sidedness and remains burdened by it.

However, if fragment 78 states that, in distinction to the human sojourn, the divine sojourn has γνώμη, and if we consider that the sojourn of the gods [351] is the presence of those who peer in, and who do so in such a way that within what is espied by them and their gaze beings first appear; if this is the case, then γνώμη, insofar as it departs from the human sojourn, cannot indicate any old capability and conduct amongst others. To be sure, the human relates to beings and espies them in the light of being. However, this light of the lightening is not something that the human accomplishes on his own: rather, he only stands within this light. The preparing of what can be seen; the originary espying whereby what can be seen first comes into the open, and through which the open itself remains: this particular preparing-beforehand of the possibility of the appearance of beings is not of human origin. It is this preparing-beforehand that is meant by γνώμη. We could translate it using the Germanic word "*Rat*" [vision], thereby understanding it as what allows the encounter with the sight and engagement with beings as such. It is within this originary vision that beings are forgathered and retained.

Fragment 41 states that this originary vision steers all things through all things. This vision, which prepares both sight and engagement and is thereby what allows for an encounter in the originary (initiating) sense, 'steers.' What does it mean 'to steer'? To steer means to forgather everything together in advance onto a pathway, and thereby, in forgathering, to point out the way and hold it gathered open in advance. In steering, presence unfolds in advance of all else: namely, that presence within which, on that steered pathway, what is encountered can presence and absence.

This originary vision steers everything in such a way that no particular being bumps up against another, and yet, each may in its own way appear conjoined with all others, and everything appears in joint (ἁρμονία) with everything else. In light of this, we ask: is the originary all-steering vision (i.e., γνώμη) something other than the presence of the originary forgathering that shelters all in its presencing and absencing? Does not the saying regarding the steering vision (i.e., γνώμη) shed some light on the essence of the Λόγος? Must not the steering vision be πάντων [352] κεχωρισμένον, i.e., the presencing region that approaches all, surrounds all, and advises all, and from out of which all directions and paths open themselves and, in this opening, grant pathways? It would initially remain an overt arbitrariness simply to equate the steering γνώμη with the Λόγος. However, because γνώμη is only suited to the divine and is related to the conjoining of the whole of beings, and because thereby the originary forgathering that prepares comes-forth from within γνώμη, we should not simply turn away from the apparently daring step of equating γνώμη θεία with the Λόγος. If we consider them both in relation to beings as a whole, and if we at the same time think the still-veiled truth of being in a Greek manner from out of ἀλήθεια and φύσις, then both γνώμη θεία and the Λόγος can tell us something essential about the essence of presence—something essential, to be sure, although perhaps not what is most fundamental, if we are even able to consider thinking toward it. However, taking the step of equating the Λόγος with γνώμη θεία becomes inescapable when we consider that the Λόγος and γνώμη, in the same way, are both called ἓν τὸ σοφόν: the One, i.e., the sole to-be-known. According to fragment 41, this knowledge consists of ἐπίστασθαι—"standing before"; now we are able to grasp this in a more originary and proper way, and not only in the later sense of ἐπιστήμη and τέχνη as being well-informed about something. To stand before means: to reside before and in the presence of the originary forgathering. γνώμη and the Λόγος are what is to be known, and, indeed, as the uniting One: the visional, advisory presence of the originary sheltering forgathering. This, however, cannot be separated and cut-off from the whole. On the contrary, it is the region that approaches all and surrounds it, dispensing all paths and directions, steering all things. The Λόγος is πάντων κεχωρισμένον. ὁμολογεῖν is the residing within the presence of the originary forgathering, a residing which is the human relation to the Λόγος.

[353] b) Reconsideration of the ὁμολογεῖν of the ψυχή and the interpretation of the self-enriching of the human λόγος as the self-forgathering residing in the presence of the originary Λόγος

The following question was posed in an earlier section:[2] how are we to prepare in advance the authentic relation of human λόγος to the Λόγος (i.e., ὁμολογεῖν)? The preliminary answer was that it is first necessary to know the relation of human

---

[2] See German page 329.

λόγος to the Λόγος: however, this means to know that, and how, the Λόγος is presence and is the region toward which human λόγος is most turned in a manner of bearing. Therefore, no matter how much the designation may suggest it, 'human λόγος' must never be thought of as a gathering relation belonging to the human which, as a peculiarly *human* relation, is somehow cut-off from its connection to the Λόγος as if enclosed by a boundary, on the other side of which is to be found a possible further relation to the Λόγος. On the contrary, the λόγος of the ψυχή, as human λόγος, is the μάλιστα διηνεκῶς ὁμιλεῖν Λόγῳ, the turning-toward the originary forgathering in a manner that bears it most of all. The human λόγος would not be λόγος at all were it not the gathering toward the originary forgathering: and it is from out of this originary forgathering, and as the relation to it, that the human has the proper essence of gathering. However, we now recognize the following: if μάλιστα διηνεκῶς ὁμιλεῖν is already a gathering, but also and more precisely a ὁμολογεῖν, then gathering and gathering are not always and exactly the same. At the same time, it also becomes apparent that the λόγος τῆς ψυχῆς—i.e., human λόγος— must always already be thought of as the gathering toward the originary forgathering. This human λόγος is itself only and precisely as the gathering toward the originary forgathering. All that continually pertains to human λόγος itself, and that which it, from out of itself and on its own accord as [354] λόγος, *is*, proceeds from out of, and resides in, the originary forgathering toward which it remains gathered.

Only when we keep all of this in mind do we remain in the realm of Heraclitean (and, more generally, Greek) thinking. Only from out of this realm can we then think-after that other saying of Heraclitus's in which he speaks of the λόγος τῆς ψυχῆς, i.e., of human λόγος. It is fragment 115, and it states:

ψυχῆς ἐστι λόγος ἑαυτὸν αὔξων.

To the drawing-in drawing-out belongs a gathering that enriches itself from out of itself.

We will now mention the saying of Heraclitus's that Hegel chose as the motto for his *Phenomenology of Spirit*, without elucidating or even translating the saying. We may assume, however, that Hegel chose precisely this saying as the motto for his work only after careful consideration, and sees within his own work the proper interpretation of this saying. In many ways, it would be illuminating to follow up on these relationships, in order to reveal in what form the Λόγος has become historically present in contemporary metaphysics, and thus in what form being addresses the contemporary human (and therefore us). However, this is not the occasion for such reflections. We must be satisfied with the suggestion that Hegel understands the Heraclitean λόγος as reason and understanding and, indeed, as the 'divine' and 'absolute.' In his *Phenomenology of Spirit*, Hegel seeks to show how absolute reason, which before all else is thought as the subjectivity of self-consciousness (in the sense of Descartes), comes to itself through the various stages of its self-appearing, and that in this developing it reveals its essence more and more. It was in view of this contemporary understanding of such a ceaselessly self-overcoming self-knowledge of the certainty of reason that Hegel [355] chose Heraclitus's saying as a motto. As a consequence of this, a strictly circumscribed meaning is imposed upon Heraclitus's saying, a meaning that remains foreign to Greek thinking in every respect. Even the common, contemporary translations of saying 115 reveal the prevalence of a metaphysical interpretation of λόγος. For example, Diels translates it as: "To the soul belongs meaning (world reason), which increases itself." By contrast, Snell translates it as: "The soul has meaning, which from out of itself becomes ever richer." Even if we keep in mind that any translation remains incomprehensible without its attendant interpretation, we may nevertheless conclude from these test cases that these translations have all arisen from out of metaphysical thinking. Insofar as this thinking understands its own history as containing within it a development toward the execution and consummation of an ever-higher self-consciousness of reason, then such a saying of Heraclitus's, notwithstanding its venerability, must appear as something provisional and incomplete beyond which Spirit has already progressed. However, Heraclitus's saying does not refer to the dialectical self-development of absolute reason: rather, it states that the essence of the human originates from out of the relation to being, and that this origin is the origin as such, insofar as it becomes ever more originary and abiding in its proper ownness. It is precisely this that remains difficult for us today to think-after, even if we do not interpolate the absolute metaphysics of reason's development into the saying (as Hegel does). There remain enough other hurdles, even if, as though doing nothing, we simply continue to cling to our conventional opining. For clearly, the word that bears the emphasis in the saying is ἑαυτόν (in its relation to αὔξων): the λόγος of the soul (i.e., the human λόγος) enriches itself from out of itself. That certainly sounds as though the human contains within himself the source from out of which, on his own accord, he himself unfolds by way of himself, thereby creating and realizing the possibilities of his existence.

[356] However, what is the human λόγος itself as this λόγος? As λόγος, it is certainly already and especially gathered toward the originary forgathering. Therefore, as the gathering relation, the self-ness of the human λόγος does not consist in it pinching and tying itself off, as it were, in order then, in seeking itself, to draw everything back toward itself. Rather, it is itself the human λόγος, and precisely as λόγος it is the drawing-out self-gathering toward the originary forgathering. It is toward this originary forgathering that the human λόγος is pointed. As the one that points in such a far-reaching way, human λόγος is pointed toward the source of enrichment. The essential depth proper to λόγος, correctly understood, harbors within itself the possibility that it enriches itself from out of itself. When and how does the human λόγος become richer? When it is more gathered toward the originary forgathering. This becoming-richer of the human λόγος is not enacted through the growing influx of beings, but rather through the usually absencing presence of 'the Λόγος' (that is, of being itself) becoming a

presencing one. The unfolding and fulfilling of the history of the human issues forth from out of the human λόγος itself as a λόγος, insofar as the Λόγος forgathers it. Owing to a pointedness toward being, and not from out of a pursuance of beings, drawing-out and drawing-in increase.

Heraclitus's saying states that the human being, in his essence, belongs to being and is determined in his gathering toward being, and that he receives his potentialities from this.

As an essential consequence of this, the human develops all manner of rigid focus upon his own abilities and competence at the expense of being: this is ὕβρις. Therefore, authentic knowledge is the following: namely, the obedient, self-gathering toward the originary forgathering. At first glance, saying 115 seems to be saying the opposite of what saying 50 says. In truth, however, the two say the same. For saying 115 does not state that the human λόγος is self-sufficient and does not require a relation to something else in order to become [357] richer. On its own—that is, in its essence—the human λόγος *is* only as the obedient self-gathering in the manner of ὁμολογεῖν as stipulated in saying 50. Conversely, the human self-gathering toward being is also not a blind sinking into, and dissipation into, the ether, but is rather the knowing turning-inward of the human into his own essence, which as λόγος is itself gathered into the presence of the Λόγος, therefore remaining distinct from it. In the self-gathering toward the Λόγος, the human forgathers himself into his own being. That toward which the soul draws-out through its λόγος—namely, being—is not something that the soul then takes back with it in the form of some kind of 'subjective experiencing.' The soul draws-in—but into *where*? Not into an inwardness meant in the subjective sense: rather, this drawing-in draws into λόγος, which in turn gathers in obedient emerging to the Λόγος.

At its core, the relation to be thought here of the human λόγος to the Λόγος is so simple that precisely its simplicity confounds our calculative thinking, which counts on stable points of reference. For our thinking immediately calls forth the conventional conceptions of a human subject whose subjectivity, for better or worse, reaches an accord with the objective. If indeed the human λόγος, and therefore the human essence, unfolds into its own richness as the relation to being (and that means, *from out of* being and not from out of beings); and if it is also the case that the human initially and for the most part remains turned toward beings, even remaining turned exclusively toward them and seeking refuge within them; if, moreover, what is always at stake for the human and, at the same time, for the proper relation to the Λόγος, is ὁμολογεῖν: if all of this is the case, then we can perhaps better understand why Heraclitus continually revisits the essence of authentic knowledge (i.e., of σοφόν). We can see more clearly why, in the characterization of the essence of authentic knowledge, λόγος and λέγειν are named. However, we can now also recognize, if only at first in a vague way, that we must think λόγος and the essence of λέγειν in the first place (and perhaps even exclusively) [358] in the light of being as experienced in an inceptually Greek way.

From out of such an understanding of the Λόγος the originary 'logic' grows, which can teach the more originary essence of thinking.

Human λόγος is the relation to being, i.e., to the Λόγος. It is this relation that determines the essence of the human. This essence unfolds its richness from out of itself. Heraclitus says (in saying 115): ψυχῆς ἐστι λόγος ἑαυτὸν αὔξων. We translate: "To the drawing-in drawing-out belongs a gathering, which enriches itself from out of itself." The self-enrichment of human λόγος is grounded upon the fact that it is itself the relation to the Λόγος, that it remains pointed toward this, and therefore receives its own λόγος-like essence—that is, it receives its self—from out of *the* Λόγος. Being a self is the state of being addressed by the Λόγος, being forgathered in its presence from out of its forgathering. The essence of the human rests within itself when it rests in a drawing-out drawing-in within the presence of the Λόγος. However, initially and for the most part, the human remains inclined toward beings, and in such a way that he believes to have found his refuge within them: that is, he thinks he has found refuge within the real understood in a contemporary way as that which acts and that which has been acted upon. The human is dispersed and dissipated in beings. It is for this reason that he does not attend to being. Moreover, it also always appears as though being is given to the human through and within beings. For, apparently, beings 'are' the same as 'being,' at least according to conventional wisdom. Beings assert themselves as 'being,' owing entirely to the way in which the human, to all appearances and in a way that renounces his nearness to being, remains allied with beings. In all of this, however, the Λόγος is already present, while nevertheless remaining absent. However, most especially, the human does not hold himself in proper knowledge (i.e., τὸ σοφόν) of the Λόγος. As such, the knowledge of the authentic to-be-known remains foreign to him. Authentic knowledge consists of attentive listening to the Λόγος (i.e., of ὁμολογεῖν). Authentic knowledge of the Λόγος and the preparing in advance of every human λόγος, which comes into its essence as ὁμολογεῖν—this preparatory [359] knowledge of the originary Λόγος is the originary 'logic.' Here, 'logic' means: to stand within the Λόγος as the presence of the originary forgathering.

c) Knowledge, the true (i.e., the unconcealed), and the Λόγος. The revealing gathering of the concealed toward unconcealment in true λόγος as the essence of knowledge (σοφία). The demand and imposition of the Λόγος

A saying of Heraclitus's that was mentioned earlier, although only in passing, can now assist us in gathering together what has been said up to this point and thinking it in a more unified way. This means: to espy more essentially what is essential within gathered thinking, and the relations therein. We are referring here to saying 112:

τὸ φρονεῖν ἀρετὴ μεγίστη, καὶ σοφίη ἀληθέα λέγειν καὶ ποιεῖν κατὰ φύσιν ἐπαΐοντας.[3]

Initially, we shall now turn toward one of the more conventional translations in order that that we may recognize how disconnected the saying remains from what is, for Heraclitus, the authentic to-be-thought (i.e., the Λόγος). However, we also turn to this rendering in order to see how hollow the saying becomes through this conventional translation—so hollow, indeed, that one is no longer inclined to attribute it to thinking. One such rendering—for example, that offered by Snell—is as follows:

> Thinking is the highest completeness, and wisdom is to say and to do the true according to the essence of things, hearkening to them.

The saying speaks of ἀληθέα—one translates this word, according to long-standing custom, as 'the true.' What this means—and, most importantly, what this means in the Greek thinking of the early thinkers—is not at all reflected upon. 'The true'—it appears as though anyone can understand what this means. 'The true'—whoever claims to know what it is makes the claim to know not [360] only what is true and of what the true consists, but also to know what truth is in general, and to know the essence of the true. In the same manner, this translation of Heraclitus's saying assumes that one is in the know when it comes to 'the true' itself, and that according to Heraclitus, all that matters is 'to say' and 'to do' what is 'the true'—that is, to say the correct correctly, and to translate it correctly into action. What matters is to heed the true in word and deed, and to put it into effect. Leaving aside for a moment the question of whether or not this hits upon Heraclitus's thinking, who could argue that in this a difficult demand is being enunciated? And yet—from where does 'the true' come to word and deed? Moreover, what is 'the true'? Heraclitus himself seems to give some information regarding this in his saying. For, according to the translation cited above, Heraclitus says: "wisdom is to say and to do the true," "according to the essence of things" (i.e., κατὰ φύσιν). Saying and doing become true and are true if they "orient themselves toward the essence of things"—that is, when they are in 'accordance' with them. Truth is the accordance of saying and doing with things. In a continuance of the thinking of Aristotle, in the medieval era one said: *veritas est adaequatio intellectus et rei*. Even Kant holds

---

[3] [Diels supplies σωφρονεῖν instead of τὸ φρονεῖν—Ed.]

fast to this determination of the essence of truth, and he takes it to be so agreed upon that an elucidation of it appears superfluous to him. It now appears, at least according to the translation cited above, that Heraclitus already knew of this essence of the truth, the knowledge of which apparently belongs to the common domain of human cognition. It is almost superfluous, then, for Heraclitus to make reference to the condition upon which this agreement with things is to be achieved—namely, that one hearken to things and thereby pick up on their quality and character.

This elucidation of the saying, derived from the guiding thought of the translation cited above, allows everything to appear in the most beautiful harmony and smoothness. However, one difficulty remains for those who attempt to think-after it. It consists [361] of the fact that the explanation for the essence of the truth given by the translation cannot be the view held by Heraclitus, owing to the fact that the reduction of the essence of the true assumed by the saying—namely, that the true is an accordance between saying, doing, and things—only comes about around the time of the formation of metaphysics in Plato and Aristotle. In short, the interpretation at work in the above-cited conventional translation of saying 112 is absolutely historically impossible, if for no other reason than that it debases the dignity of inceptual thinking in favor of a platitude. We must therefore take another way, one that has been prepared by our prior reflections.

The word in Heraclitus's saying that one commonly translates as "the true"—namely, ἀληθέα—literally and essentially means "the unconcealed." ἀλήθεια—unconcealment—is a foundational word of inceptual Greek thinking. However, no matter how familiar the translation of ἀλήθεια as "truth" may be to us, and no matter how common the determination of the essence of truth as an accordance between the assertion and the thing is, we must remain mindful of the fact that the saying is being said in the time of pre-metaphysical thinking, that is, at a time during which words, and most especially foundational words, unfolded their originary power of naming. If we now examine the entire saying again in a more careful way, we will find not only *other*, but indeed *all* of the essential foundational words of inceptual thinking conjoined by way of this saying—and no one who has come to notice this will ever cease to be amazed by it. This points to the fact that this saying, which according to its conventional translation and interpretation seems to express only something 'trivial,' in fact says something entirely other, something inceptual which, like all that is inceptual, remains to us enigmatic and inexhaustible, thinking beyond us at every turn. One finds in the saying, in addition to ἀληθέα, the words φύσις, λέγειν (λόγος), ποιεῖν (ποίησις), σοφίη, φρονεῖν, ἀρετή, and ἐπαΐω (ἀΐω). Each of these words names, in an essential way, the originary essence of [362] inceptual Greek thinking and that which it thinks. The saying itself speaks specifically only of φρονεῖν and σοφίη, of "thinking" and of "knowing": namely, it speaks of what they are. We will now translate φρονεῖν provisionally, and without elucidation, as "thinking," and σοφίη—based on prior elucidations of other sayings—as "knowing." Given all that has been elucidated thus far, one thing surely remains clear: namely, that the words 'thinking' and 'knowing' are initially only designations for questions, and, for the most part, questions that remain unasked. The translation of these words, and the other words mentioned, is almost like the translation of ἀληθέα with our word "the true." We will now attempt to head down one of many paths that are possible here, on our step-by-step attempt to elucidate this saying. We will nevertheless keep in mind that we are reflecting on this saying precisely in order to clarify the essence of the Λόγος more clearly, which is named here as λέγειν in connection with σοφόν.

The saying is comprised of two sentences. The first says something about 'thinking'; the second states of what knowing consists. The saying says nothing about the relation between 'knowing' and 'thinking,' at least not directly. Indirectly, however, we can certainly surmise enough from the saying regarding this relation, if only the saying is elucidated according to its essential aspects. Because the relation between φρονεῖν ("thinking") and σοφίη ("knowing") initially remains obscure, it is advisable to leave the καί that begins the second sentence undefined. Although καί indeed means 'and,' it almost never means *merely* 'and' in the language of Heraclitus. We will begin the interpretation of the saying with an elucidation of the second sentence, and will bring it into connection with what has already been singled out within it: namely, ἀληθέα—for it is in relation to this that the λέγειν spoken of in the saying is said. The Λόγος is encountered here in relation to ἀλήθεια. According to its conventional translation and interpretation, one understands λέγειν as "saying" and "asserting." ἀληθέα understood as "the true," in connection [363] with which saying and asserting are named, corresponds exactly to the pervasive doctrine of metaphysics, according to which 'the truth' is an inherent characteristic of asserting and belongs to it. If we direct our inquiry about the use of language by the Greeks even further back in time, then we learn that in the oldest, documented testimony—namely, in Homer—the words ἀληθέα, ἀληθές, and ἀληείη appear consistently, and do so solely in relation to expressions of saying, recounting, reporting, answering, and asserting.[4] The conventional view of ἀλήθεια, λέγειν, and their relation is thereby confirmed in the most welcoming way. And yet, ἀληθέα means the unconcealed: and what could the Greeks have meant other than *what*, and only what, their own word clearly and unambiguously says to them? What, then, becomes of our crude and late-coming interference regarding the meaning of that word? What, then, of our translated word 'the true,' to which we also affix a later, metaphysical explanation of its meaning? ἀληθέα means what is unconcealed, and for now we must hold ourselves to that. However, λέγειν means gathering and collecting, and it is *this* that we must first consider.

---

[4] Such words occur three times in the *Iliad*: ἀληθείη, at Ψ 361 and Ω 407; ἀληθέα at Ζ 382. [According to the editor's reckoning, there are 14 instances in the *Odyssey*.—Ed.]

Before all else, it is necessary to think-after whether or not there exists a more originary connection between ἀληθέα and λέγειν than the one just cited. Based upon the Homeric and Heraclitean uses of language, taken in terms of how they are conventionally understood, one could claim that, in a very general way for the Greeks, ἀληθέα—which we name the "true"—belongs in the realm of λέγειν, the realm of so-called "saying," and that it is precisely through this connection of ἀληθέα and λέγειν that the originary belonging-together of both becomes elucidated.

However, what does it mean to say that authentic knowing consists of saying the true? For 'the true' can surely only be said when it is known and when it stands within knowledge. Thus, *knowing* must exist first. And knowing *is* only insofar as it [364] has the true in its possession. Only then, when knowing *is* the having of the true, can it follow that a saying and a doing in word and deed—namely, as a realization of the true—is possible.

The saying of Heraclitus's, however, sets out to say in its second sentence what knowledge itself is. It says that knowledge itself is ἀληθέα λέγειν καὶ ποιεῖν κατὰ φύσιν. Even someone with only scant knowledge of the language of Heraclitus and the early thinkers sees immediately the way in which the saying is structured: ἀληθέα is related to λέγειν, and ποιεῖν is related to κατὰ φύσιν. Knowledge consists of λέγειν καὶ ποιεῖν, of gathering and bringing-forth. But, what is being gathered in that gathering that amounts to knowledge? ἀληθέα—the unconcealed: it is taken from out of concealment, it is unconcealed, and in such a way that it is preserved and kept safe as what has been taken out from concealment. Knowing is the revealing bringing-in and preserving of what has been taken up and out of concealment. What is unconcealed in such a way is what shows itself from out of itself, appears and, in appearing, presences. What presences in this way are beings. To know is to gather, a gathering that for-gathers what presences from out of itself into unconcealment. To this extent, unconcealment itself is what allows what presences to presence as such, preserving and forgathering what presences in its presencing. Knowing is the gathering toward unconcealment. This gathering and preserving takes in what shows itself, thereby protecting it from being withdrawn, covered over, and obscured. ἀληθέα, taken as "the true," is not grounded in λέγειν, taken as assertion: rather, λέγειν, understood as gathering, gets its essence from out of ἀληθέα, which is itself understood as what has been gathered from out of concealment and forgathered into unconcealment. What Heraclitus names as the essence of knowledge in the beginning of Occidental thinking is an essence that continues to prevail later in all Greek thought, despite all permutations. Even the beginning of metaphysics in the thought of Plato and Aristotle still thinks knowledge [365] from out of this understanding of essence: Aristotle speaks of σώζειν τὰ φαινόμενα—to save what appears, i.e., to take up and preserve the self-showing in its disclosedness. Additionally, Aristotle's metaphysics designates τὰ φαινόμενα—the self-showing, i.e., what is present in appearance—to be τὰ ἀληθῆ, i.e., what is unconcealed, with this meaning the same as τὰ ὄντα, i.e., what is present.

If we understand ἀληθέα λέγειν in the saying of Heraclitus's to be a revealing gathering of the concealed toward unconcealment, then the originary Greek answer to the question concerning the essence of knowing—which Heraclitus poses without saying it—is not our only reward. For, in the Greek interpretation attempted above, we have also stepped into the realm where Heraclitus's presentation regarding the second essential element of σοφίη (i.e., ποιεῖν κατὰ φύσιν) becomes understandable.

Given all that was said in earlier sessions about φύσις with an eye toward the elucidation of ἐπιστήμη φυσική, and given also what was said about this foundational word in connection with the elucidation of ζωή and ψυχή, there ought to be much within our memory to draw upon that can now be reconsidered. φύσις names the emerging that at the same time unfolds as a returning-back-inside-itself. In the originary oneness of both of these moments there unfolds that for which φύσις is the inceptual Greek name: namely, that which we call being. In the essence of emerging there lies a letting-go-forth into the open—i.e., revealing or, said in a Greek way, ἀλήθεια. Furthermore, in the essence of a returning-back-inside-itself there lies a taking and holding back, a covering over which the Greeks, however, did not specifically name.

This *not*-naming of the covering-over that fundamentally unfolds in all revealing is an omission and failure of enunciation, one in which the innermost secret of the fundamental essence of Greek thinking perhaps lies concealed. That is why it remains obscure to us how the inceptual thinkers of the Greeks [366] thought the essential oneness of ἀλήθεια and φύσις. The remaining fragments of the "Didactic Poems" of Parmenides are the only proof that these words gave a presaging perspective to the thought of these thinkers.

If we attend to the essential belonging-together of ἀλήθεια and φύσις, and if we consider that λέγειν as the gathering preserving is determined from out of ἀληθέα (i.e., the unconcealed and its revealing), then it becomes clear in what way the second essential dimension of knowing—the ποιεῖν κατὰ φύσιν—amounts to the same. But what does ποιεῖν κατὰ φύσιν mean in this context? ποιεῖν means "to make," "to do." The German words encompass a broad range of meanings, as do the Greek words. Nevertheless, the time has finally come to think the word ποιεῖν in a Greek way, or at least to attempt the exertion of doing so. This recurring demand here to think 'in a Greek way' is experienced and executed through the path of a dialogue with inceptual thinking, a path that is meant to lead solely toward the German thinking that has properly been assigned to us. However, what is not intended here is a correction of the historiographical understanding of a bygone Greek world. The fundamental meaning of ποιεῖν is a bringing-forth and placing-forth. It is good, and even expressly necessary, that we now take these German words seriously (i.e., 'literally') and at their word. We thereby find ourselves right in the middle of the realm that the Greeks intended, but did not specifically discuss further. *'To bring' 'forth'* from out of concealment, as in, for example, the bringing 'forth' of the visage of the god in a block of marble; thought in a Greek way, this means 'to make' a statue. All 'placing-forth' is grounded in such a bringing-forth, in such authentic ποιεῖν. In order to think it in a Greek way, we must think 'placing-forth' *thusly*: to place-forth the beams (i.e., lumber) from out of the tree trunk and its wood, and to place-forth the woodwork from out of the beams; this is the activity of bringing-forth, of placing-forth—ποίησις—the bringing of beings as beings from out of concealment and into appearance in unconcealment. Still today, we use the worn-down foreign word 'poesy'/'poetic' [367]. (We use both 'poesy' and *Dichtung* [poetry].) The doctrine and theory of the poetic arts is called 'poetics.' For the Greeks, poeticizing is also already a ποίησις, a "making": but what is actually made thereby is what is brought-forth in the sense of coming to shine forth in the poetically-said word, and thereby continuing to shine, ever anew, in the word. In the same way, 'to do' is akin to stepping into appearance and allowing to appear. ποιεῖν/ποίησις—bringing-forth/placing-forth—brings forth and places forth into unconcealment what before this had not yet appeared. ποιεῖν is primarily thought along the lines of a human comportment. In this sense, ποίησις is the essential opposite of φύσις. φύσις designates emerging-from-out-of-itself, allowing to go-forth, to bring-forth in the originary sense of bringing. ποίησις is the bringing-forth executed by the human: and such a bringing necessarily presupposes a 'harvesting' in the full sense of gathering as previously elucidated. All ποίησις is always dependent upon φύσις, but not only in the sense that the latter is a necessary prerequisite, as when, for example, the placing-forth of a ship necessitates building materials, the beams and wood which have of themselves originally emerged as tree and thereby reached presence. More importantly, however, ποίησις adheres to φύσις in the sense that what is actually being brought-forth—for example, the visage of the god in the block of marble—is what peers in, and does so in the manner of emerging from out of itself. This emerging takes place in advance and approaches the human, and human bringing-forth adheres to it. ποιεῖν takes φύσις as its measure—it is κατὰ φύσιν. Such being in *accordance* with φύσις—such *following-after* the possibilities given by φύσις and *through* its realm; all of this talk of "after," "accordance," "through," and "along"—all of this is meant by the word κατά. The one who knows is the one who brings-forth in view of what emerges-from-out-of-itself: that is, who brings-forth in view of what reveals itself and before this revealing does not appear and has not appeared. ποιεῖν κατὰ φύσιν patently does not mean "to make something in the likeness of nature," in the sense of a poor imitation of what lies before at hand.

[368] However, as we would like to argue, bringing-forth—i.e., ποιεῖν itself and as such—is not an essential element of knowing. Rather, ποιεῖν κατὰ φύσιν—i.e., placing-forth into view what emerges and what is to-be-uncovered in such a way that the human is gathered toward it—is ἀληθέα λέγειν. It is not bringing-

forth as such, therefore, that constitutes the manner of knowing obtaining to ποίησις: rather, it is bringing-forth (i.e., revealing) 'in accordance' with what emerges-from-out-of-itself.

However, thinking in such a way would mean that we would still, and in an unfortunate way, misunderstand the Greek essence of ποίησις and the Greek essence of knowing. For, understood in this way, the same thing would be said twice in the saying of Heraclitus's. In a way, this is true; in another way, it is not. It would say the same insofar as λέγειν, as the gathering preserving of the unconcealed, and ποιεῖν, as the bringing-forth from out of emerging, both show the fundamental feature of the human comportment through and in which the human allows what emerges into unconcealment to come to presence. However, it would not say the same insofar as λέγειν only preserves the unconcealed in a manner that gathers, be it that which emerges from out of itself or be it something that has been brought-forth and placed-forth, and which is thereby present. For, in that case, ποιεῖν κατὰ φύσιν, which is named as secondary, would more forcefully and authentically emphasize the moment of πρᾶξις in distinction to λέγειν, the latter of which corresponds to θεωρεῖν, i.e., pure looking at and considering.

Even though this distinction between theoretical and practical comportment originates in the metaphysics founded by the ancient Greeks, we should not superimpose it back onto Greek thinking, and certainly not in its post-Greek and contemporary iterations. Above all, even if this differentiation seems patently obvious, we should not superimpose it back onto inceptual thinking, a state of affairs that appears to be the case following the conventional translation of saying 112. For, it is the case that for Greek thought, ποιεῖν itself as ποιεῖν is primarily a knowing, [369] and not only because a certain knowledge and expertise belong to any bringing-forth and placing-forth. Rather, it is precisely because this knowledge, when experienced in a Greek way, constitutes the essential and authentic relation of ποίησις to being (i.e., to φύσις). Furthermore, it is precisely because ποιεῖν is most definitely not an effectuating making, but is, understood literally, a bringing-forth, a placing-forth and placing-there—that is, a gathering of the unconcealed as such. The Greek concept and word for what we call 'art' (and this means 'art' in the highest sense) is τέχνη, and this is a concept of cognition; such cognizing means to grasp according to the essence of knowing as the uncovering of the unconcealed. Art in its highest sense is ποίησις—poesy—and it is a knowing which, as knowing, is the gathering of the unconcealed and self-gathering to it. However, the unconcealed forgathers the corresponding self-gathering toward itself *only when* the unconcealed, as itself, has emerged from out of itself and stands within unconcealment in its own proper standing. Self-gathering toward originary forgathering does not dissolve within this forgathering. When experienced in a Greek way, the originary relation to beyng is not an indistinct dissolution into the infinite in the sense of the in-determinate. Rather, self-gathering toward being brings the latter into unconcealment, and in such a way that this gathering each time allows being to emerge as gathered into emerging beings: in other words, being is immediately defined in its scope (πέρας, τέλος), thereby bringing-forth being in such a way (i.e., into the unconcealed) and thereby not (and, indeed, never) 'making' being. This bringing-forth is the revealing of the concealed into the unconcealed. And bringing-forth is a giving that allows something to be known, and is this knowing itself. Bringing-forth in light of emerging—ποιεῖν κατὰ φύσιν—belongs to the full essence of knowing.

When Heraclitus differentiates between λέγειν and ποιεῖν, he thinks both in their originary oneness as the essential feature of knowing. And when *we* take note of this difference and hold fast to it, it is worth considering that it is *prior* [370] to the differentiation between the theoretical and the practical. The καί that stands between λέγειν and ποιεῖν does not connect, as would a mere "and," two essential pieces that comprise σοφία: rather, the καί means something akin to "and at the same time this means." The bringing-forth of emerging belongs to the full essence of λέγειν as the gathering self-gathering. That is why this particular gathering (i.e., this λέγειν), which gathers and forgathers in a more originary way than any other, is, in itself, ποίησις—namely, gathering into the word and purely as the word, and thereby coming to language in thoughtful and poetic saying. Because the word 'gathers' (i.e., harvests) the unconcealed as such in an originary and inceptually revealing way, the saying-gathering thereby becomes λέγειν in an exemplary sense: and this is why, even from early on, λέγειν as gathering also means saying. Thinking and poeticizing are, although in fundamentally different ways, originarily (and to be-gin with) the same: they are the bringing-forth of being into the word, a bringing-forth that gathers itself in the word. It is here, in the essential realm just named, where we first begin to draw nearer to the wellspring from out of which arises the mysterious interaction between Greek poeticizing and thinking in harmony with that particular bringing-forth that we know as building and creating (but which we are still far from knowing). Based on what was just said, I dare to make the assertion that still today, despite Winckelmann and Goethe (and indeed, precisely because of them), we misunderstand the entirety of Greek 'art,' not to mention Greek poetry.

However, the final determination of the essence of σοφία named in the second sentence of the saying has not yet been elucidated. This determination comes at the end of the saying and brings what has been said about σοφία into and together with something unsaid. The last word is ἐπαΐοντας—ἀΐω means 'to waft,' 'to waft back-and-forth,' 'to draw-out toward something,' 'to draw-in.' (Here one must not speak about the incipient essence of ΑΩ.) This is how we have determined the essence of the ψυχή. The ἐπί in ἐπαΐοντας properly means "toward something." We have come to experience, through saying 50, that σοφόν/σοφία (i.e., knowing) consists of the attentive listening to [371] the originary forgathering (i.e., to the Λόγος). Therefore, in saying 112, we cannot determine the "that toward which" (i.e., the ἐφ' οὗ of ἀΐοντες) in any other way than to supplement with ἐπὶ τοῦ λόγου. ἐπαΐοντας does not mean to listen attentively to things: rather, it means to listen attentively to *the* Λόγος.

With this, the circle closes itself, and its circling center enters more originarily into its encircling ground. λέγειν, which is itself at the same time ποιεῖν—i.e., the bringing-forth-gathering-self-gathering—happens ἐπαΐοντας ἐπὶ τοῦ λόγου, i.e., in the attentive drawing-out toward the Λόγος, toward the all-forgathering originary regioning presence. The Λόγος is the same as that toward which λέγειν moves according to saying 112—namely, ἀληθέα, the unconcealed as the unconcealment that is grounded in concealment. However, unconcealment is the same as that toward which ποιεῖν moves—namely, φύσις, the emerging that goes back into itself. The Λόγος, as the originary sheltering presence, is in itself the revealing that unfolds within concealing, the emerging that goes back into itself. Ἀλήθεια, Φύσις, Λόγος are *the same*: not, however, in the empty conformity of a collapsing together into the undifferentiated, but rather as the originary self-forgathering into the differentiated One: τὸ Ἕν. The Ἕν, the originary uniting One and singular, is the Λόγος as Ἀλήθεια, as Φύσις. To the One that is to be thought thusly—that is, to the Λόγος—there corresponds (in ὁμολογεῖν and as ὁμολογεῖν) that particular human λέγειν that draws-out and draws-in that is in itself at the same time ποιεῖν (i.e., bringing-forth), but is both in the manner of a hearkening harvesting of the gathered self-gathering toward the originary forgathering.

The insight into the essence of σοφία that is granted by the second sentence of saying 112—namely, the insight into authentic knowing—is what first makes it possible for us to think-after the first sentence of the saying: for it is only from out of the essence of knowing that we are able to recognize and experience what thinking authentically is, given that thinking is nothing other than the gathered-gathering standing within knowing. Thinking [372] is the care of a concernful residing within knowing. Thinking is care, and therefore also often the failure of the gathering standing-within in the self-revealing presence of being itself.

(What can still be said here—albeit at some distance—about the elucidation of saying 112 and thereby about the illumination of the originary Λόγος and, in turn, in reference to being as experienced in an inceptually thoughtful way, is certainly not fit to be quickly and deftly assessed and then sold off as some new discovery regarding Heraclitus. We can surely leave the prior historiographical interpretation of early Greek thinking as it is: for, regarding merely scholastic judgments concerning its relative correctness, nothing can result which would have the least effect on us. The sole matter of concern here is that, instead of utilizing what has just been said for 'research,' we should reflect upon it for ourselves and only in relation to ourselves, and should thereby become attentive in regard to our relation to being. However, this relation—a relation that is both thoughtful and tries to think the to-be-thought—is 'thinking' itself which, within an originary 'logic,' comes to stand within its own light, albeit not a light that it itself has made.)

We have heard that the human λόγος is a far-reaching one that has reached far. In thinking, 'the soul'—i.e., the drawing-in drawing-out from out of the originary forgathering—is called to appearance by the originary forgathering. The regioning presence of being (i.e., of the Λόγος) directs itself to thinking (i.e., to λέγειν as ὁμολογεῖν). From out of this originary demand to the human by the Λόγος, all spiritedness—i.e., that which is innermost and most expansive in the disposition of the human—is directed toward being. The spiritedness that divines what regions from out of itself and rests within itself, as well as all that is inceptually sheltered and safeguarded, is found in authentic, essential thinking—presuming that such thinking will one day be granted to the human. That which originarily shelters all and conceals it back inside itself is the precious *simpliciter*. The knowing that unfolds within authentic thinking is the highest divining of that which is precious and noble [373]. That is why Heraclitus words the first sentence of saying 112 in the following way: τὸ φρονεῖν ἀρετὴ μεγίστη. φρόνησις/φρονεῖν/φρήν is thinking in the sense of the inexhaustible meaning of our German word "*sinnen*": to reflect on something, to reflect-after it, and in this far-reaching reflecting to direct oneself toward a demand, and at the same time to mindfully consider, and in such considering enter into one's own proper essence, the ownmost characteristic of which consists precisely in a belonging to that toward which all attentive hearkening is turned. In 'reflecting' lies the abiding drawing-out of what is also meant by the Greek word φρονεῖν, which can best be translated as "reflective thinking." We can therefore express the first sentence of the saying in the following way: "Reflective thinking is the highest nobility." Upon this follows the καί, which not only joins the sentence about σοφία onto the sentence about φρονεῖν, but which connects it in such a way that the καί says: *and* this is so *because* σοφία, which concerns itself with φρονεῖν, has the essence that is now to be stated. φρονεῖν is concern for σοφία: it is concernfullness—φιλία τῆς σοφίας. It is philosophy in the originary, pre-metaphysical sense.

Only when we have once again learned to intuit the essential, authentic essence of knowing (i.e., σοφία) in a way that experiences it, will we also understand at least a little about the concernfullness for this knowing. Only then will we come to realize what is at stake in this thoughtful concern for authentic knowing, and thus what is at stake in φιλία τῆς σοφίας, 'philosophy.' Philosophy is not a 'discipline,' nor an academic 'major' or 'minor': rather, it is a *joint* in which beyng joins itself to the thinking human, presuming that beyng is the jointure that operates as this joint amongst humans.

The unspoken meaning of saying 112, which is nevertheless essential for us to speak out loud, reads thusly:

τὸ φρονεῖν ἀρετὴ μεγίστη, καὶ σοφίη ἀληθέα λέγειν καὶ ποιεῖν κατὰ φύσιν ἐπαΐοντας (τοῦ Λόγου).

Reflective thinking is the highest nobility, because knowing is the gathering of what is unconcealed (from out of its concealment) [374] within its own bringing-forth that corresponds to emerging—(all of this indeed) in the attentive hearkening to the originary forgathering.

§ 8. The human, the Λόγος, and the essence and truth of being. Final part of the interpretation of saying 112

[375] *"Far is the path one must take to the originary Λόγος."*

a) The Λόγος as ἓν πάντα: the originary forgathering presence. On the sameness of the Λόγος and being. The human as safe-keeper of being and the relation of being toward the human: the divining of the event [*Ereignisses*]

Saying 112 states:

> τὸ φρονεῖν ἀρετὴ μεγίστη, καὶ σοφίη ἀληθέα λέγειν καὶ ποιεῖν κατὰ φύσιν ἐπαΐοντας (τοῦ Λόγου).

Reflective thinking is (the) nobility, because knowing is to gather the unconcealed (from out of concealment into unconcealment) in the manner of bringing-forth into the set-forth and set-up in view of emerging (and all this, nevertheless) within the drawing-out drawing-in relation toward the originary forgathering.

According to an ancient Greek determination, the human is the ζῷον λόγον ἔχον. The ζῷον is determined by ζωή: however, ζωή itself is determined by ψυχή, the drawing-in that draws out . The ψυχή of the *human*, whose drawing-in draws out, has the manner of λέγειν in the sense of ὁμολογεῖν: what is gathered within itself gathers what, as the originary forgathering (i.e., as 'the Λόγος'), has originarily (i.e., in a manner that bestows the essential origin) directed itself toward the human. The human is ζῷον λόγον ἔχον—the drawing-in drawing-out that is gathered in itself as the gathering of the originary forgathering. The human *is* the place of the truth of being, and this is why the human can, at the same time, also be the confusion of the madness of empty nothingness. The human is what he is by constantly *not* being what he is. In fact, this 'not' is the foundation of both nobility and presumptuous mismeasurement.

[376] Following this elucidation of saying 112 and the references to the Λόγος as thought by Heraclitus that occur therein, we give the following translation of saying 50:

οὐκ ἐμοῦ, ἀλλὰ λόγου ἀκούσαντας ὁμολογεῖν σοφόν ἐστιν ἓν πάντα εἶναι.

If you have not listened merely to me, but have listened compliantly to *the* Λόγος (i.e., the originary forgathering), then the essential knowledge that subsists therein *is* (while gathered in itself) to gather the presencing of what, as the sole-One, unites all (i.e., the presence of the originary forgathering).

(See saying 32: ἓν τὸ σοφὸν μοῦνον λέγεσθαι οὐκ ἐθέλει καὶ ἐθέλει Ζηνὸς ὄνομα.

The sole-One-uniting-unifier, which alone is present in authentic knowledge, both resists gathering and grants gathering in the name of Zeus.)

The Ἓν–πάντα hides within itself a hint regarding the essence of the Λόγος itself: the Λόγος is the Ἓν, i.e., the sole-One that unfolds precisely as the One because it unites. It does not do this retroactively, but rather originarily—that is, before all else. The Λόγος is the Ἓν πάντα: the originary forgathering, the presence in which all that is present presences, the being in which all beings are.

The Λόγος is not a 'meaning,' according to which the saying 'one is all' should come about. Nor is the Λόγος that particular saying that accords with the meaning that states 'one is all.' The Λόγος is not some separate essence that pronounces, for some unknown reason, 'one is all.'

The Λόγος and Ἓν πάντα are not two separate things, but rather the same singular essence of being. Ἓν πάντα is the originary λέγειν. However, λέγειν as harvesting unites all, and does so in the sense of the safeguarding, sheltering, uncovering gathering.

[377] The Λόγος of Heraclitus's must be thought from out of what this thinker says when he names the relation of λέγειν to Ἀλήθεια and Φύσις. Ἀλήθεια and Φύσις provide a hint as to the originary, Greek essence of the Λόγος. However, the *ratio* of metaphysics and reason as subjectivity, along with the *Verbum* of Christian theology, can never relinquish their search for its determination.

The path that one must take to the originary Λόγος is far, and there are scarcely any signs indicating the way. But perhaps a reflective thinking and the proper care of its mindfulness are in fact aided by the collapse of the world: a world which, itself already groundless and empty, must bring itself to an end through the modern presumptuousness of 'creating culture,' a particular presumptuousness that first opened the gates for modern technology.

In saying 43 Heraclitus says:

ὕβριν χρὴ σβεννύναι μᾶλλον ἢ πυρκαϊήν.

The presumptuous mismeasurement it is necessary to extinguish, even more so than the conflagration.

The preceding elucidation has renounced the unreflective presumption to know what 'the true' is, and what 'saying' is, and what ποιεῖν ('to make') and 'nature' are. This particular elucidation attempts to honor the thinker by acknowledging, from the very beginning and with astonishment, that the thinker had to bring something once unsaid and never fully sayable into the word.

However, this elucidation is also aware that such an astonished withdrawal in the face of the saying can only arise if within itself there is a prior, pure thinking from out of what is to come—a thinking that renounces all support and assistance and only answers to what the saying of the thinker has said.

This elucidation rests in the knowledge that the truth of beyng needs the human who shelters it: namely, the human who is appropriate to beyng, whose essence begins with beyng and is concealed along with it, who waits and beckons with it, who is quiet with it, and who speaks with it.

This elucidation rests in the divining of the event [*Ereignis*].

[378] b) Summary of the guidelines and perspectives according to which the Λόγος, which has yet to unfold inceptually, is to be thought. The truth of being and the fate of metaphysical thinking

1. λόγος/λέγειν is harvest/to harvest, gathering/to gather.

2. The decisive determination in harvesting/gathering is conserving: namely, conserving in such a way that through this conserving something abiding remains accessible.

3. Harvesting itself is oriented in advance toward the allowing-to-presence of that which shines forth from out of the safeguarding in which it has its residing.

4. Harvesting is oriented toward the secured in such a way that, as the unconcealed (and therefore the accessible and graspable), it remains secured.

5. The essence of λέγειν is determined by what is unconcealed as such (i.e., from the unconcealment and protecting that necessarily belongs to it).

6. The essential origin of λέγειν from out of Ἀλήθεια becomes clear when we consider that all 'harvesting' is oriented toward 'beings.' However, we only first begin *to think* this when we think the common word 'beings,' and when we think it in relation to λέγειν understood in the Greek sense. Beings are what presence from out of themselves: they are what stand within unconcealment and are housed within it as the preserved, the secured, the gathered.

In order to grasp properly the essence that belongs to λέγειν, it is already enough to think-after the essence of what is to be harvested and what can be harvested (i.e., 'beings').

[379] 7. Thought more carefully and clearly, beings are what stand within unconcealment, having already emerged within unconcealment, while at the same time also being unsecure within it in a certain sense. (Light takes up that which is illuminated, and brings it to appearance against darkening and veiling. However, at the same time, the light must relinquish the illuminated.) What has emerged must be secured within unconcealment. How does this occur? Is it even possible for unconcealment as uncovering *to secure*? Where? And how?

8. Being needs λέγειν. Does being thereby not become dependent upon the human, if it is indeed the case that λέγειν is that which is 'human' about the human?

It remains to be asked: what does 'dependence' mean here? Is this dependence a belittling of being? What if being needs λέγειν *because* it (i.e., being) is the independent? What if this independence of being consists in the fact that being is the originary securer of all, and thus the harvest, and thus the gathering, i.e., the Λόγος?

9. Because being is the Λόγος, it needs λέγειν. Being needs what guarantees its independence. Here we are thinking within that realm (i.e., the realm of the truth of being) where all relations are completely different from those in the region of beings.

10. In saying 50, Heraclitus says that being is the Λόγος, and he says this by also saying at the same time what the Λόγος is: namely, the Ἕν which, as the Ἕν, *is* also at the same time πάντα. The Λόγος secures all beings as beings in such a way that, in securing, it allows beings alone to remain beings. This securing is the originary

for-gathering: it is the sublating securing that secures all within the either/or of revealing and concealing.

[380] 11. Being is pronounced in a thoughtful saying as the Λόγος. We are, if we historically *are* ourselves in our essence at all, those who think-after. We have been given the task of carrying out this thinking-after and of pondering, before any self-interest, what is inceptually said: that is, at least, if we indeed have the veneration to obey our being as historical humans.

Only as those who think-after do we think ahead of our own, long-forgotten and never expressly pronounced human essence. Only as those who think-before are we able to become aware of the saying and to remain attentive to it.

12. Whoever wishes to intuit, albeit from a distance, the Λόγος as the essence of beyng, will recognize that being, thought in this way, is foreign and ungraspable to those of us living today when approached using familiar terms. Moreover, and more importantly, one easily falls victim to the idea that the interpretation of being as the Λόγος is a making-human of being, insofar as λέγειν, as human comportment, is drawn upon and conferred upon being as its determining characteristic. However, it remains to be asked here:

a) Why is λέγειν, as the determining characteristic conferred upon being, thereby granted primacy?

b) How, then, is being understood, so that λέγειν can be conferred upon *it* and thereby determine *it*?

c) If, however, as is obvious, being itself has been thought in advance and was thereby lightened *as* being, thus becoming noticeable and distinguished, why does it now need to be conferred yet another determining characteristic?

d) Such a conferring of λέγειν onto being, so that being will thereby become the Λόγος, is impossible in every respect.

13. Being does not need the conferral upon itself of characteristics borrowed from elsewhere, characteristics which in truth have already been determined by being itself. Rather, before all else and essentially before any comportment [381] toward what has been lightened as its ground, being needs securement in the humanness of the human. However, insofar as being is inceptually lightened as the Ἕν, and thereby implicitly has not yet unfolded as the Λόγος (that is, as Ἕν πάντα), λέγειν is that which corresponds to being as the only possible human relationship to, and consummation of, securement. If it is at all possible to speak about a conferral in regard to the relation between being and the human essence, then at most what can be said is that the essence of being confers itself upon the corresponding

manner of the human comportment toward being. However, nowhere in any of this does one find a conferral. Being makes a demand of the essence of the human which, in turn, responds in a human way by offering λέγειν as its fundamental feature—a feature which is nothing other than the demand issued to it by being— and by summoning it everywhere and throughout all human comportment. This is why it remains for Aristotle the case that, albeit in a modified form, every ἐπιστήμη and σοφία, every ποίησις and πρᾶξις, is everywhere μετὰ λόγον.

14. In what way, however, do the address and the response preside in the relation between being and the human? Are the address and the response, which have been gleaned out of Heraclitus's word and saying, determinations of the originary relation of that regioning of the region toward the countering response? Certainly. But, again, that which was just named reaches out into realms that only open themselves to language for a thinking-ahead that thinks-after to a greater extent. In order to be able to follow up on this hint, our thinking must first have sloughed off a calcified perspective to which we have long grown accustomed, one which sets a limit to all thinking that seeks to think-after the relation of being to the essence of the human (and not only the relation of beings to that specific being, the human), a limit whose limitation enacts itself above all by not becoming visible as a limit.

15. When our ability to conceptualize attempts to think the relation of the human to being (proceeding from the erroneous supposition that it is precisely in this backward approach that the relation of being to the human would be grasped), it is trapped in that particular perspective that is informed by the [382] subject– object relation. The interpretation of the human essence as subject prevents an originary experience of the humanness of the human, owing to the fact that precisely what determines humanness as such—namely, both the demand of being that strikes the human, and being itself—can only be thought by the subject as an 'object' or, at most (as for Kant), as the conditionality of the object as such, i.e. as objectivity.

16. The relation of being to the essence of the human, and likewise indeed the relation itself, is, as the truth of being and as the being-there of the human, something that surpasses being and the human in their relatedness: for, prior to them both, the event [*Ereignis*] eventuates into truth as the securing of concealment and its essencing.

17. The fact that from early on λέγειν meant "to say" (i.e., 'to narrate' and similar such things), indicates that *word* and *saying* originate from out of the same essence as harvesting. However, the Greeks never truly thought-after this, which is why and how λέγειν, as originary gathering (i.e., securing into unconcealment), became

'saying,' and in such a way that λέγειν also and originally meant "to say" in a broader sense. But perhaps it is the case that the question as to how λέγειν as gathering became λέγειν as saying is an unfitting one. The securing gathering of beings as such is already originarily that sort of relation in which the human—quiescent, at first, in regard to the being of beings—per-ceives beings in their being, and therefore beings as such. This ac-quiescence to being is the originary saying and naming of beings: it is the originary word which counters the region of being—it is the first response in which any word sways as it unfurls itself in saying and sounds in the word of language. Acquiescence unfolds as the originary self-gathering of the human essence toward being, and vice versa. λέγειν, as the harvesting that secures, not only enacts itself quietly: it simply is the gathered gathering of the self-abiding quiescence. λέγειν [383] is originary quiescence. In the restraint of quiescence rests the entire self-comportment of the human to beings and, indeed, every relation to humans and gods. However, what applies to λέγειν—namely, that as originary gathering it is the securing acquiescence to being—applies in an even more originary way to the Λόγος. For, the Λόγος is the originary securing requiescence which, as such, is the fore-word to every saying of the word in the response. The fore-word is the acquieting of the stillness that unfolds in advance and before the essence of the word, a silence that must be broken only when the word is to be. The Λόγος is not the word: it is, as the foreword to any language, more originary than the word. Its claim on the essence of the human is the quieting of the fore-word that quietly sends being to the human. It is only in an ill-suited way that already depends upon the human conception of a speaking-saying that we call this quiet sending a speaking-toward and a speaking-to. In a more fitting way we could say: the Λόγος is the region that sends itself quietly to the human—i.e., it is the expanse that secures all signs and markers, the expanse that rests in itself. By quietly sending itself to the essence of the human, this region first returns back into its own stillness; and as this return, it is the parting into the preserved beginning. The truth of being that quietly sends itself to the human (therefore acquieting the humanness of the human) calls the essence of the human into the gathering toward the return in which the truth of being shelters itself in the stillness of what is always already there in advance, and which, as the originary for-gathering, preserves the tranquility as which the event [*Ereignis*] eventuates itself in order to allow all that exists to rest upon it. However, what is actually eventuated is a mutual encounter between what has been and what is to come.

18. From out of the gathering-quieting essence of λέγειν first arises what even a superficial consideration of λόγος could scarcely overlook. Such a consideration finds that λόγος as saying (in which the broken silence conceals itself) gathers in the manner of bringing-together and [384] separating. Both are the most immediately graspable characteristics of gathering. Using the terms σύνθεσις and

διαίρεσις, Aristotle identifies them as coincident moments belonging to λόγος and, indeed, to 'asserting' in the sense of demonstrating. The assertion is only able to assert something about something if it first addresses something as something. This consists of the following: something is separated off from something, and in such a way that what has been separated is precisely brought together again with the addressed. Both moments of λόγος—namely, σύνθεσις and διαίρεσις—are known already to Plato, although not as such in the construction of λόγος ἀποφαντικός.

19. A faint shimmer of the originary essence of λέγειν still shines through the determination that Kant gives to the essence of thinking when he conceives of it as "I connect," i.e., I gather. The functions of the unity of connecting—i.e., the modes of the originary for-gathering which, since Descartes, have been misplaced into the *cogito ergo sum*—are categories as concepts of understanding, through which the objectivity of objects (i.e., the being of beings in a Kantian sense) are thought. Even here, being is still grounded in a 'unity,' without, however, any question regarding the essence and the origin of this unity.

20. The faded shimmer of the inceptual Λόγος, which can still be seen in Kant's concept of the transcendental, is itself the concealed ground for the unfolding of the essence of reason in his thinking and in the speculation of absolute idealism. Reason is thought as will (Kant), as the will of the deed (Fichte), as the will of the Spirit (Hegel), and as the will of love (Schelling). As this will, reason (*ratio, logos*) is the will of 'life.' This will then appears in the following inversions which the distortions inherent to the essence of being extort from thinkers: namely, as "the will to negate life" (Schopenhauer), an inversion that, when inverted once more, consummates itself and [385] appears as the "will to power" (Nietzsche). Why does it matter that the will to power is the inversion of an inversion? What does inverting have to do with the will and its actualization? It is within this still enigmatic essence of the will of being that the essence of the will still conceals itself, and this essence of the will can only be recognized as the will to will by a thinking that thinks ahead into the truth of being. In this, the most extreme and complete counter-essence to the inceptual Λόγος lightens itself. It almost appears as though all unfolding of inceptual being has vanished within the will to will, which is why it also appears estranging when being, considered in accordance with modern metaphysics, is interpreted decisively and solely as the will (see *The History of Beyng*).[1] It appears that the only possibility is to interpret everything 'psychologically' and to declare psychology as 'metaphysics' *par excellence*. And yet, it requires only a few, simple steps undertaken by a thinking-ahead that also

---

[1] [See Martin Heidegger, *Nietzsche*, Volume II, Neske, Pfullingen, 1961, 399 ff.—Ed.]

thinks-after in order to find within the will to will the trace of the inceptual essence of being.

21. Being determines itself from out of Ἀλήθεια/Φύσις decisively as ἰδέα, οὐσία, and ἐνέργεια. This means: being signifies the going-forth into presence, presencing in the manner of self-presenting and self-representing. Therein it is determined: self-presentation and, at the same time, presenting something other (i.e., representation). Therefore, authentic beings are, in all cases, that which represents, i.e., the representatives.

According to this, being means: the decisive self-bringing, self-bringing-forth, self-bringing-through, self-carrying-through, and self-asserting into presence. From the essence of ἰδέα properly understood as the self-showing pre-forming visibility, all the way through to the predominating self-carrying-through and self-asserting, there runs a unifying essential connection in whose unfolding the willful comes forth ever more decisively. (But—why and in what way?) With the turn of the essence [386] of being toward subjectivity, the essence of the will of being is fully decided as the self re-presentation that sets-forth everything toward itself and thereby erects itself as what rules over everything placed and set forth, i.e., everything that persists. The stepping-forth and arising into the open of openness of the representing consciousness take precedence over the moment of the openness of presence. The practicing of, and engagement in, representation, within which also lies the endurance of representation, is what pushes-forth within the surge toward self-representation. Presence, and the fact that within it unfolds all surging arising-forth, retreats before this singular practice like something unimportant. But presence would not be what it is without the presencing it engages in and ceaselessly seeks anew. The fact that consummating, finalizing, and activity gain primacy everywhere, only indicates that presencing, by way of which all practicing and engaging stands and falls, is being forgotten. By unfolding as will, being demonstrates (although this is not yet recognized) that the condition for the forgetfulness of being lies within being itself.

The more willful the will becomes, the more decisively it wills, because every willing is a self-willing, i.e., as the self-willing of the will to will. However, the will surges toward the bringing-forth of the counter-will (from whence this 'counter'?), and indeed in the form that the will to will everywhere wills the same: namely, a willing that everywhere drives the sameness of the will apart into the outermost oppositions of practicing and engaging, oppositions which in truth are no such thing, but rather the willed pretenses under whose protection sameness is willed. As soon as the will to will drives itself apart into this appearance of the oppositional, it wills willing in unconditional exclusivity, solely for its own sake. The forgetfulness of being is thereby consummated, and the will to will has deluded itself into an unconditional will toward blindness.

However, being releases itself into this distortion, and it can only allow this release because it has, having taken leave from any essence of willing and its prior forms, already [387] begun to return to its own truth. In stillness, beyng turns toward the sheltering of the clearing into which it, as what is still preserved as what was always already there in advance, once gifted its grace in a manner that commences, in order to give the essence of the human a sole dignity: namely, to become the safe-keeper of the truth of beyng.

SUPPLEMENT

[391] [What follows is a first draft of a continuation of the text on German page 282, which picks up from the last line, ". . . that toward which its λόγος, as such, . . ."—Ed.]

... in its λέγειν, is related. However, this λέγειν is ὁμολογεῖν: namely, that harvesting in which the 'soul' of the human (i.e., its drawing-in drawing-out) has its fundamental feature insofar as it, by way of harvesting, gathers itself toward the Λόγος. The depth of the λόγος that the human essence 'has' determines itself from out of the expanse and concealment '*of the*' Λόγος, to which it belongs and to which it listens in a hearkening way, a hearkening and belonging-to that occurs even when it is *not* expressly and continually listening to the Λόγος. The λόγος of the ψυχή reaches toward the Λόγος, i.e., it reaches out so far toward it that the soul, itself a self-opening emerging, does not find on *its* course the outermost extremities. Moreover, it does not reach these outermost extremities when the soul embarks on its wanderings solely *from out of itself*, wandering along its ways and paths only on its own accord and according to its own measure. However, this is how the soul usually proceeds; nevertheless, its goings and wanderings are still a manner of λέγειν, of gathering and drawing-in, which does not, however, proceed from out of its own far-reaching λόγος. For this can only be what it is—namely, a ὁμολογεῖν—when the soul, instead of going down its path and ways solely on its own accord, listens *to* the Λόγος in a hearkening way. If the soul is able to do this, and is in fact to do this at all, then surely 'the Λόγος' must be perceptible, and perceptible *before* all else. This is indeed the case, according to various statements of Heraclitus's. The Λόγος to which ὁμολογεῖν must listen in a hearkening way is even nearer and more perceptible than all else that is 'near,' and all that is taken to be graspable and understandable. However, this extreme nearness of the Λόγος, before which no human may remain concealed (see fragment 16), is precisely the strange nearness that brings him to turn away from the Λόγος, ensuring that what is the most common for him and, indeed, what makes his days sacrosanct, remains foreign. The Λόγος is that which is most perceptible, and yet it is perceived the least: it is instead [392] ignored in favor of other more pressing things. The Λόγος is the originary gathering and the forgathering that rests within itself, yet which nevertheless comes up against a strange dispersal of the human essence. The manner in which the human soul 'has' its λόγος, and through this remains in a relation to the Λόγος, is estranging and counter to all expectation. However, the estranging is a sign of the extraordinary, to which the human must ceaselessly grow accustomed. This is stated in the saying that has been handed down as fragment 72:

ὧι μάλιστα διηνεκῶς ὁμιλοῦσι λόγωι τούτωι διαφέρονται, καὶ οἷς καθ' ἡμέραν ἐγκυροῦσι, ταῦτα αὐτοῖς ξένα φαίνεται.

That to which they are most turned, carrying it out ceaselessly (i.e., the Λόγος), and that which they encounter daily, appears foreign to them.

The first part of the saying contains a wordplay that is nearly impossible to replicate, for the same word is used twice, but with opposing meanings: διηνεκῶς–διαφέρω. In the first instance (i.e., in διηνεκῶς), διά means 'through,' 'along,' 'through time,' 'to carry through,' 'to bear out.' However, in its second instance, διά means 'apart': διαφέρειν means 'to carry apart/to bear apart,' 'to divide in two,' although not (and never) to separate.

Human calculating and machinating always sees the nearest and the 'near' in what comes next, the next object toward which the will wills. Thereby, the authentically near is passed over by the wanderings of the human. Even if this wandering were to wander along all paths, it would never reach what is free and expansive, and it would never reach the extremities that lead to what the human, in a concealed way, remains gathered toward. On the contrary, this wandering would bump up against the confines and constraints of its self-made limitations. That is why, instead of a calm light, there ignites a burning and scorching flame within the emerging originary self-lightening clearing of the human essence, a blaze that burns and yearns to measure these paths autonomously and selfishly, a measuring that is always merely [393] a mismeasuring and, indeed, a presumptuous one (i.e., ὕβρις). Heraclitus says the following about this in fragment 43:

ὕβριν χρὴ σβεννύναι μᾶλλον ἢ πυρκαϊήν.

The presumptuous mismeasurement it is necessary to extinguish, even before the conflagration.

The disastrous blazes that follow are all only the consequence of that burning and blazing of presumptuous mismeasurement. However, the extinguishing of the conflagration does not yet eradicate hubris, nor does it even hit upon it or consider it. The conflagration will only be extinguished through the hearkening listening to the Λόγος. *When* this listening-to comes about, there one finds authentic knowledge, i.e., τὸ σοφόν—and with it, the to-be-known and the already-known within it are manifest. It is of course difficult for the experienced and far-thinking human to recognize properly the singularity of authentic knowledge and the to-be-thought. About this, much is said, and much is discovered. In fragment 108, Heraclitus says the following about it:

ὁκόσων λόγους ἤκουσα, οὐδεὶς ἀφικνεῖται ἐς τοῦτο, ὥστε γινώσκειν ὅτι σοφόν ἐστι πάντων κεχωρισμένον.

Of the many assertions I have (already) heard, none arrives at the recognition that authentic knowledge and what is to-be-known within it are something differentiated from all else.

However, as we have heard, the to-be-known is what the Λόγος says. And this is set apart in its own unique place. However, it is not something separate: on the contrary, it is the near in all nearness. However, as such, it is inimitably singular and incomparable, and is not reachable through any mediation, nor capable of being detected through any direct or indirect equating. In its state of difference, this sole to-be-known is only accessible when the soul follows its far-reaching λόγος, instead of its customary paths and ways. The λόγος of the soul, within which alone ὁμολογεῖν comes about, is that drawing-in drawing-out that is oriented toward the free—it is authentic harvesting which, the more directly and purely [394] it adheres to itself, the more it gathers and the more it expands. That is why Heraclitus can claim the following in fragment 115:

ψυχῆς ἐστι λόγος ἑαυτὸν αὔξων.

To the soul belongs a harvesting that enriches itself.

It therefore does indeed appear as though the soul must build upon itself and follow its paths and ways in order to enrich itself. However, we must nevertheless consider that what is spoken of here is the λόγος of the soul (i.e., of that which draws out toward *the* Λόγος). And it is this λόγος, and not the self-serving and self-absorbed soul, which, as λόγος, becomes richer through its λέγειν (insofar as this constitutes ὁμολογεῖν). To the extent that λέγειν gathers itself toward the Λόγος in a hearkening way by giving itself up to it and listening solely to it, it becomes richer. The soul must abandon its accustomed ways and paths and limit itself to its singular, bare, impoverished authentic hearkening listening: for it is then, and only then, that its λόγος is enriched. The enrichening of the self-gathering toward the Λόγος consists in the fact that the former, in listening to the Λόγος, is ceaselessly overtaken by it, thereby obediently joining itself ever more simply and in a more far-reaching way to precisely that which overtakes it. And all of this takes place within the sole jointedness.

One last saying of Heraclitus's regarding the soul should be mentioned now, so that we may gain a clear perspective regarding the constantly named relations between the λόγος of the soul and its ὁμολογεῖν (in which σοφόν consists). As long as the λέγειν of the soul corresponds to 'the Λόγος,' authentic knowledge *is*. So, when and which soul is the knowing one? Is it the one that authentically and solely knows, the one that knows the most (in Greek, ψυχή σοφωτάτη)? Heraclitus tells us in fragment 118:

αὔη ψυχὴ σοφωτάτη καὶ ἀρίστη.

The sober soul is the most knowing and also the most noble.

αὔη means "dry." But, in this fragment it does not mean the dried out, the withered, or the lifeless, but rather the dry in [395] distinction to the wet in the sense of the moist, musty, bubbling, and merely inebriated. The sober soul is the one properly attuned to (and by) the voice of the Λόγος to which it listens. Once again we can glean from this saying in what way the Greeks understood the noble: it is grounded in knowledge and blooms from out of it. The nobility of the human is its originary relatedness to the One which, as the singular unifying, is all. That is why Heraclitus can say the following in fragment 49:

εἷς ἐμοὶ μύριοι, ἐὰν ἄριστος ἦι.

One counts more than ten thousand, if he is a noble one.

The disposition of the noble rests in the knowledge that a thinking—or rather, *the* thinking—exists. Thinking is life—but what kind of thinking? Precisely that thinking that follows the far-reaching λόγος in an abiding way, following it into its enrichment from out of its own depth.

We have attempted to elucidate a few sayings of Heraclitus's that speak of λόγος. Do we now know what Heraclitus thinks when he uses the word λόγος? We know some things, and yet know nothing. Above all, what little knowledge we do have does not allow us to be able to take a glancing familiarity with the λόγος of Heraclitus and then derive a definition and formula of it, as though such 'knowledge' (namely, definitional knowledge) were the most stringent of all knowledge. Perhaps this kind of familiarity with a thing is not knowledge at all, in the very same way that imprecise guessing and searching in the dark are also not knowledge.

If we look over what has been said about Heraclitus's λόγος, then it seems we have remained in the same indeterminacy that faced us in the beginning of our encounter with this word. For, on the one hand, it clearly means saying, for it is related to hearing; ὁμολογεῖν is also a saying, a speaking, in the sense of a correspondence that is attentive to what is perceptible in the Λόγος, a correspondence that follows and accedes to what is perceptible in the Λόγος and that therefore corresponds to it. Therefore, λέγειν stands together with ποιεῖν (see fragment 112) and does indeed mean saying in distinction to doing. On the other hand, however, [396] it is said of the authentic Λόγος (i.e., of the Λόγος in general) that to 'correspond' to it amounts to the knowledge that 'one is all.' The Λόγος is the One to and for the all, and is the one sole uniting unifier.

Perhaps it is indeed of benefit to us if we follow this highest of directives: namely, to adhere to the authentic Λόγος, to the unity and unifying within it. The word λέγειν itself also corresponds to it in its fundamental meaning of harvesting and gathering. Should we not finally, without reservations and sidelong glances, grasp and hold onto the fact that the Greeks in general, and the Greek thinkers before all others, whenever they thought in word and saying, and certainly whenever they wished to say the highest—that is, when they wished to say ἓν πάντα εἶναι—heard the word that corresponds purely to it: namely, λέγειν/λόγος? Should we ourselves also not make the effort to think the other meaning of λέγειν (i.e., 'saying') from out of the first meaning? However, to do this necessitates that we now think into all relations pointed to here, while at the same time eliminating from our thinking all that has been traditionally thought. We must attempt to think the Λόγος in the way that it is said, without at the same time allowing any notions of Spirit, personhood, godhood, or providence (or similar such things) to creep into our thinking in such a way that we and our conventional thinking have an easier time quickly and effortlessly imagining something in regard to the Λόγος. Does such a thinking, as ubiquitous and long-practiced as it is, amount to a serious thinking? Does it at all listen to what is said?

To be sure, it is difficult for us to think something sufficiently concrete and reliable in relation to λέγειν as "harvesting," and in the Λόγος as "harvest." For, first and foremost, the elucidation of "harvesting," and the harvest as a gathering, easily leads to one grasping λέγειν superficially in the sense of a careless snatching up and putting together of things that lie scattered about. In this way, λέγειν and the Λόγος retain the fatal feature of a merely retroactive gathering together. How can something akin to that be operative as *the* essence of the Λόγος, through whose unity everything is to [397] remain determined? It is clearly decisive that we avoid taking 'harvesting' and 'gathering' too superficially, provisionally, or emptily. 'Harvesting' in a narrow sense—namely, as the 'reading' of a script and the 'reading' of signs—is surely never a gathering together and arranging of letters. It is equally never a placing together of words to which is then, from who knows where and when, attributed a 'meaning.'

(What *is* a reading [*eine Lesung*], anyway? And, for example, what is a 'lecture' [*Vorlesung*]? Is it the mere reading off of what is written down—that is, an ordinal gathering together of written signs? Or, is it rather a gathering that, by virtue of being gathered itself, brings us to the gathering (or, at least, attempts to do so)? Lecture [*Vorlesung*] and lecture [*Vorlesung*] are not the same, and one who does not practice their difference will also never experience it, for it remains far easier for him to once again read out loud everything that he has read during the week, in order to then spew it out to the astonishment of the clueless. Lecture, reading, gathering; and then, when the school bell 'rings,' dispersal ensues and leads one to the cinema—.)

Even the most superficial taking-up and grasping of a written sign is something completely different, and it would not be what it in truth is were there not already an experience of self-showing (and showing) provisionally available for us. This provisional self-showing (and showing) counsels us in our grasping of signs, and does so even when we do not understand the sign and stand before it helplessly and without provisions. (Indeed, this is when its counsel is the most direct and unmediated.) But how in all the world does this lack of provision come to us, this failure of vision and counsel, if some sort of vision and counsel do not already exist for us beforehand?

λέγειν means "to harvest," as in to harvest ears of corn, grapes, or wood. We will now go one step further in our thinking of harvesting, and in doing so, move beyond its superficial connection to the activity of the hands. We thereby leave aside for the moment the marvel that is the hand, and our focus is solely directed toward harvesting as a gathering in the sense of a drawing-in and a bringing-in. Such harvesting prepares a provision; harvesting, in its ground, is concerned with the conserving of a provision, and this conserving is not something additional or subsequent. Proper [398] harvesting, therefore, leaves nothing out and does not allow anything to wither away. Harvesting is thus a saving. Harvesting is a gathering, i.e., a drawing-out that is already and everywhere accompanied and borne by a drawing-in and bringing-in. Harvesting is the saving of what shows itself: it is a saving and a bringing into the pro-vision. It is toward this that all proper gathering is itself already gathered: within the unity of its constancy and care it is attuned to what belongs together, to what is gathered within it and from out of it. Gathering is a bringing together and holding together, but not in a superficial or subsequent way. The shepherd gathers the herd. The herd is not some random assemblage, and the shepherd is no policeman. To gather: how can one hold together and gather, when he himself does not remain gathered toward that which is gathered within him? And how would it even be possible for there to exist a pure and highest gathering, if there does not also exist a One that before all provisions has already gathered all gathering and harvesting toward itself in advance in a provisional way? If we think from these perspectives, harvesting and gathering lose their superficial and distorted character.

The Greek thinkers speak of their thinking as being a σώζειν τὰ φαινόμενα, a saving of what shows itself. 'What shows itself' here means: that which presences from out of itself and which, as that which presences, emerges and has emerged into the unconcealed. This manner of 'saving'—namely, that which is accomplished in and through thinking—means: to bring-in the self-showing, to gather it into the unconcealed so that it may lay as a provision within the unconcealed. This saving is a gathering, a harvesting, λέγειν—namely, λέγειν τὰ ἀληθέα, *to bring the unconcealed into unconcealment*. To harvest means: the saving bringing-in of the self-showing (i.e., of signs) into the single unconcealment. Let us, for a moment, draw our attention to that saying of Heraclitus's in which he tells us of what the σοφίη of authentic knowledge consists:

καὶ σοφίη ἀληθέα λέγειν καὶ ποιεῖν κατὰ φύσιν ἐπαΐοντας.[1]

[399] And therefore authentic knowledge consists in saying and doing the unconcealed from out of, and along with, a hearkening listening that accords with what shows itself by emerging from out of itself.

ἀληθέα λέγειν καὶ ποιεῖν is thereby grasped as saying and doing (i.e., word and deed). Previously, we left it expressly undecided whether the translation of λέγειν as "to say" hits upon what is most essential. Now we clearly recognize that it does not. ἀληθέα λέγειν means to say and pronounce something more originary than merely the true, for it means to gather the unconcealed as such in a way that also brings it in, and thereby to gather oneself toward it. In short, it means 'to harvest' in the sense that is now to be thought. It is only when the saying is thought in this way that it becomes a saying capable of telling what authentic knowledge and being-knowledgeable consist in. To speak the true, as essential as that may seem, is always already something subsequent and additional, and is only possible because the true is already within knowledge. However, the true is only within knowledge when, and only when, what shows itself is saved in its unconcealedness, i.e., when it has become harvested and has thereby become the provision for all enunciating and accomplishing. Authentic knowledge, however, only *comes about* and *exists* in thinking. It is only now that we can think-after the entirety of Heraclitus's saying and can be attentive to the words that precede what has been elucidated thus far. They read as follows: τὸ φρονεῖν ἀρετὴ μεγίστη—thinking is the highest ability. Thinking *as such* is meant here, and not in the sense of a 'logic' that later develops itself, but understood as a pondering and a mindful consideration, i.e., as the self-gathering into the gathering (i.e., λέγειν).

---

[1] See above, German page 359.

Even Heraclitus already knew that bending-back and re-turning belong to the essence of the human, because the human is the one who thinks (see fragment 116):

ἀνθρώποισι πᾶσι μέτεστι γινώσκειν ἑωυτοὺς καὶ σωφρονεῖν.

To the human alone it is allotted to recognize himself, i.e., to think in a knowing way.

To think, φρονεῖν, is here [400] not meant in the sense that came to be later developed by 'logic,' for which λέγειν came only to mean 'to assert and to recite.'

Now the word λέγειν, translated as "to harvest," has an entirely different valence. λόγος is that harvesting which, in a manner that draws-out, saves and brings-in and shelters the pro-vision that before all gives vision. For this pro-vision is what originarily unites all (πάντα) in the sole oneness of what it, as the whole of beings, is. The Λόγος is the originary harvesting that draws-in within the harvest, because retained within it is all that *has* already been saved. Furthermore, this harvest saves and protects so that it may, for the first time and in its own time, be uncovered and *be* something unconcealed. However, the soul (i.e., the emerging of the human into the open and the unconcealed) has a λόγος: for its emerging unfolds as a drawing-out saving bringing-in of that point to which the soul, on its path along its outermost extremities, reached while listening to the Λόγος in a hearkening way, and with which the soul has become familiar through this harvesting.

Perhaps we may now at least attempt to make reference to the two sayings of Heraclitus's which, as those numbered fragments 1 and 2, have been placed at the beginning of the fragments handed down to us.

According to a comment of Aristotle's (*Rhetoric* III 5, 1407b16), the first fragment contains the beginning of Heraclitus's treatise. According to the oldest version recorded by Aristotle (ibid.), along with another version recorded by Sextus Empiricus (who preserves the saying's second half), the first sentence, to whose elucidation we will limit ourselves, goes as follows:

τοῦ λόγου τοῦδ' ἐόντος ἀεὶ ἀξύνετοι γίνονται ἄνθρωποι καὶ πρόσθεν ἢ ἀκοῦσαι καὶ ἀκούσαντες τὸ πρῶτον.

In relation to the Λόγος (i.e., the only one thought here and which constantly presences), humans (on their own accord, in following their own fleeting and transitory paths) arrive at an inability to bring it together, not only before they have themselves [401] heard it, but even after they have already heard it.

We will not go further into the divergent interpretations of this sentence. The conventional, albeit indefensible view is that the Λόγος is the same as what Heraclitus himself says in the saying. Accordingly, one brings the ἀεί together with the ἀξύνετοι, and thinks that Heraclitus begins his saying with the following observation: "humans will always be too foolish to understand this particular lesson of mine." It is surely foolish to believe the 'interpreters' who claim that a thinker, who according to the aforementioned fragment 50 expressly says that one must listen to the Λόγος and not what *he* himself says, would begin any writing with such a professorially vainglorious sentence. Indeed, even a glancing acquaintance with Heraclitus's own way of thinking and saying suffices to show immediately that even just the first words name something opposite to how the Λόγος stands in relation to the comportment and faculties of solely self-interested humans. ἀεί (translated as "constantly") belongs to ἐόντος, as the young Nietzsche already correctly surmised in his Basel lectures on the pre-Socratic philosophers (XIX, 172). However, it is certainly the case that this does not simply mean "to remain" (as Nietzsche suggests), but rather "to presence," i.e., to give oneself in presencing over to harvesting as the harvest. The Λόγος thus constantly presences. By contrast, all the human being accomplishes (i.e., γίνονται) on his own and on his transient way is a witless (i.e., ἀξύνετοι)[2] missing of that activity that brings about συνιεῖν, i.e., the bringing-together of what is in itself the originary gathering as the originary one and only harvest. To bring-together/not to bring-together the originary gathering of the harvest of the Λόγος with experiencing and hearkening-following are, as possibilities, in opposition to one another. Even we are still familiar with the following expression: to not and to no longer be able to bring something together, i.e., not being able to understand or follow it. We must be attuned to the oppositional sounding that sways between the Λόγος and συνιεῖν, if we are [402] readily and precisely to grasp the enigmatic relation in which the Λόγος stands to the human, and the human to the Λόγος. For how can Heraclitus say that the human does not bring together the Λόγος, even before he has properly heard it? Is it even possible to posit and intuit a bringing-together before hearing and having heard? To assume something like this is certainly senseless. To be sure, this is the case as long as one is mistaken about the Λόγος always already presencing for the human and constantly offering itself up to the human for harvest, and all of this even before the human himself has heard the Λόγος. However, according to fragment 72, the Λόγος is that with which the human is in conversation, and in a manner that constantly bears it: it is that which the human encounters every day, but does so without grasping and engaging it. But even when the Λόγος is heard expressly by the human, there is not even the slightest guarantee that he will then correspond to (and with) it—there is no guarantee that he will bring the Λόγος together into his own proper gathering. Even when humans listen with their ears, it is not guaranteed that they have listened to what they have heard, and that they have gathered themselves toward it in a hearkening way.

---

[2] Translators' note: we have supplied the word 'witless' as a translation of ἀξύνετοι, which Heidegger himself leaves untranslated.

In no way does Heraclitus wish to proclaim that humans are too dumb for this thinking. He also does not wish to claim that the foolishness of the human excludes him from the Λόγος (i.e., from the ἓν πάντα). He would rather like to say that the human, owing to his cleverness, self-interest, hasty solipsism, and self-centered stubbornness turns away from the Λόγος. By passing over the otherwise important additional sentences of the first fragment, we will now add on the second fragment, which states:

διὸ δεῖ ἕπεσθαι τῶι ξυνῶι τοῦ λόγου δ'ἐόντος ξυνοῦ ζώουσιν οἱ πολλοὶ ὡς ἰδίαν ἔχοντες φρόνησιν.[3]

---

[3] Translators' note: The 'Supplement' does not contain Heidegger's translation of this fragment (i.e., fragment 2).

[403] Editor's afterword

I.

The two lecture courses delivered by Martin Heidegger at the University of Freiburg, "The Inception of Occidental Thinking (Heraclitus)" (offered in the summer semester of 1943), and "Logic: Heraclitus's Doctrine of the *Logos*" (offered in the summer semester of 1944), appear here as Volume 55 (and as the ninth published installment) of the *Gesamtausgabe* which, beginning with the publication of Volume 24 in 1975, began to make Heidegger's works widely available.

The editor of the present volume was entrusted by Martin Heidegger himself with the editing of both lecture courses. The sudden death of the philosopher made the realization of a scheduled meeting with him regarding the present volume impossible.

The editor had access to the handwritten manuscripts of both lecture courses, as well as typewritten transcripts. The handwritten originals consist of crosswise writing and are in folio format. The left half of the page contains the continuous text, while the right half contains interlaced interpolations that intersect one another. Heidegger himself indicated the points of contact between such interpolations and the text to which they refer. The 'reviews' that appear throughout both lecture courses were drafted as separate manuscripts and were furnished with their own pagination. At the instruction of the author, they were incorporated into the text of the present volume and marked as 'reviews.' However, Heidegger did not write such 'reviews' for every lecture. Because neither the handwritten nor typewritten documents contain outlines of any kind, paragraph divisions, subdivisions, and the titles of these were left to the editor's discretion. In accordance with the author's wishes, an [404] extensive table of contents is provided in place of an index.

The manuscript for the lecture course "On the Inception of Occidental Thinking" consists of fifty-nine enumerated pages. Additionally, there are five incomplete outlined pages consisting of "indications" and "preparations." They consist of three approaches for the beginning of the lecture course, the definitive version of which is published in the present volume. The manuscript for the 'brief reviews' contains twenty pages, in addition to two crossed-out pages.

The lecture course "Logic: Heraclitus's Doctrine of the *Logos*" consists of forty-eight pages, with thirty-one pages of 'reviews.' In addition to the lectures and their 'reviews,' the editor has included a 'supplement' consisting of seven manuscript pages that were found at the end of the separately composed manuscript of the 'reviews.' Heidegger did not specify whether or not such a supplement should be included in the volume. The pages in question are a first draft for the continuation of the text from German page 282 onward (from the last line). These pages strike the editor as too valuable to withhold from the reader, and he bears the full responsibility for the inclusion of the 'supplement.'

While Martin Heidegger was still alive, the typewritten transcripts of the handwritten originals were produced by his brother Fritz under the former's own instruction, and subsequently collated by the two of them. The fact that these transcripts were authorized by Heidegger himself was of great help to the editor. Nevertheless, according to Heidegger's directives, the transcripts were twice collated to the manuscript originals. In addition to the above mentioned 'supplement,' a number of interpolations have been deciphered by the editor and, for the first time, added [405] to the text in those places where Heidegger indicated they belonged. Since no authorized afterword was provided by Heidegger, the reconstruction of an unfinished afterword was abandoned.

II.

The present volume is of fundamental importance for understanding Heidegger's other two texts "*Logos* (Heraclitus, Fragment 50)" and "*Aletheia* (Heraclitus, Fragment 16)," both of which appear in Part III of *Vorträge und Aufsätze* (Günther Neske: Pfullingen, 1954). It also provides indispensable insight into the Heraclitus seminar given by Heidegger and Eugen Fink at the University of Freiburg in the winter semester of 1966/67, which was published by Vittorio Klostermann in 1970.

On the way back into the obscurity of the inception of thinking—a way which unfolds in all of the writings of Heidegger's just mentioned—Heraclitus's fragment 16 (according to the ordering offered by Diels-Kranz) reveals itself as the first of what is to be thought inceptually.

I would like to offer a word of gratitude regarding the assistance I received during the production of the present volume. I would like to thank Frau Sylvia Neuhäuser, a Ph.D. candidate in psychology, for her conscientious review of my typescript, and for her typographical editing of the Greek passages of the text. My thanks extends to Professor Dr. F. W. von Herrmann for his indefatigable willingness to answer questions pertaining to Heidegger's estate, as well as his indispensable assistance in deciphering a number of words in the manuscript. I thank also Dr. Hartmut Tietjen for all of his help. Likewise, I extend my gratitude to Dr. Joachim W. Storck (Marbach) for further, invaluable information regarding questions pertaining to Heidegger's estate. I would also like to thank Professor [406] Dr. Bernhard Zeller from the German Literature Archive (Marbach), as well as Professor Dr. H.C. Fritz Schalk and Mr. Kenneth Stikkers for their undivided efforts concerning the verification of bibliographic matters. Last, but not least, the editor thanks DePaul University, Chicago, for generously providing a leave from my teaching duties during the production of this volume.

Concluding remark regarding the second edition from the executor of Heidegger's estate

Errors and discrepancies belonging to the first edition were corrected for this second edition. Dr. Franz-Karl Blust and Dr. Hartmut Tietjen supervised the production of this new addition with great care, for which I offer my sincere gratitude.

Hermann Heidegger

GERMAN TO ENGLISH GLOSSARY

Abendland: Occident
Abgrund: abyss; chasm
Abwesung: absencing
Abwesenheit: non-presence; absence
(das) All: the all
Anfang: inception
ansprechen: to address
Anspruch: address; demand; claim
Anwesen: essential unfolding
anwesen: to presence toward
Anwesung: presencing
aufbewahren: to conserve
aufgehen: to emerge
Aufgehen: emerging
(das) Aufgehende: the emerging thing
Aufheben: sublation; taking up
Aufenthalt: sojourn
ausholen: to draw-out
aussagen: to assert
Aussage: assertion

bergen: to cover; to secure
Beschweigen: acquiescence
Besinnung: mindful consideration
bewahren: to safeguard

Dasein: being-there
denken: to think
Denken: thinking

(das) Edel: the precious; the rare; the noble
einbringen: to bring in
(das) Eine: the One
einfach: simple; singular
Einfalt: one-fold

eigentlich: proper
Einheit: unity
einholen: to draw in
Einklang: harmony; concordance
Entspannen: un-tensing
entbergen: to uncover
Entfachen: enkindling
Entwurf: projection
Ereignis: event
Erlebnis: lived-experience
Erschweigen: acquieting
(das) Erscheinende: that which appears; the appearing thing
erscheinen: to appear

Fuge: joint
fügen: to join
Fügen: obedient joining
fügsam: compliant
Fügung: jointure; structure

geben: to give
Gefüge: configuration; combination; conjoining; structure
Gegend: region
Gegenwart: presence
gegnen: to region
Gegenwendig: counter-turning
Gesammeltheit: gatheredness
Geschichte: history
Geschick: fate
gewähren: to bestow; to grant
Grund: foundation; ground
Grundwesen: fundamental essence
Grundwort: foundational word

Grundzug: fundamental feature
Gunst: favor

herstellen: to place forth
hervorbringen: to bring forth
Historie: historiography
horchen: to hearken (obediently)

lesen: to harvest; to read
Lese / Lesen: harvest; harvesting
lichten: to lighten
Lichtung: clearing

Maß: measure

nachdenken: to think-after
Nichts: nothing
Nichtsein: non-being
Not: poverty
Notwendigkeit: necessity

(das) Offene: the open
Offenheit: openness
Ort: place, locality

Rat: vision
Rätsel: enigma; mystery

sagen: to say
Sage: saying
sammeln: to gather
Sammlung: gathering
schenken: to bestow; to give
schicken: to send
schweigen: to be silent; quiescent
Sein: being
Seiende: beings; that which is
Seieindheit: beingness
Seiendste: what is of the utmost being
Seinsvergessenheit: forgetfulness of being
Seyn: beyng
Sichbereichern: self-enriching
Sichsammeln: self-gathering
Sichverbergen: self-concealing
Sichverschließen: self-occluding
Sichzeigen: self-showing
sinnen: to reflect
Sorge: concern; care
spannen: tensing

Spruch: saying
steuern: to steer
Stimmung: mood; disposition
Streit: strife

Technik: technology

übersetzen: to translate; to interpret; to transport
unscheinbar: inconspicuous
untergehen: to submerge
Untergehen: submerging
(das) Untergehende: the submerging thing
Unterschied: difference
Unverborgenheit: unconcealment
Unwesen: distortion
Ursprung: origin

verbergen: to conceal
verborgen: concealed
Verborgenheit: concealment
verbürgen: to shelter; to guarantee
Vermessenheit: presumptuous mismeasurement
Versammlung: forgathering
Verschweigen: recquiescence
verstehen: to understand
Verstand: reason
verwahren: to preserve
verweilen: to reside
Vorrat: provision
Vorsprung: leap ahead
vorstellen: to imagine; to represent

walten: to preside
Wahrheit: truth
wahren: to safeguard
Weite: expanse
weitweisend: far-reaching
(das) Wesen: essence; unfolding
wesen: to essence; to unfold
Wesensbestimmung: essential determination
Wesensbeziehung: essential relation
Wink: hint
Wissen: knowledge
Wissenschaft: science
Wort: word

Wortgefüge: word structure/combination
Wortwesen: word essence

Zeichen: sign
Zeitwort: time-word; verb

Zier: adornment
(das) Zu-denkende: the to-be-thought
zurückspannen: to tense-back
zu-schweigen: to send quietly
Zwiefalt: two-fold

ENGLISH TO GERMAN GLOSSARY

absence: *Abwesenheit*
absencing: *Abwesung*
abyss: *Abgrund*
acquiescence: *Beschweigen*
acquieting: *Erschweigen*
(to) address: *ansprechen*
address: *Anspruch*
adornment: *Zier*
(the) all: *All*
(to) appear: *erscheinen*
(that which) appears: *das Erscheinende*
(to) assert: *aussagen*
assertion: *Aussage*

being: *Sein*
(what is of the utmost) being: *das Seiendste*
beingness: *Seiendheit*
beings: *das Seiende*
being-there: *Dasein*
(to) bestow: *gewähren; schenken*
beyng: *Seyn*
(to) bring-forth: *hervorbringen*
(to) bring-in: *einbringen*

care: *Sorge*
chasm: *Abgrund*
clearing: *Lichtung*
combination: *Gefüge*
compliant: *fügsam*
(to) conceal: *verbergen*
concealed: *verborgen*
concealment: *Verborgenheit*
concern: *Sorge*
concernful: *sorgsam*
concordance: *Einklang*
configuration: *Gefüge*

conjoining: *Gefüge*
(to) conserve: *aufbewahren*
countering-turning: *das Gegenwendige*
(to) cover: *bergen*

demand: *Anspruch*
difference: *Unterschied*
disposition: *Stimmung*
distortion: *Unwesen*
(to) draw-in: *einholen*
(to) draw-out: *ausholen*

(to) emerge: *aufgehen*
emerging: *Aufgehen*
(the) emerging thing: *das Aufgehende*
enigma: *Rätsel*
Enkindling: *Entfachen*
(to) appear: *erscheinen*
(to) essence: *wesen*
essence: *Wesen*
essential determination: *Wesensbestimmung*
essential relation: *Wesensbeziehung*
(to) essentially unfold: *anwesen*
event: *Ereignis*
expanse: *Weite*

far-reaching: *weitweisend*
fate: *Geschick*
favor: *Gunst*
forgathering: *Versammlung*
forgetfulness of being: *Seinsvergessenheit*
foundation: *Grund*
foundational word: *Grundwort*
fundamental essence: *Grundwesen*
fundamental feature: *Grundzug*

(to) gather: *sammeln*
gathering: *Sammlung*
gatheredness: *Gesammeltheit*
(to) give: *geben*; *schenken*
(to) grant: *gewähren*
ground: *Grund*
(to) guarantee: *bergen*; *verbürgen*

harmony: *Einklang*
(to) harvest: *lesen*
(the) harvest: *die Lese*
(to) hearken (obediently):
    horchen
hint: *Wink*
historiography: *Historie*
history: *Geschichte*
(to) imagine: *vorstellen*
inception: *Anfang*
inconspicuous: *unscheinbar*
interpret: *übersetzen*

(to) join: *fügen*
joint: *Fuge*
jointure: *Fügung*

knowledge: *Wissen*

leap ahead: *Vorsprung*
lightening: *Lichten*
lived-experience: *Erlebnis*
locality: *Ort*

measure: *Maß*
mindful consideration:
    Besinnung
mood: *Stimmung*
mystery: *Rätsel*

necessity: *Notwendigkeit*
noble: *das Edel*
non-presence: *Abwesenheit*
non-being: *Nichtsein*
nothing: *Nichts*

obedient joining: *Fügen*
Occident: *Abendland*
(to) oscillate: *schweben*
(the) One: *das Eine*
one-fold: *Einfalt*

(the) open: *das Offene*
openness: *Offenheit*
origin: *Ursprung*

place: *Ort*
(to) place forth: *herstellen*
placing there: *herstellen*
poverty: *Not*
precious: *das Edel*
(to) presence toward: *anwesen*
presence: *Gegenwart*
presencing: *Anwesung*
(to) preside: *walten*
(to) preserve: *verwahren*
presumptuous mismeasurement:
    Vermessenheit
projection: *Entwurf*
proper: *eigentliche*
provision: *Vorrat*
(to be) quiet; quiescent: *schweigen*

(to) quietly send: *zu-schweigen*

rare: *edel*
reason: *Verstand*
recquiescence: *Verschweigen*
(to) reflect: *sinnen*
region: *Gegend*
(to) region: *gegnen*
(to) represent: *vorstellen*
residing: *Aufenhalt*

(to) safeguard: *bewahren*
(to) say: *sagen*
saying: *Sage*
saying: *Spruch*
science: *Wissenschaft*
(to) secure: *bergen*
self-concealing: *Sichverbergen*
self-enriching: *Sichbereichern*
self-gathering: *Sichsammeln*
self-occluding: *Sichverschließen*
self-showing: *Sichzeigen*
(to) send: *schicken*
(to) shelter: *verbürgen*
sign: *Zeichen*
(to be) silent: *schweigen*
simple: *einfach*
singular: *einfach*

sojourn: *Aufenhalt*
(to) steer: *steuern*
strife: *Streit*
structure: *Fügung; Gefuge*
sublation: *Aufheben*
(to) submerge: *untergehen*
submerging: *Untergehen*
(the) submerging thing: *das Untgergehende*

(to) take up: *aufheben*
technology: *Technik*
(to) tense: *spannen*
(to) tense-back: *zurückspannen*
that-which-is: *das Seiende*
(to) think: *denken*
(to) think-after: *nachdenken*
thinking: *Denken*
time-word: *Zeitwort*
(the) to-be-thought: *das Zu-denkende*

(to) translate: *übersetzen*
(to) transport: *übersetzen*
truth: *Wahrheit*
two-fold: *Zwiefalt*

unconcealment: *Unverborgenheit*
(to) uncover: *entbergen*
(to) understand: *verstehen*
(to) unfold: *wesen*
unfolding: *Wesen*
unity: *Einheit*
un-tensing: *Entspannen*

verb: *Zeitwort*
vision: *Rat*

word: *Wort*
word essence: *Wortwesen*
word structure/combination: *Wortgefüge*